COM AND DCOM
MICROSOFT'S VISION FOR DISTRIBUTED OBJECTS

Roger Sessions

WILEY COMPUTER PUBLISHING

John Wiley & Sons, Inc.
New York • Chichester • Weinheim • Brisbane • Singapore • Toronto

Publisher: Robert Ipsen
Editor: Theresa Hudson
Managing Editor: Frank Grazioli
Illustrator: John Hubbard
Text Design and Composition: Benchmark Productions, Boston, MA.

Designations used by companies to distinguish their products are often claimed as trademarks. In all instances where John Wiley & Sons, Inc., is aware of a claim, the product names appear in initial capital or ALL CAPITAL LETTERS. Readers, however, should contact the appropriate companies for more complete information regarding trademarks and registration.

This book is printed on acid-free paper. ∞

Library of Congress Cataloging-in-Publication Data:

Sessions, Roger
    COM and DCOM: Microsoft's vision for distributed objects /
Roger Sessions.
        p. cm.
    Includes index.
    ISBN 0-471-19381-X (pbk. : alk. paper)
Electronic data processing—Distributed processing. 2. Object-oriented programming (Computer Science) 3. Microsoft software.
I. Title.
QA76.9.D5S47   1998
004' .36—dc21   97-33993
                                                                      CIP

10 9 8 7 6 5 4 3 2

About the Author

Roger Sessions is one of the leading experts in distributed object technology. He is the author of three other books and over 20 articles on Java, COM/DCOM, CORBA, object-oriented programming, and distributed objects. He has spoken at dozens of conferences throughout the world.

Sessions has over 15 years of industry experience including 5 years at IBM. He has served as one of the lead architects for OMG's Object Persistence Service specification, one of the CORBAServices, and as one of the lead architects of IBM's CORBA project.

He is now Principal of ObjectWatch, Inc., a company specializing in training, consulting, and mentoring to companies adopting distributed object technology. He publishes an Internet newsletter dedicated to distributed object technology.

He lives in Austin, Texas, the live music capital of the known universe, and feels sorry for anybody who doesn't. Sessions can be reached through ObjectWatch, Inc., in Austin, or at roger@objectwatch.com .

CONTENTS

[v]

Preface

I worked at IBM from 1990 through 1995, a period during which IBM was fixated on Microsoft. IBM was afraid Microsoft would dominate the desktop with Windows NT and eliminate OS/2 as a viable operating system. Stopping Microsoft was deemed crucial to IBM's future.

By the end of 1996 it was clear that IBM's greatest fears had become reality. In the last half of 1996, the last remaining OS/2 magazine and the last remaining OS/2 conference both announced they were closing their doors for lack of interest. Within IBM, it is universally acknowledged (at least privately) that OS/2 had been a complete failure. Even while executives like John W. Thompson, the Vice President of Software, and John Slitz, the Vice President of Object Marketing, assured a skeptical public that IBM was fully committed to OS/2, behind the scenes all major software development was being retargeted from OS/2 to Windows NT.

During the years in which Microsoft held IBM's undivided attention, Microsoft was, in fact, in no way a threat to IBM. IBM never made a profit from OS/2, never even came close. IBM squandered billions of dollars on OS/2 and related technologies like Taligent, OpenDoc, and SOM. Had Microsoft succeeded in preempting OS/2 as early 1992, Microsoft would have done IBM a tremendous favor and saved IBM huge sums of money. If Microsoft hurt IBM, it was only in not killing OS/2 soon enough.

IBM always perceived Microsoft as a competitor for the desktop operating system. Once IBM gave up on OS/2, IBM lost interest in Microsoft. The IBM philosophy today is that the desktop never was important anyway. After all, IBM is a mainframe company, and that is where Corporate America runs its business.

IBM is making another serious blunder. IBM's perception of Microsoft today is just as wrong as it was during the OS/2 years. Then, Microsoft was perceived as an enemy, whereas, in fact, it was harmless. Today, Microsoft is perceived as benign, whereas, in fact, it is threatening the very existence of IBM.

Microsoft is paving the way for a new revolution in computer technology. This revolution, if successful, will have three profound effects:

1. It will begin a new era in which desktop machines running NT form the backbone of distributed commerce applications.

2. It will destroy the last refuge of the large mainframe machines.

3. It will expand Microsoft's sphere of influence far beyond anything that has yet been seen.

Microsoft is attempting nothing less that a complete redefinition of the software basis for corporate computing. The underpinnings of this architecture include DCOM, the fundamental Microsoft mechanism for distributed components. The middle layers include sophisticated transactional and clustering technologies, applied for the first time to desktop systems. The high levels include frameworks for cooperation among applications, including technology for sophisticated message queuing and provisions for complex interactions between far-flung components.

The Microsoft vision is a compelling one. Microsoft promises us a world in which hugely complex transactional commerce systems are run on desktop-class machines that are banded together, tied into the Internet, and coordinated by a family of closely related products.

Many will dismiss the Microsoft vision as just another Microsoft attempt to take over the world. Of course, there is some truth in this. Microsoft, like any company, needs to be profitable, and a company is only profitable if it is successful. But the success of this vision would bring benefits to everybody, not just Microsoft. And ultimately, that is the best way for a company to be successful.

There is no place for IBM in this world. Should Microsoft prove successful in bringing this vision to reality, IBM will find itself in a rapidly declining market. Mainframes will be replaced by clusters of NT servers. CICS, the main IBM transactional system and a primary IBM revenue generator, will be replaced by Microsoft cluster, transaction, messaging, and database technology. Using mainframes for managing the flow of commerce will seem as quaint as programming with punch-cards.

Its hard to pin Microsoft down on terminology. Terms like ActiveX, DCOM, OLE, and ActiveX Servers are used to mean different things by different people and in different technical and historical contexts. Therefore, I am coining a new term, one which I believe is still up for grabs. I will use the term *Microsoft Distributed Component Architecture* (MDCA) to include all the technology that Microsoft has created to enable distributed commerce applications based on components. At the low level, this includes Java, COM, and DCOM. At the highest level, this includes coordinating technologies like transactions, clusters, and security, to name but a few.

This book describes the Microsoft vision for distributed commerce-oriented applications. It gives an overview of the technology I call MDCA. It gives a background to the technical issues involved, analyzes the different layers of the Microsoft solution, describes how these layers work together, and predicts how this architectural vision will influence the software industry. This book is for planners, technical managers, and software developers who are looking for a detailed overview of the Microsoft architecture for large-scale, distributed applications. This architecture will impact the entire software industry. This book provides an essential road map to that architecture.

Naming this book was very difficult. I would have like to have named it *the Microsoft Vision for Distributed Components*, or something like that, but nobody would have known what I was talking about. I finally chose the name it has today, knowing that COM and DCOM are only part of what this book is about, but they are a very critical part.

The main reason Microsoft's Java, COM, and DCOM are so exciting is not because they are wonderful technologies in and of themselves. If we want nothing more than Java programming, Sun offers a better integrated solution. If we want nothing more than distributed components, CORBA is a better programming model than DCOM. What makes Java, COM, and DCOM so exciting is how they feed into a whole vision of how to write distributed applications. This vision includes sophisticated security, an entirely new model for efficient management of shared objects, and an incredible idea of clustered workstation machines, to name but three.

To examine Java, COM, and DCOM in isolation of these other MDCA technologies is to completely miss the point of what Microsoft is doing. It is like trying to understand the construction of a guitar by examining only three of its strings. Three strings by themselves may be able to vibrate, but they can't make music. The strings need an instrument and a musician. Microsoft has provided the instrument. I hope this book shows you how to become the musician.

I am determined to write an easy-to-read, jargonless book. Microsoft, like any good vendor, has created a sea of acronyms, quite capable of drowning the unwary. Yet I believe the underlying ideas behind the MDCA are simple. I have tried to strip my explanations of overly complex polysyllabic words, on the one hand, and trivialized fooBar examples on the other. I hope I have managed to convey the heart of this exciting architectural vision.

Acknowledgments

Many people have been generous with their time. I particularly appreciate Brad Merrill and Mark Ryland, both of Microsoft, who spent many hours on the phone helping resolve programming issues, finding information, and discussing architectures. However, the opinions I have expressed in this book should in no way be attributed to them or anybody else at Microsoft. I am very grateful to Jack Swan, Tom Kennedy, and John McCullagh, three friends, for their time reviewing code and math formulae. John Wiley & Sons has been a total delight to work with. Terri Hudson, who first nurtured this book into existence, Frank Grazioli, who was my managing editor, and John Hubbard, my highly talented artist, have been an exceptional team who have put their hearts and souls into this book.

But all of this would have been for nothing without the continuing support of my family. My children, Emily and Michael, have been patient and understanding, but mostly I have depended on the encouragement and love of my wife, Alice. More than anybody else, she made this book and so many other things possible.

Code Samples

All of the code samples in this book are available as a Zip file on the Web. Go to www.wiley.com/compbooks/, and follow the link to book code.

Book Outline

This book describes the many layers of the MDCA and how these many layers work together to form a unified architectural vision. Each of these layers forms a coherent subplot that can be examined and appreciated on its own, but can be more richly appreciated in the context of the whole drama.

I have written this book in much the same way. The chapters by and large form complete units. One can pick and choose those chapters that are of interest and read them independently of the others. But keep in mind that there is a larger vision behind all of this, one that can only be seen when the chapters are read in relation to each other. To paraphrase Shakespeare, "The MDCA is but a stage, and the individual layers merely players on it."

Now let me introduce you to the players.

Chapter 1: Architectural Overview

Gnomes are cute, furry, imaginary creatures. What are they doing in a book about a distributed component architecture? It turns out that the rules governing the mythical kingdom of gnomes exactly parallel the rules governing software components. This chapter introduces gnomes, uses them to define the problems that commerce systems must solve, and describes how they can be used as the building blocks of complex commerce systems. The result is an overview by analogy of all of the major ideas and pieces of the MDCA including components, interfaces, COM, DCOM, transactions, security, databases, clusters, scalability, and three-tier architectures.

Chapter 2: COM/DCOM Issues

Underneath it all are components. This chapter discusses the important ideas behind components, how one goes about distributing these components, and some of the reasons behind Microsoft's architectural decisions. You will see the gnomes a lot in this chapter, as we continue borrowing on their expertise for explaining performance, implementation, sharing, birth, death, and other issues critical to working with components.

This chapter also introduces a commerce example we will use extensively throughout the rest of the book. This system is a brokering system, and is designed to match up buyers and sellers, and coordinate the transfer of goods for money. In this chapter we introduce this system using gnome theory.

Chapter 3: The Java Layer

Components can be built with many languages, but one language stands out. Java is the best choice for creating components because it is an easy language, it is a good fit with the Microsoft component model, and is widely supported. Java complements COM/DCOM very nicely. The most complicated features about COM/DCOM are eliminated when using Java as the implementation tool, and the most complicated features about Java are eliminated when you can assume the components will be running in the MDCA environment.

This chapter describes Java's history, gives an overview of the Java technology, and describes Microsoft's J++ product. We then look at using the object-oriented features of Java to implement components, first with some very simple components that illustrate general ideas, and then by looking at our first full implementation of the brokering system.

This chapter focuses on Java concepts that are particularly important to component development. One such example is the relationship between interfaces and classes. Another is control of the point of instantiation. These concepts are generally neglected in traditional Java programming books that lack the component focus.

Chapter 4: Components

Once Java has been used to implement algorithms, that code must be enclosed within a COM wrapper. This chapter explains some of the advantages of creating COM wrappers for Java objects, and walks through the actual process.

One advantage of creating COM wrappers is that the Java code then becomes accessible to other programming languages. One of the most important languages with which we would like Java to interact is Visual Basic. The combination of these two languages gives us access to one of the best languages for developing user interfaces and one of the best languages for implementing business algorithms. The Visual Basic/Java pair is a formidable team, and one I consider basic to developing applications for MDCA. This chapter therefore also describes Visual Basic, and gives an introduction to creating sophisticated user interfaces in this very-easy-to-master environment.

To pull everything together, we return to our brokering system. We reexamine our Java code to discover areas poorly designed for COM wrapping. We then reimplement those areas, create COM wrappers, and use Visual Basic to design and implement a visually appealing interface to our brokering system.

Chapter 5: Persistence

Starting in this chapter, we move to higher-level issues. The first area we look at is persistence; that is, why you want to store component data, and how you go about doing so. We explore briefly the idea of object-oriented databases and show why they have not measured up to their hype. We look at the so-called ActiveX framework for persistence that defines interfaces for object persistence and provides basic support for storing and restoring object data. Finally, we add persistence to our brokering system, and look at some of the benefits this introduces.

Chapter 6: Sharing and Scalability

The MDCA is specifically designed to work with distributed components. The problems one must face in working with distributed components are unique in many ways. Two of the biggest are efficiency and scalability. Efficiency refers to the number of clients a given configuration of distributed components can support. Scalability refers to the ability to support more clients by spending more money. These topics are closely related.

You might assume that it is obvious that if you spend more money, you can support more clients. But this is not, in fact, the case. It is perfectly possible to spend more money without gaining the ability to support more clients. This chapter will help you understand what you will and won't get for your money.

The MDCA has taken a unique approach to sharing component objects. This approach is called object pooling, and has significant implications on how components must be designed. The result of this approach is that component-based systems run very efficiently and scale extremely well. Pooling is the domain of the Microsoft Transaction Server (MTS).

This chapter describes the issues involved with efficiency and scalability, describes the MTS approach to remote object management, and describes the design considerations of which implementors need be aware. As a sample case, we reimplement the brokering system so that it can participate in object pooling.

Chapter 7: Transactions and Databases

Transactions are central to commerce, and have been since the first caveman traded an arrowhead for a mastodon tusk. As soon as a second caveman became interested in that same tusk, we needed record locking, and as multiple arrow-heads and multiple tusks became involved, we needed techniques to coordinate additional trading systems.

This chapter uses gnomes to give a nontechnical description of the basic laws of transactional commerce, and the algorithms that enforce these laws. The most important of these algorithms include record locking, deadlock detection, and two-phase commits.

Then we look at the layers of the MDCA that provide distributed transactional support, the Microsoft Distributed Transaction Coordinator (MS-DTC), and how this product is integrated with Java, COM, and DCOM. MS-DTC supports a variety of database products. One of these products is another of the MDCA layers, SQLServer. SQLServer is a relational database. We discuss what it means to be a relational database, how this works within the overall transactional framework, and how we might modify the brokering system to make use of SQLServer technology.

Chapter 8: Multi-Tier Architecture

So far, we have looked at implementing user interfaces in Visual Basic, implementing components in Java/COM/DCOM, and storing component data in SQLServer. Now we look at a formal structure for organizing these technologies called multi-tier architectures. Multi-tier architectures refer to a software organization in which user interfaces run on small, cheap desktop machines, Java/COM/DCOM objects run on component servers, and databases run on data management servers.

This chapter describes multi-tier architectures, gives them some historical context, and describes the glue MDCA provides to coordinate the activity of the different tiers.

Chapter 9: Security

We can't have commerce without trust or security. Since commerce includes used car dealers, we can eliminate trust. So let's focus on security. This chapter describes the basic security issues and the two main mechanisms MDCA provides for making components secure.

The first mechanism involves protecting interfaces within the Microsoft Transaction Server environment. This environment protects interfaces through both client authorization and client impersonation. We discuss both, and the advantages and disadvantages of each.

The second mechanism is called the CryptoAPI, which supports a wide range of cryptographic functionality. This chapter looks at the architecture, purpose, and algorithms of this extensive and important API.

Chapter 10: Clustering

A great deal is being made of NT scalability, an important function of the MDCA. The MDCA answer to scalability is clusters. Wolfpack is the layer of the MDCA that provides cluster support. Wolfpack is at the very heart of Microsoft's battle against the mainframes. If Wolfpack fails, then clusters fail, scalability fails, and NT fails. There is no room, in the field of commerce, for systems that cannot scale. And Microsoft wants this market.

This chapter gives a nontechnical description of why a clustered architecture performs better, operates more reliably, and costs less than a mainframe architecture. This chapter includes an introduction to the mathematics of clusters, presented to be understandable by anybody with high-school algebra, and includes tables and rules you can use to accurately predict failure rates of different cluster configurations. This chapter describes the architecture Wolfpack uses to support clusters.

Chapter 11: Message Queuing

Java/COM/DCOM technology is basically a synchronous messaging system. Much of commerce runs on asynchronous messaging. MDCA provides an asynchronous message system under the name of the Microsoft Message Queue Server (MSMQ), otherwise known as Falcon. This chapter describes the differences between synchronous and asynchronous messaging, how MSMQ supports asynchronous messaging, and how MSMQ fits together with the rest of MDCA. Just as important, the chapter describes where the fit is less than perfect, and speculates on how MSMQ might be better integrated with MDCA in the future.

Chapter 12: Wrap-Up

This chapter wraps up the book. It describes the two competitive technologies to MDCA, Java the megasystem and CORBA. This chapter is intentionally provocative, laying down opinions that will inflame, amuse, and perhaps even illuminate. In this chapter, I explain it all. Why CORBA has failed. Why Java has had exactly the opposite effect Sun intended. The major problems with MDCA. Who won. Who lost. What the future holds for us all.

This book concludes with my 10 must-follow rules for developing distributed component systems within the MDCA. If the first half of the chapter left you in a state of distress, I hope to make it up to you here.

We have many stops to make on this journey. Now let the tour begin.

ARCHITECTURAL OVERVIEW

Some say the *Microsoft Distributed Component Architecture* (MDCA) is a revolutionary advance in computer science. They point out that, if Microsoft delivers on its promises, we will see cheap Windows NT workstations become the systems of choice for running large, complex, distributed, commerce-oriented applications. Expensive mainframes will be history. Corporate computing will never be the same. These people say Microsoft is brilliant—a truly visionary company.

Others say the MDCA is just a rehash of existing technologies. They say Microsoft has just stolen ideas from object-oriented programming, distributed programming, transaction processing, clustering, security, client-server architectures, queuing, directory services, and *RASS* (Reliability, Availability, Scalability, and Serviceability). These people believe Microsoft is an intellectual thief—the lowest of the low.

I agree with both camps. There are very few novel ideas in MDCA. We have used most of these basic concepts for decades in large, mainframe systems and have tested them repeatedly in the unforgiving world of computerized commerce. However, the MDCA is the first serious attempt to build commerce-enabling systems out of computers that many mainframe programmers still regard as glorified PacMan entertainment modules.

In this chapter, I give an overview of the Microsoft architecture for distributed component applications—the architecture I call MDCA. The M is for Microsoft, obvious enough, the contender for the throne of commerce computing. The D stands for Distributed, because this architecture is about enabling distributed commerce-oriented applications. The C stands for Component, because this architecture uses, as its fundamental building blocks, component-based software. The A stands for architecture, because this is much more than a technology for objects, user interfaces, remote methods, or even components. It is a technology for enabling components to work together in ways unheard of just a few years ago and, in many camps, still thought impossible.

This architecture uses *DCOM*, the Microsoft technology for distributing components across process spaces, which in itself uses *COM*, the Microsoft component model. It also works best (but not exclusively) with Java for component development, and Visual Basic (also not exclusively) for user interface development. So, to do justice to the MDCA, we must also spend time with Java, COM, DCOM, and Visual Basic. Then we must see how these components are coordinated by Microsoft's Distributed Component Management System, which they have misnamed the *Microsoft Transaction Server* (code-named "Viper"). We must see how these coordinated components are organized into Microsoft's Reliability, Availability, Scalability, and Serviceability Framework, which they call *Clusters* (code-named "Wolfpack"). And we must see how these components can send messages back and forth reliably and securely, using the Microsoft technology called *Message Queuing* (code-named "Falcon").

Individually, these names are just confusing acronyms. Together, they form a vision. To study Java or Visual Basic without studying COM is like examining a leaf and never the branch. To look at COM alone from DCOM is like looking at a branch and never a tree. To understand DCOM without understanding the Transaction Server is like understanding a tree but not the forest. And so on. All of these are the pieces of MDCA, Microsoft's vision for the next generation of computing. MDCA is the ecosystem that Microsoft has planned for all of our futures.

But enough of this: Java, COM, DCOM, Wolfpack, Viper. . . . It's enough to make one's head spin. I said in the Preface that I wanted to keep this book simple, so let's start by talking about simple things. Let's talk about commerce. And let's talk about gnomes.

Electronic Commerce

MDCA enables *electronic commerce*. This is its purpose. But what is electronic commerce?

Electronic commerce is just commerce conducted over computer networks. Commerce is the transfer of valuables between individuals or organizations. Sometimes these valuables are goods. Sometimes they are services. Sometimes they are money. Sometimes they are just the promise of money. Sometimes they are information.

For example, I give $2.50 to Dave at Texpresso for a cappuccino. That is commerce. I transfer $103.12 to my stockbroker in exchange for a 1/1,195,188,000th ownership in Microsoft. That is commerce. I ask a bank to transfer money from my savings account to my checking account. That is commerce. I give John Wiley, Inc., the right to publish my future bestseller on COM/DCOM and MDCA in return for an advance against future royalties. That is commerce. Electronic commerce is just commerce managed by computer.

Computers are useful to manage commerce exchanges when the volumes involved are very high. When I agree to write a book in return for future royalties, I participate in an exchange that happens perhaps four or five times a decade. We don't need a computer for this exchange (although we use e-mail extensively). When I buy a piece of Microsoft, my $103.12 may be only a drop in the $727,701,562.50 bucket that will trade hands as bits and pieces of Microsoft are bought and sold today. Managing daily exchanges of 700 million anything requires sophisticated, reliable computers. And lots of them.

Electronic Commerce Requirements

Let's look at some of the requirements for electronic commerce systems.

Electronic commerce systems must be available. When I ask to buy a share of Microsoft, I don't want to hear that the stock exchange system is down for the month of February.

Electronic commerce systems must always see an exchange through to a logical conclusion. If I ask to buy a share of Microsoft for $103.12, I expect one of two things to happen. Either I will end up owning a share of Microsoft and my account will be debited by $103.12, or I will not own a share of Microsoft and my account will not be debited by $103.12. I prefer the first outcome, but either outcome is acceptable. I will not accept having my account debited by $103.12 without getting a share of Microsoft. And my stockbroker will not accept the reverse.

Electronic commerce systems must not forget things. If I successfully purchase one share of Microsoft, I don't expect to hear the next day that the computer has forgotten about the exchange.

Electronic commerce systems must be both trustworthy and suspicious. If I am going to give my credit card number to a system, I want to be sure the system is what it claims to be. And if the system is going to ship merchandise to me based on my credit information, it wants to be sure I am who I claim to be.

With the advent of the Internet, we are seeing a whole new set of expectations being placed on electronic commerce systems. Now I expect to buy my share of Microsoft not through a phone call but through a Web page. This requires interfaces that are easy to use and highly adaptable to the whims of fickle consumers.

Because customers are waiting for orders, performance is important. A customer entering information at a Web page has limited patience. If the system does not respond within seconds, the customer will probably quit and not return.

In many cases, electronic commerce systems need the flexibility to interact with other software systems. In the near future we may be doing much of our purchasing using agent software. Agents are more or less autonomous processes. I ask an agent to do something and then let it loose on the Internet. It worms its way around from one electronic commerce system to another, seeking the best possible strategy to fulfill my request. Travel systems seem particularly amenable to this approach. I give my software agent some parameters, such as:

- I want to go from Austin to Stockholm.
- I want to arrive before 2:00 P.M. on Friday.
- I want to keep the cost below $700.

Now I send the agent off on its merry way: "Wake me up when you are done, thank you." My software agent may have many negotiations with many unrelated commerce systems before it finds a series of flights that can get me from Austin to Stockholm on time and within my budget.

So, if we are looking at a software architecture that supports electronic commerce, we expect provisions for the following:

Availability, so that whenever a customer is ready to place an order the system is up and running.

Performance, so that customers do not have to wait.

Durability, so that when the system accepts an order, the system never forgets that order, no matter what.

Predictability, so that no matter how many customers are interacting with the system, every customer gets an outcome that is predictable and reasonable. This does not mean the system must accept every order (the system may, for example, refuse an order because it doesn't approve of a customer's credit history), but it does mean the system can't either refuse an order and debit the customer's account, or accept the order and not debit the customer's account.

Security, so that both the system and the customer (or the customer's agent) can be sure they are working with trustworthy partners.

Scalability, so that I can plan for increased system capacity as I increase my customer load.

Adaptability, so that I can rapidly evolve my system as the needs of my customers change.

Flexibility, so that my system can work with order entry clerks, customers, or other software systems.

Any software architecture for electronic commerce, like Microsoft's Distribution Component Architecture, must solve these problems. Let's see how Microsoft addresses each of these issues, starting from the bottom, and working our way up.

Gnomes

We are competing in a fast-paced world. Our competitors are constantly coming up with better products and better strategies for selling those products. We need not only to build electronic commerce systems, we need to build them quickly and change them quickly as the needs of our customers and the capabilities of our competitors evolve.

The use of components allows us to build and rebuild software quickly. MDCA is all based on component technology. So let's talk about components. I think of a component as being the software equivalent of a *gnome*. So let's start by talking about gnomes.

A gnome is a soft, furry creature that can do things for you. They look a lot like the creature in Figure 1.1. Gnomes have two particularly endearing qualities. First, they are very good at following instructions. Second, they work for almost no pay. Gnomes are not, however, creative. They need specific and well-defined instructions in the form of instruction booklets.

Let's say I want a gnome that knows how to manage credit card purchases. I can create a credit card management instruction booklet that explains to gnomes how to respond to specific commands relating to credit cards. The instruction booklet might include details on processing the following requests:

- Charge a purchase of x amount.
- Credit a payment of x amount.
- Tell me the credit available.
- Tell me the outstanding balance.

I might also want a gnome that knows how to manage store purchases. Now I have to create a detailed instruction booklet for store purchases.

The hard part of working with gnomes is not the communication with the gnome, but the process of writing the instruction booklets. Remember, gnomes are not smart, just diligent. My instructions need to be very precise, and need to include detailed information about how to handle unforeseen conditions. When a gnome makes a mistake, it is rarely the fault of the gnome, but rather the fault of the person writing the instruction booklet. For example, my instructions for "charge a purchase of x amount" must include not only the obvious instructions

Figure 1.1 Gnomes.

on subtraction, but also the minutiae on what the gnome should do in any of the following situations:

- I mistakenly give a negative amount.
- I make a purchase that exceeds my credit limit.
- I make a purchase that is unusually large.
- The log where my credit card information is stored was eaten by my dog.

Writing instruction booklets is difficult. First of all, gnomes don't speak English. They speak Gnomish. Gnomish is very confusing for people, so people typically use machines to translate from English (or some human language) to Gnomish. The people who write these instructions and use these translators are highly skilled and highly paid professionals, and even then it is a tortuous process. Clearly, the business I want to be in is using the gnomes. The business I *don't* want to be in is writing instruction booklets for gnomes.

Buying prepared and tested gnome instructions is getting easier and easier. Many companies make their living selling gnome instruction booklets. Let's say I want a creditManager gnome. I get the catalog for Gnomics, Ltd., one of many companies writing gnome booklets. I look for an instruction booklet that teaches how to manage credit cards. I will probably have many from which to choose. I buy the one best suited for my system. The booklet has already been translated into Gnomish, so I just bring the booklet home, give it to my gnomes, and I have a working system.

Buying prepackaged gnome instruction booklets is a good deal both for me and for Gnomics, Ltd. I get to buy a well-tested instruction booklet at a fraction of what it would have cost me to develop. Gnomics, Ltd., gets to sell its booklet to many customers, eventually making up the cost of the booklet development and a tidy profit besides.

Interface

Buying a gnome instruction booklet does not completely solve the problem of working with gnomes. There are really two aspects to working with gnomes. First, I need to know how to communicate requests to my gnomes. Second, my gnomes need to know how to process these requests. The gnome instruction booklet solves the second problem, but not the first.

I might try to figure out how to communicate with creditManager gnomes by looking at the credit card instruction booklet. But remember, the instruction booklet is in Gnomish. While there are translating machines that can translate from English to Gnomish, there are none that can satisfactorily perform the reverse operation.

We deal with this problem by using something we call an *interface definition*. An interface definition is a formal way of describing how to communicate with gnomes. It is written in English, not Gnomish. A given instruction booklet will always include an interface definition. An interface definition for a creditManager gnome (a gnome that is following the credit card instruction booklet) might look like this:

```
interface creditManager
{
    chargePurchase(creditCardNumber, amount, store);
    creditPayment(creditCardNumber, amount, store);
    getCreditAvailability(creditCardNumber) returns
        creditAvailability;
    getBalance(creditCardNumber) returns balance;
}
```

This interface tells me how to communicate with a creditManager gnome. It says, for example, that the proper way to ask a gnome to charge a 10-dollar purchase to credit card number 1234 and credit the store named Gnobles is chargePurchase(1234, 10, Gnobles). It also says that the proper way to get credit card 1234's available credit is to ask an appropriate gnome to getCreditAvailability(1234), and the gnome will return the answer.

This example shows just one possibility for an interface language. The exact language we use for defining an interface is not important. What *is* important is that we agree on that language. We'll see the official Microsoft language for describing interfaces (Interface Definition Language, or IDL) when we get to the chapter on COM.

An interface for a stockClerk gnome (a gnome that knows how to request delivery of a specific stock item to a specific customer) might look like this:

```
interface stockClerk
{
```

```
    getStockItem(customerName, stockNumber, quantity);
}
```

An interface for a informationGatherer gnome (a gnome that knows how to take an order from a customer) might have this interface:

```
interface informationGatherer

{
    getOrder()returns customerName, creditCardNumber,
        stockNumber, quantity, totalCost;
}
```

Encapsulation

There is bad news and good news about purchased gnome instruction booklets. The bad news is that we don't know how gnomes perform the operations defined by the creditManager interface, because the booklets are written in Gnomish. The good news is that we don't care how the gnomes perform these operations. This is the basic idea we describe as *encapsulation*. Encapsulation says that we get to know only what a gnome *does*, not *how* a gnome does it.

You might think that encapsulation constricts your freedom to use gnomes in creative ways. Let's say you know that the directions for chargePurchase involve updating a particular piece of paper. You might be tempted to go directly to that paper and update the information yourself. "Why not?" you might say. After all, any later requests to that gnome will still work, and this will improve your system's performance.

In fact, encapsulation is a liberator. Because I cannot know what instructions are used for any of these creditManager operations, I must rely only on the published creditManager interface when I build my system. This ensures that I can replace the instruction booklet used by my creditManager gnomes with new instruction booklets, as long as those new instruction booklets honor the same interface as the first.

Let's say that I become unhappy with the credit card instruction booklet purchased from Gnomics, Ltd. Perhaps it doesn't perform well when I ask my gnomes to process more than 50 purchases per minute. I look in the catalog for a competing company, say, Gnometrics, Inc., and I see another instruction booklet. This booklet uses the same creditManager interfaces, but claims to process purchases at a rate of 5000 per minute.

I can easily replace my old instruction booklets with these new instruction booklets. All I know about my creditManager gnomes is that they respond to specific requests, like chargePurchase(1234, 10, Gnobles). This is true of gnomes using either the old instruction booklets or the new improved versions. From my perspective, these booklets are interchangeable. As you can see in Figure 1.2, I can replace my old booklets with new versions without having to change how I interact with the gnomes themselves.

Figure 1.2 Booklet replacement.

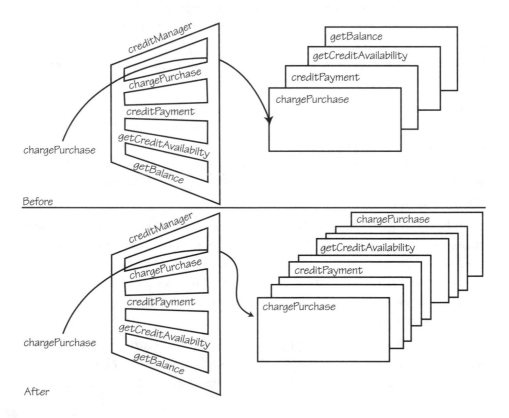

Adaptability

A system built from gnomes is very adaptable. I can build such systems easily, and modify them quickly as my needs change. Most of my work involves directing the interactions between gnomes. Let's say I have instruction booklets for creditManager, stockClerk, and informationGatherer gnomes. Remember, these three interfaces look like:

```
interface creditManager
{
    chargePurchase(creditCardNumber, amount, store);
    creditPayment(creditCardNumber, amount, store);
    getCreditAvailability(creditCardNumber)
        returns creditAvailability;
    getBalance(creditCardNumber) returns balance;
}
interface stockClerk
{
    getStockItem(customerName, stockNumber, quantity);
}
interface informationGatherer
{
    getOrder()returns customerName, creditCardNumber,
        stockNumber, quantity, totalCost;
}
```

I can create three gnomes, say, Cred, Stockard, and Crusty. I will ask Cred to follow the credit card instructions, Stockard to follow the stockClerk instructions, and Crusty to follow the informationGatherer instructions. Given these three gnomes, I can create a store system just by asking these gnomes to perform the appropriate operations in the appropriate order.

A request to a gnome has to include various pieces of information. This includes the following:

- The gnome to which I am making the request.
- The operation I want the gnome to perform.
- The information the gnome needs to perform the request.

The syntax I will use (at least for now) to describe a request, say, to Cred, to charge credit card 1234 with a 10-dollar purchase crediting Gnobles, is as follows :

```
ask Cred to chargePurchase(1234, 10, Gnobles);
```

The syntax I will use (at least for now) to describe a request that returns information, say, to Crusty, to get the next customer order, is as follows:

```
ask Crusty to getOrder()
    getting customerName, creditCardNumber,
    stockNumber, quantity;
```

Given that I have purchased the instruction booklets for all three of my gnomes, it is very easy to write a system to manage a customer purchase. My high-level instructions might be no more complicated than the following:

```
create Cred as a creditManager gnome;
create Stockard as a stockClerk gnome;
create Crusty as a informationGatherer gnome;
ask Crusty to getOrder() getting
    customerName, creditCardNumber, stockNumber,
    quantity, totalCost;
ask Cred to chargePurchase(creditCardNumber, totalCost, Gnobles);
ask Stockard to getStockItem
    (customerName, stockNumber, quantity);
```

These instructions are so simple, I might even decide to create a higher-level gnome that encapsulates this instruction set; for example, salesRep:

```
interface salesRep {
    takeCustomerOrder();
}
```

Once I have taken my instruction set, translated it to Gnomish, and used it to implement the salesRep interface, it becomes even easier to create a system to take customer orders. The system now collapses to these two instructions:

```
create Stacy as a salesRep;
ask Stacy to takeCustomerOrder();
```

So, although the system looks very simple to us, the reality is much more complicated, as shown in Figure 1.3.

Every gnome has (at least) one interface that describes operations that gnomes can process. It is very important that the right gnome be asked to perform the right operation. Cred is a creditManager gnome. Therefore, you can ask him to chargePurchase. Crusty is *not* a creditManager gnome. It makes no more sense to ask Crusty to chargePurchase than it makes to ask me to flyToTheMoon (a request that might be completely appropriate for a rocketPilot gnome).

When developing gnome-based systems, I may not always be able to buy the instruction booklets I need. If my application is highly specialized, I might need to write my own instruction booklets. If so, I can try to create general interfaces that I can reuse in later systems. I might even be able to sell these booklets to others working in a similar field. Between the ever-increasing availability of booklets on the open market, and the library of booklets I have created for past projects, I can built a large number of systems as easily as I built the store system.

Figure 1.3 Stacy behind the scenes.

Stacy as We See Her

Cred

Stockard

Stacy as She Really Is

Crusty

Remember the discussion on encapsulation earlier in the chapter? We said encapsulation ensured that we could replace instruction booklets without impacting those using the gnomes. You can see this in the store system. I can change the instruction booklet used for, say, creditManager gnomes. The store system works without change as long as the new instruction booklet honors the same interface as the original.

The importance of encapsulation can hardly be overemphasized. There are hundreds of possible instruction booklets for any given interface. Because we see an instruction booklet only through its interface, we are able to treat all of the instruction booklets associated with a given interface as equivalent and interchangeable. There may be performance or quality reasons why one booklet is better than another, but from an interface perspective, they are the same.

Gnome Locality

In general, gnomes are cute but simple creatures. One of their drawbacks is their limited communication abilities. Gnomes know how to respond to requests from people when physically located in the same room. If Cred, Crusty, and Stockard are all located in the same room as I am, everything works fine. But this may not be a very efficient way of running things.

Suppose the instruction booklet for getStockItem, one of the operations of the stockClerk interface, looks something like this:

```
Pull items from shelve;
Slap customer sticker on items;
Place items in chute;
```

The location of the store showroom (where the customer is located) is probably far away from the location of the store warehouse (where the merchandise is located). So when I blithely ask Stockard, the stockClerk gnome, to "Pull items from shelf," I may well be asking for something more like the following:

```
1.      Walk out of the showroom;
2.      Take the escalator to the first floor;
3.      Say "hello" to Sam in Lady's Hats;
4.      Go to the employee's entrance;
5.      Take the elevator to the tenth floor;
6.      Grab a cup of coffee;
```

```
7.       Go through the double doors to the warehouse section;
8.       Find the appropriate isle;
9.       Tie your shoes;
10.      Pull items from shelf;
11.      Slap on customer sticker;
12.      Place in chute;
13-21.  Reverse 1-9 to return for your next instructions;
```

Of these 21 instructions, only 3 (10–12) are directly involved with fulfilling our request. The rest have to do with moving Stockard from one place to another. Obviously, it would be much more efficient if Stockard stayed in the warehouse and we phoned to ask that the item be pulled. But Stockard doesn't know how to talk on the phone. How do we manage this?

An obvious solution is to add instructions to the stockClerk booklet that explain to Stockard how to use communications equipment. But this has a problem. We didn't write the instruction booklet, remember? We purchased it from Gnomics, Ltd. And the version we have isn't in English. It has already been translated into Gnomish. There is no way we can work with Gnomish instructions, so we are stuck.

You might think that I could have bought a different stockClerk instruction booklet from Gnomics, Ltd., one that would have included communications instructions. But this also has a problem. There is no standard for communications equipment. Gnomics, Ltd., is trying to write generic instructions for stockClerk gnomes that can be sold to as many stores as possible. Some stores use push-button phones, some use dial phones, some use intercoms, some use walkie-talkies, some use PA systems. If Gnomics, Ltd., were to include communications instructions for a specific communications medium, say, dial phones, in the stockClerk instruction booklet, it would limit the stores that could make use of this booklet, and thereby limit its potential customer base.

There is another problem with adding communications instructions to gnome instruction booklets. Communications instructions, even when you know the medium, are very complicated. There are all kinds of things that can go wrong, and all kinds of conditions that need to be checked. You need to worry about the volume of the receiver, missing dial tones, lost lines, static, broken equipment, and a hundred other details. If we are to add these instructions to every booklet for every type of gnome that might ever need to work remotely, we will have an explosion in both the size and cost of instruction booklets.

We aren't finished. There is yet another problem with teaching gnomes to communicate, and that is that stores are constantly updating their communications systems. If I purchased gnome instruction booklets hard-wired for, say, intercoms, and then update my store to use cell phones, I have a lot of expensive instruction booklets to throw away. Stores cannot afford to throw away entire systems every time they upgrade their communications technology.

So, obviously, we aren't going to teach our gnomes to use phone lines. What are we going to do?

The answer to this is in a clue I gave in the section on "Gnome Locality." I said "Gnomes know how to respond to requests from people or other gnomes physically located in the same room." So, since we can't teach Stockard, the stockClerk, to use the phone, we will buy some new gnomes that can use the phone. Then we will teach these gnomes to talk to Stockard. Figure 1.4 shows the interactions between these gnomes.

Figure 1.4 Stockard and the telephone.

These new phone-savvy gnomes are like any other gnomes. They also need instruction books. But these instruction booklets are very complicated and very specialized. Gnomics, Ltd., specializes in instruction booklets for various types of store gnomes. Now we are talking about gnomes that know how to coordinate activity between gnomes in stores. For these booklets, we will go to a specialist. We will go to Micrognome.

Micrognome is a company that specializes in gnome-based commerce-enabling systems, including communications. Communications is one of the most basic layers of this gnome-enabling technology. We will see many more layers of Micrognome technology before we are done.

It may not be clear what we have gained by adding phone-savvy gnomes. We have already abandoned the idea of adding communications knowledge to our existing gnomes because of complexity, equipment specialization, and obsolescence. These phone-savvy gnomes would seem to have many of these same problems.

However, there is a major difference between phone-savvy gnomes and phone-savvy stockClerks. Phone-savvy gnomes only know about communications (specifically, communications over phones). They don't know, for example, how to be a stockClerk. A phone-savvy stockClerk, on the other hand, has to know about both phones and stockClerking.

The difference between having, on the one hand, phone-savvy gnomes *and* stockClerk gnomes, and having, on the other hand, phone-savvy gnomes that *are also* stockClerks, is subtle. It turns out that there are many advantages to having the two separated. Let's consider a few.

Let's say my business is writing instruction booklets for different types of gnomes involved in stores (stockClerks, informationGatherers, etc.). I may have a lot of different instruction booklets. I don't know exactly how my customers will choose to use these booklets in their systems. There is no way I can predict which booklets are going to be used for local gnomes, and which are going to be used for remote gnomes. There is also no way to know what communications system (if any) will be used by the people buying my instruction booklets. If I can assume that any customers using remote communications systems buy the communications-related instruction booklet elsewhere, then I can greatly reduce the amount of work (and therefore, the cost) of my own instruction booklets.

This separation between store gnomes and communications gnomes also benefits me as a system developer. If I can purchase store instructions separately from communications instructions, then I can easily upgrade my communications equipment. When I replace my communications equipment, I also replace my communications instruction booklets, without having to replace my huge investment in both purchased store-related instruction booklets, and the gnome systems I have built based on these instructions are protected.

Finally, there is a booklet size issue. Let's say an average store instruction booklet contains 10,000 instructions, and, on average, it takes 20,000 instructions to deal with communications equipment. If I have 20 store-related instruction booklets, and these booklets include communications instructions, I will have a total of $20 \times [10,000 + 20,000]$ instructions, or 600,000 instructions. If I have 20 store-related instruction booklets and the communications instructions are packaged separately, then I will have a total of $20,000 + [20 \times 10,000]$ instructions, or 220,000 instructions, as you can see in Figure 1.5. This is a huge reduction in instruction size. Instruction size is directly related to both the initial cost of booklets and to the

Figure 1.5 Instruction booklet size.

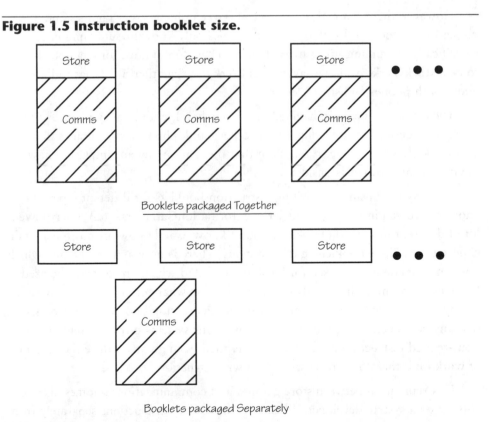

Booklets packaged Together

Booklets packaged Separately

ongoing cost of booklet maintenance. Therefore, this reduction in instruction size will have a large impact on both my immediate and long-term costs.

Needless to say, the techniques used for hooking up communications-savvy gnomes to regular gnomes is a topic in itself. We will examine the Micrognome technology for working with remote gnomes in other rooms in detail in Chapter 4.

Predictability and Durability

At the beginning of the chapter we identified two requirements for commerce. We called them *durability* and *predictability*. Durability means that once something happens, it does not spontaneously *un*happen. Predictability means that the number of possible system outcomes is limited to a subset that makes sense.

There is some relationship between durability and predictability. If we include future outcomes in predictability, then we would certainly predict that things in the future will not change without warning. If I am told that I have purchased an airline ticket and my credit card has been debited, I don't expect to arrive at the airline and hear there is no record of my purchase. Even not being charged for the ticket isn't going to mollify me. I expect to get on that plane. Period.

What makes this outcome not acceptable is the fact that somebody promised me I could have that airline ticket. If, when I first made the purchase, I was told the ticket was not available and I would not be charged, I might have been unhappy, but I would have accepted this outcome. Once I am promised the ticket is mine, I am getting on that airplane. That ticket has been committed. We don't break commitments and stay in business for very long.

We might think of this as a gradual reduction in the set of possible outcomes. Let's go back to our store gnomes. Without any durability and predictability there are four possible outcomes, the combination of possible outcomes from my interactions with each gnome. Cred (the creditManager gnome) might and might not debit my account. Stockard might and might not deliver my purchase. These possible outcomes, then, are as follows:

1. Cred debits and Stockard delivers.
2. Cred doesn't debit and Stockard doesn't deliver.
3. Cred debits and Stockard doesn't deliver.
4. Cred doesn't debit and Stockard delivers.

With predictability, I can eliminate outcomes 3 and 4 as being unexpected. With long-term predictability (or durability), I can further say that to whichever of outcomes 1 or 2 the store committed, the store had better follow through. If Cred debits my card, then Stockard had better deliver. If Stockard can't deliver, then Cred had better not debit my card.

It's quite possible to build a system that ensures predictability and durability, but the instructions are going to be a lot more complicated than these instructions, first presented earlier in the chapter.

```
create Cred as a creditManager gnome;
create Stockard as a stockClerk gnome;
create Crusty as a informationGatherer gnome;
ask Crusty to getOrder() getting
    customerName, creditCardNumber, stockNumber,
    quantity, totalCost;
ask Cred to chargePurchase(creditCardNumber, totalCost, Gnobles);
ask Stockard to getStockItem
    (customerName, stockNumber, quantity);
```

Look at all the things that can go wrong with these instructions! Crusty could get some bad information from the customer. Cred could get a credit refusal. Stockard could find the item out of stock. Any of these failures and a hundred others would make these instructions fail the predictability and/or durability test.

We need a lot of instructions if we want predictability and durability. We need instructions to verify all of Crusty's information. We need Cred to let us know whether or not the charge was successful, and if not, why not. We need Stockard to let us know whether or not he can deliver the purchase, and if not, why not. We will need to create back-up systems so that if anything goes wrong with Cred and Stockard's notes, we won't lose the information on this interaction. This is more than a bunch of instructions. This is a *very big* bunch of instructions. And it is a very difficult bunch to get right. You might think of a hundred points of failure, but the one you miss will be the one that will bill your customer $10,000 for a delivery that will never be made.

So, what is the solution? How can we create a system that ensures predictability and durability without adding mountains of instructions? Once again, it is Micrognome to the rescue. Micrognome provides a transactional framework, the purpose of which is to ensure predictability and durability. We will describe this framework in detail in Chapter 7, but let's take a quick preview here.

The main purpose of transactional frameworks is to allow predictability and durability to be added to systems as easily as possible. Perhaps the easiest way to do this is to go back to Stacy. Remember Stacy? We discussed her earlier in the chapter, where we proposed encapsulating in her instruction booklet all of the knowledge about managing a customer order. Her interface looked like this:

```
interface salesRep {
    takeCustomerOrder();
}
```

Using Stacy, our store system collapsed to just a few instructions:

```
create Stacy as a salesRep;
ask Stacy to takeCustomerOrder();
```

Stacy then interacts with Cred, Crusty, and Stockard to get the customer information, process the credit card, and pull the merchandise.

The Micrognome architecture allows us to declare that takeCustomerRep() is to be considered a transaction. With this declaration, we get two important guarantees. First, the system guarantees either operations will be conducted in their entirety or they will not be conducted at all. Second, the system guarantees that whatever the outcome, that outcome will never be lost. Never. No matter what.

Keep in mind that the system doesn't guarantee that the charge card will be debited and the purchase delivered. It can't guarantee that. It has no control over too many unknowns, like the validity of the charge card. What the transactional system guarantees is that either Cred will debit the charge card and Stockard will deliver the order, or Cred will not debit the charge card and Stockard will not make the delivery. Everything will happen. Or nothing will happen. And whatever happens, once it happens, it will never be lost.

This is a remarkable result, and almost magic when you think of all the things that could go wrong. We have gained a great deal with the simple declaration of an operation as being a transaction. We will see just how much we have gained when we look at this topic in more depth in Chapter 7.

Security

Electronic commerce systems must be secure. I don't want anybody stealing my credit card number. I don't want Stockard to send my purchase to somebody else.

Security is easy to ensure when all of the gnomes work together in the same room. I can see which gnomes I am talking to, and they can see me. Security becomes very complex when some gnomes (like Stockard) work remotely. Let's consider an architecture in which Stacy (the salesRep), Cred (the creditManager gnome), Crusty (the informationGatherer), and Stockard (you know who Stockard is) are all working in different rooms and using phones to communicate back and forth. To simplify this discussion, we will assume the gnomes can directly use the phones, and ignore the role of the phone-savvy gnomes.

The single instruction

```
ask Stacy to takeCustomerOrder();
```

is going to generate a lot of conversation among these gnomes, as predicted by the instructions implementing takeCustomerOrder:

```
1.   create Cred as a creditManager gnome;
2.   create Stockard as a stockClerk gnome;
3.   create Crusty as an informationGatherer gnome;
4.   ask Crusty to getOrder() getting
          customerName, creditCardNumber, stockNumber,
          quantity, totalCost;
5.   ask Cred to chargePurchase(creditCardNumber, totalCost, Gnobles);
6.   ask Stockard to getStockItem(customerName, stockNumber, quantity);
```

In order to accomplish instruction 4, Stacy phones Crusty and asks for the customer information. Line 5 has Stacy phoning Cred and telling him some information returned by Crusty, along with the name of the store. Line 6 has Stacy phoning Stockard and passing on more of the other information returned by Crusty.

Consider this system from Cred's perspective. He gets a phone call. He answers the phone. The caller says she is Stacy, and asks him to charge a purchase of some amount to some credit card number, crediting a particular store. Cred knows nothing about the previous interactions between Stacy and Crusty.

Consider this system from Stockard's perspective. He gets a phone call. He answers the phone. The caller says she is Stacy, and asks him to remove a quantity of a particular stock item, slap on a customer sticker, and send the item(s) off for delivery. The system as it should look is shown in Figure 1.6.

Consider this system from Stacy's perspective. She dials Cred's phone number. Somebody answers the phone. He says he is Cred. She gives him a valid credit card number and asks him to charge a purchase of some amount crediting Gnobles. Now she dials Stockard. Somebody answers the phone He says he is Stockard. She gives him a customer name, stock item, and quantity, and he says he will send off the item(s) for delivery.

Now consider this system from the perspective of Dred, a depraved human being. Dred avoids work whenever possible. Dred steals. Dred is not nice. How can Dred bend this system to his own evil purposes? Now, gnomes are good. They do what they are told, and *only* what they are told. Once a gnome has learned his or her instructions, he or she will not learn new instructions. Gnomes cannot be bribed. So what can Dred do?

Dred has a huge number of possibilities open to him. Let's say he wants to take items from the store without being charged. He might consider bribing Cred to ignore purchases made on his credit card number, but we know Cred would never do that. So instead, Dred knocks Cred over the head and replaces him by Fred. Fred is also a creditManager gnome, in that he follows an instruction booklet in which interactions are described by the creditManager interface. But Fred's instruction booklet looks a lot different than Cred's.

Figure 1.6 Stacy and Cred.

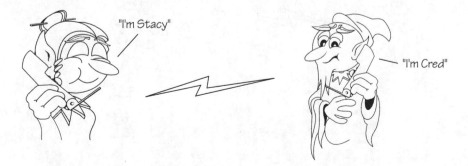

So Stacy dials Cred's phone number. But now Fred answers the phone. He says he is Cred. Stacy gives him a valid credit card number and asks him to charge a purchase of some amount crediting Gnobles. But Fred's instructions say that the purchase should be ignored if the credit card number belongs to Dred. Stacy, assuming Dred charged the purchase, calls Stockard and asks for the delivery. Dred gets the merchandise, but never gets charged. This breach of the system is shown in Figure 1.7.

Dred can also replace Stockard with a look-alike. The Stockard replacement might decide to send Dred a color TV every once in a while, or perhaps a car. Dred can even replace Stacy. Since Stacy controls all the gnome interactions, a Stacy look-alike can do almost anything. Both of these are shown in Figure 1.8.

Dred can also work at the communications layer. He might reroute wires so that, for example, when Stacy thinks she is dialing Cred, she really dials Fred. And we know what Fred does. Dred might decide to steal nothing, but just monitor the phone lines. Then, when he finds a customer making an embarrassing purchase, he jots down the information and blackmails the customer. Or perhaps he just notes the number of the credit card being passed to Cred and uses it himself later.

Believe it or not, we have just scratched the surface of security concerns. Obviously, real commerce systems can't go out the door with such weaknesses.

Figure 1.7 Stacy and Fred.

Figure 1.8 More bad news from Dred.

Dred Replaces Stockard

Dred Replaces Stacy

Fortunately, Micrognome provides an easy-to-use security system that makes the following guarantees:

- *Gnomes are who they say they are.* If a gnome tells Stacy his name is Cred, she can be sure it is really Cred.

- *Requests are coming from people or gnomes that have the authority to make those requests.* If Cred is asked to debit a credit card, he can be sure the person or gnome making that request has the authority to do so.

- *Information passing through the system is kept confidential.* If I am making a purchase, I can be sure nobody is listening on the line.

We will look more closely at security in Chapter 9.

Record Management

Our gnomes need to access and store information. In many cases, processing information is their primary task. We can imagine, for example, that when Cred charges a purchase, he needs to verify the credit card number, add a purchase description to the customer's file, and place an entry into a billing file. All of this involves processing information. How might this information be stored?

Let's say Cred has three huge filing cabinets. One has credit card information, one has customer files, and one has billing files. Cred's instruction booklet or, more precisely, the creditManager instruction booklet, could include directions on storing and retrieving information from these files. Sounds straightforward. To read, you open a file and remove a record. To write, you open a file and add a record. To update, you open the file, remove a record, update it, and return it. What could be simpler?

If our store is small enough, record management might just be this simple. But if our store is this small, we probably aren't investing in gnomes. If we are investing the big bucks it takes to set up a gnome system, then we are probably processing thousands of customer purchases every day, maybe every hour. And then our recordkeeping needs to be just a little more complicated. Let's look at some of the things we need to consider.

First of all, there is performance. How long does it take Cred to process a typical request? Let's make some assumptions about how long it takes to do different information management tasks. Here are some hypothetical values:

- Finding a particular file (say, a customer file) in a cabinet: 4.5 seconds.
- Finding a particular record in a file: 1.0 seconds.
- Reading a record: 1.0 seconds.
- Writing a record: 2.0 seconds.
- Returning a record to a file: 1.0 seconds.
- Returning a file to a cabinet: 3.0 seconds.

There are basically two categories of information management tasks. There are *read* tasks and *write* tasks. Each takes the following amount of time:

Read task: Finding a file (4.5 seconds), finding a record (1.0 seconds), and returning the file to the cabinet (3.0 seconds). Total time: 8.5 seconds.

Write task: Finding a file (4.5 seconds), writing a record (2.0 seconds), returning a record to the file (1.0 seconds), and returning a file to the cabinet (3.0 seconds). Total time: 10.5 seconds.

Now let's take a guess at the information management involved in making a charge against a credit card. Let's say there are three parts to this task: verifying the credit card number, updating the customer file, and updating the billing file. Verifying the credit card number is a read task and takes 8.5 seconds. Updating the customer file is a write task and takes 10.5 seconds. Updating the billing file is also a write task and takes 10.5 seconds. Therefore, the total time required to process a credit card purchase is 8.5 + 10.5 + 10.5 seconds, or 29.5 seconds, or just a tad under 1/2 minute.

You might assume from this analysis that our store can process 120 customer purchases per hour, or 1200 in a 10-hour day. But this is wrong. The truth is that Cred can process *at most* 120 customer purchases per hour. And this doesn't include a lot of overhead, such as the cost of communicating with Cred in the first place.

If store customers were nice enough to enter the store at a constant flow throughout the day, then Cred's peak flow would be the same as the number of customers that could be processed per day. Unfortunately, customers don't work that way.

Customers arrive in herds. For many stores, the biggest herd arrives around lunch time. If you were to chart the number of customers arriving in a given 1-hour period, your chart would look something like the one shown in Figure 1.9.

With Cred's peak flow of 120 customers per hour, we are going to lose 180 customers between 12:00 P.M. and 1:00 P.M., and another 30 from 1:00 P.M. to 2:00 P.M. It would be nice if these customers would just hang around until Cred is free, but they won't. They will get frustrated and leave. Customers are like that. So, even though Cred theoretically could have handled 1200 customers in a 10-hour day, because of the herding effect he was able to handle only 440 of the 650 customers who actually walked through the door. More than 200 customers angrily walked out of the store, never to return.

You can see that performance is more complicated than you might think. Systems are rarely limited by their theoretical throughput. They are usually limited by their peak throughput. In Cred's case, his actual throughput (440 customers per day) is barely one-third of his theoretical throughput (1200 customers per day).

Figure 1.9 Herd movement of customers.

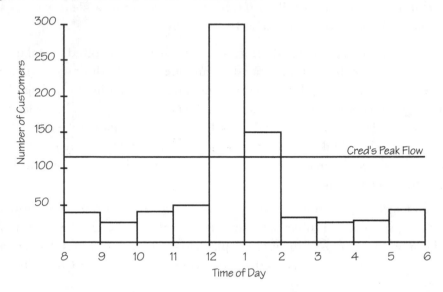

One way to deal with this performance issue is to buy two more Creds. Or, more specifically, buy two more checkBook gnomes. Let's call these new gnomes Crud and Crum. Between Cred, Crud, and Crum we have maximum throughput of 360 customers per hour. This is enough to handle our lunch-hour rush. Things should be fine now, right?

Well, yes and no. Remember we only have one set of files. This means Cred, Crud, and Crum have to sit in the same room and use the same files. You can imagine the chaos that ensues as all three gnomes are rushing back and forth, opening and closing file cabinets, pulling and returning records, and all the while trying to keep up with the relentless flow of customers. If you can't imagine this, just take a look at Figure 1.10. The more gnomes we throw into this room, the more chaos we are going to have, and the more difficult it will be to coordinate their activity.

There is another issue the gnomes have to deal with. There is always the possibility that two people in the store will be making a purchase with the same credit card number at the same moment. Not likely, but it can happen, and you can imagine how that affects our harried gnomes.

Figure 1.10 Cred, Crud, and Crum.

Let's say Cred and Crud are both asked to charge purchases of $300 and $20, respectively, to credit card 1234 with a starting balance of $100. Cred goes to the file cabinet and looks up the balance for card 1234. He finds the balance is $100. He goes back to his desk to add $300 to $100.

In the meantime, Crud is asked to charge a purchase of $20 to the same credit card number. He looks up the balance and also finds the number is $100. He goes back to his desk to add $20 to $100.

Cred finishes his calculations. He comes up with $400 ($300 + $100). He goes back to the file system, finds the record for credit card 1234, crosses out the old balance, and enters $400.

Then Crud finishes his calculations. He also started out with $100, added $20, and came up with $120. He goes back to the file system, finds the record for credit card 1234, crosses out the old balance, and enters $120.

The problem is that when Crud crosses out the old balance, the number he crosses out is the number Cred just entered! So, credit card 1234 started out with a balance of $100, made two purchases of $300 and $20, and ended up with a balance of $120. Not a bad deal.

Clearly, the instructions necessary to have a robust record management system are very complex. Once again, we are faced with the question of where these instructions should live. Should they be added to the checkBook instructions, the salesRep instructions, or someplace else?

If we place these instructions in any of the gnome booklets, we have three problems. First, the complexity of the gnome booklets has greatly increased. Second, the instructions have to repeated in every gnome booklet that is involved with recordkeeping. Third, the gnomes have become tied to a particular style of record-keeping. Should the store change its recordkeeping system, the gnome booklets have to be completely trashed. That's a major investment down the drain.

By now these problems should sound familiar. We saw exactly the same issues arise when we discussed security and predictability earlier in the chapter. So, it should come as no surprise that the solution for record management is similar to the solutions for predictability and security. Once again, we find ourselves looking to Micrognome to provide an easy-to-use system that will have minimal impact on the instruction set used by our gnomes and our store system. We will look at the Micrognome solution to record management in detail in Chapter 7, in the discussions about databases.

Scalability

Let's switch gears for a moment. We have been talking a lot about the gnomes' problems. Let's look at things from the perspective of the store owner. We are now the store owner, and we want to know what this system will cost.

If our store is big enough to need gnomes, it is probably pretty big. It may have anywhere from 10 and 50 departments, each with a departmental station where customers can place orders and make payments. Each of these stations needs to have contact with different gnomes.

One possible configuration is that each station is using its own private Stacy (or Stacy equivalent). Remember Stacy? She is a salesRep gnome. The salesRep interface looked like:

```
interface salesRep {
    takeCustomerOrder();
}
```

The takeCustomerOrder operation is where we had placed all the coordination of the informationGatherer, creditManager, and stockClerk gnomes.

When we first showed Stacy being used, we proposed the following instructions for a store system:

```
create Stacy as a salesRep;
ask Stacy to takeCustomerOrder();
```

The takeCustomerOrder operation has these instructions:

```
create Cred as a creditManager gnome;
create Stockard as a stockClerk gnome;
create Crusty as a informationGatherer gnome;
ask Crusty to getOrder() getting
    customerName, creditCardNumber, stockNumber,
    quantity, totalCost;
ask Cred to chargePurchase(creditCardNumber, totalCost, Gnobles);
ask Stockard to getStockItem(customerName, stockNumber, quantity);
```

Let's modify this slightly. Now we will assume that when Stacy is finished with one customer, she should immediately prepare for the next. She should then continue doing this until we are ready to close the store. Our new instructions for takeCustomerOrder look like this:

```
create Cred as a creditManager gnome;
create Stockard as a stockClerk gnome;
create Crusty as a informationGatherer gnome;
repeat until (store is ready to close) {
    ask Crusty to getOrder() getting
        customerName, creditCardNumber, stockNumber,
        quantity, totalCost;
    ask Cred to chargePurchase(creditCardNumber, totalCost, Gnobles);
    ask Stockard to getStockItem(customerName, stockNumber, quantity);
}
```

This is a very logical structure for a store system. It creates four gnomes for every departmental station. The salesRep gnome, Stacy, is local, because she is coordinating details for this particular station. The informationGatherer gnome, Crusty, is local, because she is gathering information from the customer. The creditManager gnome is remote, because he needs to be in the room where the records are kept. The stockClerk gnome is remote, because he needs to be in the room where the stock is kept.

The cost of your gnome system is primarily determined by the size of the rooms you must build in which to house your gnomes. We can simplify the cost analysis by assuming that space for local gnomes is free, because we already have the departmental stations. The cost of the system is therefore determined by the cost of the remote gnomes and the rooms in which they live. We will focus here on the creditManager gnomes, and assume that a similar analysis for stockClerk gnomes would give a similar result.

The creditManager gnomes live in the recordkeeping room. Let's say it costs $5,000 to build a recordkeeping room large enough for five gnomes, and $10,000 to build a recordkeeping room large enough for ten gnomes. In other words, the recordkeeping room costs about $1,000 per gnome.

We said creditManager gnomes working at full capacity, or 100-percent efficiency, can process 120 purchases per hour. If we need to process 360 purchases per hour, how large a room do we need? Gnomes take up the same amount of space regardless of whether or not they are actually doing anything, so the amount of space we need depends on how efficiently our gnomes work. The more efficiently the gnomes work, the fewer of them we need to process the workload. Here are several possibilities:

- If our gnomes work at 100-percent efficiency, then we need a room big enough for three gnomes. This room costs $3,000.
- If our gnomes work at 50-percent efficiency, then we need a room big enough for six gnomes. This room costs $6,000.
- If our gnomes work at 10-percent efficiency, then we need a room big enough for thirty gnomes. This room costs $30,000.

If we plot this, as in Figure 1.11, we see a exponential relationship between cost and gnome efficiency.

Efficiency

Now here is a very simple question. As the store owner, which of these rooms would we prefer to build?

Figure 1.11 System cost and gnome efficiency.

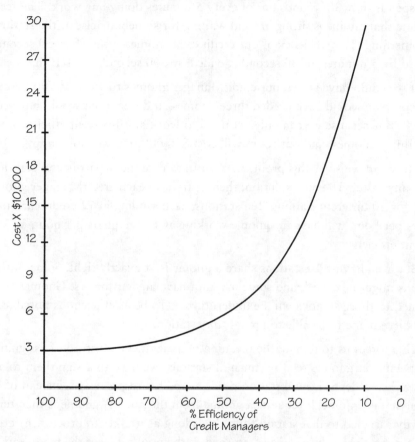

Clearly we want our gnomes to work at 100-percent efficiency. The less efficiently they work, the larger and more expensive will be their room. So what *is* the efficiency at which our gnomes work?

Let's make some reasonable assumptions. Earlier in the chapter we proposed that it takes Cred about 30 seconds to process a credit card purchase. Let's say it takes Crusty 1.5 minutes to take an order; Stockard 1.5 minutes to get the item; and the human being actually working with the customer 1 minute to package the merchandise and say good-bye to the customer. Therefore, an average departmental station takes 5 minutes to completely process a customer.

The remote gnome assigned to process that station's credit card purchases then spends only 30 seconds out of every 5 minutes doing any work. The rest of the time that gnome is sitting around waiting for somebody else at the station to do something. The efficiency of our credit card gnomes is therefore 30 seconds divided by 5 minutes, or 30 seconds divided by 300 seconds, or 1/10th.

If we could have gotten our creditManager gnomes to work at 100-percent efficiency, we would have needed three gnomes, and our room would have cost $3,000. But because we can only get them to work at 10-percent efficiency, we need thirty gnomes, and our room will cost $30,000. Do we look happy?

How can we solve this problem? We can't make the departmental stations work any faster. The only solution, then, is to have each creditManager gnome work for 10 different stations. Ten stations, each sending in 12 credit card purchases per hour, will have the gnome working at 120 requests per hour, or 100-percent efficiency.

But even having 10 stations share a gnome isn't exactly right. Some of those stations might be closed, and some may not have any customers. Gnomes assigned to those stations will be underutilized. To be as efficient as possible, we want *any* gnome to be able to process *any* station.

This forces us to rethink the meaning of assignments. Instead of assigning creditManager gnomes to departmental stations, we need to assign them to a pool. When a departmental station needs a credit card processed, instead of using a preassigned gnome, it requests a gnome from the pool. A gnome is then temporarily assigned to that station for only as long as it takes to process the credit card request. Then the gnome is returned to the pool to await the next request. This is shown in Figure 1.12.

What happens if a station requests a gnome and all the gnomes are busy processing other requests? Then that station waits on a queue for the next available gnome. But it won't be long. It only takes a gnome 30 seconds to process a request, and we have three gnomes. Even when all the gnomes are working, a gnome becomes available every 10 seconds. Typically, a station waits at most a few seconds for a gnome. What's a few seconds to a station that is going to take 5 minutes to process a customer?

You can see that pooling our creditManager gnomes is much more efficient than preassigning gnomes to departmental stations. It allows our gnomes to work

Figure 1.12 The gnome pool.

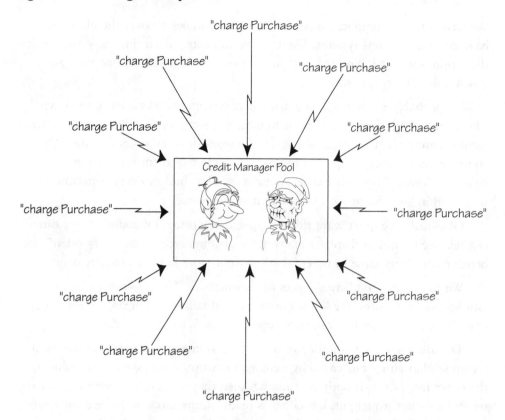

at very close to 100-percent efficiency, and allows us to build the recordkeeping room as cheaply as possible.

This efficiency is not free. It is much more difficult to manage a pool of gnomes than it is to preassign gnomes to stations. We need a lot of instructions to manage the pool, make temporary gnome assignments, return gnomes to the pool, keep track of which stations are waiting for gnomes, and a hundred more details. Who is going to write all these instructions? Us? Gnomics, Ltd.?

This is a rhetorical question. By now, I know you know the answer. Micrognome is going to write these instructions. This is all part of the commerce-enabling structure for gnome management that we will be purchasing from Micrognome. We will look at the Micrognome architecture for gnome pooling in detail in Chapter 6.

Availability

We have a pretty complicated system. We have gnomes all over the place. We have communications systems. We have file cabinets. Given time, any and all of these things will fail. Nothing lasts forever. Gnomes get sick. Phone lines go down. File cabinets get stuck.

It's probably not a problem when a departmental workstation goes down. There are plenty more to service customers. But suppose the file cabinets in the record management room get stuck. Or the stock delivery system crashes. Or the communication lines going to either the record management room or the stock room go down. When this happens, our system has had it. Every departmental workstation goes down. Our store might as well close.

Obviously, we don't want this to happen very often. Of course, "very often" is a relative term. But there are many areas of commerce where "very often" had better mean "very close to never." Let's say our store has such requirements.

We have three conflicting pieces of information. We know we will have gnome-related failures. We know gnome-related failures will bring down our system. We know our system can never come down. What can we do?

The answer is to maintain parallel gnome systems. The parallel systems are set up so that either one can fully manage the store. If one system goes down, the other takes over. If both are running, then they can both be used to improve overall system throughput, but either is ready at any moment to be a fully functioning, autonomous system.

There is still a chance that both systems will go down at the same time, but this is unlikely. Let's say either system has a 1/25 chance of going down on a given day. Then the chances of both systems going down is about $1/25 \times 1/25$, or 1/625. A system with a 1/25 chance of going down on a given day will be down on average once every 3 1/2 weeks. But both systems (and the store as a whole) will be down only once every 2 years or so.

We can reduce the downtime even further. If we have three parallel systems, then the chances of all three being down is about $1/25 \times 1/25 \times 1/25$, or 1/15,625, or an average of once every 43 years. This is good enough for almost any store.

You can imagine how difficult it is to coordinate these parallel systems. Both systems must always be up to date. As soon as one system has a failure, the remaining system must take over. Once the sick system has recovered, it needs to be brought up to date so that it is ready to take over. This is a lot of work, but part of what we need if our gnomes can work in the exacting world of commerce. And this is part of what we can get from Micrognome. We will look closely at this topic in Chapter 10.

Three-Tier Architecture

There are many types of gnomes. In our store system, we have seen four *explicit* gnome types, and a very large number of *implicit* gnome types. Our explicit gnome types have been the creditManager, stockClerk, informationGatherer, and storeRep. Our implicit gnomes have been those anonymous gnomes managing the recordkeeping system, the creditManager gnome pools, the security system, and all the other commerce-enabling gnome systems provided by Micrognome.

All gnomes have to live someplace. So far, we have described two possible places where gnomes can live. The first is in the departmental stations. The second is in the records room (or the equivalent for the stockClerk gnomes). We have already said the gnomes directly interfacing with customers will live at the departmental stations. And, obviously, stockClerks and creditManagers live in the stock room and records room, respectively. But where do all the myriad anonymous gnomes live that maintain our system?

Perhaps they live at the departmental workstations. But we said that the tasks these gnomes perform are highly complex. We can therefore assume that there is a large number of these gnomes. Departmental stations are small, barely enough room for a human being and the few gnomes that must work directly with the customer. Definitely no room for a small army of system gnomes.

Perhaps they live in the record management room with the creditManagers. But at least some of their tasks will involve coordination of gnomes in different rooms. We discussed one example of such cross-room coordination earlier in the chapter. There we described how the system ensures that either the customer's credit card is debited and a purchase delivered, or the customer's credit card is not debited and the purchase not delivered. So, these gnomes need to live someplace where they have an equal overview of both the record management and the stock rooms.

Putting these system gnomes in the record management room gives them a good overview of the creditManager gnomes, but very little visibility into the lives of the stockClerk gnomes. Of course, putting them into the stock room has the opposite problem.

There is also a space issue. When we built the record management room, we built it large enough to hold the three (or whatever) creditManagers. There isn't room for all of our system gnomes. Similarly, there is no room in the stock room.

So, if we can't put our system gnomes in the departmental station, and we can't put them in the recordkeeping room, and we can't put them in the stock room, what's left?

The answer is to build them a room of their own. This has a lot of advantages. We can ask Micrognome how big the room needs to be, and design one that exactly meets their needs. We can place this room in a location where it can have a good overview of both the record management room and the stock room, and where it can also communicate with the departmental stations.

By building the system gnomes their own room, we end up with a three-layered architecture. At the bottom layer we have the gnomes working at record management and stock movement. At the middle layer we have the system gnomes. At the top layer we have the departmental workstations. Figure 1.13 shows a picture of these three layers. We will describe the Micrognome support for this architecture in detail in the chapter on three-tiered architecture.

Software Components

I hope I have convinced you that gnomes are cute, furry, and very useful creatures. But not everybody has the magic necessary to find these mythical beings. What are the rest of us to do?

Fortunately, there is another entity that is very similar to gnomes. These entities are cheap, readily available, and follow the same rules as do gnomes. These entities are called *software components*. If you liked gnomes, you will love software components. Software components are just like gnomes, except they aren't furry and, even more importantly, they aren't mythical.

Like gnomes, software components need instruction booklets, interfaces, and coordinating systems. The coordination issues components face are exactly like

Figure 1.13 Three-layered gnome architecture.

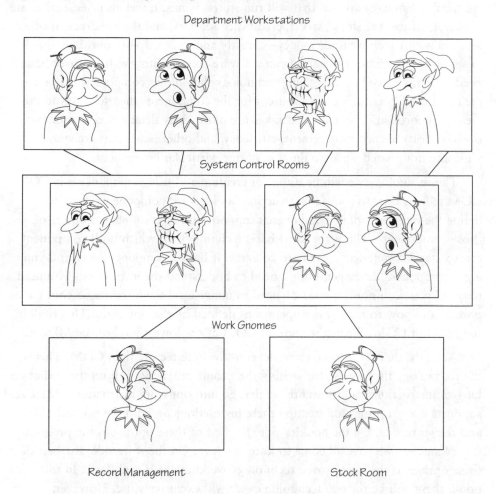

Department Workstations

System Control Rooms

Work Gnomes

Record Management   Stock Room

those faced by gnomes: the need to deal with locality, communications, security, record management, and efficiency. If you understand the problems of gnomes, then you understand exactly the problems faced by components. A component is just a non-hairy gnome.

Like gnomes, components can do specific tasks. You can buy software components that know how to manage credit card purchases, display stock tickers, process calendars, and create sophisticated user interfaces. The list of available components increases daily.

From our perspective, the most important use of components is to build the electronic commerce systems that will run stores, banks, travel agencies, real estate brokerage firms, the stock market, credit card services, and the hundreds of other services with which we trade money—directly and indirectly—in our daily life. In order to built commerce systems from software components, we have three basic needs. First, we need an underlying technology that allows components to be created and used. Second, we need sources for the components themselves. And third, we need coordinating systems that take care of the dirty details of communications, security, record management, efficiency, and other issues that are system-wide and not related *per se* to the task of one particular component.

The technology we will be using for creating and using components is COM. COM tells us how to package instruction booklets for components, how to define the interfaces those components support, and how to make requests of those components. This is the most basic technology on which both component creators and component users need to agree. If I am a component user and you are a component developer, I don't need to understand the instructions you used to build your component, but I do need to understand the interface of your component and how to request the operations defined by that interface. This is all in the realm of COM. We might think of COM as the lowest level of the MDCA.

Actually, there is an even lower level of the architecture than COM. This is the technology that we use for writing the gnome instructions, both those that go into an instruction booklet and those that go into our store instructions. MDCA supports many options for creating these instructions on both the booklet side and the store side. On the booklet side, the best of these options is the programming language we have all come to know as Java. On the store side, the best of these options is the long-proven technology we know as Visual Basic. In this book, these will be the two technologies we will exclusively use. However, MDCA does not require either Visual Basic or Java and, therefore, strictly speaking, they aren't part of MDCA.

An important part of MDCA is the ability to move components out of our immediate space. For gnomes, "space" means rooms and buildings. For components, "space" means processes and machines. We put Cred in the room that contained file cabinets. We put the component equivalent of Cred in a process running on the same computer that manages the databases. Just like we want Cred the gnome to live where he can most efficiently manage his records, we want Cred the component to live where it can most efficiently work with its data source.

The technology that allows us to work with components in different processes and machines is DCOM. Since the ability to work with remote components is fundamental to commerce systems, we might think of DCOM as the second level of the MDCA, the level just above COM.

When we couple COM and DCOM together with the various system levels provided by Microsoft, we get the MDCA. This gives us the systems required to

Figure 1.14 Commerce systems from a gnome's perspective.

Credit Manager

Stock Clerk

Sales Rep

Figure 1.15 Commerce system from a component's perspective.

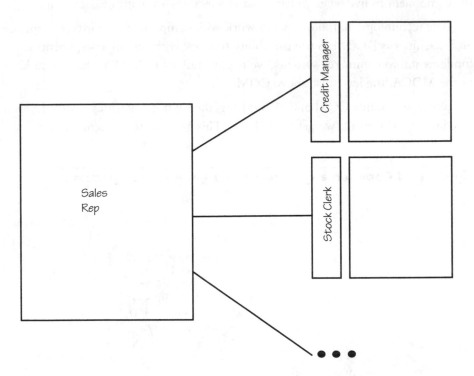

create and distribute components, and systems required to coordinate those components, giving us capabilities such as predictability and security. Just as our gnome-based store system needs to ensure that all of our gnomes are well coordinated, our component-based store system needs to ensure that our software components are well coordinated. For components, this coordination is ensured by the MDCA.

Systems like transactions and security work at a level between the user interface and the actual components. We therefore describe these systems as the MDCA middle layer, or just the MDCA middleware. The middleware includes transactions, databases, security, clustering, and others. The main emphasis of this book is on the COM and DCOM, and how they relate to the MDCA middleware.

Summary

We see that gnomes and components are very similar, so similar that we can learn most of what we need to know about components by studying gnomes. Both have well-defined operations, interfaces to describe those operations, and systems necessary to coordinate their usage in the development of commerce systems. Figure 1.14 shows a typical commerce system from a gnome's perspective. Figure 1.15 shows that same commerce system from a component's perspective.

COM/DCOM ISSUES

COM stands for *Component Object Model*. You wouldn't think these would be fighting words, but a great deal of ink has been spilled over the words *Component Object Model*. Is COM really about components? Does COM have anything to do with objects? What is an object, anyway? For that matter, what is a component? How can COM call itself a model?

This chapter describes COM, some of the issues COM deals with, and why Microsoft has made the COM design choices it has made. We will start by describing many of the issues COM addresses in the context of the mythical gnome world we introduced in Chapter 1. Gnomes can help us clarify issues without getting bogged down in either technical details or academic debates about the meaning of words like *object*.

DCOM stands for *Distributed COM*. This chapter covers DCOM as well as COM. Most books treat these as two separate topics; however, the beauty of DCOM is that it appears so much like COM. In fact, it's fairly arbitrary to say where COM ends and DCOM begins. The demarcation between these two is much more a matter of historical accident than technical foresight.

COM, DCOM, ActiveX, and OLE

In Microsoft's world-class collection of truly confusing technologies, there is probably nothing more confusing than the relationship between what it calls COM, DCOM, ActiveX, and OLE.

COM is the technology that one uses to define components. It is not a technology for implementing components. For this you would use Java (your best choice), C++, Visual Basic, or some other language with COM support. COM is also the technology that one uses for manipulating components, but in a similar vein, it is not a technology one uses for writing client programs. Think of COM as a shell that one wraps around components, and that defines how communication is passed between clients and component objects. This is shown in Figure 2.1.

DCOM is the technology that extends COM to allow component objects to live on remote machines. Microsoft often describes DCOM as "COM with a longer wire." In future releases from Microsoft, I would expect the distinction between COM and DCOM to be de-emphasized and eventually disappear, as Microsoft seeks to position remote component objects as natural extensions of local component objects. DCOM is shown in Figure 2.2.

OLE is a obsolete term used to describe the precursor to ActiveX, back when ActiveX was intended primarily to facilitate the embedding of applications within documents: for example, spreadsheets within word-processing documents.

The term *ActiveX* has succeeded OLE, but is much broader. It includes a hodgepodge of frameworks designed for many different, and often unrelated, purposes. I expect the term *ActiveX* also to become obsolete once Microsoft begins to focus more and more on distributed commerce applications, although it

Figure 2.1 The COM component shell.

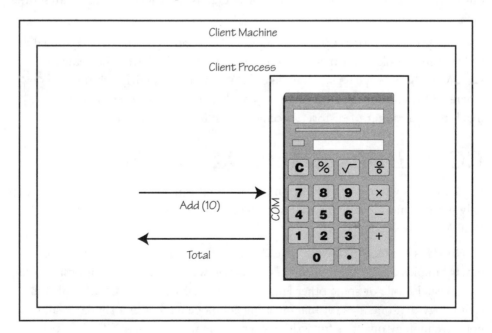

Figure 2.2 DCOM.

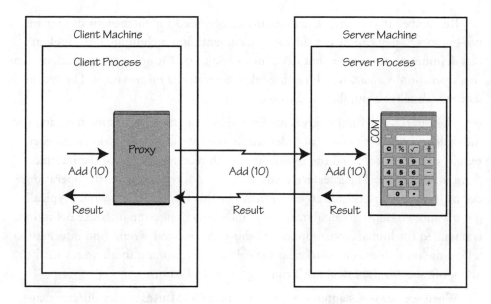

is possible that Microsoft will use ActiveX as a kind of brand name to embrace its distributed commerce frameworks.

Efficiency of Operation Lookup

Let's start by looking at one of the major goals of COM: to allow methods to be invoked on component objects as efficiently as possible.

Let's look at Cal. Cal is a calculator gnome. Knowing that Cal is a calculator gnome tells us two things: First, we know we have a booklet that instructs gnomes on how to act like a calculator. Second, we know we have a calculator interface defined someplace.

The calculator interface definition could look like this:

```
interface calculator {
    clear();
    add(number operand);
    subtract(number operand);
    devide(number operand);
    multiply(number operand);
```

```
total() returns number;
};
```

Remember that interface definitions are provided for the benefit of humans, not gnomes. They can be considered a documentation technique. I can look at this definition and assume that calculator gnomes will support six operations. The first operation is *clear*, which neither takes nor returns information. The second is *add,* which takes a number, and so on.

The interface definition gives me limited information. It tells me the names of the operations, their numerical order within the interface, the information each requires to do its job, and the information each returns. That's all the interface definition tells me. The interface definition does not tell me what the operations do, or how they are related to each other. For this information I would typically go to a more extensive calculator user's guide which, like the interface definition, is intended for human consumption. In this user's guide I would find information telling me that *clear* is used to clear the calculator's running total, *add* is used to add a number to the calculator's running total, and so on.

When we get to Chapter 4, we will see that COM uses a very different language for defining interfaces. The language it uses today is called IDL, for *Interface Definition Language.* But COM could easily support other languages. In the past, its language of choice was called OIDL, for *Object Interface Definition Language.* I expect IDL to undergo a metamorphosis, and probably a name change, in the future as Microsoft seeks tighter integration with Java.

But although it looks different, it contains the same kind of information we are showing here. And the particular language used to define interfaces is not important. What *is* important is the concept by which the interface is defined, in whatever language.

Based on the calculator's interface definition and the user's guide, I can understand how to work with a calculator gnome. Let's say I want to add together the numbers 10 and 15. Conceptually, I will be writing directions like this:

```
create Cal as a calculator gnome;
ask Cal to clear();
ask Cal to add(10);
ask Cal to add(15);
ask Cal to total() getting totalValue;
```

When we ask Cal to perform one of these operations, for example, add(10), he needs to do two things. First, as we discussed in Chapter 1, he needs to find the section in the instruction booklet that contains the *add* instructions. Second, he needs to execute those instructions. The total amount of time required for an *add* operation will therefore be the sum of the time required for the *lookup* and the time required for the *execution*.

These two functions, lookup and execution, are controlled by different layers of the MDCA (Microsoft Distributed Component Architecture, remember?). *Lookup* is part of what COM provides. *Execution* is ultimately controlled by the Java code (or whatever implementation language has been used).

There is little we can say about the execution time. This is largely determined by the skill of the calculator instruction booklet author and the efficiency of the language. Authors who know what they are doing write efficient instructions. Those who don't, don't. So, let's look at the time COM *can* influence, the lookup time. In order to understand how to perform lookup efficiently, we need to understand something about how instruction booklets are organized.

Instruction booklets are made up of pages. The instructions related to a given operation (e.g., *add*) always begin at the top of a page and continue for one or more pages. The first page of the booklet is reserved for a table of contents. The table of contents lists each instruction by name and the page number where its section begins. It's a lot like the book you are now reading, if you think of chapter headings as being analogous to gnome operations.

So, when I ask Cal to add, how might he go about finding the page containing the *add* instructions? He might start thumbing through the whole book, looking at the top of each page to see if it contains the *add* instruction. Or he might scan the table of contents looking for the word *add*, and then go directly to the correct page number. Or we might, instead of asking Cal to add, just gave him the page number with the *add* instructions. What is the relative speed of these three techniques?

Lookup Strategies

You can perform a simple experiment to compare the costs of a full book scan versus the cost of using a table of contents, versus the cost of going directly to a page. Here is what you do. Take three index cards. On the first, write

"Efficiency." On the second, write "Three-Tier Architectures." On the third, write "Lookup Strategies" and the page number you are now reading.

Now find a stopwatch and an innocent bystander (a.k.a. "subject"). Tell the subject you want to time how long it takes to find a particular section in this book. Show your subject what a section looks like both within the book and in the table of contents.

Hand your subject the first card, and time how long it takes to find the section written on that card. Most likely your subject will first look up the name of the section in the table of contents and then go to the correct page. If your subject doesn't do this, find another subject. We will call this lookup technique *name lookup*.

Now take back the book and Krazy-Glue together the pages containing the table of contents. Hand your subject the modified book and the second card, and time how long it takes to find the correct page for that section. We will call this lookup technique *full book scan*.

Now hand your subject the third card (the one with the section name *and* page). Again, time how long it takes to find the correct page for that section. We will call this lookup technique *direct page lookup*. Figure 2.3 compares these three lookup approaches.

When I performed this experiment with a randomly chosen subject (my daughter, Emily), I got the following results. Direct page lookup: 5 seconds. Table of contents lookup: 20 seconds. Full book scan: 180 seconds (and a highly annoyed daughter).

We can draw several conclusions from this experiment. First, full book scans take too long to ever be practical. Second, direct page lookups are the fastest way to find a section. Third, name lookup, while slower than direct page lookup, is fast enough for situations in which speed is not absolutely critical. Because the organization of gnome instruction booklets is similar to the organization of this book, we can use the results of these experiments to predict the speed with which gnomes can find the pages where operations are described using different search strategies, and why COM has made the choices it has made.

At the conclusion of this experiment you will need to purchase a second copy of this book to replace your ruined table of contents. But I honestly feel this is a small price to pay for the important knowledge you will have thus gained.

Figure 2.3 Comparison of three lookup approaches.

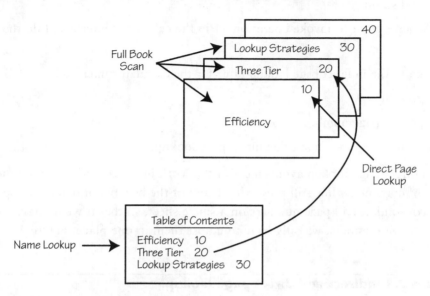

Indirect Page Lookup and VTBLs

Name lookup, although slower than direct page lookup, does have several advantages, primarily from the gnome user's perspective. Name lookup allows the gnome user to request operations by their names, an intuitive mechanism for the user. With direct page lookup, the user must request operations by page number.

Requesting operations by page number has two problems. First, it isn't obvious how users even find page numbers for operations, since instruction booklets are designed for gnomes, not humans. Second, a user may request operations in many places, and each of these will require a page number. If that page number changes for some reason, there are many places where that change must be propagated.

There is a compromise lookup strategy that is almost as fast as direct page lookup and almost as intuitive as name lookup. I call this compromise strategy *indirect page lookup*. Every interface is given a special page I call an *indirect page lookup table*, and every gnome operation of that interface is assigned a sequence number within that page. The indirect page lookup table has one line per operation. Each line contains a page number. The first line contains the page number for the instructions that implement the first operation. The second line contains the page number for the instructions that implement the second operation, and so on.

When I want to invoke operation #1 in the calculator interface, I do the following:

1. I go to the indirect page lookup table for the calculator interface.
2. I go to line #1.
3. I get the page number.
4. I request the operation using direct page lookup.

Indirect page lookup avoids most of the work involved with scanning the table of contents, while still preserving many of the benefits of name lookup. It also consolidates all page numbers on a single sheet, so that if we do have to adjust page numbers, we only have to adjust them in one place. Figure 2.4

Figure 2.4 Indirect and direct page lookup.

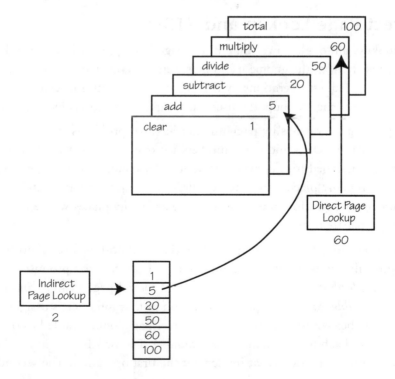

compares indirect page lookup with direct page lookup. And once the gnome user remembers that, say, *add* is operation 2, it becomes almost as easy to request operation 2 as it is to request an *add* instruction.

There is only one last issue we need to resolve. How does the gnome user figure out that *add* will be, by convention, operation 2? Well, it turns out we already have a convenient way of identifying operation sequence numbers. We can use our *interface definition*. Remember the definition for the calculator interface? It looked like this:

```
interface calculator {
    clear();
    add(number operand);
    subtract(number operand);
    devide(number operand);
    multiply(number operand);
    total() returns number;
};
```

We can use this interface definition to assign sequence numbers to operations using the simple convention that the nth operation in the interface definition is assigned the nth sequence number: *clear* is assigned 1, *add* is assigned 2, and so on. Now, as long as both the gnome user and the creator of the indirect page lookup table use the same interface definition, we are all set.

Using the interface definition in this way has one important implication. Once it has been handed out to potential gnome users, it had better not change. Imagine what would happen if a gnome user had been given this interface definition:

```
interface calculator {
    clear();
    add(number operand);
    . . .
```

while the indirect page lookup table was constructed using this definition:

```
interface calculator {
    check();
    clear();
    add(number operand);
    . . .
```

The results of this mix-up are shown in Figure 2.5. With these incompatible versions of the calculator interface definition, the gnome user will assume the *add* operation is assigned sequence 2, while the indirect page lookup table will be constructed assuming that *add* is assigned sequence 3. If I use the indirect page lookup table to get the page for operation 2, thinking operation 2 is *add*, I will in reality get the page for the *clear* operation. That will certainly be a surprise!

The COM Approach(es)

COM supports two techniques for mapping methods invocations to actual code. The first is exactly what I have described as indirect page lookup table. COM calls this *VTBL binding*. The second is a variant on what I have called *name lookup*. COM calls this *IDispatch Binding*.

VTBL, also written vtable, binding makes use of tables containing addresses of code. Like our indirect page lookup table, there is one table per interface, and

Figure 2.5 Incompatible indirect page lookup tables.

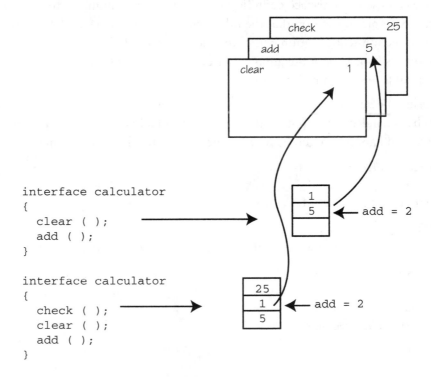

the offset within the table is indicated by the sequence number of the operation. The table is called a VTBL because it is modeled after C++ virtual method tables. This is shown in Figure 2.6.

VTBLs are particularly efficient for compiled languages, like Java or C++. When the Java compiler sees code like this:

```
calculator myCalc = new Calculator;
myCalc.clear();
```

it can automatically make the following adjustments:

- Determine that calculator is a COM-defined component.
- Adjust myCalc to automatically refer to the VTBL for the calculator interface.
- Determine which operation corresponds to *clear*, and replace *clear* by the corresponding sequence number.

The reality is a little more complicated than this, but this gives the general idea.

Interpreted languages have trouble with VTBLs. Because they do not go through a compile phase, it is much more difficult to make these kinds of adjustments. Instead, they use the *IDispatch mechanism*.

Figure 2.6 VTBL for calculator.

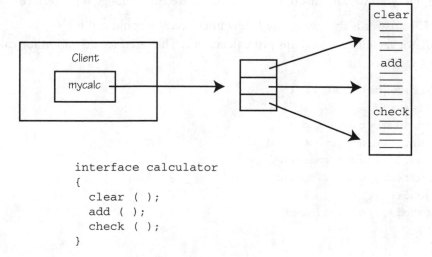

```
interface calculator
{
    clear ( );
    add ( );
    check ( );
}
```

Components that support the IDispatch mechanism include some special operations. These operations basically tell the component what method is being invoked, and the component itself takes care of the dispatching. It's kind of like name lookup, where the component does the lookup. In the case of Java, these operations are automatically implemented by the Java runtime—yet another reason to choose Java for implementing COM components.

When defining an interface, one has to say if the component will support VTBL dispatching, IDispatch, or both. If you follow the guidelines in this book, all of your components will automatically support both dispatch mechanisms. If you are invoking methods from Java, you will automatically use VTBL. If you are invoking methods from Visual Basic, you will automatically use IDispatch, and you will never have to be aware of which is which.

Interface Versions

In the last section, we saw the damage that can be caused when indirect lookup tables are inconsistent. This brings us to a rule about interface definitions. Once an interface definition is released, it is never changed. Any changes would cause grave problems for existing users, so changes must not be allowed.

Let's say we are the company that wrote the calculator instruction booklet and interface definition, and we want to add new functionality to our calculator. Suppose we want to add a square operation that multiplies the running total by itself. How do we add this to the calculator if we can't change the interface?

The answer is that we create a new interface. We could call it calculatorVersion2, or perhaps just calculator2. The interface definition for calculator2 will look like this:

```
interface calculator2 {
    clear();
    add(number operand);
    subtract(number operand);
    devide(number operand);
    multiply(number operand);
    square();
    total() returns number;
};
```

Creating a new version of an interface does not mean we have to rewrite the calculator instruction booklet. All we need to do is create a new interface definition adding the square operation, and create a new indirect page lookup table. This is shown in Figure 2.7.

Now, you might think that all we would have to do to use calculator2 is to rewrite line 1 in our user directions, which had looked like this:

```
create Cal as a calculator gnome;
ask Cal to clear();
ask Cal to add(10);
ask Cal to add(15);
ask Cal to total() getting totalValue;
```

The new line 1 would look like:

```
create Cal as a calculator2 gnome;
```

Figure 2.7 Replacing an interface definition.

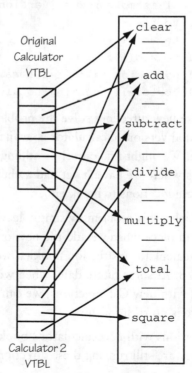

Now I should be able to write directions utilizing the new square operation:

```
ask Cal to clear();
ask Cal to add(10);
ask Cal to add(15);
ask Cal to square();
ask Cal to total() getting totalValue;
```

But in reality, we must do a little more than simply change Cal's type. It is likely that our gnome directions will have to run in many different gnome locations. Some of these locations may not have purchased the new instruction booklet for calculator2. These locations only have available the original instruction booklet for calculator.

In order for our directions to work with either calculator version, we need to create Cal as the most recent calculator version available, and then check his version wherever we are about to request some version-specific operation (like square). Conceptually, our gnome directions now look like this:

```
create Cal as most recent version of calculator gnome;
ask Cal to clear();
ask Cal to add(10);
ask Cal to add(15);
if (Cal's version is at least calculator2) ask Cal to square();
ask Cal to total() getting totalValue;
```

These new directions solve the problem of using Cal at locations where only the original version of calculator is available. But we could also have the opposite problem. We might find ourselves adding the calculator2 instruction booklets to locations where we haven't yet had a chance to update Cal's directions. We don't want these locations to break either.

We solve this problem by simply leaving the original calculator instruction booklet in place when we add the new one. In other words, we don't replace the original calculator instruction booklet, we add another one. This is shown in Figure 2.8. At some future date, when we are sure all of our locations have been updated with new Cal directions, we can remove the original calculator booklet. But there is no rush for this.

Locations with new calculator2 booklets and old Cal directions now work fine. They are still running these directions:

Figure 2.8 A new and an old calculator booklet coexisting.

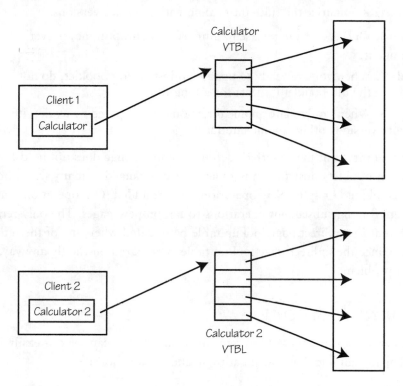

```
create Cal as a calculator gnome;
ask Cal to clear();
ask Cal to add(10);
ask Cal to add(15);
ask Cal to total() getting totalValue;
```

Since we still have the original calculator booklets available, these directions work fine. Once we replace these directions by the new Cal directions:

```
create Cal as most recent version of calculator gnome;
ask Cal to clear();
ask Cal to add(10);
ask Cal to add(15);
if (Cal's version is at least calculator2) ask Cal to square();
ask Cal to total() getting totalValue;
```

we will automatically start picking up the new calculator2 booklet.

So, let's summarize the rules for dealing with interface versions.

- Rule 1. Once you have released an interface definition, never ever change it.
- Rule 2. When you are ready to update an instruction booklet, do not remove the old booklet (at least for a long time).
- Rule 3. When you update gnome directions, be prepared to work with earlier versions of the gnome interface.

The requirement that interface definitions not change does not hold for instruction booklets. Instruction booklets can be changed in many ways. Books can be combined or split. New operations can be added. Old operations can be rewritten, forcing subsequent operations to fall on new pages. The only requirement is that the indirect page lookup table be updated when any of these things happen. Since the indirect page lookup table is prepared on-the-fly anyway, this is not a problem.

Gnome Memory

As a general rule, gnomes need to remember things. You can see this easily in Cal, our calculator gnome. Look again at these gnome directions:

```
create Cal as calculator gnome;
ask Cal to clear();
ask Cal to add(10);
ask Cal to add(15);
ask Cal to total() getting totalValue;
```

These directions assume that when Cal is asked to clear, he is clearing his memory. When he is asked to add(10), he is adding 10 to the result of his last operation, which is 0 from the clear. When he is asked to add(15), he is adding 15 to the most recent result, 10. If Cal had no memory, the total operation would return either 0 or gobbledygook. The correct working of the total requires Cal to keep track of what has happened.

We often have more than one of a given gnome type. For example, these directions use two calculator gnomes. The first keeps track of the total number of customers who have entered our store. The second keeps track of the total amount of money they spent.

```
create TotalCustomers as calculator gnome;
create TotalMoney as calculator gnome;
ask TotalCustomers to clear();
ask TotalMoney to clear();
repeat until (no more customers) {
    ask TotalCustomers to add(1);
    ask TotalMoney to add(purchase of customer);
}
ask TotalCustomers to total() getting NumberOfCustomers;
ask TotalMoney to total() getting TotalPurchases;
```

These directions require not only that calculator gnomes have memory, but that they have individual memory. In these directions, TotalCustomers' memory is different from TotalMoney's memory. If they shared the same memory, these directions wouldn't work.

But I have a surprise for you. In reality, gnomes *do not* have a good memory. In fact, gnomes do not have *any* memory. But clearly, our usage of gnomes requires that gnomes have the ability to remember things. How do we reconcile these facts?

It turns out that gnomes are a lot like me. I also have a bad memory. However I, like gnomes, can give the appearance of total recall. I can do this not because I have a good memory, but because I have a good filing system.

I should warn you that we are about to get into some complex material; however, the good news is that there is nothing in the rest of this section you need to understand in order to use COM/DCOM/Java. The most important point has already been made, and that is that gnomes (components) *do* have memory. There is a lot of confusion in the industry as to whether or not COM components are able to remember things, and many falsely have concluded that they can't. Therefore, I feel compelled to spend some time making the point that indeed they *can* remember, and explain a little of the process they use for doing this. Having said all this, I will add to the confusion by saying that although they can remember things, they shouldn't, for reasons we will explore in Chapter 6. OK, back to the story.

There are many pages of information of which gnomes make use. We have already discussed how the gnome instructions are kept in pages in books. The instructions for each operation start on a new page. An operation can be uniquely identified by the page and the book in which its instructions are located. For example, the instructions for the *add* operation might be found in the calculator book on page 100.

There is another book that is very useful. This book is not assigned to any interface and can be used by anybody for virtually any purpose. Like other books, this book has pages, and these pages can be uniquely identified by the book name and the page number. We will call this book the *scratch pad*.

The scratch pad is the key to gnome memory. Every gnome takes over one or more pages in the scrapbook. Like operation sections, each gnome section begins at the start of some page. Now you might think that gnomes would at least be able to remember where their pages start. After all, even *I* can remember this much about my filing system. But gnomes can't. So, when you ask gnomes to perform operations that require using their memory, you must give them a gentle reminder to help them find their assigned pages.

A request to a gnome to perform an operation requires two components. The first requirement is the book and page number containing the operation instructions, as we discussed earlier in the chapter. This number we look up on the spot in the indirect page lookup table. The second requirement is the page number within the scratch pad that the gnome is using for memory.

When we first create Cal as a calculator gnome, he finds the next available page in the scratch pad and takes it over. We know that whenever we ask Cal to do anything for us, we will have to remind him of what page he is using. You might think that remembering this should be Cal's responsibility, but it isn't. It is ours. If Cal could remember this, he would. But he can't.

We will be using Cal quite a bit. What information do we need to use Cal? We need two numbers. We need the number of the page on which the indirect page lookup table is located, and we need the number of the page that Cal is using for his memory.

Two numbers are too much for us to remember. We are a bit better in the memory department than gnomes, but one number is about our limit. Yet we can't use Cal unless we can remember two numbers: the page of the indirect page lookup table and Cal's memory page. What are we to do?

We are going to steal a trick from Cal. We are going to get an unused page in the scrapbook. We will write two numbers on that page. The first number will be the page of the indirect page lookup table associated with Cal. The second number will be Cal's memory page. Now the only thing we need to remember about Cal is the page number of this page in the scrapbook. This page will be so intimately associated with Cal in our mind that we will even name it our Cal page. This is shown in Figure 2.9.

If we have two calculator gnomes, say Cal and Clare, we will use two pages in the scrapbook. Our Cal page has two numbers. The first number is the page of the indirect page lookup table. The second is Cal's memory page. Similarly, our Clare page has two numbers. The first is the page of her indirect page lookup table, and the second is her memory page.

Let's think for a moment about the nature of indirect page lookup tables. If we have two gnomes, Cal and Clare, both of which are calculator gnomes, how many indirect page lookup tables do we have?

Figure 2.9 The Cal page.

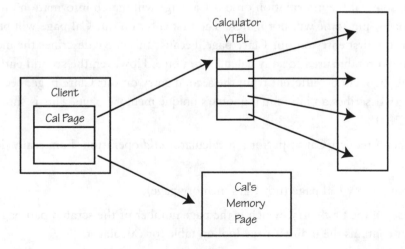

Remember that page lookup tables are driven by two things: the interface definition and the location of operations in the instruction booklet. The calculator interface is

```
interface calculator {
    clear();
    add(number operand);
    subtract(number operand);
    devide(number operand);
    multiply(number operand);
    total() returns number;
};
```

Based on the calculator interface, we know there will be exactly six entries in the indirect page lookup table. We know the first will contain the page number in the calculator booklet containing the instructions for the *clear* operation. We know the second will contain the page number in the calculator booklet for the *add* instruction, and so on.

There is nothing gnome-specific about this table. The entries for Cal will be exactly the same as the entries for Clare. Therefore, there is no reason to maintain two separate indirect name lookup tables. Although we need as many indirect name lookup tables as we have interfaces, all the gnomes of a given interface can share the same table.

So, some of the information on our Cal page will match information on our Clare page, and some will not match. The first entry on our Cal page will be the same as the first entry on our Clare page, because this entry describes the indirect name lookup table used for any calculator gnome. However, the second entry on our Cal page will be different from the second entry on our Clare page, because this entry describes an individual gnome's unique memory page. This is shown in Figure 2.10.

When I request Cal to perform a calculator *add* operation, I am really doing the following:

1. Going to my Cal page (not Cal's memory page).

2. Reading the first entry, which is the page number of the scratch pad page that contains the indirect page lookup table for calculator.

3. Reading the second entry, which is Cal's memory page.

4. Reading the second entry of the indirect page lookup table for calculator, which I know from the interface definition is the entry corresponding to the *add* operation. This entry is the page number in the calculator booklet where the instructions for *add* begin.

5. Requesting Cal to execute the instructions on the *add* page in the calculator booklet, and reminding him that his memory page is the number I looked up in step 3.

The procedure for directing Clare to perform an *add* operation is identical, except that in step 1 I go to my Clare page rather than my Cal page. This process is summarized in Figure 2.11.

Keep in mind the differences between the Cal page and Cal's memory page. I use the Cal page to store the page number on which the indirect page lookup table resides and the page number of Cal's memory page. I own the Cal page. Cal never sees this page and has no idea how I have it organized. Cal uses Cal's memory

Figure 2.10 Cal's and Clare's pages.

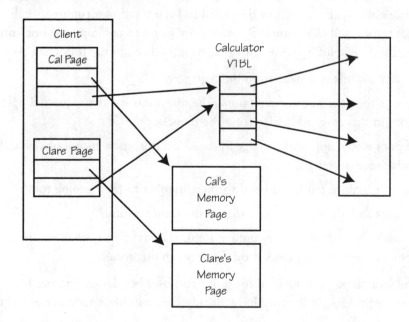

Figure 2.11 Closeup of an *add* request.

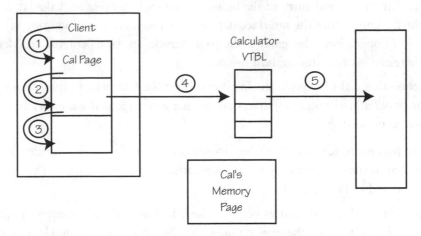

page to store any information he needs to track between operation requests. Cal owns Cal's memory page. I never see this page (except for its page number) and I have no idea how Cal has it organized.

Let's consider all this from the perspective of Cal. Cal is a calculator gnome, and all calculator gnomes know they need to keep track of a running total. Therefore, they will all organize their memory pages to contain only one entry, a running total. When Cal is asked to add, he goes through the following six steps:

1. He gets his memory page from the requester.

2. He gets the page number containing the directions for the requested operation (in this case, *add*), also from the requester.

3. He goes to the appropriate page in the calculator instruction booklet and reads the instructions.

4. The instructions tell him to add the new number to the running total.

5. He goes to his memory page and gets the running total.

6. He adds the number to the running total, erases the entry that was in his memory page, and replaces it by the new running total.

The scratch pad can be used for other purposes besides by gnomes for remembering things. In fact, we have already seen another important use of the scratch pad. The scratch pad is where the indirect page lookup table is located or, more accurately, where the indirect page lookup tables are located, since there is one table for each interface.

We are getting close to some very metaphysical questions, such as "Do gnomes really exist?" and "What is the ultimate nature of reality?"

. . . but we are going to postpone these just a little longer.

Gnome Names

There is nothing special about the gnome names. I can choose any name that appeals to me. Often we choose gnome names that help us remember the purpose to which we are putting the gnome. I can name my gnomes Cal and Clare. I can name my gnomes TotalCustomers and TotalMoney. The gnomes don't care. These directions:

```
create TotalCustomers as calculator gnome;
create TotalMoney as calculator gnome;
ask TotalCustomers to clear();
ask TotalMoney to clear();
repeat until (no more customers) {
    ask TotalCustomers to add(1);
    ask TotalMoney to add(purchase of customer);
}
ask TotalCustomers to total() getting NumberOfCustomers;
ask TotalMoney to total() getting TotalPurchases;
```

work every bit as well as these:

```
create Cal as calculator gnome;
create Clare as calculator gnome;
ask Cal to clear();
ask Clare to clear();
repeat until (no more customers) {
    ask Cal to add(1);
    ask Clare to add(purchase of customer);
}
ask Cal to total() getting NumberOfCustomers;
ask Clare to total() getting TotalPurchases;
```

but the first set of directions is easier for humans to understand, and it is we humans who will have to maintain these directions.

Introduction to Broker System

Up until now our gnomes have been fairly simple, and we have been fairly loose about their use. We have had gnomes related to our store system and our calculator gnome, all of which had limited ability to interact. We used them because they demonstrated basic concepts of gnome usage. But no more kiddie stuff. We are ready for some advanced concepts, and we need a grown-up example.

In this section I introduce a new application. This application is as simple as possible, so you won't have to plow through thousands of lines of gnome instructions, and you should by now have little trouble understanding it. Yet this example is still rich enough to form the start of thread we can follow for the remainder of this book. This example is a sales brokering system that matches up buyers and sellers.

Let's say I want to buy a vintage VW, and I'm willing to pay up to $5,000. I create a gnome that is a buyer's agent. I tell the gnome what I want to buy (vintage VW), and the maximum price I am willing to pay ($5,000). I then register this gnome with the broker system as my buyer's agent. There may be many buyer's agent gnomes registered at any one time, one for each item that somebody wants to buy.

Let's say you want to sell a vintage VW, and you want at least $4,500. You create a gnome that is a seller's agent. You tell the gnome what you want to sell (vintage VW), and the minimum price you are willing to take ($4,500). You then register this gnome with the broker system as your seller's agent. There may be many seller's agent gnomes registered at any one time, one for each item that somebody wants to sell.

The broker system is run by a broker gnome. The broker gnome is responsible for registering and matching up buyers and sellers. A buyer and seller are considered a match if they agree on the item they want to trade (vintage VW), and the buyer's offered price is at least the seller's requested price. If the buyer and seller match, the broker will "negotiate" a price midway between the offered and requested prices. The deal is done, and the two agent gnomes are unregistered.

Interfaces of Broker System

Let's look at the interfaces. The first interface describes operations clients use to interact with their agents:

```
interface: EmployeeInterface;
{
    employee() returns employeeName;
    item() returns itemName;
    price() returns price of item;
    otherName() returns other gnome's name;
    negotiatedPrice() returns brokered price;
    employee(name);
    item(itemName);
    price(newPrice);
}
```

The buyer, say, Charlotte, uses the last three operations to tell her agent her name ("Charlotte"), the item she wants bought, and the maximum price she is willing to pay. Charlotte uses otherName() to find out the name of the seller, if there is one yet, and negotiatedPrice to find out how much she is obligated to pay.

From Charlotte's perspective, she would use instructions like the following to make a buy request:

```
get Broker;
create Choxy supporting EmployeeInterface;
request employee("Charlotte") on Choxy;
request item("1973 VW Bug") on Choxy;
request price(5,000) on Choxy;
request registerBuyer(Choxy) on Broker;
```

Assuming negotiatedPrice returns 0 if the transaction hasn't completed, she can periodically check on the status of the transaction using this operation:

```
request negotiatedPrice() on Choxy getting myPrice;
if (myPrice greater than 0) ...
```

If Meredith wanted to sell her 1973 VW Bug, she would use commands like these:

```
get Broker;
create Moxy supporting EmployeeInterface;
request employee("Meredith") on Moxy;
request item("1973 VW Bug") on Moxy;
request price(4,000) on Moxy;
request registerSeller(Moxy as a SellerAgent) on Broker;
```

The next interface describes operations used by the broker to interact with the agents, in other words, Choxy and Moxy.

```
interface: AgentInterface;
{
    employee() returns employeeName;
    item() returns itemName;
    price() returns price of item;
    otherName() returns other gnome's name;
    negotiatedPrice() returns brokered price;
    negotiatedPrice(newPrice);
    otherName(newName);
}
```

If the broker is trying to negotiate a deal, he needs to know two things: Does the item offered match the item wanted, and is the price offered at least as much as the price wanted? When item is invoked on a buyer's gnome, it returns the name of the item the buyer wants to buy. When item is invoked on a seller's gnome, it returns the name of the item the seller wants to sell. Similarly, price invoked on a buyer and seller gnome returns the price offered and wanted.

In negotiating a deal, the broker will look through all registered buyers and all registered sellers, looking for gnomes that agree on item and whose price is within each other's range. When a match is found, he can broker a deal by, say, choosing a number in between the offered price and the wanted price. The broker then invokes otherName on each of the gnomes, to tell them who their trading partner is, and negotiatedPrice, to tell them the result of the brokered deal.

Once Charlotte and Meredith have prepared their agent gnomes, they interact with the broker using the BrokerInterface operations. The registerBuyer operation is used to register a gnome as a buyer's agent, and the registerSeller operation is used to register a gnome as a seller's agent. We will introduce some more operations in the next chapter, but for now, we will leave it at this:

```
interface: BrokerInterface
{
    registerBuyer(buyer);
    registerSeller(seller);
}
```

Implementation of Broker Operations

The instructions for most of these operations are fairly obvious. For example, consider the first employee operation on EmployeeInterface, the one that takes a parameter, and the second, which doesn't. The first might be implemented by the gnome using these instructions:

```
Go to my memory page;
Go to the entry where I store my name;
Update this entry with my name;
```

The second might be implemented by the gnome using these instructions:

```
Go to my memory page;
Go to the entry where I store my name;
Return to my client this entry;
```

Most of the operations are no more complicated than these. In fact, if one is using Java as the programming language, even these details are hidden. In Java, these implementations would look like:

```
public String employee ()
{
    return myEmployeeName;
}
public void employee (string name)
{
    myEmployeeName = name;
}
```

Pretty simple, isn't it? Very much like absolutely run-of-the-mill Java programming.

However, there are a few tricky implementations, primarily in the BrokerInterface. Let's look at registerBuyer. One of many possible implementations of this operation, using a Java pseudocode, is:

```
request item from BuyerAgent getting ItemToPurchase;
repeat until (no more agents on sellerAgentQueue);
    get next SellerAgent from sellerAgentQueue;
    request item from SellerAgent getting ItemToSell;
    if (ItemToSell matches ItemToPurchase) {
        request price from SellerAgent getting PriceWanted;
        request price from BuyerAgent getting PriceOffered;
        if (PriceOffered is at least PriceWanted) {
            set Price to halfway between
                    PriceOffered and PriceWanted;
            request name from BuyerAgent getting BuyerName;
            request name from SellerAgent getting SellerName;
            request otherName(SellerName) on BuyerAgent;
            request otherName(BuyerName) on SellerAgent;
            request negotiatedPrice(Price) on BuyerAgent;
            request negotiatedPrice(Price) on SellerAgent;
            log transaction in broker log;
            remove SellerAgent from sellerAgentQueue;
        }
    }
    If (no Seller found) {
    then place BuyerAgent on buyerAgentQueue;
}
```

The implementation of registerSeller would look very similar to this.

Features of Broker System

There are many features of this application we haven't seen before. The features are generally characteristic of a large number of applications and, in particular, of those applications having to do with commerce. We will look at most of these features in detail, but let's take a quick overview here.

Client Location. In order to interoperate efficiently, the broker and agents need to be in one location. The actual clients (the ones on whose behalf the agents are operating) will be in locations that are both remote and unpredictable.

Building Block Mentality. One can easily imagine using the broker system as a building block for some other systems, such as stock trading or car brokering.

Multiple Interfaces. Many of these gnomes has more than one set of operations. The buyer agent, for example, has one interface for interacting with its client and another set for interacting with the broker.

Unpredictable Time Frame. The buyer and seller clients have no way to predict how long their agents will take to complete their task. They could take seconds, minutes, hours, days, or they might never complete their task. We need an efficient procedure for letting clients know when their requests have been processed.

Multiple Implementations. We can imagine more than one implementation of these interfaces. For example, the EmployeeInterface's price operation is responsible for returning the amount the buyer client is ready to pay. This operation could be implemented so that it immediately offers less money at first, maximum, and then increases its offer after it has been turned down. It could also be implemented to take into account how long it has been waiting for a sell offer and weight its offer accordingly.

Gnome Sharing. We have operations in the broker interface that take, as part of the information they are given, a gnome with which to interact. There is a long period of time in which a given gnome may be getting requests from two different sources. The broker may be making requests in order to process a transaction, and the gnome's client may be making requests to find out how negotiations are going.

Life Cycle Issues. Gnomes must be created before they can be used, and they must be dematerialized when they are no longer needed. When the gnome is shared, it is important that the gnome not be dematerialized until everybody has finished making requests of that gnome. Making requests of a gnome that has been already dematerialized is very disrespectful.

Performance Bottlenecks. New requests to register buyer and seller agents are blocked until the previous request has been fully processed, either successfully or unsuccessfully. In order for the broker to work efficiently, we need a mechanism for processing more than one request at the same time.

Multi-Language Support. If I am a seller, I want to sell to anybody, not just other English-speaking people. Similarly, if you are a French buyer, you want to be able to buy from anybody, regardless of their native language. Neither of us cares what language was used for developing the various gnome instruction booklets. The system must therefore be language-insensitive. Extending this logic to components means that the programming language used to develop the client must be independent of the programming language used to develop the component. It's well worth noting that this is not the situation we have today with vanilla Java or vanilla C++.

Pyramid of Complexity. There is a pattern to the instruction complexity. As you get closer to the actual clients of this system (Charlotte and Meredith), the number of instructions one must write become fewer, and the complexity of those instructions becomes simpler. Somebody implementing a broker instruction booklet might be looking at a several-person-year project. Somebody implementing a buyer agent might be looking at a several-person-week project. Charlotte and Meredith will be able to implement their instructions in a few minutes.

Client Location

We started discussing the concept of gnome location back in Chapter 1. We were a bit tongue-in-cheek. Let's look a little more seriously at this issue.

In order for the broker system to be useful, we need it to be accessible to clients in different locations. We can imagine our system's configuration looking something like that shown in Figure 2.12.

We have to put the agent gnomes someplace. We have two obvious choices. We can place them on the client machine, or we can place them on the broker

Figure 2.12 Broker system configuration.

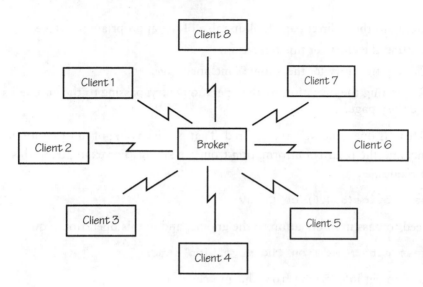

machine. One way or the other, these gnomes are going to have to deal with remote communications. Either they will be communicating remotely with their client or they will be communicating remotely with the broker. Or perhaps, even both.

What are the performance implications of these choices? First, we have to make some assumptions about the relative cost of local and remote operating requests. Let's look a little more closely at what's involved with a remote operation request.

We said back in Chapter 1 that run-of-the-mill gnomes, like agent gnomes, don't know how to use communication systems. We mentioned that we would need to make use of specialized communications gnomes. Now it's time to look more closely at this architecture.

Passing Information Locally

The fundamental basis for all work with gnomes is the operation request. We have already discussed most of the mechanics of making an operation request earlier in the chapter. As we said, an operation request consists of the following steps:

- Going to the indirect page lookup table of the appropriate interface.
- Getting the entry for this operation.
- Getting the entry for the gnome's memory page.
- Requesting the operation by the operation entry, passing to the gnome its memory page.

There is one issue we have ignored. That is the passing of information to the gnome, and the return of information from the gnome. For example, in this operation request

```
request price(5,000) on Choxy;
```

we need to pass in information to the gnome, and in this operation request

```
request otherName() on Choxy getting name;
```

we need to get information from the gnome.

Once again, we are getting into an area with more detail than you need to use COM. Everybody needs to understand the concept of passing information to and from methods. But the *how* is definitely only for those with a "need" to know.

One way we could pass this information back and forth is to use another page in the scratch pad. Let's call this the *information transfer* page. Then we need to agree with the gnome (or more precisely, the gnome instruction booklet) on how we will find this page, and what the entries on that page will represent. Conceptually, we could find this page by passing the gnome the page number, exactly as we did with the gnome's memory page.

Now when we request an operation, we need three pieces of information. We need the operation page number, which we get from the indirect page lookup. We need the number of the gnome's memory page. And we need the page number of the information transfer page.

Once we know the page number of the information transfer page, we can easily agree on how we will use that page. The price operation, for example, requires the transfer of one piece of information from the client to the gnome. This information is the price the client is willing to pay for the desired item. A reasonable protocol would be for the client to insert the price in the first entry in the information transfer page before requesting the price operation.

The gnome can also use the information transfer page to return information to the client. For example, the otherName operation could use the protocol that the first entry in the information transfer page will be used to return the name of the trading partner. This is shown in Figure 2.13.

Notice that a gnome cannot use the information transfer page as a substitute for the gnome's memory page. The information transfer page will be reused on the next operation request, which may or may not even be to the same gnome. So, if the gnome wants to "remember" any of the information that was passed in, the gnome needs to be sure to transfer that information from the information transfer page to the gnome's memory page.

Just as a gnome cannot rely on the permanence of information in the information transfer page, neither can the client. The next operation request will probably overwrite the information on that page, so Charlotte or Meredith must be sure to remember any information they need for later use.

Figure 2.13 Information transfer page.

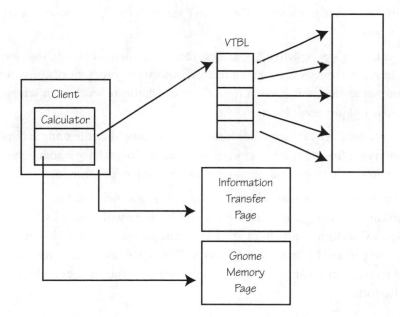

Like I said, if you find that the use of the information transfer page is too complicated to understand, don't worry. Java and Visual Basic will handle all of these details for you.

Passing Information Remotely

Let's consider remoteness from a very simple perspective. Let's assume Charlotte wants to request the price operation on her agent. Normally, she would use this command:

```
request price(5,000) on Choxy;
```

Now let's assume that Choxy lives in a different location from Charlotte. We already know several things, including:

- Charlotte will need to use some kind of communications system to work with her agent.
- Making either Charlotte or Choxy communications-savvy is not a good idea.

From Charlotte's perspective, the easiest mechanism would be one that looks as much as possible like the local case. In other words, it would be nice if the same directions that work when Choxy, her agent, is local, also work when Choxy is remote.

From Choxy's perspective, the easiest mechanism would be one that looks as if the operation requests are coming from Charlotte. In other words, it would be nice if the same mechanisms used to respond to Charlotte work even when Charlotte is in a different location.

Let's see how we can accomplish this. Let's assume that the underlying communications is a phone system, to keep this simple. So we have phone-ignorant Charlotte in one location and phone-ignorant Choxy in another location.

The solution is to use another pair of gnomes, gnomes that know how to do communications. The gnome that lives with Charlotte will look, to Charlotte, just like Choxy. Charlotte can then interact with this gnome just as if the gnome was Choxy. The gnome that lives with Choxy will look just like Charlotte. Choxy will respond to requests coming from this gnome just as if they had actually come from Charlotte.

Let's call the communications gnome that lives with Charlotte a proxy gnome. A gnome that is a proxy for an Employee gnome we will call an Employee Proxy. Every remote gnome with which Charlotte interacts has a proxy living with Charlotte. The Employee Proxy that is the proxy for Choxy we will arbitrarily call ChoxyProxy.

The communications gnome that lives with Choxy is a DoorKeeper gnome. We really only need one DoorKeeper gnome in a given location. Let's call the DoorKeeper gnome that lives with Choxy (and, therefore, the broker) Daryl. Just as Charlotte can communicate with any number of local gnomes at her location, Daryl can communicate with any number of local gnomes at his.

Of course everything that applies to Charlotte applies also to Meredith. The only exception is that Meredith uses a SellerAgentProxy named MoxyProxy. Since Charlotte's and Meredith's agent gnomes both live in the same location (with the broker gnome), they both make use of Daryl. Figure 2.14 shows the relationship between all of these gnomes.

Figure 2.14 Relationship between gnomes.

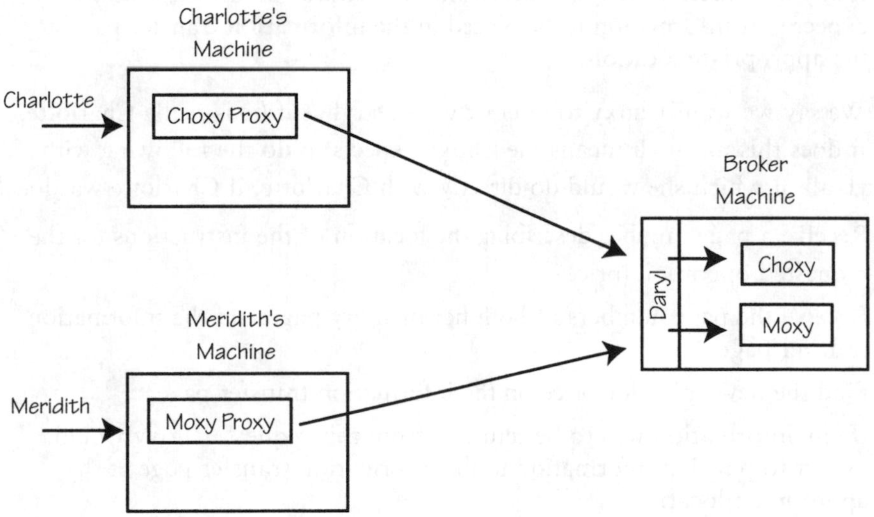

Now, the key to understanding the interactions between everybody is in understanding the basic rule of remote gnome communications. The basic rule is this: Adding communications to a system should have no impact on existing interactions. Charlotte wants to interact with ChoxyProxy as if it is the real Choxy. And Choxy wants to interact with Daryl as if he is really Charlotte. From the perspective of Charlotte and Daryl, local interactions should look just like remote interactions. This concept is shown in Figure 2.15.

We say we want Charlotte to interact with ChoxyProxy as if it is the real Choxy. What does this mean exactly? It means Charlotte expects to do the following with ChoxyProxy, all of which she would do directly with Choxy, if Choxy was local:

- Find an indirect page lookup table for the ChoxyProxy, the layout of which is described by the interface definition for EmployeeInterface.

- Request an operation, say, price, by passing the third entry in the indirect page lookup table corresponding to the location of price in the interface definition.

- Pass in the page number of both the gnome's memory page (that is, the Choxy's memory page) and the information transfer page, which would contain the value of price.

- If any information was returned from this request, Charlotte would expect that information to be placed in the information transfer page at the appropriate location.

We say we want Choxy to interact with Daryl as if he is really Charlotte. What does this mean? It means the Choxy expects to do the following with Daryl, all of which she would do directly with Charlotte, if Charlotte was local:

- Receive a page number describing the location of the instructions for the requested operation (price).

- Receive the page numbers of both her memory page and the information transfer page.

- Find the new value for price on the information transfer page.

- If any information was to be returned from this request, Choxy would expect to put that information in the information transfer page at the appropriate location.

It is clear that the expectations of Charlotte and Choxy don't come even close to the reality of working with telephones. Telephone communications use dialing

Figure 2.15 Comparison of local and remote gnome interactions.

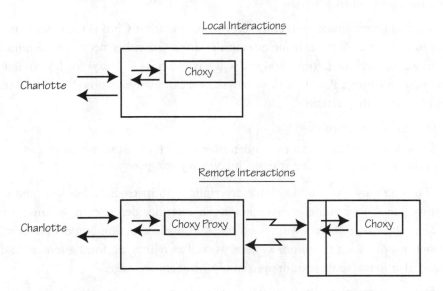

and speaking. There is no such thing as passing book pages through a phone line. And there is no way somebody on one side of a phone line can either examine or write on pages in a book located on the other side of the phone line.

This is the purpose of ChoxyProxy and Daryl: to hide the phone system from Charlotte and Choxy. But don't think of ChoxyProxy and Daryl as magical beings, they aren't. They are just like any other gnomes. They are described by an interface. They get their instructions from an instruction booklet. They have an associated memory page. They know how to work with information transfer pages.

There are three important differences between Choxy and ChoxyProxy. The first is the instructions that implement their respective Employee operations. The second is the information they store on their memory pages. ChoxyProxy's instruction booklet is not going to contain instructions for acting as a proper buyer's agent. It is going to contain instructions for using telephones. And her memory page is not going to store information used by buyer's agents. It is going to store information used for communication with Daryl. The third difference between Choxy and ChoxyProxy is that the latter's interface is constructed automatically, rather than being defined in an interface definition written by a person.

We can pretty much predict the type of information ChoxyProxy needs to store in her memory page. It includes information she either needs for communicating with Daryl, or information she will have to pass to Daryl for his communications with Choxy. Based on this analysis, we can assume ChoxyProxy will store the following information:

- Daryl's phone number.
- Some key that Daryl can use to determine which of his many local gnomes is the gnome for which ChoxyProxy is a proxy.

Daryl will also have an interface description, an instruction booklet, and a memory page. We can pretty much ignore his interface description, because it is used only by ChoxyProxy. We can assume that his instruction booklet contains instructions on using the phone system, as well as managing local gnomes. And we can also make some assumptions about his memory page.

Daryl's memory page will contain a table containing one entry for each local gnome. Let's call this table the *local gnome table*. Each entry in the local gnome table will contain several pieces of information. Let's consider the entry for Choxy. It will need to contain the following:

- The page number of Choxy's indirect lookup page table or, more accurately, the page number of the indirect lookup page table for the EmployeeInterface interface.
- The page number of Choxy's memory page.

Daryl's local gnome table is organized by keys. He can use a given key to locate the entry for a given local gnome. His usage of keys needs to match ChoxyProxy's usage of keys. There are many possible ways the local gnome table could be keyed. We are not going to discuss them here, because the keys are the private business of Daryl and ChoxyProxy. Neither Charlotte nor Choxy ever has to deal with these keys. Daryl's local gnome table is shown in Figure 2.16. Once again, we are in a detail area you don't need to understand to effectively use components.

We have various pages and tables in use. Figure 2.17 summarizes their purposes.

Now we have all the pieces together to follow through a remote request. Let's look at what happens when Charlotte asks her agent to set a price of $5,000.

Figure 2.16 Local gnome table.

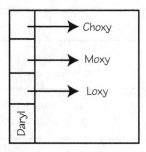

1. Charlotte looks at the interface definition for EmployeeInterface and sees that price is the third operation.

2. Charlotte goes to the indirect page lookup table and finds the third entry.

3. Charlotte gets ChoxyProxy's memory page.

4. Charlotte prepares an information transfer page with 5000 as the first entry.

5. Charlotte requests the operation by page number, passing in the memory page number and the information transfer page number.

6. ChoxyProxy phones Daryl.

7. ChoxyProxy tells Daryl the key for Choxy, the name of the operation requested (price), and reads the first entry on the information transfer page.

8. Daryl uses the key to find the entry for Choxy in his local gnome table.

9. Daryl prepares an information transfer page with the entry ChoxyProxy read him on the phone.

10. Daryl finds Choxy's indirect page lookup table, and finds the entry for "price." This is the third entry (as usual).

11. Daryl finds Choxy's memory page from her entry in his local gnome table.

12. Daryl requests the operation on Choxy via the page number of the page containing the instructions for price.

13. If Choxy had any information to return, she would place that information in the information transfer page, which would be returned to Daryl at the end of the operation. He would then read it back to ChoxyProxy who would return it to Charlotte via her information transfer page.

Figure 2.17 Purpose of pages and tables.

Page or Table	Purpose
Indirect Page Lookup Table	Access to Gnomes instructions. A Gnome equivalent of a VTBL.
Information Transfer Page	Used to transfer information between clients and gnomes. Looks a lot like a procedure call.
Local Gnome Table	Used to keep track of which Gnomes exist on which machine.
Gnome Memory Page	Where a Gnome stores his information.
VTBL	A component's equivalent to an indirect Page Lookup Table.

From Charlotte's perspective, this system works the same, regardless of whether she is interacting with Choxy or ChoxyProxy. The differences are in the implementation of ChoxyProxy. Figure 2.18 contrasts the local and remote interactions.

This proxy business adds considerable flexibility to our system, allowing us to interact with gnomes living virtually anywhere. Proxy gnomes also add considerable complexity. Fortunately, Charlotte doesn't have to be aware of the proxy mechanism at all. She can think of ChoxyProxy as Choxy herself. After all, ChoxyProxy responds to the same operations as does Choxy, with the same net result. The fact that ChoxyProxy can respond to price only by phoning her friend Choxy is really none of our business. If we define ourselves by our behavior, then ChoxyProxy is, to all intents and purposes, an Employee gnome, and indistinguishable from Choxy.

Gnome Sharing

Sometimes you want to share a gnome, and sometimes you don't. What does it mean to share a gnome? It means that more than one person wants to make

Figure 2.18 Local and remote gnome interactions.

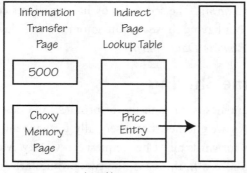

Local Interactions

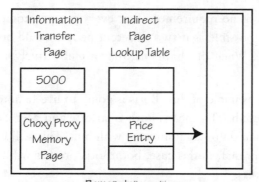

Remote Interactions
(Looks pretty much the same, doesn't it?)

requests of the same remote gnome. The primary reason for using shared gnomes is to set up a public arena in which private gnomes can meet and interact.

Boris the Broker is such a public arena. He takes on the role of coordinating interactions between private gnomes like Choxy and Moxy. Charlotte asks Boris to register her buyer agent. Meredith asks Boris to register her seller agent. Boris then coordinates the buy/sell activity between these two gnomes. If Charlotte and Meredith can't agree on sharing a common broker, they can't interact. If Charlotte registers her agent with one broker, and Meredith registers her agent with another broker, their respective agents will never know about each other. So, Charlotte and Meredith need a mechanism with which to share Boris.

There are two ways for multiple clients to share gnomes. The first is by having the client's proxies all communicating to the same remote gnome. I will call this *Remote Gnome Sharing*. The second is by having clients connected to different remote gnomes, but having those remote gnomes share their data storage area. I will call this *Remote Data Sharing*.

Remote Gnome Sharing

The key to sharing gnomes is through use of proxies. As I described in the last section, proxy gnomes are gnomes that essentially forward all requests to another gnome. ChoxyProxy forwards all of her requests to Choxy. MoxyProxy forwards all of her requests to Moxy. In this case, the two proxies are going to two different gnomes.

However, there is no requirement that every proxy gnome forward to a different gnome. It is possible that two different people could both have proxies to the same gnome. When this happens, they are effectively sharing that gnome.

Boris is a good example of this. Boris is going to live remotely from both Charlotte and Meredith. This means both Charlotte and Meredith will need to use the proxy mechanism to communicate with him. This will work just like their agent proxies, except that, in this case, both Boris proxies will be forwarding to the same gnome, Boris.

Proxies are always used for interacting with remote gnomes. This is true whether or not the gnomes are shared. If a gnome is reachable by only one proxy, then that gnome is *private*. If a gnome is reachable by more than one proxy, then that gnome is *shared*. This is illustrated in Figure 2.19.

Remote Data Sharing

When sharing is accomplished with Remote Data Sharing, rather than Remote Gnome Sharing, the sharing occurs at the data level. Two (or more) gnomes appear to behave as if they were shared, because they all read and write to the same data area. In a sense, it is as if they are using the same memory pages to store their information, except that these memory pages, rather than located on scratch books, are located in sharable persistent data storage. This is shown in Figure 2.20.

Figure 2.19 Private versus shared gnomes.

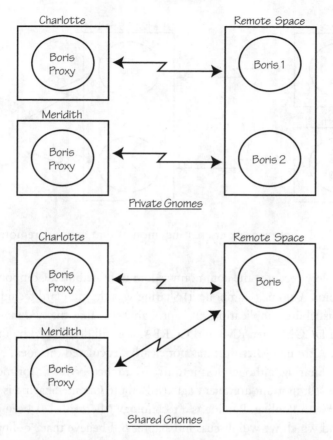

There are some disadvantages to Remote Data Sharing. These include the following:

- Every method in a sharable gnome must read its "memory" from storage at the beginning of its method, and write it back to storage at the end of its method. However, it turns out this is a requirement for transactional processing anyway, which we will cover in Chapter 7.

- The data storage system must have provisions for high-quality sharing. However, it turns out that the data storage systems we would most likely use for this already support high-quality sharing, as we will also cover in Chapter 7.

Figure 2.20 Remote data sharing.

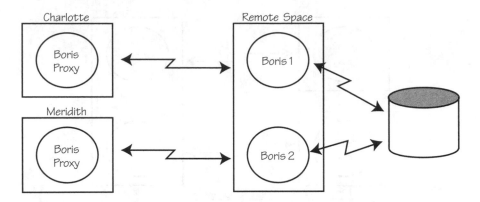

We will look more closely at creating gnomes that support remote data sharing in Chapter 5.

Up until very recently, the common wisdom in Distributed Components/Objects was that Remote Gnome (Component) Sharing was the standard technique for developing distributed applications. It is probably true that the two main competitors to COM/DCOM, Java RMI and CORBA, are still dominated by this faulty line of reasoning. Although Microsoft has not clearly articulated this idea, I believe that Remote Data Sharing, although less intuitive, is a much better fit for most applications. The most important argument against Remote Gnome Sharing is that it is incompatible with Pooling. Pooling is a technology Microsoft has been pushing, rightly so, and which we will discuss in Chapter 6. I believe that Pooling is an essential requirement for any serious commerce-oriented application. This book, therefore, will use Remote Data Sharing exclusively as its gnome-sharing strategy.

Where Little Gnomes Come From

This discussion about proxies and gnomes raises an interesting question. How does one get a proxy to a gnome? But there is really nothing special about proxies. Remember that proxies are just one of many types of gnomes. So, when we ask where proxies come from, we are really asking the question "Where do gnomes come from?"

Gnomes come from other gnomes. There are other possibilities, but this is the most rewarding. You are probably starting to think that maybe there is a whole other side to being a gnome, and maybe being a gnome isn't so bad after all. I say "Shame on you." Gnomes are highly moral and respectable, and would never consider doing You Know What. Besides, this is a family book.

Gnomes come from special gnomes I think of as *wizard gnomes*. Microsoft, in its boring style, calls these *class factories*. A wizard gnome is a specialized gnome. Its purpose in life is to create other gnomes. Some wizards are very specific about the type of gnomes they will create, and some are less fussy. To simplify the discussion, we are going to assume that a given wizard creates one given type of gnome.

The process of creating a remote gnome is therefore a two-wizard process. One wizard creates the gnome in the remote location. Another wizard creates the proxy in our location. We might imagine that the line Charlotte uses for creating a remote gnome:

```
create Choxy as a EmployeeInterface;
```

expands to something like this:

```
get Gandolf, a wizard for EmployeeInterfaces;
get Gwen, a wizard for proxies;
request create on Gandolf returning Choxy;
request create on Gwen returning ChoxyProxy;
link ChoxyProxy to Choxy;
```

But these directions have two problems. One, they have Charlotte making use of Choxy, a gnome that can be accessed only from the remote location. Second, they require Charlotte to use "remote specific" directions. These directions presume Charlotte knows Choxy is going to be remote, violating the stated goal that one should be able to use remote gnomes without knowing whether they are local or remote.

In order to maintain local/remote transparency we need to hide the proxy creation. We can do this by expanding the line:

```
create Choxy as a EmployeeInterface;
```

into these two lines:

```
get Gwen, a wizard for EmployeeInterfaces;
request create on Gwen returning Choxy;
```

The only problem with these directions is that, deep down inside, we know they are a lie. Even though they say Gwen is returning an EmployeeInterface, we know that can't really be true. In order for this system to work, Gwen must really return a EmployeeInterfaceProxy. But what about the fact that the second line says she is returning Choxy? Is this a lie? Shouldn't the line say Gwen is returning ChoxyProxy?

Saying that Gwen returns Choxy rather than ChoxyProxy is more of a white lie than an all-out lie. Choxy is, after all, just an arbitrary name. I say, if Charlotte wants to think of the gnome that Gwen returns as Choxy rather than ChoxyProxy, what's the harm?

In fact, from Charlotte's perspective, there is no difference between ChoxyProxy and Choxy. ChoxyProxy supports all of the operations Choxy supports. When Charlotte makes a request of ChoxyProxy, the request is processed as if it had been made to Choxy. Why confuse Charlotte by making her know anything about ChoxyProxy?

Charlotte's naiveté on the issue of gnomes and proxies can work to her advantage. Now she can use these directions:

```
get Gwen, a wizard for EmployeeInterfaces;
request create on Gwen returning Choxy;
get Broker;
request employee("Charlotte") on Choxy;
request item("1973 VW Bug") on Choxy;
request price(5,000) on Choxy;
request registerBuyer(Choxy as a BuyerAgent) on Broker;
```

These directions now work fine, regardless of whether the gnome Gwen returns is local or remote. In fact, we can go a step further and say that it is none of Charlotte's business whether Gwen decides to create a local EmployeeInterface or to create a remote EmployeeInterface and return a EmployeeInterfaceProxy to Charlotte. Unless Charlotte is very inquisitive, she will never know the difference.

Once again, Java and Visual Basic to the rescue. Both of these languages have much simpler mechanisms for creating component objects and proxies. You will never see wizards (or class factories). But the relationship between remote objects, proxies, and automatic proxy construction is still as described here.

Location Registration

We've already decided that Gwen, the EmployeeInterface wizard, can make the decision as to whether the gnome returned to Charlotte will be a local EmployeeInterface (local Choxy) or a EmployeeInterfaceProxy (ChoxyProxy) to a remote EmployeeInterface (remote Choxy). We can take this a step further. If Gwen decides to make Choxy in a remote location, then Gwen can even decide which location that will be.

This sounds like Charlotte isn't getting much say in Choxy's location—not an insignificant matter. Charlotte is, after all, a human. Perhaps we feel that Gwen, a gnome, shouldn't be making such weighty decisions. But who said Charlotte is human? Perhaps Charlotte is herself a gnome, playing her small part in some master scheme. In this case, it is very convenient to have Charlotte deal only with very simple issues and not try to keep track of every possible location in which she might need to create a buyer agent. In fact, even humans might find this a bit much to keep track of!

This brings us back to the idea of location transparency. We have already said we would like to *use* a gnome without having to know where that gnome is located. Now we are going to extend this concept. Now we are saying we want to *create* a gnome without knowing where that gnome will be created.

Although we say that Gwen will decide where Choxy is going to be located, we are obviously not going to let her make this momentous decision without a great deal of help. We need a mechanism to tell her what the choices are.

How are we going to tell Gwen where Choxy should be created? We don't want to tell her directly. First of all, she may not even exist when we are ready to make that decision. Second, we may have no direct access to Gwen. Third, we may have many wizards involved in our overall system, and we need one mechanism to let them all know what's happening. Fourth, we would like to localize this information, so that we need look in only one place to find out how our gnomes are going to be distributed.

The easiest way to manage this is to have one gnome at each location responsible for knowing how gnome creation requests at that location should be managed. Let's call this gnome a *registrar*, and name our registrar Regis.

Now we are set. I let Regis know where buyer's agents should be created. I can let Regis know this at any time, perhaps when I first install the instruction booklets. When Gwen is ready to create Choxy, she checks with Regis to find how creation requests for EmployeeInterfaces emanating from this location should be resolved. Regis now serves as a central communications point between whatever person is responsible for making these decisions for this location and the individual wizard gnomes used at this location.

The Many Faces of Gnomes

Gnomes can take on more than one role. Choxy, for example, can interact with Charlotte as an *Employee*, that is, a gnome that supports the operations defined by the EmployeeInterface. Choxy can also interact with Boris as an *Agent*, that is, a gnome that supports the operations defined by the AgentInterface. We need to ensure that Boris is using AgentInterface operations, and not EmployeeInterface operations. How can we do this?

Let's review how operations are requested in gnomes, a topic we covered in detail earlier in the chapter. When we request an operation on a gnome, we need these pieces of information:

- *The indirect page lookup table for the correct interface.* This table contains the page numbers of the operation instructions in the appropriate instruction booklet, with the *n*th entry in the table containing the page number of the nth operation in the interface definition.

- *The page number of the gnome's memory page.* This page is used by the gnome to store information.

- *The page number of the information transfer page.* This page contains information the client (Charlotte) wants passed to the gnome, and information the gnome (Choxy) wants transferred back to the client.

If a gnome supports two interfaces, then that gnome can be associated with two indirect page lookup tables. When Charlotte invokes operations on Choxy, she will do so by the indirect page lookup table for the EmployeeInterface. When Boris invokes operations on Choxy, he will do so by the indirect page lookup table for the AgentInterface. But given a pointer to the indirect page lookup table for one interface, how does one get the indirect page lookup table for another?

The answer is, you ask Choxy. Every interface, including the EmployeeInterface, includes operations defined in a default interface, which I would have called BasicObject, but Microsoft calls IUnknown. One of these operations can be used to retrieve page numbers of indirect page lookup tables for other interfaces that gnome supports. I would have called this operation getInterface, but Microsoft called it QueryInterface. This operation takes an operation ID and returns a pointer to the VTBL for that object for that interface.

Because Java clients can avoid the complexity of IUnknown entirely, and Visual Basic clients can avoid it usually, we are not going to discuss it further in this book, but include it here for completeness. If you have the misfortune to be using C++ for your development language, you will have to understand IUnknown and many other details from which Java programmers are luckily shielded.

Extending Interfaces

Earlier in this chapter we introduced two interfaces used in the broker system: EmployeeInterface and AgentInterface. These were their definitions:

```
interface EmployeeInterface
{
    employee() returns employeeName;
    item() returns itemName;
    price() returns price of item;
    otherName() returns other gnome's name;
    negotiatedPrice() returns brokered price;
    employee(name);
    item(itemName);
    price(newPrice);
}
interface AgentInterface
{
    employee() returns employeeName;
    item() returns itemName;
    price() returns price of item;
    otherName() returns other gnome's name;
    negotiatedPrice() returns brokered price;
    negotiatedPrice(newPrice);
    otherName(newName);
}
```

Notice that there is a lot of overlap here. The first five operations are the same in both interfaces. The way we usually deal with this discovery is to factor out the common operations into another interface. Since we know that Employees and Agents are both Gnomes, we will call this common interface GnomeInterface. The GnomeInterface contains those operations that are common to both Employees and Agents. It looks like this:

```
interface GnomeInterface
{
    employee() returns employeeName;
    item() returns itemName;
    price() returns price of item;
    otherName() returns other gnome's name;
    negotiatedPrice() returns brokered price;
}
```

Having made this change, we can rewrite EmployeeInterface and AgentInterface like this:

```
interface EmployeeInterface extends GnomeInterface
{
    employee(name);
    item(itemName);
    price(newPrice);
}
interface AgentInterface extends GnomeInterface
{
    negotiatedPrice(newPrice);
    otherName(newName);
}
```

There are several ways you can read this. One is rather matter-of-factly. That is, GnomeInterface defines these five operations, and EmployeeInterface includes those operations in addition to the three it defines. Another way you can read this is as a way of categorizing the world of objects. We can read this as saying that there are Gnomes, and some of these Gnomes are also Employees, and some of these Gnomes are Agents.

Graphically, we can show this in several ways. Figure 2.21 shows this using subset diagrams. Figure 2.22 shows this using a derivation hierarchy commonly used in software documentation.

Some gnome aficionados describe this extension idea using other terminology. Many people will say that EmployeeInterface is *derived* from GnomeInterface.

Figure 2.21 Interface extension.

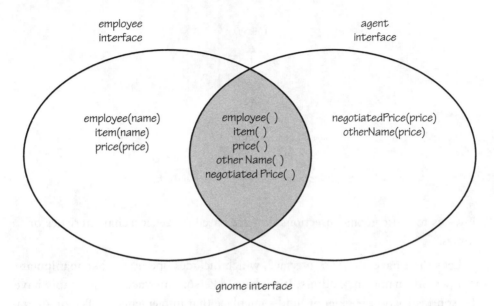

gnome interface

Others say that EmployeeInterface *inherits* from GnomeInterface, a description that I think is particularly nonintuitive. Some (including me) describe GnomeInterface as the base interface and EmployeeInterface as the derived interface. Others describe GnomeInterface as the super interface and EmployeeInterface as the sub interface (again, not very intuitive).

We have already pointed out that all interfaces are derived from IUnknown, the ultimate base interface. And we have also said that we are going to create all of our components to support IDispatch, which is itself derived from IUnknown. We can extend the derivation hierarchy to include both of these interfaces, as shown in Figure 2.23.

Thinking about interface hierarchies as ways of categorizing things is very helpful. It facilitates thinking of an interface in the most generic possible way, and

Figure 2.22 Derivation hierarchy.

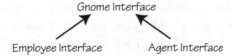

Figure 2.23 Extended interface hierarchy.

allows us to reuse gnome directions that are based on generic characteristics of gnomes.

Let's say I have a Person interface, which includes operations like manipulating a person's name and address. If we have a Person interface, we probably have a Person instruction booklet around someplace that implements the Person operations, and we probably have a bunch of client-side directions that know how to work with Person.

Now, let's say we want to have an Employee interface. Employees also have names and addresses. In fact, despite rumors to the contrary, every Employee is also a Person. Back when I was an Employee of IBM, if I went to Texpresso and ordered a cappuccino, I was treated like a Person. Dave at Texpresso interacts with his customers in the most generic way possible, regardless of whether they are Employees, BankPresidents, AirlinePilots, or Clerks. As far as Dave is concerned, they are all Persons.

Of course, not everybody treats Persons as Persons. Managers interact with Persons as Employees. If somebody accidentally threw a BankPresident in a tank with a manager, chaos would ensue. The manager would assume he was interacting with an Employee, and the BankPresident would assume the manager had lost his mind.

Dave (at Texpresso) and my manager interact with people at different levels of abstraction. Dave deals with only the most generic characteristics of all people. Therefore, his interactions are appropriate for both Employees and BankPresidents. My manager deals with much more specialized characteristics,

characteristics that only some people have. Therefore, his interactions are appropriate for only that subset of people who are also Employees.

This ability to work with the level of abstraction that is appropriate for a particular situation is an important concept. It allows us to reuse a great deal of instructions. We don't need one set of coffee shops for BankPresidents and another set of coffee shops for Clerks, because coffee shops deal with only a generic level of Person abstraction. As directions deal with lower and lower levels of abstraction or, we might say, more and more specialized types of people, the number of different people for whom those directions are appropriate becomes smaller and smaller.

The formal specification for interface extension makes these relationships very clear. When we see these definitions:

```
interface Person
{
  . . .
}
interface Employee extends Person
{
  . . .
}
```

we immediately understand that any Employee is also a Person, and that anything that one can do generally to a Person one can also do specifically to a Employee. We also immediately understand that people in general will not allow themselves to be treated as Employees. It takes a special breed.

Gnome Death

Benjamin Franklin said, "In this world nothing can be said to be certain, except death and taxes." Fortunately for gnomes, they do escape the latter. Unfortunately for gnomes, they don't escape the former. All gnomes die. Choxy, Moxy, and Boris will eventually go to their final resting place. There is no point in being maudlin about this, and the fact is, if they are going to die anyway, it might as well be at a convenient time for us. After all, gnomes take up a lot of resources, and once a gnome has fulfilled his or her purpose in life . . . well, you get the picture.

Gnomes have a very effective recycling system. Once a gnome has died, the gnome's resources are made available to become the stuff of future gnomes. This includes the gnome's memory page and any entries referring to that gnome in the local gnome table (as we discussed earlier in the chapter). Recycling is good, because it is an efficient use of resources. But it is dangerous, because if we try to talk to a dead gnome, we can get some nasty surprises. We may find that whereas we thought we were talking to Choxy (a BuyerAgent) we are in reality talking to a resource that has since turned into Ira (an InternalRevenueServiceAgent).

Even with our simple broker system, things can get tricky. Let's say Charlotte creates Choxy, her Buyer Agent, and registers her with Boris, the Broker. Then Charlotte changes her mind about the purchase, and tells Choxy her services are no longer needed. Choxy then pulls her own plug. But in the meantime, Boris has matched Choxy with a SellerAgent and begins to negotiate with Choxy, unaware that Choxy is no more than a memory. Who or what is Boris negotiating with? The answer is, "Who knows?"

You might think this could be solved by insisting that only Boris make the decision about Choxy's demise. But this also causes problems. Choxy includes operations for future discussions with Charlotte, her mistress. Should Charlotte try to have these discussions with Choxy after Boris has given the word, she is going to be heading for the land of unknown instructions.

So, the Micrognome infrastructure dictates that nobody can tell a gnome when to die. What people *can* do is say is that as far as they are concerned, the gnome can die. When there is nobody left who still cares whether or not the gnome lives or dies, the gnome becomes history. I call this the *Tinkerbell Strategy* to life cycle. When there is nobody left clapping, the gnome just sort of fades away.

Now think about this from a gnome's point of view. Choxy is trying to figure out if anybody still cares about her, so she can decide if life is still worth living. She has gotten two "don't care" votes. But how does she know if those are all the people to whom she was once important? Maybe there is still another soul out there clapping his heart out.

Micrognome therefore provides two related gnome operations. One operation is used to tell the gnome that you are one of the people (or gnomes) with a vested interest in that gnome's life. The other operation is used to tell the gnome you don't care any more. Choxy keeps track of how many people (or gnomes) want her to stay alive, and how many don't care. When the number that don't care is equal to the number that wanted her alive in the first place, she knows her time has come. As long as there is even one person for whom Choxy's life still has meaning, Choxy will stay with us.

So, let's see how this works in the interactions between Charlotte, Boris, and Choxy. Charlotte creates Choxy. Creation automatically registers interest in the gnome. Boris is then asked to registerBuyer, at which time he is first told about Choxy. The first thing Boris should do is tell Choxy he cares about her. This will ensure that Charlotte cannot pull the rug out from underneath him.

At some point, Boris needs to say his affair with Choxy is over. He should do this when he has successfully negotiated a deal between Choxy and Moxy.

Charlotte also needs to let Choxy that her services are no longer needed. She should do this either when she receives word that a deal has been made, or she decides the purchase is no longer worth pursuing.

Choxy is responsible for keeping track of her own life. She heard from two sources that she was important. These two sources were Charlotte and Boris, but she doesn't know that. When she hears from two sources that she *isn't* important, she will make her exit, quietly and with nobility.

You can see a few things that might go wrong here. Charlotte or Boris might forget to register interest. Or Charlotte or Boris might register lack of interest more than once. Either of these errors will cause Choxy to die prematurely. On the other hand, Charlotte or Boris might register interest more than once. Or Charlotte or Boris might forget to register lack of interest. Either of these errors will cause Choxy to live forever, tying up resources that could have been used for new gnomes. It is very important that both Charlotte and Boris scrupulously fulfill their responsibilities.

One last question. We know Charlotte and Boris must let Choxy know whether or not they care. Therefore, there must be two operations: one to let Choxy know that somebody cares, and one to let Choxy know that that same somebody doesn't care anymore. For now, let's call these operations *ICare* and *IDontCare*. But in which interface should these operations live?

We don't want to place these operations in the BuyerAgent interface for two reasons. First, these operations are very general, and could be used to control the life cycle of any gnome. Second, these operations need to be invoked from people or gnomes that may not be using the BuyerAgent interface (like Boris).

The logical interface in which to place these operations is the Basic Gnome interface, or what Microsoft calls IUnknown. Remember IUnknown? This was the interface that we discussed earlier in the chapter. Then it was used for another generic gnome capability: to return a page number for another interface supported by the gnome. That capability was encapsulated in the operation QueryInterface, which also solved a problem faced by all gnomes.

So, now the Gnome interface defines three different operations.

QueryInterface. Used to find the page number of another of the gnome's interfaces.

ICare, or what Microsoft calls **AddRef.** Used to tell the gnome you care about his or her life.

IDontCare, or what Microsoft calls **Release.** Used to tell the gnome you no longer care about his or her life.

It may occur to you that this life cycle business is very tricky. Bad things happen when either you forget to tell a gnome that either you care or don't care, or you tell a gnome too many times that you care or don't care. The good news is that Java programmers don't need to worry about life cycle at all. This whole business is tightly integrated into the Java life-cycle and garbage-collection scheme, and if you are a Java programmer, you can forget you ever read this chapter. If you are a C++ programmer, all I can say is, "my condolences."

Summary

COM and DCOM are important technologies. They give you the capability to define a programming language neutral mechanism for clients and components to interact. They give you the ability to move components around from one computer to another, and to work with components on machines far from your own.

COM objects are defined by interfaces. They contain state. They respond to method invocations by their clients. They can be used as building blocks for complex applications.

COM and DCOM are not without problems. Instantiating objects, object life cycle, and finding specific object interfaces are tricky-client side business. Dealing with dispatching is tricky implementation business. Fortunately, the correct choice of programming languages can go a long way toward simplifying COM/DCOM programming. The choice today is Java for component implementation, and Visual Basic.

THE JAVA LAYER

Time to get serious. In the last chapter, we described a fictional gnome-based system for matching sellers and buyers. In this chapter, we are leaving the land of make-believe. We will look at an actual implementation of this system in a real object-oriented programming language.

I could have written this system in any of several programming languages. C++ would be an obvious choice, since it has the longest historical relationship with the ActiveX architecture. However, I have chosen Java for the following reasons:

- Java is the newest, most exciting development in programming languages in many years.

- Java programming is much easier than C++ programming, and far more suited to my lazy personality.

- Java is a much cleaner fit with the distributed ActiveX architecture than is C++.

- Microsoft has anointed Java as the language of choice for writing distributed ActiveX applications. A lot of this is future hype, since many of the necessary tools are still in their infancy. Nevertheless, it is clear that Microsoft has seen the future, and the future is Java.

Now this is not a book on Java programming. Therefore, I will focus on those features of Java that are of special interest to distributed applications programmers. Features that are reasonably obvious or well covered in the many introductory Java books I will discuss only briefly.

The Big Picture

This book is about writing distributed applications using the Microsoft Distributed Component Architecture (MDCA). MDCA includes many pieces, one of which is Java. Where does Java programming fit into this overall picture?

As shown in Figure 3.1, MDCA can be pictured as a many-layered ball, kind of an onion without the tears (or perhaps, not entirely without the tears). At the outer layers we have coordinating technologies like the *Transaction Server* (or "The Service formally known as Viper"), *messaging* ("Falcon"), and *clustering* ("Wolfpack"). At the next layer, we have the capability to transmit method invocations across machine boundaries. This technology is often referred to as *DCOM* (Distributed Component Object Model). At the next layer, we have the ability to work with *components*. A component is a blob that can do something for you, and with which you interact through strictly defined interfaces. This layer has historically been referred to as *COM* (Component Object Model), and the interfaces are described as *COM interfaces*. At the lowest level, you have programmers implementing these blobs. Where you have programmers, you must have programming

Figure 3.1 The many layers of the Microsoft Distributed Component Architecture (MDCA).

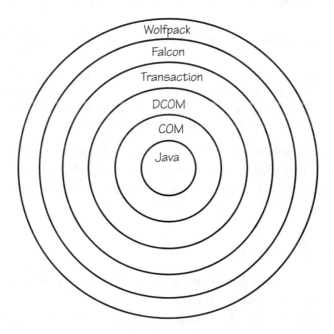

languages. And this is where Java enters the picture. Java is the language of choice for implementing blobs. It's the center of the onion. We will start there, and work our way out.

The History of Java

When I was a child, our morning ritual included throwing Wonder Bread under the broiler. Usually what came out was either raw Wonder Bread or charcoal. If what came out was something between these extremes, we called it "toast" and considered the day off to a wonderful start.

Today, toast is held to a different standard. It must be a perfectly controlled shade of brown. It must eject at a precisely defined moment in time. And, of course, the toast is useless unless coordinated with the automatic cappuccino machine.

This new ideal for toast has spawned a market for technologically advanced toasters. These toasters need much more than heating coils. They need timers, sensors, attenuators, circuit breakers, converters, phase shift adjusters, multiplexers, LAN connections, data converters, and who knows what other techno-baubles. And of course, they need a computer to coordinate all of this frenetic activity.

Where there is a computer, there must be a computer language. And where there is a computer language, there must be a language designer. Enter SunSoft. Their challenge: to design the language to run the computers to control the toasters. The result: an incredibly underwhelming new language called Oak.

At some point it occurred to somebody that the Internet is a lot like a toaster. It must support a lot of different manufacturers. It must run on itsy bitsy little machines. It must not electrocute the end user. If a language could run on a CPU embedded in a toaster, then surely it could run on a machine connected to the Internet. And so, Oak was renamed Java, and the rest, as they say, is history.

Of course, the technology didn't stop with a new language. Any self-respecting language requires a bunch of libraries, programming environments, bridges to other systems, and programming methodologies. So what started out as an attempt to make perfect toast rapidly evolved into the ultimate, full-featured, maxed-out, language theme park we know today as Java.

IBM, never one to miss the obvious, soon decided that Java was of interest to the technical community. Even more important, IBM decided Java might represent its last chance to derail Microsoft in its rapid ascent to total domination of the operating system market. So, IBM joined forces with SunSoft and officially "bet the company" on Java. Having presumably paid off its "bet the company" wagers on OS/2, SOM, OpenDoc, and who knows what else, IBM decided that Java is the answer for which it had been seeking all along.

IBM is not the only company to see the future in Java. Java has forced every major software company to reevaluate its plans. Never in the history of software has a programming language come even close to Java in either the immediacy or the scope of its influence.

It is tempting to explain the unprecedented interest in Java as a testimonial to its technical superiority. But this misses by far the most important allure of Java. Companies are not drawn to Java the language because of its superior features. Better languages than Java have come and gone without leaving so much as a whiff of their passing. Companies are drawn to Java the banner, Java the unifier, Java the equalizer in what these companies see as their common struggle against the dark one, against Microsoft.

Microsoft was thus instrumental in the early adoption of Java the language. It reminds me of the famous play *Waiting for Godot*. Like Godot, Microsoft never appeared on the Java stage and, like Godot, Microsoft was never out of the minds of either the cast or the audience. It is safe to say that no other company played such a pivotal role in Java's acceptance. Even SunSoft, the company that first introduced Java, was a minor character in this drama compared to Microsoft, and IBM's role, despite its huge investment, would barely warrant a mention in the playbill. No, this drama was about one thing. This drama was about the war against Microsoft.

In order to understand why these companies saw Java as their answer to Microsoft, we need to look at the underlying Java technology.

The Technology behind Java

Java is far from perfect. It is still a hodgepodge of mostly incomplete pieces, many of which are not well coordinated, and some of which are actually at odds with each other. However, the fundamental design of Java has both a seductive simplicity and a remarkable richness—a combination guaranteed to intoxicate any true techie.

The most basic Java design principle is the underlying architecture. The Java architecture consists of a language definition, a compiler, a set of class libraries, and a so-called "virtual machine," or an interpreter.

Programmers write Java code following the precepts of the language definition. The Java language is basically a much simpler C++. In the design of Java, every C++ feature was subjected to a worthiness test. If it didn't provide true value for its cost, out it went. Among the casualties were pointers, multiple inheritance, operator overloading, and the oft-maligned goto. Features of other languages were examined and, if found useful, were added. In came automatic garbage collection, dynamic class loading, and interfaces.

Once Java code is written, it is processed by the Java compiler. The Java compiler is not exactly a compiler in that it doesn't produce machine code. Instead, it produces something between Java Code and machine code. This something is called *Java bytecode*.

Java bytecode is, in a sense, machine code, but it is for a machine that doesn't actually exist. It is for a hypothetical machine that has been theoretically optimized for running Java code.

Since there is no machine that can actually run Java bytecode, the Java bytecode needs to be run on a simulator. The simulator, or interpreter, is called the *Java Virtual Machine*. One of the major tasks of porting Java to a new machine lies in porting the Java Virtual Machine.

The Java bytecode is carefully specified by SunSoft, as is the interface to the Java Virtual Machine. Any Java Virtual Machine, regardless of the underlying operating system, can run the bytecode generated by any Java compiler. This ensures that you can download a Java application developed and compiled, say, on an Apple system and run it on a Java Virtual Machine for, say, NT.

Because the Java Virtual Machine is dependent only on Java bytecode, it is, in some sense, independent even of the existence of a Java compiler. Any technology that can generate Java bytecode can produce programs that can be run on a Java Virtual Machine. One could redesign compilers for other languages, say, C++, to generate Java bytecode. One could create GUI packages that directly produce Java bytecode. Any of this Java bytecode, regardless of origin, is fair game for any Java Virtual Machine. This is shown in Figure 3.2.

Figure 3.2 Overview of Java architecture.

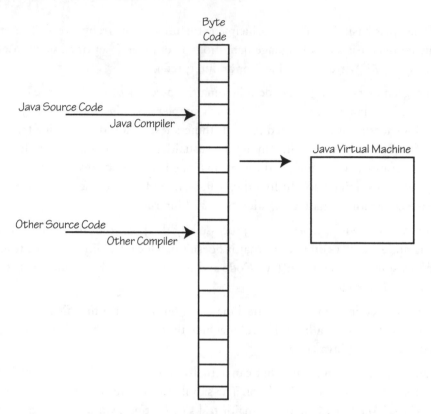

The Java Virtual Machine does not have to be a standalone application running directly on the operating system. It can be embedded in some other application. When this is done, that other application can directly run Java bytecode.

The most famous, and most important, example of embedding a Java Virtual Machine into some other application is that of Netscape Navigator, and now, Microsoft's Internet Explorer. Both of these products are Web browsers, and both include a Java Virtual Machine. This gives the Web browser the ability to run Java bytecode. Since, as we discussed, this bytecode can come from any Java compiler, the Web browser can download the bytecode as needed, as long as it has some way of knowing *which* bytecode is needed and *where* that bytecode can be found. The answer to "which bytecode and where" is given directly in the HTML, the standard specification for a Web page.

There is a serious issue that must be dealt with when downloading Java applications intended to be run within a Web browser. This issue is security. We all know how dangerous it is to download programs from the Internet. Who knows what these programs will really be doing when we think they are merely playing our favorite games.

There are three general techniques used to prevent Java Web applications (called *applets*) from behaving maliciously. One is through the language specification, and the other two are through the Web browser.

The protection through the language specification has mainly to do with memory pointers. Neither Java nor the Java bytecode specification support memory pointers. This automatically eliminates one of the standard techniques used by hackers to penetrate systems.

The Web browser provides protection by one of two techniques. One of these has to do with disallowing selected Java capabilities, such as reading and writing data files, for Web-based applets. This technique is often referred to as *Sandbox Security*, because it treats applets as if they were untrustworthy children who must be kept in a secluded environment for their own and the rest of the world's protection.

Recognizing the great limitation of Sandbox security, Microsoft has been pushing an alternative technology, *Digital Signing*. The idea here is that applets can be signed in such a way that you can verify their point of origin. Presumably, if you can be sure who created the applet, and it is somebody you trust, then you will be willing to let the applet out of the sandbox.

It is very unusual to write a Java program that is fully self-contained. Any interesting Java program will have dependencies on the Java libraries. These libraries are distributed in bytecode format, and one can assume that they are available to any Java Virtual Machine.

Since one never knows exactly which Java Virtual Machine will be running a given program, and almost all programs have dependencies on Java libraries, it stands to reason that these libraries must be carefully standardized if they are to be generally useful. And standardized they are.

Libraries in Java are organized into what are called *packages*. There are eight packages that are part of the standard Java library collection. Each package is organized around specific tasks. Briefly, the six most important of these packages are these:

Applet package. This is used for creating applets to be run within a Web browser.

awt (Abstract Windowing Toolkit) package. This is the package used for creating graphical user interfaces.

io (Input/Output) package. This is similar to the C++ streamio package, used for doing basic I/O to the terminal and to files.

lang (Language) package. This includes classes that are tightly coupled to the Java language, including wrapper classes for the basic types, classes involved with exceptions, and classes used for creating Java threads.

net package. Classes involved in creating network applications.

util package. A useful group of miscellaneous classes such as collection classes, a date class, and a random number generator.

The Java language, compiler, virtual machine, and libraries are all reasonably well established at this point, and should see limited changes. The next group of Java-related technologies is mostly either still in, or just barely out of, the specification stage, and will likely be undergoing significant changes in the next six months. Despite their immaturity, they are very important, and will likely play heavily in future matches of Microsoft versus The World.

JavaBeans is a set of mostly vaporware libraries that together will allow Java components to interoperate over a network. JavaBeans is subdivided into libraries responsible for Component Interface Publishing and Discovery, Event Handling, Persistence, Layout, and Application Builder Support. Most of these systems are in conflict with specifications being developed by the Object Management Group, which virtually all of the anti-Microsoft companies, most notably SunSoft and IBM, claim to also support. The libraries include the following:

- The *CORBA* Java bindings will allow Java to plug into the distributed object architecture as defined by the Object Management Group. This architecture is called CORBA (Common Object Request Broker Architecture).

- The *JDBC* (Java Database Component) package will give Java programmers a standard interface for accessing persistent object data in databases.

- *Java Commerce* is a collection of classes intended to support serious, Internet-based commerce applications. IBM is especially involved in this effort.

- *HotJava* is a set of building blocks intended to be used to develop customizable network-aware applications.

- *RMI* (Remote Method Invocation) will define how a Java object will be able to invoke methods on objects living on remote machines. This work is in conflict with the CORBA Java bindings.

- The JavaOS is a thin client operating system designed to support HotJava applications, and little else. In a press release dated November 6, 1996, IBM announced that is it licensing both JavaOS and HotJava, is "evaluating HotJava for use in future offerings," and that it will offer JavaOS as an option for future network computers. A Network computer is another technology related to Java. It refers to a new class of very inexpensive computers intended exclusively for running either HotJava applications or Web browsers. From IBM's perspective, any computer running JavaOS is one less royalty payment to Microsoft.

So, where is all this leading us? This is the Java world vision:

- Tools are relatively standardized.
- Everything is plugged into the Internet.
- Any application can run on any machine.

And surprisingly, Microsoft fully supports this vision. Well, at least all but the last bullet. But two out of three ain't bad, unless you happen to be the opposition.

The Java Battleground

Because Java is interpreted, a Java program can run on any machine that supports the Java interpreter. And because the Java interpreter is highly portable, it is available for just about every machine type. Java programs do not have to be recompiled, just downloaded and run. There is absolutely no difference between a Java program for Unix and a Java program for Windows NT.

Java's "download and run" capability is an essential part of the "stop Microsoft" strategy. Operating systems are successful because of the number of applications they support. In order to host many applications, an operating system vendor must convince software vendors to write applications for its platform.

Developing a large application involves writing a large amount of operating system-specific code, and porting from one operating system to another is extremely expensive. Software vendors, therefore, preferentially write for those operating systems that have the largest installed base, because the larger the installed base, the larger the pool of potential customers for that vendor's product.

Once an operating system has obtained more than 50-percent penetration of the computer market, a psychological trigger is touched off. At 50-percent penetration, that operating system owns as much of the computer market as all of its competitors combined. And it has a huge advantage in the war for software vendor loyalty. No vendor can possibly afford to ignore 50 percent of the market. The Microsoft Windows family of operating systems has achieved this level of penetration.

So, the non-Microsoft operating systems are at a huge disadvantage, and in a no-win situation. They cannot compete for market share without applications. And they can't convince vendors to write those applications because they don't have the market share. They are in a downward spiral. As more and more vendors abandon them, they have a harder and harder time holding on to what little market share they have, and this further erodes their remaining vendor loyalty. This is the classic pattern that killed OS/2 and is now killing Apple.

But suppose a new technology came along that would allow any program to be run on any computer, regardless of the underlying operating system. This is very attractive to applications vendors. Now they can write their code once, avoid the huge porting expenses, and sell their products to anybody. This is the promise of Java, and you can see its attraction.

The minority players in the operating system arena have a huge stake in Java. They now have a way of courting applications developers. Don't worry about the operating system, they say, just develop to Java and we will port Java to our system. Suddenly the advantage of being number 1 has evaporated, and for numbers 2–100, this is a dream come true.

The minority players still have one problem. If Microsoft owns more than 50 percent of the market, then even with a combined Java strategy they can't offer the platform coverage that Microsoft can. So, it was actually to their benefit to make sure Java was available on the Microsoft platform. This placed them in a funny situation. They needed to make sure that their dreaded competitor had technology that was every bit as sophisticated as what they themselves could offer. Because only if Java was successful on Microsoft platforms would Java be treated as a viable development tool by vendors, and only then could these wanna-be operating systems offer potential customers the applications coverage they needed to survive.

So, the original drive to make Java a useful tool on Microsoft operating systems came not from Microsoft but from SunSoft, the developer of Java, and a competitor to Microsoft. In fact, SunSoft gave the Microsoft version of its Java tools as high a priority as it did those for its own operating system (Solaris). SunSoft had nothing to gain from the Microsoft versions (in fact, it gave them away free), but these versions were necessary if anybody would consider writing applications for Java a real option.

So, let's summarize the wanna-bes' strategy. Their plan was this:

1. Make Java available on as many platforms as possible, including those of the enemy.

2. Popularize the Java virtual machine as the platform of choice for developing applications.

3. Ensure that any Java applications developed for Microsoft operating systems could also run on their operating systems.

4. Erode the advantage Microsoft enjoyed as the operating system supporting by far the largest number of applications.

This strategy relied on two conditions: First, Java had to be ubiquitous. Second, Java had to be the same for all platforms. Java's pervasion was guaranteed by the widespread industry belief that it represented the last stand against Microsoft. Java's uniformity was to be guaranteed by legal ownership of the Java standard by SunSoft.

The Java Wake-Up Call

How would Microsoft respond to the rebel alliance? Microsoft basically had two choices:

- Microsoft could ignore Java, and hope it would eventually go away.
- Microsoft could embrace Java, and make Java its own.

For a while, Microsoft tried the first strategy and downplayed the significance of Java. Java was a new language, Microsoft said. It doesn't fit well with COM.

Nobody wants to rewrite all their applications. Java applets can't be used with Internet Explorer. And so on. However, industry interest in Java continued to snowball, and Microsoft had to reconsider its position.

By early 1996, Microsoft had reconsidered its position. With the agility of a speedboat and the force of a battleship, Microsoft made a complete about-face. Cornelius Willis, the Group Product Manager for the Internet Platform and Tools Division at Microsoft, clearly outlined the Microsoft strategy in a letter dated August 9, 1996, and posted to many bulletin boards. In this letter he said:

> . . . *Microsoft and Sun have absolutely conflicting visions of the future of networked computing.*
>
> *Microsoft believes in giving customers the option of leveraging the hundreds of billions of dollars that they have invested in desktop, server, and portable computers. We know that the 60+ million people who bought PCs and Macs last year will not be satisfied with applications constrained to the least common denominator that Sun has proposed. Programmers and content developers will continue to build great apps and Web sites that take full advantage of today's high-performance Windows and Macintosh architectures, and Microsoft's goal is to make sure those applications can leverage the Internet. Given the rich, interactive multimedia capabilities provided by even today's lowest-cost PC, this approach will enable a whole new generation of more exciting and useful Internet content and applications. These new applications will drive user and developer investments for decades to come. We think the future belongs to a richer, fuller-featured, and lower-cost computing model, rather than the more centralized, controlled, and constrained model.*
>
> *It's worth noting that Sun couches this discussion in terms of Java versus ActiveX. (We couch this discussion as the PC versus Sun.) At this point, Sun is marketing so many technologies under the Java brand name that is difficult to tell where one stops and the next begins. To sort this out more clearly:*

The Java Language. *We think this is a great and exciting technology, for lots of reasons documented elsewhere. We've made sure that Microsoft Visual J++ is the best Java development tool on the planet. . . .*

Cross-platform bytecodes and accompanying Virtual Machine technology. *This is also great. It gives our customers a cross-platform development tool and run time. Of course, it's important to note that there are engineering tradeoffs in using any cross-platform subset. In the case of Java, today it means that you only get four fonts. You get no right mouse button. No QuickTime. No Sound. No printing. . . . In short, there is no way on earth you can create a competitive Macintosh, Windows, or even Solaris (The SunSoft operating system) application. But in many cases, developers will want to trade off rich functionality to support multiple platforms, and for these scenarios Java is a great solution. Of course, we've made sure that Windows is a great, high-performance execution environment for Java bytecodes by making substantial performance enhancements in the Microsoft implementation of Java. . . .*

The Java operating system and chipset. *Now, this Microsoft unapologetically and enthusiastically competes against. We're in the operating system business today; we intend to be in the operating system business in the future. And now that we've dissected Sun's marketing strategy so that real comparisons can be made, compare the JavaOS against what Windows or the Mac, or any other competitive system platform offers in terms of user experience, third-party application support, developer support, price/performance, choice of hardware and peripherals, choice of tools, and all the other factors that customers use to evaluate operating systems. To say the least, Microsoft feels pretty comfortable with this comparison. . . .*

So, about JavaBeans. As a Java customer we are deeply disappointed by the way Sun has managed the introduction and development of JavaBeans. There has been no design review, no open process, not even a private technical briefing, and certainly no spec. Only a press release and a marketing white paper. We certainly can't make any commitments to support or ship it until Sun provides us with an actual specification for it. . . .

Right now we don't see how JavaBeans adds value over and above the ActiveX support already in Java. . . . It's also important to note that we've provided the source implementation for our ActiveX support for Java back to Sun so that Sun can distribute it to other licensees, if they choose to. . . .

Does anybody really buy this stuff anymore? Certainly not the customers who had been paying for Sun's proprietary chipset, proprietary hardware, and proprietary OS, and who are now buying equivalent or faster, "open" Windows NT machines. And spending much, much less money on them.

So, the Microsoft Java strategy can be summarized as follows:

- Make sure generic Java runs at least as well on Microsoft's platforms as on anybody else's.

- Extend Java on Microsoft, so that you can do much more with Java on Microsoft platforms than you can do on anybody else's platforms (including support the distributed commerce framework that is the topic of this book).

- Make sure that the Microsoft extensions to Java work only on Microsoft or, at least, work only on platforms that are paying license fees to Microsoft.

Of course, Microsoft doesn't have a patent on this strategy. There is nothing to prevent anybody else from attempting this. But the reality is that only Microsoft has the huge installed base that makes this strategy feasible.

The Java Religion

Java is more than a programming language. It is a religion. Of course, this is true of most programming languages so, in that sense, there is nothing special about Java. Java the religion comes complete with its own doctrines of infallibility, apotheosis of The Great Ones, public conversions of the newly reformed, excommunication of the rabble-rousers, and a general assortment of ascetics, charismatics, and heretics vying for attention. One person's orthodoxy is an other's blasphemy, so keeping track of the true doctrine is not always an easy task. But there is some general agreement, at least among the rebel alliance, on the following precepts:

I believe that Java is the one language that shall be used by all systems.

I believe that the one true doctrine comes from Cupertino, from the mouth of Sun.

I believe that all operating systems are equal in the eyes of the bytecode.

I believe that the meek shall inherit the earth.

It's easy to see why Microsoft is considered a pariah among the faithful.

Overview of Microsoft Visual J++

When you are working on Java, you will most likely be doing so in the Microsoft Visual J++ environment. Without going into a lot of detail about Visual J++, it's worth giving a quick tutorial and overview of its basic features.

Visual J++ organizes your Java work into projects. Here we will run through the process to create a new Java project, add a class, and do some debugging.

After you bring up Visual J++, you will get a window like that shown in Figure 3.3.

The first thing you will do is start up a new project. You do this by pulling down the File menu, and then choosing New. This will bring up the window shown in Figure 3.4. You will highlight Java Project, enter a location, choose a project name, and click OK.

Figure 3.3 Visual J++ startup.

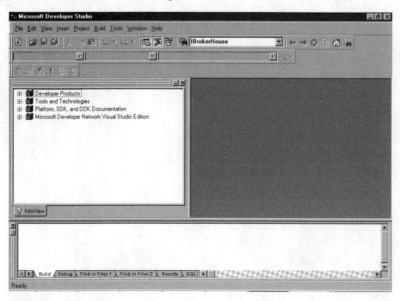

Figure 3.4 The New window.

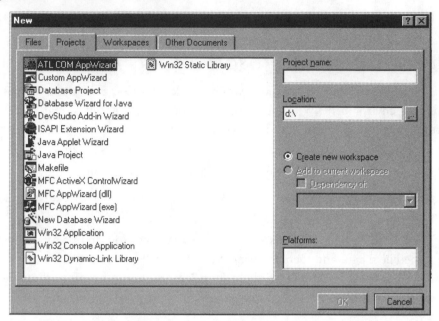

You are now ready to start adding Java source files to your project. First pull down New, then choose Java Source File, the name of the Java class file (in this example, I am using *dog*), then click OK.

Now you want to get into your dog.java file. To do this, choose the FileView thumb tab, click the + in front of Test Files, and double-click on dog.java. Your cursor will now be on the right-hand side of the screen, waiting for you to type. Enter the following:

```
public class dog {
   String bark ()
   {
      return "Woof Woof Woof Woof"
   }
   public static void main(String args[])
   {
      dog myDog = new dog();
      String myDogsBark;
      myDogsBark = myDog.bark();
   }
}
```

Notice there is a missing parenthesis after the Woof string, but leave that off for now just to see what errors look like. You can now compile the class any number of ways, but do it by pressing CTRL-F7. You will now see your error information in the lower part of the screen, as shown in Figure 3.5.

You can go directly to the error by positioning your cursor over the 5,2 in the error message below and double-clicking. Correct the error by adding ; to the end of the line, and recompile.

Now you are ready to execute the program. You can put a break point in the program so you can see the result of the assignment by positioning the cursor on the line following this line:

```
myDogsBark = myDog.bark();
```

and choosing the hand icon. The line will now be preceded by a red dot. If you press F5, you will start up debugging. The first time, you will get a window requesting some debugging information, as shown in Figure 3.6. For the Class file, enter the name of the Java file containing the main routine, which is dog.java. For Run program under, choose Stand-alone interpreter. The program will run

Figure 3.5 A dog with errors.

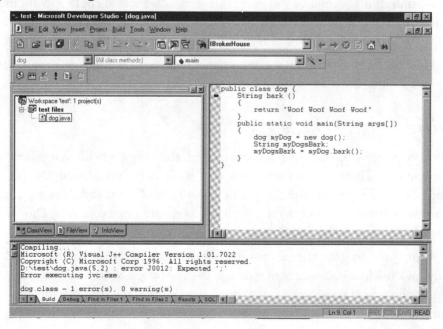

Figure 3.6 Getting debug information.

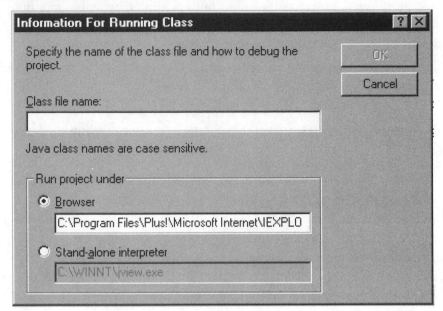

and break on the requested line. If you float the cursor over the word *myDogsBark*, in a second or so you will see a message screen come up with the value of the variable. It should look like Figure 3.7. If you then press Shift+F5, you will stop the debugger.

This should be enough information to get you started with Visual J++, and/or give you an idea of the work environment.

Object Interfaces

Let's review a few basics about Java. In general, this is not a book about Java programming. There are many excellent such books. However, I want this book to be readable by people with no specific knowledge of Java, and there are a few Java details about which even the so-called experts are often confused. One of these is the role of interfaces.

Many Java programmers do not understand the purpose of interfaces, and many Java books discuss them in passing. The reason for this is that one can write sophisticated programs without ever using interfaces. Although any program would greatly benefit from careful organization of interactions between

Figure 3.7 Running the debugger.

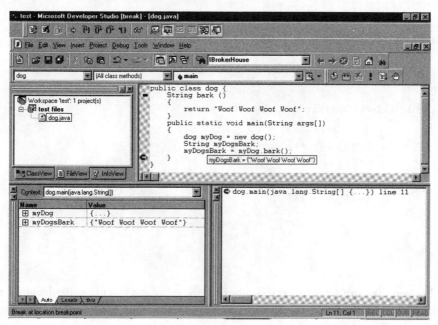

objects as well-defined interfaces, Java does not enforce this. But when it comes to distribution, interfaces are critically important. All interactions with distributed objects *must* go through interfaces.

This reminds me of a sign I once saw in a restaurant men's room: "Employees *must* wash hands. Everybody else *should*." This is true for the relationship between interface and distributed objects: Interactions with distributed objects *must* go through interfaces. All other interactions *should*. But what does it mean to go through an interface instead of a class? And why should one use interfaces instead of classes?

Let's look at a very simple class. This code is in the Chapter03-01 directory in the web zip file. Consider a calculator class, similar to the one we described in the last chapter, but with the ability to only multiply. Suppose Micrognome came out with such a calculator that looked like this:

```
public class MicrognomeCalculator {
    private long first;
    private long second;
    public void setFirstMultiplier(long n1)
```

```
{
    first = n1;
}
public void setSecondMultiplier(long n2)
{
    second = n2;
}
public long multiplyNumbers()
{
    long result = 0;
    long n;
    for (n=0; n<second; n++) {
        result += first;
    }
    return result;
}
}
```

Let's make sure we understand what's happening here. This code declares a public class called MicrognomeCalculator. Declaring the class public means that it can be used by anybody. There are no interfaces involved here.

This class declares some *private data*. Private data is data that will be contained in every object of this class. Declaring the data private means that it can be accessed only by code in this class. Data does not have to be private, but it is a violation of the rules of encapsulation to make it anything else. The state of the private variables of a given object can be considered synonymous with the current state of that object.

This class declares and implements three methods: setFirstMultiplier, setSecondMultiplier, and multiplyNumbers. These are the methods that clients will use to work with MicrognomeCalculators.

In order to use this calculator, you follow the following sequence. First, you instantiate a MicrognomeCalculator. Instantiating a MicrognomeCalculator means creating a new object that looks, smells, feels, and behaves according to the rules of the MicrognomeCalculator class. Second, you tell the calculator to set the first number. You do this by invoking the method setFirstMultiplier with the argument of the number you want set. Third, you tell the calculator to set the second number using the method setSecondMultiplier. Finally, you ask the calculator to multiply the two numbers using the method MultiplyNumbers. The following program demonstrates this. Pay particular attention to the code in getResult():

```
public class MainProgram {
    public static long getResult(
        MicrognomeCalculator calc, long n1, long n2)
    {
        calc.setFirstMultiplier(n1);
        calc.setSecondMultiplier(n2);
        return calc.multiplyNumbers();
    }
    public static void main (String args[])
    {
        MicrognomeCalculator calc = new MicrognomeCalculator();
        System.out.println("4 X 5 = " + getResult(calc, 4, 5));
    }
}
```

Now suppose a competing company, say, ObjectWatch, comes out with a new calculator, greatly streamlined, and with a more efficient implementation of multiply. Their calculator looks like this:

```
public class ObjectWatchCalculator {
    public long multiplyTwoNumbers(long n1, long n2)
    {
        return n1 * n2;
    }
}
```

Clearly, this is a better calculator. It uses a greatly reduced instruction set, and a much more efficient algorithm. So we rush out and buy this new calculator, and now we want to modify our program to use it. How many lines of code do we need to modify? Let's look at the program again, this time with line numbers.

```
1.    public class MainProgram {
2.    public static long getResult(
3.    MicrognomeCalculator calc, long n1, long n2)
```

```
4.     {
5.         calc.setFirstMultiplier(n1);
6.         calc.setSecondMultiplier(n2);
7.         return calc.multiplyNumbers();
8.     }
9.   public static void main (String args[])
10.    {
11.        MicrognomeCalculator calc = new
               MicrognomeCalculator();
12.        System.out.println
               ("4 X 5 = " + getResult(calc, 4, 5));
13.    }
14.}
```

Let's enumerate the required changes.

1. The type declaration of calc in line 11 is wrong. It must change to ObjectWatchCalculator.

2. The constructormethod in line 11 is wrong. It must change to ObjectWatchCalculator().

3. The function that actually uses the calculator, getResult(), declares the wrong type of calculator. It must change to declare an ObjectWatchCalculator.

4. The method invocation setFirstMultiplier() is no longer valid. It must be removed.

5. The method invocation setSecondMultiplier() is no longer valid. It must be removed.

6. The method invocation multiplyNumber() must be changed to multiplyTwoNumbers().

7. The numbers to multiply must be added to the newly changed multiplyTwoNumbers().

The new program would look like this:

```
public class MainProgram {
   public static long getResult
        (ObjectWatchCalculator calc, long n1, long n2)
```

```
    {
        return calc.multiplyTwoNumbers(n1, n2);
    }
    public static void main (String args[])
    {
        ObjectWatchCalculator calc = new ObjectWatchCalculator();
        System.out.println("4 X 5 = " + getResult(calc, 4, 5));
    }
}
```

Seven code changes is a lot of changes, considering the program required only 14 lines in the first place. Had this program required 1000 lines of code, we would likely be looking at close to 500 code changes. Not an amusing prospect.

How could interfaces have helped? In the most optimistic scenario, Micrognome and ObjectWatch could have agreed to disagree on the implementation of multiplication, but could have at least agreed on the interface to multiplication. Suppose they had agreed that the following interface would be used by all calculators:

```
interface Calculator {
    public long multiply(long n1, long n2);
}
```

Micrognome can still use its odd implementation, writing its new class as:

```
class MicrognomeCalculator implements Calculator {

    public long multiply(long first, long second)
    {
        long result = 0;
        long n;
        for (n=0; n<second; n++) {
            result += first;
        }
        return result;
    }
}
```

And ObjectWatch can use its improved algorithm:

```
class ObjectWatchCalculator implements Calculator {
    public long multiply(long n1, long n2)
    {
        return n1 * n2;
    }
}
```

The code shown is part of the web zip file, in the Chapter03_02 directory. These new implementations have the following changes:

- *An interface definition has been introduced.* Interfaces look a lot like classes, except that they have no code for the methods. They define methods, but do not implement them.

- *The classes have been rewritten to implement the interfaces.* When a class says it implements an interface, this constitutes a promise on the part of the class to provide code for all of the methods defined in the interface.

What, you may ask, has this change brought the consumer? With the Calculator interface being the guaranteed user interface, the client code would now look like this:

```
public class MainProgram {
    public static long getResult(Calculator calc, long n1, long n2)
    {
        return calc.multiply(n1, n2);
    }
    public static void main (String args[])
    {
        Calculator calc = new MicrognomeCalculator();
        System.out.println("4 X 5 = " + getResult(calc, 4, 5));
    }
}
```

So again, why is this an improvement? The reason is that now we can switch from using the bad old Micrognome calculator to the good new ObjectWatch calculator by making only one change in the whole program. The change is in this line:

```
        Calculator calc = new MicrognomeCalculator();
```

which needs to change to this:

```
Calculator calc = new ObjectWatchCalculator();
```

That's it. That's the only change. And suddenly we have a new calculator that performs much faster.

So this works fine as long as Micrognome and ObjectWatch are willing to agree on the interface. But suppose one or both is unwilling to cooperate (as hard as this is to imagine in the computer industry). Are we stuck?

It turns out we can still make good use of interfaces. Let's say we make a corporate-wide decision that all calculators are going to support the Calculator interface, and all code we write will be written against that interface. Since we can't get Micrognome and ObjectWatch to use that interface, we can wrap their code ourselves with the calculator interface. A wrapper class for the Micrognome calculator looks like this:

```
public class MicrognomeCalculatorWrapper implements Calculator {
    private MicrognomeCalculator realCalc;
    MicrognomeCalculatorWrapper()
    {
        realCalc = new MicrognomeCalculator();
    }
    public long multiply(long n1, long n2)
    {
        realCalc.setFirstMultiplier(n1);
        realCalc.setSecondMultiplier(n2);
        return realCalc.multiplyNumbers();
    }
}
```

Notice three things about this class. First, it supports the Calculator interface. Second, it contains a reference to a Micrognome calculator, which it sets up at object instantiation time (when MicrognomeCalculatorWrapper will automatically be invoked). Third, it doesn't contain any real calculator code, it simply delegates all calculator invocations off to the Micrognome calculator. A similar wrapper for the ObjectWatch calculator looks like this:

```
public class ObjectWatchCalculatorWrapper implements Calculator {
    private ObjectWatchCalculator realCalc;
```

```
ObjectWatchCalculatorWrapper()
{
    realCalc = new ObjectWatchCalculator();
}
public long multiply(long n1, long n2)
{
    return realCalc.multiplyTwoNumbers(n1, n2);
}
}
```

The same three observations we made about the
MicrognomeCalculatorWrapper apply here as well. This new version of the calculator code is in the Chapter03_03 directory of the web zip file.

Having written these two wrappers, we can now write code that can easily be
ported from one to the other. This program uses the Micrognome calculator:

```
public class MainProgram {
    public static long getResult(Calculator calc, long n1, long n2)
    {
        return calc.multiply(n1, n2);
    }
    public static void main (String args[])
    {
        Calculator calc = new MicrognomeCalculatorWrapper();
            System.out.println("4 X 5 = " + getResult(calc, 4, 5));
    }
}
```

And by changing this one line:

```
        Calculator calc = new MicrognomeCalculatorWrapper();
```

to:

```
        Calculator calc = new ObjectWatchCalculatorWrapper();
```

we have made a total switch in calculator implementations.

Obviously, the best of all worlds is for the world's calculator manufacturers
to agree on interface standards for their products. But even if they refuse to do so,
we can still gain a huge amount of independence by developing our own interface
standards, and then wrapping the code we buy to force it to meet these standards.

We can use very similar techniques for wrapping legacy systems, which becomes very important as companies switch over to the new technology of MDCA (Microsoft Distributed Component Architecture).

Point of Instantiation

Invoking methods through interfaces is very interesting business. Let's look again at this code:

```
public static long getResult(Calculator calc, long n1, long n2)
{
    return calc.multiply(n1, n2);
}
```

When we invoke calc.multiply, we are invoking a method. But what method? The multiply() method is defined on the Calculator interface, but interfaces by definition do not include implementations of methods. So what implementation are we invoking?

The variable *calc* contains a reference to an object. This code has no way of knowing to what object that reference will be set at run time. However, the code does know that whatever object calc is set to, that object will be one supporting the Calculator interface, and therefore supporting the multiply() method. The actual implementation of the multiply method might end up being the MicrognomeCalculatorWrapper implementation, or it might end up being the ObjectWatchCalculatorWrapper implementation, but there will be *some* implementation.

Exactly which implementation will eventually be used is undetermined at compile time. There is no way this can be predicted by looking at the preceding four lines. This determination is made at run time, at the *Point of Instantiation*. The point of instantiation, in this code, occurs when the statement shown in bold is executed *at* run time:

```
public static void main (String args[])
{
    Calculator calc = new MicrognomeCalculator(); // POI
    System.out.println("4 X 5 = " + getResult(calc, 4, 5));
}
```

At the point of instantiation, an object reference is assigned a value. Even though typically the object reference will be declared to be an interface (e.g., Calculator), at the point of instantiation that variable will be set to be an instance of a class (e.g., MicrognomeCalculator, or ObjectWatchCalculator, or MicrognomeCalculatorWrapper, or ObjectWatchCalculatorWrapper). The variable *must* be set to a class, because only classes contain method implementations.

There are many techniques for controlling the actual class of an object at the point of instantiation. We will see more when we discuss DCOM. However, every technique embodies these two important principles:

- The object reference is declared to be an interface.
- The object reference is set to an instance of a class at the point of instantiation.

Program Description

Enough background. Let's see what our serious Java program looks like. In this chapter we will look at the Java code it takes to implement the gnome brokering system described in the last chapter. This implementation is Java only, and makes no use of COM/DCOM. We will add COM/DCOM in the next chapter.

This actually parallels the way you will usually build distributed systems. First, you create a nondistributed version in standard Java (or whatever programming language you are using). Second, you create the COM/DCOM interfaces and test the software within a single process. Third, you move the distributed objects to another process on the same machine. Finally, you move the objects to another machine. This gradual distribution makes testing and debugging considerably easier.

This program is a brokering system between buyers and sellers. It is the Java implementation of the Gnome Broker system we discussed in Chapter 2. The program loops, and in each loop, a user can do any of the following:

- Register to buy something.
- Register to sell something.
- Check to see if any of the sellers and buyers "match."
- List the status of the sellers and buyers.
- Quit the program.

A seller and a buyer "match" if the following conditions are true:

- The seller and buyer agree on the item.
- The buyer is willing to pay at least what the seller wants.

If the program finds a match between a seller and a buyer, the program negotiates a price midway between the buyer's and seller's prices, and tells the buyer and the seller the deal has been consummated.

The buy requests and sell requests are both represented by gnomes. Gnomes know the name of the person they represent, the item they want to sell (or buy), and the price they want to get (or are willing to pay).

Gnomes are implemented as Java Language Objects. The use of the word *object* is confusing, because it is used to refer to both Java-type objects and Component (COM)-type objects. I will generally distinguish between these two types of objects by calling the former *language objects* and the latter *component objects*, but in cases where the context makes it obvious which is being discussed, I will often revert to the common practice of just calling the thing an *object*.

The brokering is done by a Broker language object. The Broker keeps track of all outstanding buyers and sellers. It looks for buyer/seller matches whenever a new buyer or seller is registered, or whenever a request is made for an explicit check for matches.

Clients interact with a user interface language object called *UserSide*. UserSide collects information from the user and transmits that information to the Broker. The Broker then processes that information and returns results to UserSide, which in turn presents the results to the end user. For now, the user interface is made very simple, since user interfaces aren't the focus of this chapter. In a later chapter, we will discuss Microsoft technology that can be used to build a much more interesting user interface.

A typical run of this program looks like this:

```
0-Quit, 1-Buy, 2-Sell, 3-Check, 4-List: 1

What is your name?    Michael
What are you buying? dog
What will you pay?    10
```

With the first loop shown, a buyer named "Michael" registers to purchase a dog for $10. The program then continues with the next loop:

```
0-Quit, 1-Buy, 2-Sell, 3-Check, 4-List: 2

What is your name?    Emily
What are you selling? dog
What is your price?   5
```

In the second loop, Emily registers to sell a dog for $5. Because a buyer has already registered to buy the item Emily is selling, and because the price the buyer will pay ($10) exceeds the asking price ($5), the system considers Emily and Michael a match. We can see this either by choosing option 3 (which will display "match found"), or option 4, which will list all of the matching buyers and sellers:

```
0-Quit, 1-Buy, 2-Sell, 3-Check, 4-List: 4

BUYERS
Michael|dog|10|jane|7|

SELLERS
Emily|dog|5|roger|7|
```

From the listing just shown, we can see that the seller Emily has been matched with the buyer Michael, and that the negotiated price was $7, more or less midway between what Emily was asking and what Michael was willing to pay.

Had Emily been greedier and wanted $15, the system would not have been able to match, even if Michael and Emily agreed that the item of interest was a dog. In this scenario, the final listing would have looked like this:

```
0-Quit, 1-Buy, 2-Sell, 3-Check, 4-List: 4

BUYERS

SELLERS
```

That's what the program does. Let's look at some Java code.

Broker Interfaces

Now that you have a good understanding of Java interfaces, and the relationship between interfaces and classes, let's look at some of the broker interfaces. The code shown in this section is in the Chapter03_04 directory of the web zip file. You will find that much of the discussion in this section parallels that of the section "Extending Interfaces." This is because we purposely chose a language for describing gnome interfaces that looked much like Java, even though this meant putting off a discussion about the real language used for describing COM interfaces until Chapter 4.

Gnomes are used to represent buyers and sellers. Gnomes have two interfaces. Their EmployeeInterface is used by sellers and buyers to tell the gnome the seller's (or buyer's) name, the item he or she wishes to sell (or buy), and the acceptable price. The AgentInterface is used on the broker side to broker the agreement. These two interfaces have a lot of common functionality; that is, functionality used by both the employee and the broker. This common functionality is factored out into a base interface called GnomeInterface, which is a base interface for both EmployeeInterface and AgentInterface. This is very much like the discussion we had in the section "Extending Interfaces" in Chapter 2.

Here is the common GnomeInterface used by both the EmployeeInterface and the AgentInterface.

```
interface GnomeInterface
{
    public String employee();
    public String item();
    public long price();
    public String otherName();
    public long negotiatedPrice();
}
```

The methods in GnomeInterface return the following information:

employee(). The name of the gnome's employee.

item(). The name of the item the employee wants sold (or bought).

price(). The price the seller wants (or the buyer is willing to pay).

otherName(). The name of the employee who bought (or sold) this item, null if no transaction has been completed.

negotiatedPrice(). The price the broker negotiated for this item, zero if no transaction has been completed.

This is the EmployeeInterface, used by the buyer or seller:

```
interface EmployeeInterface extends GnomeInterface{
    public void employee(String newName);
    public void item(String newItem);
    public void price(long newPrice);
}
```

The EmployeeInterface method names looks similar to those in the generic GnomeInterface. Both, for example, declare a method named employee. But keep in mind that Java is like C++, in that both support so-called overloaded method names. This means that methods are differentiated not only on their name, but on their parameter types. Therefore, a method named employee that takes no parameters is different than a method named employee that takes a String parameter. With this in mind, the EmployeeInterface methods have the following purposes:

employee(String). tells the gnome the name of the employee.

item(String). sets the name of the item to sell (or buy).

price(long). sets the price of the item.

The next interface defines those methods used by the broker to coordinate the deal-making. This interface is the AgentInterface. It looks like this:

```
interface AgentInterface extends GnomeInterface {
    public void negotiatedPrice(long newPrice);
    public void otherName(String other);
}
```

These methods defined in this interface have the following purpose:

negotiatedPrice(long). Used by the broker to tell the gnome what price the broker negotiated.

otherName(String). Used by the broker to tell the gnome the name of the other party in the transaction. Both this and the other method are used only when a transaction has been successfully negotiated.

The three interfaces discussed illustrate a common theme, that of a single object supporting multiple interfaces. In this case, the object is a gnome that will represent a buyer or a seller. The gnome has one interface (EmployeeInterface) that is used in its interactions with the person who is setting up the buy (or sell), one interface (AgentInterface) that is used in its interactions with the broker of the system, and one interface (GnomeInterface) that can be used by anybody.

We sometimes describe interfaces as contracts with particular types of users. In this terminology, the EmployeeInterface represents a contract with buyers and sellers, and the AgentInterface represents a contract with the broker. GnomeInterface is part of both of these contracts. By organizing the methods into multiple interfaces, we are able to present to the buyer/seller only those methods that are of interest to the buyer/seller; and to the broker only those methods of interest to the broker. We can further use inheritance to conveniently locate those methods of interest to more than one type of user in a base interface.

A good example of these contracts is in the concept of pricing. The price(long) method is used to set the price of the item being sold (or bought). Clearly, this should be done only by the person setting up the transaction. On the other hand, everybody needs to be able to check on the price, so the price() method is included in the generic GnomeInterface. The negotiated price, however, cannot be set by the employee. Only the broker can determine a fair price midway between the one offered by the buyer and the one requested by the seller. However, once this price has been determined, everybody needs to know what it is. So, in which interfaces would you expect to see negotiatedPrice(long) and negotiatedPrice()? Obviously, in AgentInterface and GnomeInterface, respectively.

Because the broker object interacts only with employees, it only has one interface. The BrokerInterface looks like:

```java
public interface BrokerInterface
{
    public EmployeeInterface getEmployee();

    public void registerBuyer(GnomeInterface newBuyer);
    public GnomeVector getBuys();
    public boolean anyBuys();

    public void registerSeller(GnomeInterface newSeller);
    public GnomeVector getSells();
    public boolean anySells();
}
```

The purpose of these methods is as follows

getEmployee() creates a new object supporting an EmployeeInterface.

registerBuyer(GnomeInterface) registers a new gnome representing a buyer.

getBuys() gets a vector of all gnomes representing buyers that have found a matching seller.

anyBuys() returns *true* if there are any matched buyers, *false* otherwise.

registerSeller(GnomeInterface) registers a new gnome representing a seller.

getSells() gets a vector of all gnomes representing sellers that have found a matching buyer.

anySells() returns *true* if there are any matched sellers, *false* otherwise.

Broker Code

These four interfaces (GnomeInterface, EmployeeInterface, AgentInterface, and BrokerInterface) tell you almost everything you need to know about this system. There are a few missing details, such as exactly what is meant by a GnomeVector (as returned by getSells()), but by and large, we know everything we need to create a brokering system given objects supporting these interfaces.

To give a complete picture of creating a distributed system based on Java classes, we will next look at the files that implement the interfaces we have just finished discussing.

At the lowest level, we have the GnomeVector. This is a class that acts as a Java Vector, which is specifically designed to hold Gnomes and adds one piece of additional piece of functionality to standard Vectors. Vectors are well documented in any documentation on the standard Java libraries, and we won't cover them here, other than to note that they essentially act as a smart array. The GnomeVector class contains a reference to a standard Vector and, for most of its methods, simply passes through to the actual Vector. The GnomeVector implementation is as follows:

```java
import java.util.Vector;
class GnomeVector
{
    private Vector myVector;

    public GnomeVector duplicateVector(boolean remove)
    {
        GnomeVector newVector = new GnomeVector();
        GnomeInterface gnome;
        for (int n=size()-1; n>=0; n—)
        {
            gnome = getGnome(n);
            newVector.addGnome(gnome);
            if (remove) myVector.removeElementAt(n);
        }
        return newVector;
    }
    public GnomeVector()
    {
        myVector = new Vector();
    }
    public GnomeInterface getGnome(int n)
    {
        GnomeInterface gnome;
        gnome = (GnomeInterface) myVector.elementAt(n);
        return gnome;
    }
    public void addGnome(GnomeInterface gnome)
    {
        myVector.addElement(gnome);
    }
    public void removeGnome(int n)
    {
        myVector.removeElementAt(n);
    }
    public int size()
    {
        return myVector.size();
    }
}
```

Let's go through each of these methods.

duplicateVector returns a new GnomeVector, which is a duplicate of this one. The Boolean parameter *true*, causes the Gnomes in the original Vector to be deleted as they are added to the new Vector. For now, that functionality is not helpful, but it will be used to modify this code in later chapters.

GnomeVector is the constructor for a new GnomeVector. Constructors are those methods that are automatically invoked on newly instantiated objects. They always have the same name as that of the class. If you aren't familiar with this concept, consult any standard book on Java.

getGnome returns Gnome, which is stored in the vector as the location specified by the parameter. This method returns an object that supports the GnomeInterface. In fact, this object will support even more specialized interfaces (namely, EmployeeInterface and AgentInterface), but this is more specialization than need concern the GnomeVector.

addGnome adds a Gnome into the end of the vector. It is a pass-through method.

removeGnome removes a Gnome from specified location in the vector.

size returns the number of Gnomes in the vector.

The Broker class implements the various BrokerInterface operations. It makes use of the GnomeVector for storing Gnomes. The Broker implementation starts like this:

```
import java.util.Vector;
public class Broker implements BrokerInterface
{
    private GnomeVector pendingBuys;
    private GnomeVector pendingSells;
    private GnomeVector oldBuys;
    private GnomeVector oldSells;
```

You can see in the preceding code fragment that the Broker implementation will use four GnomeVectors to store buyers waiting for sellers (pendingBuys), sellers waiting for buyers (pendingSells), buyers who have been matched with sellers (oldBuys), and sellers who have been matched with buyers (oldSells). The first method is the class constructor, which sets up these variables.

```java
public Broker()
{
    pendingBuys = new GnomeVector();
    pendingSells = new GnomeVector();
    oldBuys = new GnomeVector();
    oldSells = new GnomeVector();
}
```

The getEmployee() method is straightforward. It will be used to instantiate Gnomes. We could have done without this at this point, but eventually we are going to add more code in here as the Broker needs prime employees with specific information.

```java
public EmployeeInterface getEmployee ()
{
    Gnome gnome = new Gnome();
    return (EmployeeInterface) gnome;
}
```

The next four methods just return references to the private GnomeVectors.

```java
public GnomeVector getPendingBuys()
{
    return pendingBuys;
}
public GnomeVector getPendingSells()
{
    return pendingSells;
}
public GnomeVector getOldBuys()
{
    return oldBuys;
}
public GnomeVector getOldSells()
{
    return oldSells;
}
```

The next two methods return a Boolean telling whether or not there are any matched buyers or sellers, and the following two return arrays containing the matched buyers and sellers.

```
public boolean anyBuys()
{
    GnomeVector v = oldBuys.duplicateVector(false);
    if (v.size() > 0) return true;
    else return false;
}
public boolean anySells()
{
    GnomeVector v = oldSells.duplicateVector(false);
    if (v.size() > 0) return true;
    else return false;
}
public GnomeVector getBuys()
{
    GnomeVector v = oldBuys.duplicateVector(true);
    return v;
}
public GnomeVector getSells()
{
    GnomeVector v = oldSells.duplicateVector(true);
    return v;
}
```

You are probably looking at these methods and wondering why we bothered with duplicating the arrays, instead of just using the original sizes. This code is basically set up to simplify some work we will be looking at in later chapters, and we are trying to keep the code as parallel as possible. So be patient for a while on this.

The next two methods are used for registering buyers and sellers. Both are very simple, because they relegate the real work to a private method, lookForMatches(), which we will see in a moment.

```
public void registerBuyer(GnomeInterface newBuyer)
{
    pendingBuys.addGnome(newBuyer);
    lookForMatches();
}

public void registerSeller(GnomeInterface newSeller)
{
```

```
        pendingSells.addGnome(newSeller);
        lookForMatches();
    }
```

Finally, the only two methods that do any real work. Both are private, meaning two things. First, they can be invoked only from other methods of this class. Second, they do not appear in the interface (since they are not part of any contracts). Because they are really an implementation detail of this class, we will not step through their code here. It is all standard Java fare. The first method is just a loop controller, preparing each buyer and seller for a match check.

```
private void lookForMatches()
{
    int nSellers;
    int nBuyers;

    AgentInterface buyer, seller;

    check:
    for (nSellers = 0; nSellers < pendingSells.size();
         nSellers++) {
       seller = (AgentInterface)
            pendingSells.getGnome(nSellers);
       for (nBuyers = 0; nBuyers < pendingBuys.size();
            nBuyers++) {
          buyer = (AgentInterface)
               pendingBuys.getGnome(nBuyers);
          if (lookForMatch(buyer, seller)) {
             pendingSells.removeGnome(nSellers);
             pendingBuys.removeGnome(nBuyers);
             break check;
          }
       }
    }
}
```

The next method does the actual match check and, if found, updates the buyer and seller object.

```
private boolean lookForMatch (
      AgentInterface buyer, AgentInterface seller)
```

```
    {
        String itemToSell;
        String itemToBuy;
        long sellPrice;
        long buyPrice;
        long midPrice;
        String buyerName;
        String sellerName;

        itemToSell = seller.item();
        itemToBuy = buyer.item();

        if (itemToSell.compareTo(itemToBuy) != 0) {
            return false;
        }

        sellPrice = seller.price();
        buyPrice  = buyer.price();

        if (buyPrice >= sellPrice) {
            buyerName = buyer.employee();
            sellerName = seller.employee();
            midPrice = (buyPrice + sellPrice)/2;

            seller.negotiatedPrice(midPrice);
            buyer.negotiatedPrice(midPrice);
            seller.otherName(buyerName);
            buyer.otherName(sellerName);

            oldBuys.addGnome((GnomeInterface) buyer);
            oldSells.addGnome((GnomeInterface) seller);

            return true;
        }
        return false;
    }
}
```

The Gnome class implements three interfaces: GnomeInterface, EmployeeInterface, and AgentInterface. These interfaces represent the different roles Gnomes can play. Note that the Gnome class doesn't explicitly state that it implements the GnomeInterface, but this is implied by the fact that both of the other interfaces are derived from this one. The code here is very simple. It does no more than update private variables.

```java
class Gnome implements AgentInterface, EmployeeInterface
{
    private String myEmployeeName;
    private String myItemName;
    private long myPrice;
    private long myNegotiatedPrice;
    private String otherName;

    public Gnome()
    {
        myEmployeeName = "Unknown";
        myItemName = "Unknown";
        myPrice = 0;
        myNegotiatedPrice = 0;
        otherName = "None";
    }
    public String employee()
    {
        return myEmployeeName;
    }
    public void employee(String employeeName)
    {
        myEmployeeName = employeeName;
    }
    public String item()
    {
        return myItemName;
    }
    public void item(String itemName)
    {
        myItemName = itemName;
    }
    public void price(long price)
    {
        myPrice = price;
```

```
    }
    public long price()
    {
        return myPrice;
    }
    public String otherName()
    {
        return otherName;
    }
    public void otherName(String newName)
    {
        otherName = newName;
    }
    public long negotiatedPrice()
    {
        return myNegotiatedPrice;
    }
    public void negotiatedPrice(long newPrice)
    {
        myNegotiatedPrice = newPrice;
    }
}
```

Finally, we have the UserSide class, with which clients interact. This is an interesting class because it shows many problems with this code that COM will help solve. The two biggest problems are the code complexity and the poor-quality user interface. The class starts out with:

```
import java.io.*;
public class UserSide
{
    private BrokerInterface broker = null;
    final static int done = 0;
    final static int buy = 1;
    final static int sell = 2;
    final static int check = 3;
    final static int list = 4;
```

The first three "methods" are intimately associated with the main program. Java proponents are fond of saying that Java is fully object-oriented, because everything is a class and all code is embodied in the method in some class. A careful look at this code (and almost any Java code) should convince you of the absurdity of this argument. In reality, Java is no more or less object-oriented than any other language (although it does have other redeeming features, especially as it relates to COM).

```java
public static void main(String args[])
{
    UserSide myUserSide = new UserSide();
    myUserSide.runit1(args);
}
private void runit(String args[])
{
    int next;
    while (true)
    {
        next = seeWhatToDo();
        if (next == done) break;
        else if (next == buy)   prepareBuyOrder();
        else if (next == sell)  prepareSellOrder();
        else if (next == check) checkStatus();
        else if (next == list)  listStatus();
    }
}
private int seeWhatToDo()
{
    int next = -1;
    while (next < done || next > list) {
        next =
        readNumber("0-Quit, 1-Buy, 2-Sell, 3-Check, 4-List: ");
    }
    return next;
}
```

The next four methods correspond to the four menu choices. The first asks if there are any buyers or sellers in the Vectors of buyers and sellers who have been matched.

```java
private void checkStatus()
{
```

```
BrokerInterface myBroker = getBroker();
if (myBroker.anyBuys() || myBroker.anySells()) {
    System.out.println("Match found");
}
else {
    System.out.println("No match found");
}
}
```

The next method is used to list the matched buyers and sellers. It gets copies of the vectors in question and turns them into strings. There is no reason at this point to make copies of the vectors, but there will be in later versions of this code, and we are going for consistency here.

```
private void listStatus()
{
    String sellerText, buyerText;

    BrokerInterface myBroker = getBroker();
    GnomeVector v = myBroker.getSells();
    sellerText = getGnomeVectorString(v);

    v = myBroker.getBuys();
    buyerText = getGnomeVectorString(v);

    System.out.println("BUYERS");
    System.out.println(buyerText);
    System.out.println("SELLERS");
    System.out.println(sellerText);
}
```

The next method gets a new employee from the broker object, sets up information for a buy, places that information in the Employee, and registers the Employee with the broker as a buyer.

```
private void prepareBuyOrder()
{
    String name, item;
    int price;
```

```
    BrokerInterface myBroker = getBroker();
    EmployeeInterface agent =
         myBroker.getEmployee();

    System.out.println("");
    name =  readLine  ("What is your name?   ");
    item =  readLine  ("What are you buying? ");
    price = readNumber("What will you pay?   ");
    System.out.println("");

    agent.employee(name);
    agent.item(item);
    agent.price(price);
    myBroker.registerBuyer((GnomeInterface) agent);
}
```

This method is almost like the last, except that the Employee is eventually registered as a seller rather than a buyer.

```
private void prepareSellOrder()
{
    String name, item;
    int price;
    BrokerInterface myBroker = getBroker();
    EmployeeInterface agent= myBroker.getEmployee ();

    System.out.println("");
    name =  readLine  ("What is your name?   ");
    item =  readLine  ("What are you selling? ");
    price = readNumber("What is your price?   ");
    System.out.println("");

    agent.employee(name);
    agent.item(item);
    agent.price(price);
    myBroker.registerSeller((GnomeInterface) agent);
}
```

The next method is used to get a broker object. For now it does very little, but it will be the focus of a lot of attention in later chapters.

```
private BrokerInterface getBroker()
{
    if (broker == null) broker = new Broker();
    return broker;
}
```

The remaining methods are totally uninteresting, but included for completeness:

```
private String getGnomeVectorString(GnomeVector v)
{
    String s = "";
    EmployeeInterface gnome = null;
    int nsize = v.size();
    for (int n=0; n<nsize; n++) {
        gnome = (EmployeeInterface) v.getGnome(n);
        s = s + getEmployeeText(gnome) + "\n";
    }
    return s;

}
private String getEmployeeText(EmployeeInterface gnome)
{
    String s =
            gnome.employee()           + "|"
            +gnome.item()              + "|"
            +gnome.price()             + "|"
            +gnome.otherName()         + "|"
            +gnome.negotiatedPrice()   + "|";
    return s;
}
```

That's it for the interfaces and code. Kind of a cute little application, but with many problems including these:

- *This application doesn't store any data.* Every time the application starts up, it starts with a fresh set of data.

- *This application can run on only one terminal.* There is no provision for this program running on multiple terminals with coordinated data.

- *There is no provision for distributing this application.*

- *The user interface is pathetic, and Java is limited in its ability to support state-of-the-art user interfaces.* Visual Basic is great for user interfaces, but you can't manipulate Java classes with Visual Basic.

- *The UserSide class is too complicated for run-of-the-mill programmers to modify.*

- *This program is a Java-only solution.* There is no provision for using any of these code pieces with other languages.

- *The program does not include transactional guarantees.* One can imagine scenarios in which a buyer is told the buy went through, but the seller never gets told.

- *The program does not scale well.* We will go into more detail later.

In the following chapters, we will see how MDCA can be used to solve all of these problems, and more.

Summary

Only a few years ago the world could be divided into those who were against Java and those who were for it. In other words, Microsoft and the rest of the world. Then a funny thing happened. Microsoft discovered that Java is a pretty cool language. Much cooler, in fact, than C++, which had been up until then Microsoft's flagship language. And much better suited to the kind of components technology Microsoft was pushing. Microsoft saw the light—Microsoft became a Java junkie.

On one level, Microsoft doesn't care about Java. Microsoft is out to dominate the high-end commerce market. If it is are successful, then the Microsoft of tomorrow will dwarf the Microsoft of today. But Java is a perfect fit in Microsoft's overall game plan. It is an easy-to-use, object-oriented language with excellent support for many features, such as interfaces, that are critical to distributed technology. In the next chapter, as we look more closely at COM/DCOM, we will see just how close a fit Java is.

It is a safe bet that Microsoft is not going to be derailed by Java. Not in our lifetimes.

COMPONENTS

We have looked quite a bit at objects and developing systems using object-oriented technology. We have looked at objects from perspectives ranging from the furry theoretical to the Java practical. In this chapter we are going to add an important new layer on top of objects. This layer is called the *components* layer, and it is the layer that makes objects usable.

The component idea is crucial to MDCA. It is the foundation upon which all of the commerce-enabling layers are built. In some sense, it is even more basic than Java, which is really a technology for building components. To understand components is to understand the philosophy of Microsoft.

Problems with Objects

Object-oriented systems are big, complicated, and tedious. People who work with object-oriented systems are also big, complicated, and tedious. They use incomprehensible phrases, like "polymorphic method resolution," hoping that you will go away and not bother them. They actually enjoy arguing about the relationship between overloading and overriding. Obviously, these are not well people.

Anybody who does object-oriented programming has to understand all of the following concepts:

Classes

Interfaces

Objects

Methods

Inheritance

Vectors

Java Programming Language

This understanding is *over and above* any business logic needed for the problem at hand. If this is the state of the art, then every programmer who wants to slap an interface on some code is going to have to start out getting a Ph.D. in abstract formalism. Clearly, there is something wrong with this approach.

A component is like an object in many superficial ways. Components have interfaces. Components can do things for you. But components differ from objects in some fundamental ways.

Components are easy to use. Components are much easier to use than objects. An object-oriented program is typically constructed of a large number of interfaces, classes, and instantiated objects. A component system is typically constructed of a single component definition with a very small number of interfaces.

Components are language independent. A class in an object-oriented system can be used only from the programming language that was used to implement the class. Java classes can be used from only Java. C++ classes can be used only from C++. A component can be used from any programming language, and even from programming environments that do not use programming languages at all, like Visual Basic.

Components are end-user focused. Components are intended to be used by user interface code. Objects are intended to be used by programmers. Objects are easy to implement and difficult to use. Components are difficult to implement and easy to use. Components are written for the benefit of the client, not the implementer.

So, if components are so much better than objects, why have we been stressing objects all along and, in particular, the development of objects in Java? The answer is that writing components is hard work. Components are intricate, elaborate, and abstruse. Components have a lot of code. Object-oriented programming is the best tool we have for designing and implementing complex code systems, and a component is a complex code system. Java is also a possible choice for manipulating components, but this is a much rarer scenario. Java's place in MDCA is as an implementation vehicle for components; especially non-GUI-oriented components.

Client/GUI Programming

Java is a great language. Java really stinks.

Both of these statements are true. If you try implementing a serious business-oriented component (like our broker system) in C++, C, Visual Basic, and Java, it will take you no time to conclude that Java is by far the best choice. But if you try implementing a serious client user interface in C++, C, Visual Basic, and Java, it will take you no time to conclude that Java is by far one of the worst choices (followed closely by C++ and C).

Microsoft distributes a book named *Learn Java Now* along with Visual J++. In this book is an example of a simple Java application called *ScreenType* that allows you to type keystrokes in a window. This example takes almost 100 lines of code, including this method, which is used to process a key being pressed:

```
public boolean keyDown (Event evt, int nKey)
{
    // add key at the current location
    m_vKeys.addElement(new Key(nKey, m_dimLoc));

    // now update the location for the next character
    // by moving it over the width of this character
    // (remember that different characters are different
    // widths )
    m_dimLoc.width += m_fm.charWidth(nKey);

    // okay to repaint now
    repaint();
    return true;
    }
}
```

The following method from this example is used to repaint the window containing the text:

```
public void paint (Graphics g)
    // loop through the saved Key objects
    int nSize = m_vKeys.size();
    for (int i = -; i < nSize; i++)
    {
        // get the key
        Key key = (Key) m_vKeys.elementAt(i);

        // from the key get the keystroke and the location
        Dimension dimLoc = key.GetLoc();
        char[] cKey = key.GetKey();

        // output the key and location
        g.drawChars(cKey, 0, 1, dimLoc.width, dimLoc.height);
    }
}
```

Now, let me go out on a limb here. Despite all the claims by Java Heads to the contrary, I say this is ugly code. And having to write code like this to do the simplest of text displays (I can't even call it "text processing") is bad for your health. Let's contrast this to the code you have to write in Visual Basic to accomplish the same thing. Here is the equivalent Visual Basic Code:

Wasn't much to it, was there? Which would you prefer to write, 100 lines of Java code or 0 lines of Visual Basic code? And which would you prefer to maintain?

User Interfaces and Business Components

So, Java is a horrible language for writing *user interfaces*. But it is a great language for writing *business components*. What is the difference between a user interface and a business component?

A user interface is a piece of code, the primary purpose of which is to interact with, and collect data from, an end user (otherwise known as a "person"). A business component is a piece of code, the primary purpose of which is to encapsulate the rules for running the business. A user interface is designed by an expert at presentations. A business component is designed by an expert in the rules of a particular business. User interface experts worry about the best organization for their pulldown menus. Business component experts worry about using seismic data to predict the size of oil fields.

The brokering system we have been discussing requires both user interface and business component expertise. The user interface expertise goes into designing easy-to-use screens for collecting buy/sell information. The business component expertise goes into figuring out how a broker keeps track of 10,000 outstanding buy/sell requests, efficiently makes matches between buyers and sellers, and scales up to 50,000 people demanding instant gratification.

Where COM Fits In

So, we have come to several conclusions. First, systems need both user interfaces and business components. Second, user interfaces are best written in Visual Basic. Third, business components are best written in Java. Fourth, user interfaces must interoperate with business components. None are useful without the others.

But there is a major problem here. Visual Basic and Java are incompatible. There is no way a Visual Basic program can coordinate with a Java component. Visual Basic programs cannot instantiate Java objects. Visual Basic programs cannot invoke methods on Java objects. Visual Basic programs don't understand Java interfaces.

Fortunately, both Visual Basic and Java do have one thing in common: They both understand COM. Java understands both how to be and how to use a COM object (although we will focus on the former). And Visual Basic understands how to be and how to use a COM object (although we will focus on the latter).

Another way to think about this is that Visual Basic knows how to instantiate and invoke methods on COM objects. COM has a technology for wrapping Java classes so that method invocations on the COM object are delegated to a Java object. The Java object returns information back to the COM wrapper, which returns it to the Visual Basic client. This is shown in Figure 4.1.

It turns out that Visual Basic, Java, and COM complement each other very well. Visual Basic is great for user interfaces. Java is great for business components. COM is great for packaging components. Figure 4.2 gives a summary of

Figure 4.1 COM wrapping Java.

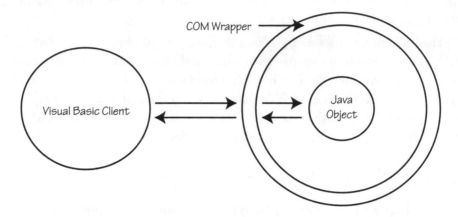

where each of these three pieces fits into the overall MDCA puzzle. You can see that although no one of these three is very strong in every critical area, the group as a whole satisfies each critical area. Oddly enough, no more than one of the three is strong in *any* given area, which gives an amusing illusion that Microsoft actually planned this whole strategy in advance.

Figure 4.2 Java, Visual Basic, and COM comparison.

	Visual Basic	Java	COM
User Interfaces	very strong	weak	none
Business Logic	weak	very strong	none
Language Independence	none	none	very strong
Distribution	none	none*	very strong
Scalability	very weak	very weak	very strong
Secure	weak	weak	very strong

* excluding add-on Remote Method Invocation (RMI)

Visual Basic/COM/Java Example

Let's start by looking at a very simple example of Visual Basic and Java communicating with each other through COM. We will start with a simple Java class, look at a prospective Visual Basic client program, and then go through the steps necessary to create a COM wrapper to make the Java class accessible from Visual Basic. The code for this example can be found in the code zip file under Chapter04_01.

The Original Java Class

The first stop in this example is most likely an existing Java class. Here is a nice, simple, little Java class.

```java
package HelloTest;
public class SayHello
{
    public String speak(String in)
    {
        return "You say " + in + " and I say hello";
    }
}
```

The *speak* method of the SayHello class takes a single String parameter. It then returns a new string that consists of "You say [input parameter] and I say hello." We can see this class working in the following Java client:

```java
import HelloTest.*;
class Client {
    public static void main(String args[])
    {
        String text;
        SayHello myhello = new SayHello();
        text = myhello.speak("goodbye");
        System.out.println(text);
    }
}
```

The output from this program is:

```
You say goodbye and I say hello
```

The Perspective Visual Basic Client

Now let's say we have a Visual Basic program that knows how to create a window that looks like that shown in Figure 4.3.

This window has an area for input text, output text, and Execute and End buttons. It would certainly be nice to put together the Visual Basic screen and our Java class. A logical relationship between the two would be to have our Visual Basic window instantiate the Java SayHello class. Then, when the user clicks on the Execute button, the text in the input area would be passed into SayHello's speak method, and the text returned from speak would be displayed in the output area.

Of course, we know we can't really do this, since Visual Basic can't invoke Java methods. So we need to create a COM component that wraps the Java class.

Creating an IDL Wrapper Definition

The first step in getting our Visual Basic window to work with our Java class is to define a COM component in a language COM understands. It would be nice if COM understood Java, and perhaps someday it will. But for now, it doesn't. The lingua franca for COM is IDL. So, we define our wrapper class for SayHello in IDL. I will number the lines for future reference. Here is the file HelloTest.idl:

```
1.   #include <JavaAttr.h>
2.   [
3.     uuid(1F60FB52-D7D3-11d0-BAFA-000000000000),
4.     version(1.0),
5.     helpstring("HelloTest Type Library Version 2")
6.   ]
7.   library HELLOTESTLib
8.   {
9.     importlib("stdole2.tlb");
10.    [
11.      object,
12.      uuid(1F60FB50-D7D3-11d0-BAFA-000000000000),
13.      dual,
14.      helpstring("ISayHello Interface"),
15.      pointer_default(unique)
```

```
16.    ]
17.    interface ISayHello : IDispatch
18.    {
19.      import "oaidl.idl";
20.      HRESULT speak([in] BSTR instr, [out, retval] BSTR* out-
str);
21.    };
22.    [
23.      uuid(1f60fb51-d7d3-11d0-bafa-000000000000),
24.      helpstring("Hello Class"),
25.      JAVACLASS("HelloTest.SayHello"),
26.      PROGID("HelloTest.Hello")
27.    ]
28.    coclass CSayHello
29.    {
30.      [default] interface ISayHello;
31.    };
32.  };
```

Let's go through these lines, and describe the major functionality.

Line 1 causes a header file to be included. This header file (JavaAttr.h) defines some Java-related macros used later in the IDL file (for example, line 25).

Lines 2 through 6 are a set of modifiers that relate to the COM library we are creating. A library is a COM entity in which COM components live.

Line 3 assigns a unique identifier to this library ("uuid" stands for universally unique id). This unique identifier is the key used within COM to identify this

Figure 4.3 Visual Basic user interface.

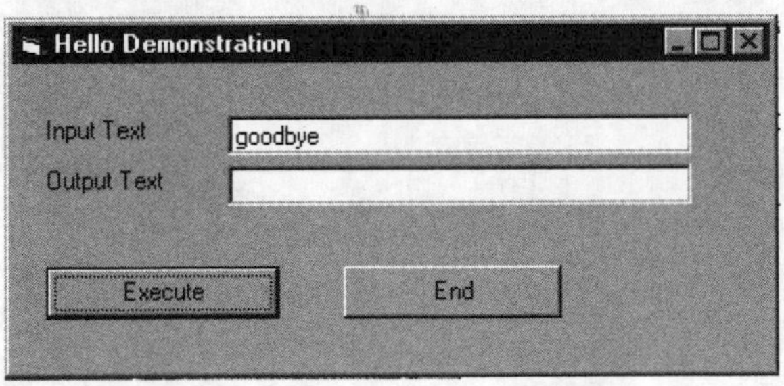

library. This unique identifier must be unique throughout the world to guarantee
this library does not clash with one created elsewhere. Keep in mind that these
libraries will eventually get distributed to who knows where, so this really
becomes a worldwide issue. In theory, this is more than a world issue, it is a *universe* issue (which is why it's called a *universally* unique id). But, to the best of
my knowledge, Microsoft's influence is still limited to the planet Earth and its
subsidiaries, at least as of press time for this book.

You have probably already figured out that you can't just make up any old
32-character number and expect it to be a unique identifier. The easiest way to
acquire an id that is guaranteed unique throughout at least *our* world is to use
one of the Microsoft tools to generate it. The most accessible tool is part of
Visual J++.

If you bring up Visual J++, and pull down the Tools menu, you will find an
option called Create GUID. If you choose this, you will get the screen shown in
Figure 4.4. Push the button for registry format. That will copy the new uuid
shown at the bottom of the screen to the clipboard. Then bring up your IDL file
in the text editor and paste it in the appropriate place. Change the brackets to

Figure 4.4 GUID tool.

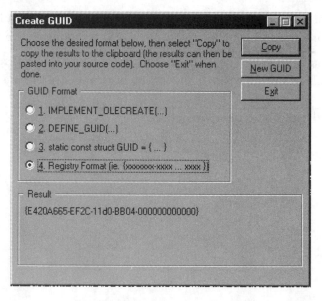

parentheses, and you are set. You will notice there are three places you need uuids in the IDL file. Don't reuse the same one. Generate a new one each time.

Lines 4 and 5 are documentation lines that show up in various tools, and need not concern us here.

Line 7 starts the definition of the HELLOTESTLib library. This library will contain one interface definition and one class definition. The interface will be called ISayHello, and the class will be CSayHello. Line 20 defines the method of ISayHello. Line 30 declares that CSayHello implements the ISayHello interface.

So, we see an important idea about the relationship between classes and interfaces. Interfaces *define* methods, and classes *implement* one or more interfaces. Notice how similar this is to the philosophy espoused back in Chapter 3, which argued for the same relationship between Java classes and interfaces.

Line 17 declares that the ISayHello interface is derived from the IDispatch interface. Back in Chapter 2 we discussed the IDispatch interface. We said that this interface is provided for the benefit of Visual Basic to do its own special form of method dispatching, which closely resembles name lookup. We will never see this interface in use or have to implement any of the methods (as long as we are working in Java), but we do need to make sure our interfaces support IDispatch, and this is how we do so.

Backing up a bit, Lines 11–15 are modifiers on the ISayHello interface. Line 11 says this library is one of custom OLE interfaces, rather than DCE RPC interfaces, which is its etymology. Line 12 gives a uuid for the ISayHello interface. The discussion on the library uuid also applies here.

Line 13 declares this interface as being "dual." A dual interface is one that supports both IDispatch (used by Visual Basic clients) and VTBL binding (used by Java clients), as we discussed back in Chapter 2. I suggest you have all interfaces support both binding styles, since you just never know.

Line 14 is a documentation line, similar to line 5. Line 15 says that the default for pointers is unique, which describes how pointers and memory will be managed. This is probably the most reasonable default. The Microsoft documentation describes the various alternatives.

Line 17 starts the formal definition of the ISayHello interface. This name is arbitrary. I chose one that would match my Java class. Line 19 imports some definitions.

Line 20 declares the single method of this interface. It returns an HRESULT, a standard error-passing mechanism for Visual Basic. You should declare all of your methods to return HRESULTs. The name of the method is *speak*. It transfers two pieces of information. The first is input, and this is of type BSTR. BSTR is a wide, double-byte (Unicode) string that corresponds to the Java String type. The second information is output from the method, and will come in the form of a pointer to a BSTR. The keyword *retval* indicates that this is returned from the Java method. This definition of ISayHello corresponds to this Java equivalent:

```
interface ISayHello {
    String speak(String instr);
}
```

It's very important that the IDL definition correspond exactly to the Java class for which it will wrap. Since IDL, as you may have noticed, looks as much like Java as English looks like Klingon, getting these two to match up is not necessarily a piece of cake. One has to assume that Microsoft is not unaware of this miserable state of affairs. Since Java is not likely to change, one might hope that Microsoft will eventually come up with a better mechanism for defining COM interfaces. But who knows? Anyway, we are getting sidetracked.

Most, but not all Java parameter types have corresponding COM types. And it is important that you stick with those that do. The acceptable Java types, and their COM equivalents, are shown in Figure 4.5.

Lines 22–27 are modifiers on the class CSayHello. Line 23 is its uuid and line 24 is its documentation string. Line 25 defines the Java class that will provide the implementation for this class. Remember that COM doesn't have any mechanism for implementing classes, just for defining them. Line 26 is the Program ID, which can be used in client programs to instantiate an object of this class. We will see how it is used when we get to the Visual Basic client.

Line 28 is where the class is declared. The keyword *coclass* declares the class. Line 30 declares the interfaces this class supports (only one in this case). The default keyword indicates that this is the default interface for this class.

Working with IDL is clearly an art form, an art form that most of us have no desire to master. The chances are good that by the time you master it anyway, Microsoft will have changed to something better. My recommendation is that

---

Figure 4.5 Type equivalents between Java and COM.

Java	COM
boolean	boolean
char	char
double	double
int	int
int64	long
float	float
short	short
byte	unsigned char
string	BSTR
pointer to interface	unknown*
void	void

you understand how the types match between IDL and Java, and that you use this IDL file and the others in this book as a pattern for creating wrappers for your Java classes.

Creating the Type Library

An IDL file is intended to be read by humans (perhaps not very happy humans, but humans nevertheless). Type Libraries are intended to be read by computers. Visual Basic, and other software that makes use of so-called "automation," or basically, IDispatch binding, uses the Type Library to figure out how to invoke methods. At this stage, it isn't worth worrying a lot about what a type library is, other than to realize that Visual Basic wants it. So, we are going to create it.

To generate a Type Library from the HelloTest.idl file we created earlier, we use this command:

```
midl HelloTest.idl
```

This generates the file HelloTest.tlb, which is the Type Library corresponding to our IDL file.

Checking the Java Wrapper

At this point, it's worth checking to make sure the Java wrapper you are generating is a good match with your actual Java class. A good match could loosely be defined as a class where the method names and signatures are the same in both the Java class and the wrapper class. In the original Java class we had one method, which was defined as

```
String speak(String);
```

The easiest way to check the wrapper class is to use a Java tool called javatlb. This tool has other purposes, but for now we will use it to check the wrapper. Giving the command

```
javatlb /U:T HelloTest.tlb
```

will cause the following events to happen:

1. The type library HelloTest will be parsed.

2. A file named summary.txt will be generated.

3. This file will be placed in %SystemRoot%\java\trustlib\package, where *package* is the directory corresponding to this package. We have created our SayHello as a standard Java package called HelloTest, so, in our case, javatlb will place summary.txt in %SystemRoot%\java\trustlib\HelloTest.

If we look at summary.txt, this is what we see:

```
public class hellotest/CSayHello extends java.lang.Object
{
}
public interface hellotest/ISayHello extends com.ms.com.IUnknown
{
    public abstract java.lang.String speak(java.lang.String);
}
```

The interface definition is the wrapper definition corresponding to the interface section of the input IDL file. You can see that this definition, although more verbose than ours, exactly matches our Java class. The same number of methods, the same names, and the same signatures. We know we are on the right track. This file serves no more purpose. We can delete it now if we choose.

Creating Dummy Java Classes

Next, we will create some dummy Java classes that are used by COM. To create these classes, use the following command:

```
javatlb /d . /p HelloTest /p:b- HelloTest.tlb
```

Again we see the javatlb tool. The options have the following meanings:

/d tells the directory you want used for output. By default, this would go to %SystemRoot%\java\trustlib\package. I find it easier to work in my local directory until I am sure everything is working okay.

/p gives the name of the package, which should correspond to the package used in the original Java class. The package in the original Java class was given in the first line of the SayHello.java file:

```
package HelloTest;
public class SayHello
{
    public String speak(String in)
    {
        return "You say " + in + " and I say hello";
    }
}
```

/p:b- says you don't want the base name as the package name.

If everything has gone well, you should now have two new files in your package (HelloTest) directory. These files are CSayHello.class and ISayHello.class. They correspond to the interface(s) and class(es) you defined in your IDL file.

Modifying the Original Java Files

You now need to make one modification to your Java files to tell Java that this class is an implementation of a COM interface. You do this by adding an implements clause to your class declaration. Your original file looked like:

```
package HelloTest;
public class SayHello
{
```

```
    public String speak(String in)
    {
        return "You say " + in + " and I say hello";
    }
}
```

Your new version looks like this, with the changed section shown in bold:

```
package HelloTest;
public class SayHello implements ISayHello
{
    public String speak(String in)
    {
        return "You say " + in + " and I say hello";
    }
}
```

Recompiling Your Java Classes

Now is a good time to recompile your Java classes. To do this, go into your package directory and issue the following command:

```
jvc SayHello.java
```

You should get a clean compile with no errors.

Copying Your Classes

Next you need to copy your Java "package" (class files) to a well-known directory. The easiest way to do this is to copy everything in your HelloTest directory to %SystemRoot%\java\trustlib\HelloTest\.

Registering Your COM Classes

You will need to register your COM classes in the system registry. This is where COM will look when trying to finding these classes. The command to do this is:

```
javareg /register /class:HelloTest.SayHello /progid:HelloTest.Hello
/clsid:{1f60fb51-d7d3-11d0-bafa-000000000000}
```

This should be one line. The options to javareg have the following meanings:

/register says to register this class.

/class:HelloTest.SayHello is the name of the Java class, including the Java package name. This should match the JAVACLASS(HelloTest.SayHello) directive in the IDL file.

/progid:HelloTest.Hello describes the id that will be used by Visual Basic to instantiate the class. This should match the PROGID(HelloTest.Hello) directive in the IDL file.

/clsid:{...} is the uuid for the class, and should match the uuid of the coclass in the IDL file.

The Java Client

Before we test this class in Visual Basic, we should test it in the simpler environment of Java. To do this, we can modify our original Java test program to use the newly created COM wrapper. Our original test program looked like this:

```
import HelloTest.*;
class Client {
    public static void main(String args[])
    {
        String text;
        SayHello myhello = new SayHello();
        text = myhello.speak("goodbye");
        System.out.println(text);
    }
}
```

The COM wrapper version, with changes shown in bold, looks like this:

```
import HelloTest.*;
class Client {
    public static void main(String args[])
    {
        String text;
        ISayHello myhello = new CSayHello();
        text = myhello.speak("goodbye");
```

```
        System.out.println(text);
    }
}
```

Notice that the only changes are in the declaration of myhello, which is now declared to be the COM-created interface; and the instantiation, which is now declared to be the COM-created class. This program should give the same output as our original test program, namely:

```
You say goodbye and I say hello
```

Keep in mind that, although this program looks like a Java program, it is actually a COM client. It is using the Java class, true, but through the COM wrapper.

Batching the Wrapping Process

This probably sounds like a lot, and it is, but there are two points worth keeping in mind. The first is that Microsoft will probably find ways to streamline this process. The second is that repetitious parts can all be placed in batch files and automated.

The batch file I use for this is:

```
rem Create HelloTest.tlb
midl HelloTest.idl

rem Create CSayHello.class and ISayHello.class
javatlb /d . /p HelloTest /p:b- HelloTest.tlb

rem del classes from trustlib
del %SystemRoot%\java\trustlib\HelloTest\*.class

rem Compile local class
jvc HelloTest\*.java

rem Compile client
jvc Client.java

rem Copy local class to trustlib
```

```
copy HelloTest\*.class %SystemRoot%\java\trustlib\HelloTest\

rem Register java class
javareg /register /class:HelloTest.SayHello
/progid:HelloTest.Hello /clsid:{1f60fb51-d7d3-11d0-bafa-
000000000000}
```

The Visual Basic Side

Remember the original point of this exercise? We wanted to hook our Java class to our Visual Basic window. Let's take another look at our Visual Basic window, as shown again in Figure 4.6.

This window includes the following components:

- The window has a high-level label, called Hello Demonstration.
- It has standard Windows controls for minimizing, maximizing, and closing of the window.
- It has a label area, where the text "Input Text" is displayed.
- It has a text input area, where text can be typed.
- It has a label area, where the text "Output Text" is displayed.
- It has a text output area, where text can be displayed.
- It has a button labeled Execute, which can be pressed.
- It has a button labeled End, which can be pressed.
- The window can be moved around the screen, and automatically redraws itself as necessary.

Figure 4.6 Visual Basic user interface.

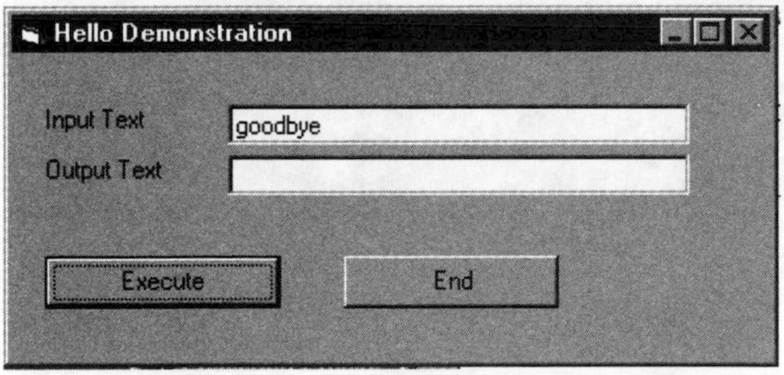

Creating this window in Java would be a tedious process. How much work is it to create in Visual Basic? Surprisingly, there is no coding involved at all.

Starting a New Visual Basic Project

Let's start with a brand new Visual Basic project. The Visual Basic code and forms for this are in the code zip file under Chapter04_01, as was the Java code. If you start up Visual Basic and ask it to start a new "executable" project, you will get a window like that shown in Figure 4.7.

At this point, we have a new form with no elements (except for the form itself). Adding an element to the form consists of these four steps:

1. Click on the element. The collection of possible elements is shown on the left edge of the window.

2. Draw that element over to the form.

3. Drop the element where you want it.

4. Size the element.

Figure 4.7 A New Visual Basic project.

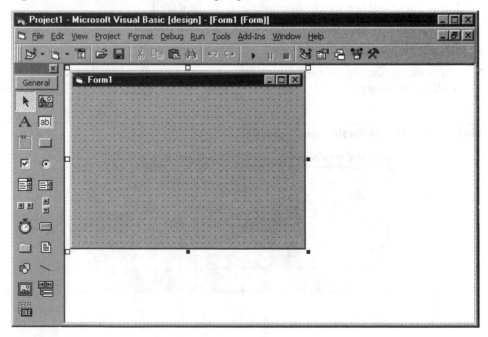

We will use three different elements in this form. Labels can contain text. Their icon is the one with the large A in the middle. Text fields can be used for both input and output text. They are shown by the icon with the ab in the middle. Buttons are able to be pressed or clicked. They are shown by the button icon just below the text field icon. Figure 4.8 shows the new form as we are in the process of sizing our first label.

When you have finished adding all the elements, you will have a form that looks like the one shown in Figure 4.9.

The next thing we want to do is change the text on the labels, buttons, and text fields to match our expectations. We do this by changing the properties associated with each form element. We bring up the properties window by choosing the View drop-down menu, and then the properties window option. This changes our Visual Basic window to look like that shown in Figure 4.10.

As we click the mouse on different elements of the form, the property window changes to the property window associated with that form element. Each of these elements has many properties. We need to find the one associated with the

Figure 4.8 Adding the first element.

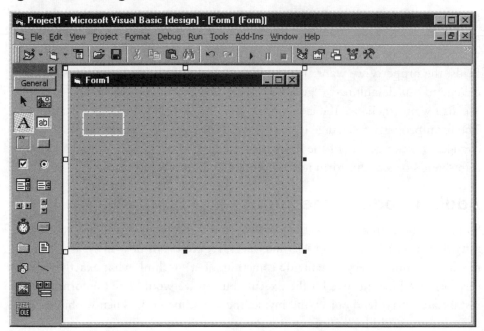

Figure 4.9 Form with all elements in place.

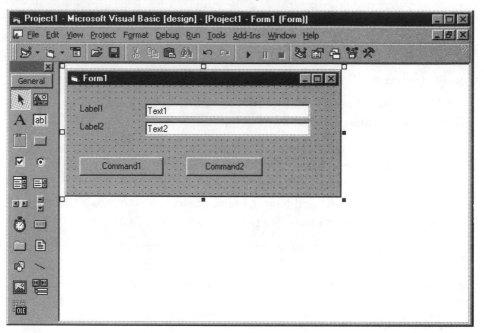

text we want changed, and change the value in the property window. For the text labels and the buttons, the property we want changed is the one called Caption. If you double-click on caption, you can change the text as desired. For the text fields, the property we want changed is the "Text." The first text field we will change to our default text ("goodbye"), and the second we will change to blank. We also want to change the label on the form itself to "Hello Demonstration." The form property to change is "Caption." When we have finished with these changes, we can get rid of the properties window by clicking on the x in its upper right-hand corner. Our form now looks like that shown in Figure 4.11.

Adding Code to the Form

So far, we have, in almost no time and without writing any code, created quite a nifty little user interface. But user interfaces, regardless of how nifty, aren't of much value unless they actually do something. Let's rethink what exactly we want this form to do. When we hit the Execute button we would like the form to instantiate a SayHello object and invoke the speak method. When we hit the End button we would like the form to disappear.

Figure 4.10 Form with Properties window.

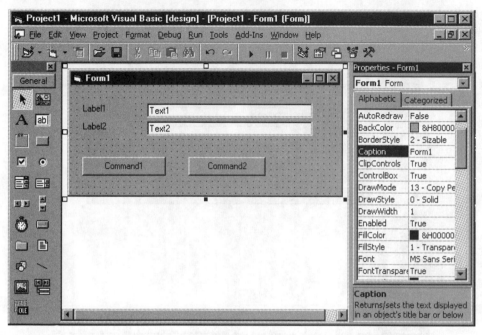

We have already done all of the background work. We have written the Java class, written an IDL definition, created Java/COM wrappers, and registered our work. Now we just need to add a few lines of code to our Visual Basic screen.

In Visual Basic, we have two different views of a screen. One is the *object view*, and the other is the *code view*. The object view is what we have been looking at up until now. This is the view that shows us the form, and allows us to drag, resize, and move form elements. The code view is where we get to look at the Visual Basic code associated with each event that can occur with each element.

There are several ways of moving back and forth between object and code view. The easiest is probably to do so through the View pulldown menu.

One can get quite carried away with element events. A button, such as our Execute button, recognizes over a dozen events, including DragDrop, DragOver, and LostFocus. But we are going to keep it simple. All we care about is the event that occurs when somebody clicks the button. When somebody clicks our Execute

Figure 4.11 Form with all properties updated.

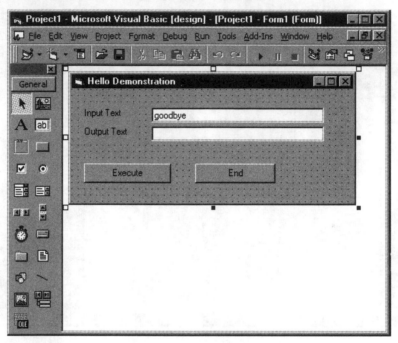

button, we will instantiate the object and call the method. The Visual Basic code for this is:

```
Private Sub Command1_Click()
    Dim myHello As ISayHello
    Set myHello = CreateObject("HelloTest.Hello")
    Text2.Text = myHello.speak(Text1.Text)
End Sub
```

The first line of code declares that the variable myHello refers to an object that can support the ISayHello interface, which, if you remember, was declared in our IDL file. This would be equivalent to this line of Java code:

```
ISayHello myHello;
```

The second line of code instantiates an object whose program id is HelloTest.Hello. If you recall, this is the program id we assigned our COM class.

The third line of code is the one doing all the work. It says to invoke the speak method on myHello; pass in the text found in element Text1.Text, which is the text shown in the first of the text fields on the form; and take the information returned by the COM object (wrapping the Java class) and place it in Text2.Text, which is the text area associated with the second of the text fields on the form.

When somebody clicks our End button, we will end the program. The Visual Basic code for this is:

```
Private Sub Command2_Click()
    End
End Sub
```

We only have one line of code here, and that is the line that says to end the program.

For both of these routines, Visual Basic provided the declaration and end of the routine, and we just enter the body of the routines, or the indented sections.

If we go to the code view and enter the lines just shown, our Visual Basic window will look like Figure 4.12.

We can now go ahead and run the Visual Basic program. One way to do this is through the Run option of the Run menu. If we do this, a little window pops up that looks like the one shown in Figure 4.13.

If I push the Execute button, the window changes to the one shown in Figure 4.14.

Of course, there is nothing sacred about the word *goodbye*. I can replace that word with anything I like, such as shown in Figure 4.15.

Now I get the result shown in Figure 4.16 when I press Execute.

Not a bad program for only four lines of code, wouldn't you say? See how many lines of Java code it would take to create this interface!

We now have a system in which the business logic is encapsulated into a COM component, and the user interface is taken care of by Visual Basic. Perhaps more importantly, the user interface part of our project is completely separate from the business logic. We can work in these two areas completely independently.

Suppose, for example, somebody complains about the placement of the buttons. This is in the domain of the user interface. The business logic (Java) programmer doesn't have to be bothered by this. The user interface programmer brings up the Visual Basic form and drags the buttons around until the user is

Figure 4.12 Visual Basic code view.

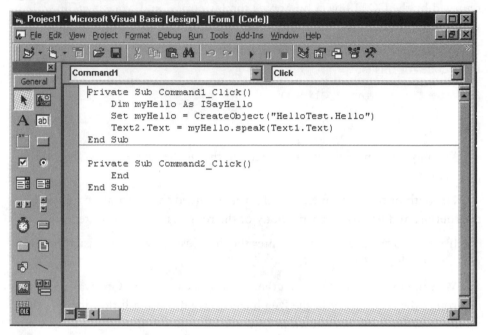

happy. Let's say the user likes the buttons as placed in Figure 4.17. Fine. No problem. The Java programmer couldn't care less.

Point of Instantiation

Back in Chapter 3, we saw how interfaces and classes relate to each other in Java. We saw how we could have many classes implement a given interface,

Figure 4.13 Hello demonstration program.

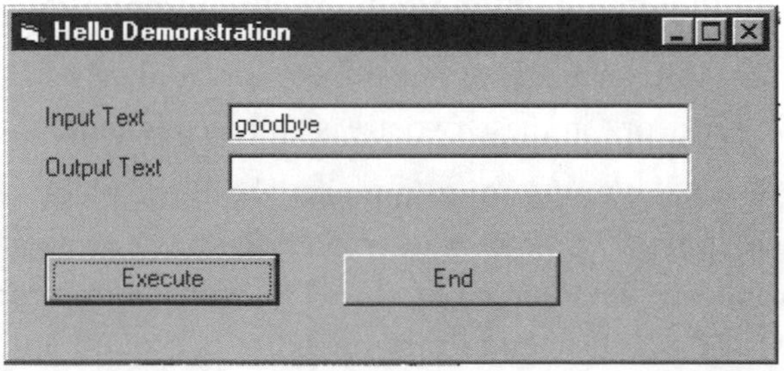

Figure 4.14 Hello demonstration program (2).

each with different implementations of the methods defined in the interface. We saw that when a client invokes a method, the actual method invoked is the one associated with the class of the object. We also saw that the class of the object is not determined by the declaration of the object reference, which is, after all, an interface, not a class. The class of the object is determined at the *point of instantiation*.

This works the same in Visual Basic. When we see the lines:

```
Dim myHello As ISayHello
Set myHello = CreateObject("HelloTest.Hello")
```

it is the second line, not the first, that determines the class of the object. We can create two COM classes that both support the ISayHello interface, as shown in this IDL file:

```
// HelloTest.idl
//
#include <JavaAttr.h>
[
    uuid(1F60FB52-D7D3-11d0-BAFA-000000000000),
    version(1.0),
    helpstring("HelloTest Type Library Version 2")
]
library HELLOTESTLib
{
    importlib("stdole2.tlb");
```

```
[
    object,
    uuid(1F60FB50-D7D3-11d0-BAFA-000000000000),
    dual,
    helpstring("ISayHello Interface"),
    pointer_default(unique)
]
interface ISayHello : IDispatch
{
    import "oaidl.idl";
    HRESULT speak([in] BSTR instr, [out, retval] BSTR* outstr);
};
[
    uuid(1f60fb51-d7d3-11d0-bafa-000000000000),
    helpstring("Hello Class"),
    JAVACLASS("HelloTest.SayHello"),
    PROGID("HelloTest.Hello")
]
coclass CSayHello
{
    [default] interface ISayHello;
};
[
    uuid(DC7FA621-E8BB-11d0-BB04-000000000000),
    helpstring("Hello Class2"),
    JAVACLASS("HelloTest.SayHello2"),
    PROGID("HelloTest.Hello2")
]
coclass CInsecureSayHello
{
    [default] interface ISayHello;
};
};
```

The difference between this and the last IDL is the inclusion of the second coclass, the one called CInsecureSayHello, along with the modifiers that precede it. So now we have two classes that implement ISayHello: our original CSayHello class, which we will call the *secure* version; and CInsecureSayHello, which we

Figure 4.15 Hello demonstration program (3).

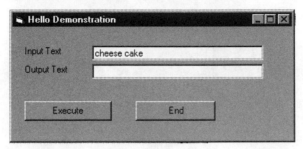

will call the *insecure* version. The code we are working with now is part of the code zip file under Chapter04_02.

We now have two Java classes to register with javareg. Notice that the clsids match the uuids in the IDL file for those class definitions.

```
javareg /register /class:HelloTest.SayHello
/progid:HelloTest.Hello /clsid:{1f60fb51-d7d3-11d0-bafa-
000000000000}


javareg /register /class:HelloTest.InsecureSayHello
/progid:HelloTest.InsecureHello /clsid:{DC7FA621-E8BB-11d0-BB04-
000000000000}
```

The Java implementation of the secure SayHello, our original version, is unchanged. Our insecure implementation looks like this:

```
package HelloTest;
public class InsecureSayHello implements ISayHello
{
    public String speak(String in)
    {
        return "I thought you said " + in + "," +
        " but I wasn't really sure." +
        "... In any case, I wanted to say hello." +
        "... I hope that's ok." +
        " Did you say " + in + "?";
    }
}
```

Figure 4.16 Hello demonstration program (4).

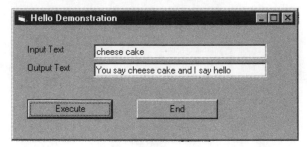

We can demonstrate both implementations of the ISayHello interface in our Visual Basic program. First, we add a pulldown menu to let our user choose between the secure and the insecure version. Then we increase the size of the output text field to accommodate either. The new version of the form is shown in Figure 4.18.

Figure 4.17 Modified button placement.

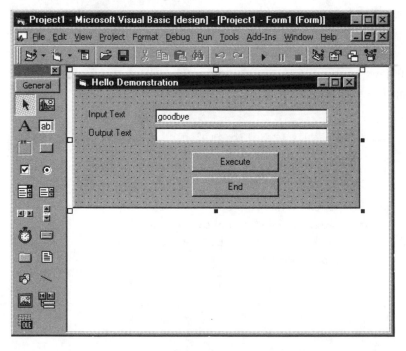

Figure 4.18 Modified form.

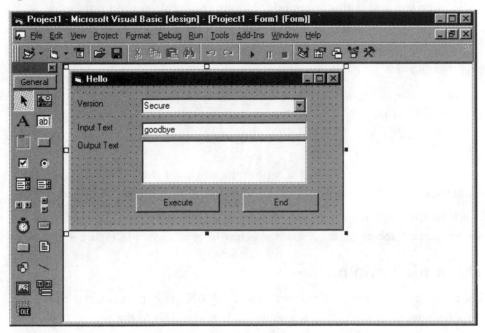

There are a few modifications we need to make in our Visual Basic code. First, we will use our newly created combo box to control the actual class of the instantiated object. The new code is as follows:

```
Private Sub Command1_Click()
    Dim myHello As ISayHello
    If (Combo1.Text = "Secure") Then
        Set myHello = CreateObject("HelloTest.Hello")
    End If
    If (Combo1.Text = "Insecure") Then
        Set myHello = CreateObject("HelloTest.InsecureHello")
    End If
    Text2.Text = myHello.speak(Text1.Text)
End Sub
```

Look carefully at the line of code that actually invokes the speak method. It is an unconditional invocation. It doesn't care whether we instantiated the secure or the insecure version. Whatever we instantiate will support some implementation of the speak method. That is guaranteed by the fact that both classes support the same interface, and that is the interface where the speak method is declared.

We will also add code to the Form Load event, which is the event that occurs when the form is first loaded. This is where we prime the combo box with the possible choices:

```
Private Sub Form_Load()
    Combo1.AddItem ("Secure")
    Combo1.AddItem ("Insecure")
End Sub
```

When we run our form again, we get the original behavior if we choose the secure version (which is our old implementation). This is shown in Figure 4.19.

If we choose the insecure version, we get an entirely different behavior when we press the Execute button. Now the behavior is as shown in Figure 4.20.

Dynamic Loading

Let's look again at the code that instantiates an object. Remember, this code not only instantiates the object, but also determines the class of the object. Although there are several mechanisms for doing this in Visual Basic, the most common is to use the CreateObject function, as shown here:

```
Set myHello = CreateObject("HelloTest.Hello")
```

Notice the type of the parameter passed to CreateObject. It is a string.

Figure 4.19 The secure version.

Figure 4.20 The insecure version.

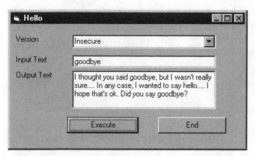

The fact that a string is passed to CreateObject has immense consequences. There are a lot of ways to create a string, and any of these are fair game for creating the string that will be passed into CreateObject. This means that the class of the object instantiated can be totally determined at run time. For example, either of the following Visual Basic code lines would be just as acceptable:

```
Set myHello = CreateObject(Text1.Text)
Set myHello = CreateObject(myObjectType)
```

Java also allows the type of an object to be determined at run time, but using a much, much weaker mechanism. In Java, code such as the following is legal:

```
ISayHello myhello;
if (...) myhello = new CSayHello();
if (...) myhello = new CInsecureSayHello();
```

Notice how much more constrained the Java code is. The programmer basically has to enumerate all possible instantiations, and use program control to determine which will be used. There is no way to add in new classes after the program code has been completed.

In Visual Basic, we don't have to have a clue as to the possible classes of the object when we write our code. We can slip in new implementations of COM interfaces *at any time*. This truly allows us to write code that is extensible in a very powerful way. We can use dynamically determined instantiation in the broadest possible sense.

Actually, this ability to do dynamic instantiation is not exclusively a feature of Visual Basic. This is a capability of COM. We can use dynamic instantiation even inside of Java programs, as long as the objects we are instantiating are COM objects rather than Java objects. COM provides Java the equivalent of CreateObject for instantiating COM objects. My assumption is, however, that dynamic instantiation will be far more common on the Visual Basic side of the equation than on the Java side.

Errors

Errors are a fact of life, and a fact of programming. We need a mechanism to return error information from one section of code to another. In Java, we typically use exceptions for this purpose. In the COM wrappings for Java, Microsoft has provided a mapping between Java exceptions and Visual Basic errors. The code here is in the Chapter04_05 section of the web zip file.

In Visual Basic, one checks for error using an "On Error" section, which behaves somewhat like a Java *catch* clause. In this section of code, we set up an Error Management section, to which control will be transferred upon encountering an error in any part of the routine:

```
Private Sub Command1_Click()
    On Error GoTo ErrorHandling
    Dim myHello As ISayHello
    Set myHello = CreateObject("HelloTest.Hello")
    Text2.Text = myHello.speak(Text1.Text)
    Exit Sub
ErrorHandling:
    Dim msg As String
    msg = "You entered " + Text1.Text
    msg = msg + "... I don't think that's a good idea."
    MsgBox (msg)
End Sub
```

On the Java side there are several ways we can indicate an error, but the easiest is just to throw in a com.ms.com.ComFailException, as shown here:

```
package HelloTest;
public class SayHello implements ISayHello
{
```

```
public String speak(String in)
{
    if (in.compareTo("Howard Sterns")==0)
        throw new com.ms.com.ComFailException();
    return "You say " + in + " and I say hello";
}
}
```

If we now rerun the Visual Basic form, we still get our old behavior when errors *don't* occur, as shown in Figure 4.21. But if we enter information that the Java code chokes on, we get an error condition raised. Instead of putting any text in the output area, our form now pops up an error window, as shown in Figure 4.22.

Thinking Like a Component

Now we understand the basic idea of wrapping Java classes as COM components, and using component objects from Visual Basic. Let's go back to our brokering system. What would it take to use Visual Basic with that system?

The first step in becoming a component is thinking like a component. But what is a component? We said earlier in the chapter that components are typically described by a single interface, and are simple to use. How well have we accomplished this with our brokering system, as written in Chapter 3?

We can best answer this question by looking at the system from the perspective of someone trying to use the system: the developer of the UserSide class. How much work did that person have to do, and much expertise did that person have

Figure 4.21 Typical behavior of new form.

Figure 4.22 The Howard Stern error window.

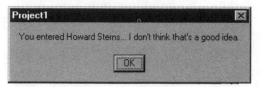

to have? Let's look at what this programmer had to do to find matched buyers and sellers. This required three methods and almost 40 lines of code including vector manipulation, program loops, and three different objects and interfaces, not to mention the Java idiosyncrasies of public versus private methods and class-level versus object-level scoping:

```java
private void listStatus()
{
    String sellerText, buyerText;

    BrokerInterface myBroker = getBroker();
    GnomeVector v = myBroker.getSells();
    sellerText = getGnomeVectorString(v);

    v = myBroker.getBuys();
    buyerText = getGnomeVectorString(v);

    System.out.println("BUYERS");
    System.out.println(buyerText);
    System.out.println("SELLERS");
    System.out.println(sellerText);
}
private String getGnomeVectorString(GnomeVector v)
{
    String s = "";
    EmployeeInterface gnome = null;
    int nsize = v.size();
    for (int n=0; n<nsize; n++) {
        gnome = (EmployeeInterface) v.getGnome(n);
        s = s + getEmployeeText(gnome) + "\n";
```

```
        }
     return s;

   }
   private String getEmployeeText(EmployeeInterface gnome)
   {
     String s =
         gnome.employee()              +  "|"
        +gnome.item()                  +  "|"
        +gnome.price()                 +  "|"
        +gnome.otherName()             +  "|"
        +gnome.negotiatedPrice()       +  "|";
     return s;
   }
```

True, this is not the worst code in the world, and certainly is much simpler than, for example, the code needed to look for matching buyers and sellers in the broker class. But it is still too complicated for use by Visual Basic programmers.

So, the first thing we need to do is rethink the organization of the brokering system. Instead of thinking of it as a collection of objects, we need to think of it as a system that can do things for us. What do we want it to do for us? There are basically five things we want. We want to ask the system to buy something for us. We want to ask the system to sell something for us. We want to know if any of our transactions have been completed. If we are a buyer, we want to see from whom we have bought. If we are a seller, we want to see to whom we have sold. Let's start to think of the system as a broker house that can do these five things for us.

A Java interface for our compartmentalized broker house looks like this:

```
public interface BrokerHouseInterface
{
    public boolean prepareCheckStatus();
    public void prepareBuyOrder
          (String name, String item, int maxPrice);
    public void prepareSellOrder
          (String name, String item, int minPrice);
```

```
public String getSellerText();
public String getBuyerText();
}
```

The purpose of these five methods is as follows:

prepareCheckStatus returns a Boolean telling us if any of our transactions have been completed.

prepareBuyOrder takes a string describing the name of the buyer, a string describing the item to be purchased, and a number describing the price we are willing to pay.

prepareSellOrder takes a string describing the name of the seller, a string describing the item to be sold, and a number describing the price we want.

getSellerText returns a text string describing the sellers whose transactions have been completed.

getBuyerText returns a text string describing the buyers whose transactions have been completed.

This is a much simpler system than the labyrinth of objects and interfaces our client had to work with in the last chapter. And implementing these methods isn't too difficult. In fact, it is mainly a matter of separating the non-user interface code from our old UserSide class and moving it in to the BrokerHouse class. The new version of the brokering system is given in Chapter04_03 of the web zip file. For those of you interested in the programming details, we'll look at the BrokerHouse code shortly. For those of you who aren't, you can take on faith the following points:

- The BrokerHouse code is much more complicated than the SayHello code.

- Despite this complexity, it has only four public methods. From the client perspective, BrokerHouse is nothing more than an implementation of the BrokerHouseInterface.

- The complexity is in the implementation of these methods, not in the definition or use of these methods.

- From the client perspective, the interface of BrokerHouse is hardly any more complicated than the interface of SayHello. It has five methods instead of one, but this is hardly a big deal.

Keep in mind the purpose of BrokerHouse. It basically packages up in a neat little bundle our entire brokering system, and presents it in a way that is *much* easier to use than our original system. You can see this in Figure 4.23, which compares the old and new brokering systems as seen from the client's perspective. Keep in mind that the simplification is not in the code, it is in the packaging of that code. The old and new systems are equally complex, and equally difficult to maintain. In fact, if anything, the new system is even more complex, since it introduces more interfaces. But the new one is a lot easier to use.

The next question we need to answer is this: If we want to turn this system into a COM component, which set of classes should componentized? For that

Figure 4.23 A client's perspective.

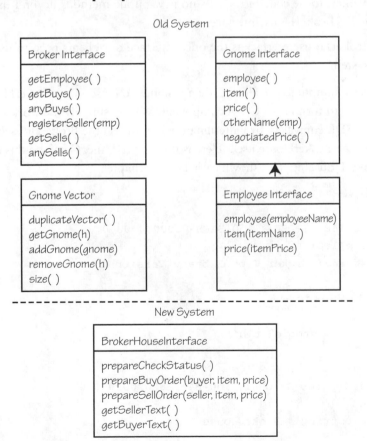

matter, what does it mean to componentize a class? It means that we will do the following:

- Define an equivalent COM IDL definition.
- Create COM wrapper classes.
- Modify the original Java classes to implement the COM wrapper interfaces.
- Register the wrapper class with the system registry.

Let's make a couple of assumptions, which we will validate when we look at the BrokerHouse code in detail. Let's assume that:

1. The BrokerHouse code fully implements the BrokerHouseInterface (shown earlier).

2. The BrokerHouse code introduces no new public methods beyond those defined in BrokerHouseInterface.

3. The BrokerHouseInterface is the only interface our clients need to use the new system.

If these assumptions are all true, then it stands to reason that BrokerHouse is the class we want to turn into a COM component. We can simplify the work necessary to create an IDL equivalent by patterning the IDL file on the BrokerHouseInterface, rather than the BrokerHouse itself. Here is the new IDL file. Compare this IDL file to the BrokerHouseInterface shown earlier in the chapter.

```
#include <JavaAttr.h>
[
    uuid(C414B3D1-DB01-11d0-BAFB-000000000000),
    version(1.0),
    helpstring("Broker Type Library Version 1")
]
library BrokerLib
{
    importlib("stdole2.tlb");
    [
        object,
        uuid(C414B3D2-DB01-11d0-BAFB-000000000000),
        dual,
        helpstring("IBrokerHouse Interface"),
```

```
        pointer_default(unique)
    ]
    interface IBrokerHouse : IDispatch
    {
        import "oaidl.idl";

        HRESULT getSellerText([out, retval]BSTR *text);
        HRESULT prepareSellOrder
                ([in] BSTR p1, [in] BSTR p2, [in] long p3);
        HRESULT prepareCheckStatus([out, retval]long* status);
        HRESULT prepareBuyOrder
                ([in] BSTR p1, [in] BSTR p2, [in] long p3);
        HRESULT getBuyerText([out, retval]BSTR *text);
    };
    [
        uuid(C414B3D3-DB01-11d0-BAFB-000000000000),
        helpstring("Broker House Class"),
        JAVACLASS("Broker.BrokerHouse"),
        PROGID("Broker.Broker")
    ]
    coclass CBrokerHouse
    {
        [default] interface IBrokerHouse;
    };
};
```

You can see that although the BrokerHouse system as a whole is much more complicated than SayHello, the format and complexity of the IDL files describing the two systems are about the same.

Adding the User Interface

Now, what are we going to do about our user interface? Remember the user interface for this system as we last left it? Not very attractive.

```
0-Quit, 1-Buy, 2-Sell, 3-Check, 4-List: 1

What is your name?   Michael
What are you buying? dog
```

```
What will you pay?    10

0-Quit, 1-Buy, 2-Sell, 3-Check, 4-List: 2

What is your name?     Emily
What are you selling? dog
What is your price?    5
```

So, if we want a state-of-the-art user interface, we need a state-of-the-art user interface programming system. Enter Visual Basic.

Figure 4.24 shows one possible user interface for the brokering system, one that can be created using the simplest Visual Basic functionality. It contains space for a user to enter a name, item, and a price. The user can then press the Buy button, if the item is being purchased, or Sell, if the item is being sold. There is also a Check button, which will see if there are any outstanding matches between buyers and sellers, and a Display button, which will display any matches.

Let's walk through some of the Visual Basic code needed to implement this interface. I actually had to write 25 lines of Visual Basic code to make this interface work. Another 12 lines were supplied automatically by Visual Basic, for a total of just over 35 lines. Figure 4.25 shows Visual Basic up and running, and ready to work on this form.

Figure 4.24 One user interface for the brokering system.

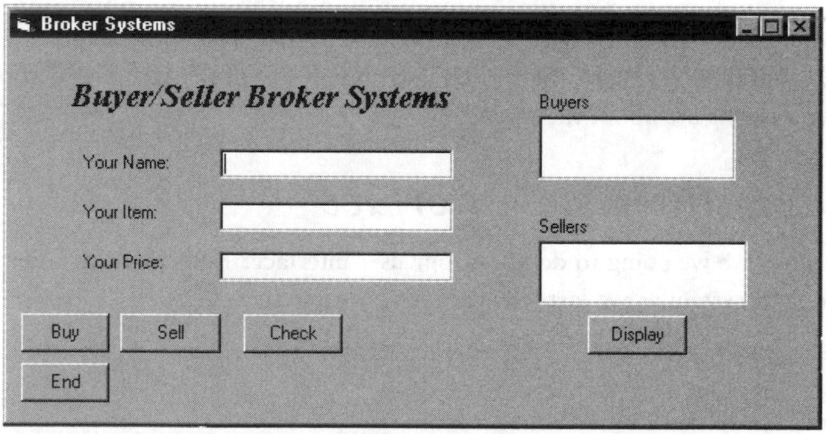

Figure 4.25 Visual Basic and the brokering system form.

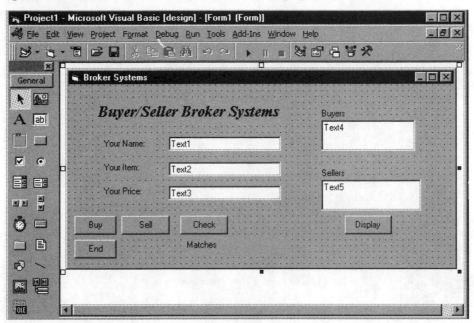

If I switch Visual Basic over to the Code view (as we discussed earlier in the chapter), I can start adding the code associated with various form events. A Code view of this system is shown in Figure 4.26.

Notice in the upper part of the Code view there are two pulldown menus: one containing Command1, and the other containing Click. These two pulldown menus allow you to navigate to the code associated with any possible form event easily and quickly. The first pulldown menu allows you to choose among all of the form elements, and the second pulldown menu allows you to choose among all possible events for the element chosen in the first menu.

These two Code view menus greatly simplify working with code, since I don't have to remember the names of the somewhat obscure procedure names. If I want to work with the event associated with a user clicking the Buy button, I pull down Command1, and then Click.

It is also possible (and recommended) to give user-friendly names to the form elements. This would allow you to name, for example, Command1 (the

Figure 4.26 Code view of the brokering system.

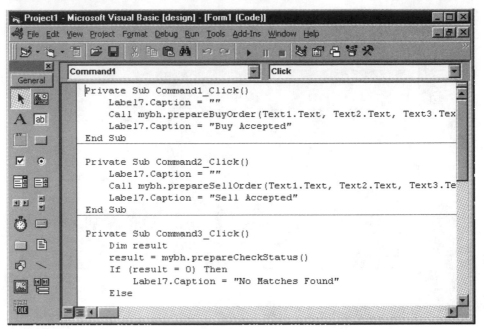

default name of the first command button), as "cmdBuy." Then when you pulled down the Object menu, you could choose cmdBuy, which is easier to remember than Command1. However, in a perhaps misguided effort to minimize the amount of Visual Basic you need to understand this book, I have stuck with the default names.

This is all of the code I had to write to implement the Buy functionality:

```
Private Sub Command1_Click()
    Label7.Caption = ""
    Call mybh.prepareBuyOrder(Text1.Text, Text2.Text, Text3.Text)
    Label7.Caption = "Buy Accepted"
End Sub
```

This code assumes that the first text field contains the buyer's name, the second text field contains the item name, and the third field contains the price the buyer is willing to pay.

Notice this code assumes that a mybh (for my BrokerHouse) object has already been instantiated. Where is a logical place to instantiate this object? Unlike our simpler SayHello example, it doesn't make sense to instantiate this at the time the event occurs. The reason for this is I don't want different events working with different instances of the BrokerHouse object. The BrokerHouseObject contains state. It knows who has previously registered as buyers and sellers, and depends on being able to compare the new entry to those it has stored away in the past. So I need to instantiate the object once, and then use that instantiation throughout.

The SayHello object didn't work this way. In the code for that form, I instantiated the object every time I dealt with a Click event. Why could I get away with reinstantiations in that code, and not here?

The difference between the BrokerHouse object and the SayHello object is that the former contains state, and the latter doesn't. In Chapter 2, I mentioned that there is debate in the industry about whether or not COM objects can have memory (or state). If you weren't convinced by that discussion, you should definitely be convinced by this example. There is no possible way this BrokerHouse example could work unless the BrokerHouse object keeps track of its state. We will give a twist to the whole issue of state in Chapter 6.

Now, back to the instantiation of the BrokerHouse. We want this to happen in an event that occurs only once, at the start of the system. There is a load event associated with the form as a whole, which is a perfect place to insert this type of initialization code. In this event, I have placed the instantiation and initialization of several text fields:

```
Private Sub Form_Load()
    Set mybh = CreateObject("BrokerHouse")
    Text1.Text = ""
    Text2.Text = ""
    Text3.Text = ""
    Text4.Text = ""
    Text5.Text = ""
    Label7.Caption = ""
End Sub
```

There is one more issue with which we must deal relating to the mybh variable, and that is its *declaration*. Variables declared inside of event code are considered private to that section of code. To make a variable public, we need to declare it in a special area that contains information public to the whole form. This area is called a *module*.

The declaration of public variables involves the following:

1. Pulling down the Project menu

2. Choosing Add Module

3. Adding the declaration of the variable

Figure 4.27 shows the view of the module with the declaration of the mybh variable.

If you understand the Visual Basic code we have seen so far, the remaining Visual Basic code is straightforward. The next event is triggered when the Sell button is clicked:

```
Private Sub Command2_Click()
    Label7.Caption = ""
    Call mybh.prepareSellOrder(Text1.Text, Text2.Text, Text3.Text)
    Label7.Caption = "Sell Accepted"
End Sub
```

The next event is triggered when the Check button is clicked:

```
Private Sub Command3_Click()
    Dim result
    result = mybh.prepareCheckStatus()
    If (result = 0) Then
        Label7.Caption = "No Matches Found"
    Else
        Label7.Caption = "Matches Found"
    End If
End Sub
```

The next event is triggered when the Display button is clicked:

```
Private Sub Command4_Click()
    Text4.Text = mybh.getBuyerText()
    Text5.Text = mybh.getSellerText()
    Label7.Caption = ""
End Sub
```

Figure 4.27 Module view.

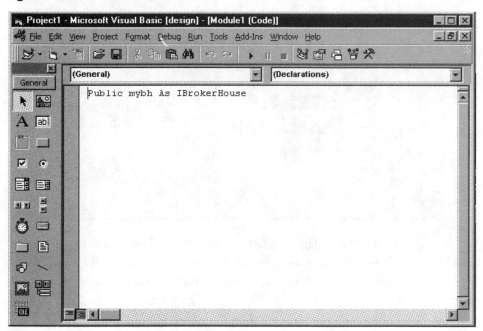

The next event is triggered when the End button is clicked. It ends the program.

```
Private Sub Command5_Click()
    End
End Sub
```

That's all there is to the user interface.

There are two ways I can run this interface. The first is from inside Visual Basic, which is most convenient when I am still in debug mode. The second is by saving the project as an executable, which can then be run completely independently of Visual Basic.

The next series of figures demonstrates this interface at work, and interacting with our BrokerHouse Java class. Figure 4.28 shows the interface as it first starts up. Figure 4.29 shows the system after I have entered the information for a planned purchase. Figure 4.30 shows the system after I press the Buy button. Notice the "Buy Accepted" message in the lower part of the screen.

Figure 4.31 shows the interface after Jane finished entering the information needed to sell a dog, and after pressing the Sell button.

Figure 4.28 Startup.

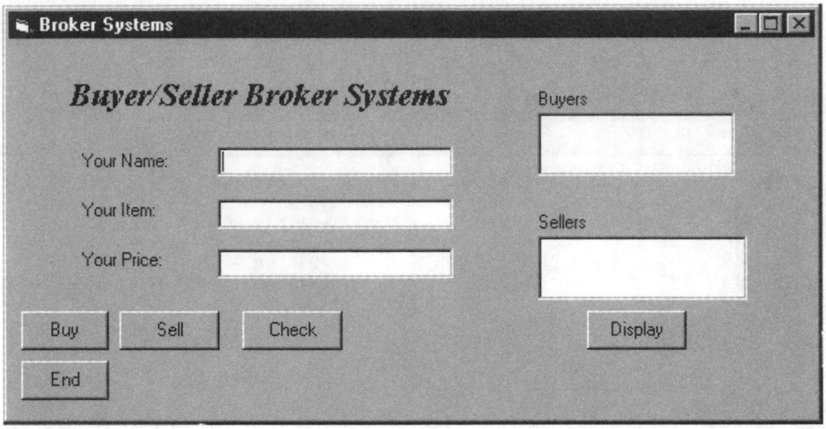

We can now ask the system to check for matches by pressing the Check button. This system says matches were found, because I want to buy the same thing Jane wants to sell, and our prices are within each other's range. Figure 4.32 shows the system at this point.

If I now ask the system to display the matches, by pressing the Display button, the system shows the matched buyers and sellers, as shown in Figure 4.33. The text display isn't very good, but it was cheap. We could add more Visual Basic code to clean this up, but it doesn't serve any pedagogical purpose, so we haven't bothered.

Figure 4.29 Ready for purchase.

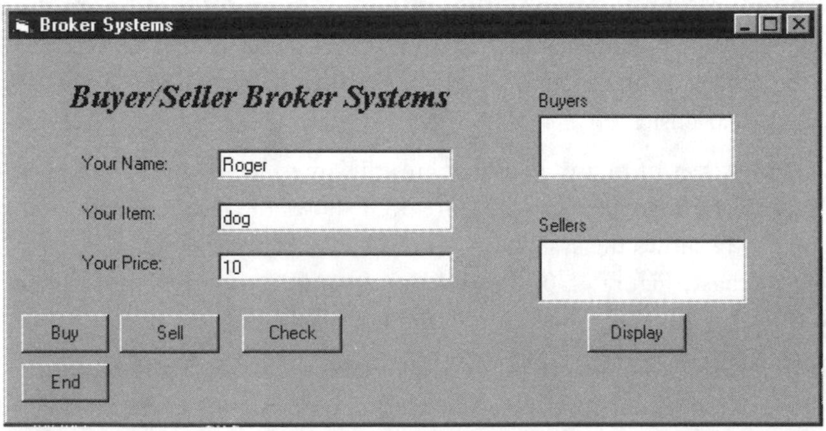

Figure 4.30 After submitting Buy.

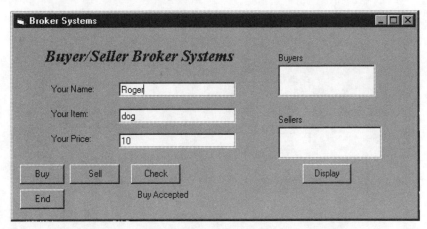

Separation of User Interface and Business Component

We have now achieved several important goals. First, and most obvious, we have created a much more attractive user interface to our Java broker system. Second, we have achieved a clean separation between the user interface and the business component. This clean separation is shown in Figure 4.34.

Figure 4.31 After submitting Sell.

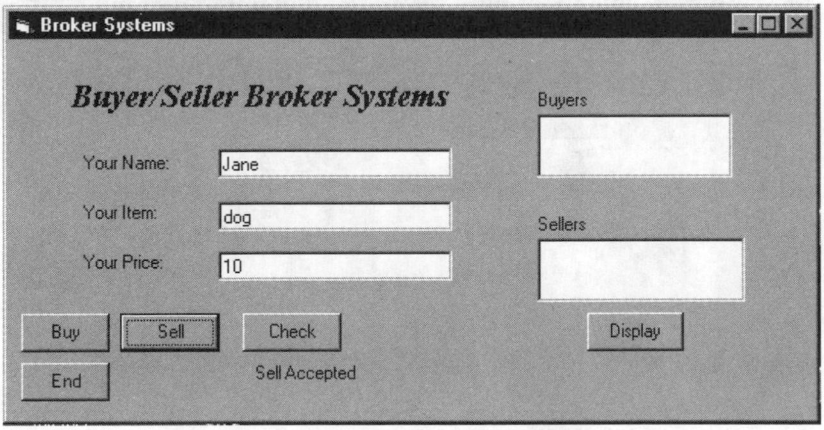

Figure 4.32 After checking.

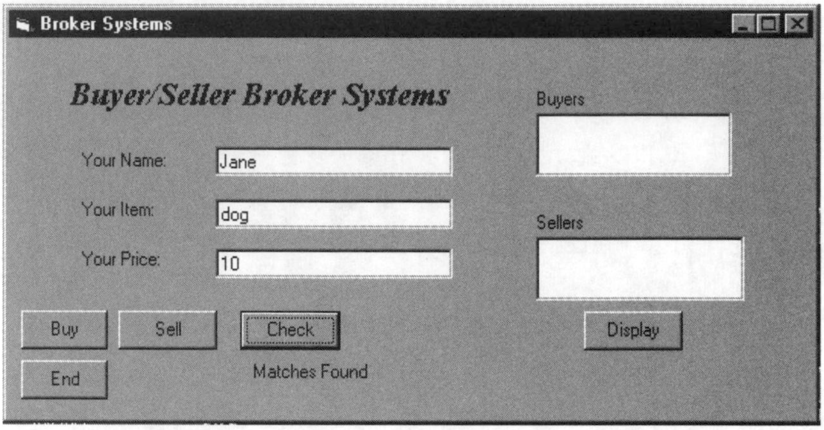

Because of the separation between user interface and business component, we can work on these two areas completely independently. For example, suppose the user interface programmer decides to attack the problem of item names. With the current system, if one person tries to sell a "dog" and another tries to buy a "Dog," the system will not consider them a match. Even adding case insensitivity won't go far here, if one tries to sell a "little dog" and another tries to buy a "small dog."

Since this is basically a user interface issue, we might attack this by not allowing people to type in their buy/sell item, but instead have them choose one from a

Figure 4.33 After displaying matches.

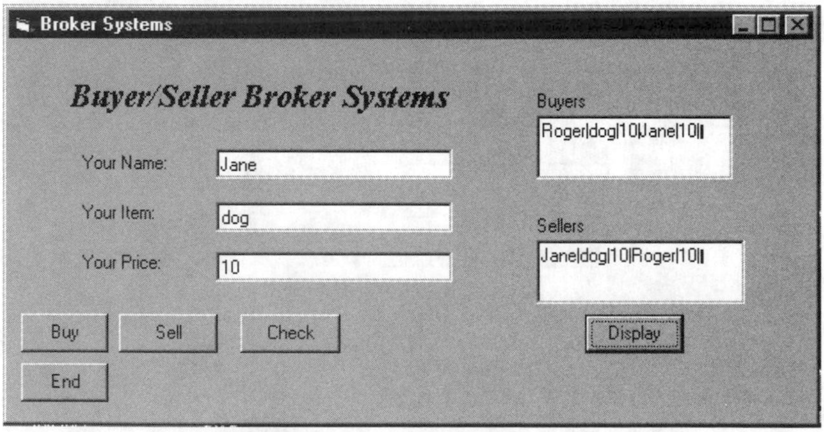

Figure 4.34 Separation of user interface and business component.

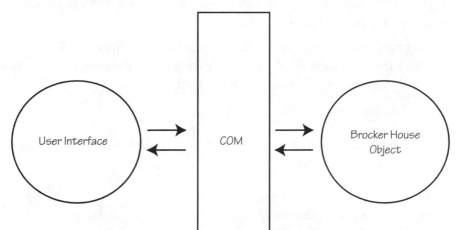

preapproved list. We can redesign our form, replacing the item text box by what is called a *combo box*. In Visual Basic, this new form design looks similar to our old design, but we can now see the combo box in place. This is shown in Figure 4.35.

Figure 4.35 User interface with a combo box.

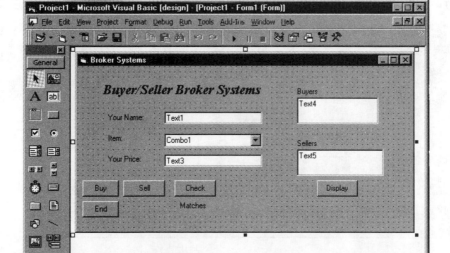

When users run this newly designed form, they don't type in the name of an item. They pull down a menu, and click on an item. Figure 4.36 shows a user choosing an item using this new interface.

Changing from a text box to a combo box is surprisingly easy in Visual Basic. Other than replacing the element by deleting it and choosing a combo box, we need only replace the parameter shown in bold:

```
Private Sub Command1_Click()
    Label7.Caption = ""
    Call mybh.prepareBuyOrder(Text1.Text, Combo1.Text, Text3.Text)
    Label7.Caption = "Buy Accepted"
End Sub

Private Sub Command2_Click()
    Label7.Caption = ""
    Call mybh.prepareSellOrder(Text1.Text, Combo1.Text, Text3.Text)
    Label7.Caption = "Sell Accepted"
End Sub
```

We also need to prime the combo box, which is done at form load time (again in bold):

```
Private Sub Form_Load()
```

Figure 4.36 Choosing an item.

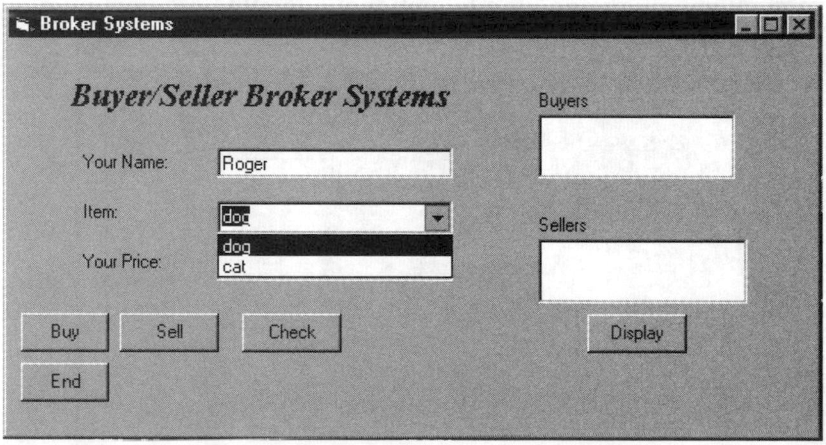

```
        Set mybh = CreateObject("BrokerHouse")
        Text1.Text = ""
        Text3.Text = ""
        Text4.Text = ""
        Text5.Text = ""
        Label7.Caption = ""
        Combo1.Text = "dog"
        Combo1.AddItem ("dog")
        Combo1.AddItem ("cat")
End Sub
```

It's really quite amazing that a change as significant as this can be made with so little actual work.

Location Independence of the BrokerHouse

We haven't talked much about location lately. But keep in mind that from either the user interface or the component perspective, there is no difference between so-called COM and so-called DCOM. The component object may be in the same process as the user interface, another process on the same machine, or a process on some other machine. This should be seen as just a configuration detail that doesn't impact either the user interface or the component itself.

New Broker Code

For those of you interested in looking at the brokering system in more depth, I'll go through the new code here. Keep in mind the overall strategy we took.

First, we created a new interface definition, BrokerHouseInterface, which would package together the entire brokering system.

Second, we created an IDL definition corresponding to this interface.

Third, we generated our Java wrapper interface and class.

Fourth, we created a Java class, BrokerHouse, which implemented this interface. This class was a reorganization of code from our old UserSide class. That is the code we will look at now.

The public methods are these:

```java
package Broker;
import java.io.*;
public class BrokerHouse implements IBrokerHouse,
BrokerHouseInterface
{
    private BrokerInterface broker = null;
    public int prepareCheckStatus()
    {
        BrokerInterface myBroker = getBroker();
        if (myBroker.anyBuys()) return 1;
        if (myBroker.anySells()) return 1;
        return 0;
    }
    public void prepareBuyOrder
        (String name, String item, int maxPrice)
    {
        BrokerInterface myBroker = getBroker();
        EmployeeInterface agent =
            myBroker.getEmployee();

        agent.employee(name);
        agent.item(item);
        agent.price(maxPrice);
        myBroker.registerBuyer((GnomeInterface) agent);
    }
    public void prepareSellOrder
        (String name, String item, int minPrice)
    {
        BrokerInterface myBroker = getBroker();
        EmployeeInterface agent= myBroker.getEmployee ();

        agent.employee(name);
        agent.item(item);
        agent.price(minPrice);
        myBroker.registerSeller((GnomeInterface) agent);
    }
```

```
public String getSellerText()
{
    BrokerInterface myBroker = getBroker();
    GnomeVector v = myBroker.getSells();
    return getGnomeVectorString(v);
}
public String getBuyerText()
{

    BrokerInterface myBroker = getBroker();
    GnomeVector v = myBroker.getBuys();
    return getGnomeVectorString(v);
}
```

The following private methods are used in the public methods, but do not appear as part of the public interface in the Java interface, the Java class, or the COM IDL definition.

```
private BrokerInterface getBroker()
{
if (broker == null) broker = new Broker();
return broker;
}
private String getGnomeVectorString(GnomeVector v)
{
String s = "";
EmployeeInterface gnome = null;
int nsize = v.size();
for (int n=0; n<nsize; n++) {
    gnome = (EmployeeInterface) v.getGnome(n);
    s = s + getEmployeeText(gnome) + "\n";
}
return s;
}
private String getEmployeeText(EmployeeInterface gnome)
{
    String s =
        gnome.employee()              + "|"
```

```
            +gnome.item()              + "|"
            +gnome.price()             + "|"
            +gnome.otherName()         + "|"
            +gnome.negotiatedPrice()   + "|";
    return s;
    }
}
```

This is the new UserSide class, which we keep around for simple debugging purposes. Notice it is now much simpler than the old version shown back in Chapter 3.

```
import java.io.*;
import Broker.BrokerHouse;

public class UserSide
{
    private BrokerHouse myBrokerHouse;
    final static int done = 0;
    final static int buy = 1;
    final static int sell = 2;
    final static int check = 3;
    final static int list = 4;

    private void runit(String args[])
    {
        int next;
        myBrokerHouse = new BrokerHouse();

        while (true)
        {
            next = seeWhatToDo();
            if (next == done) break;
            else if (next == buy)   prepareBuyOrder();
            else if (next == sell)  prepareSellOrder();
            else if (next == check) checkStatus();
            else if (next == list)  listStatus();
        }
```

```java
    }
    public static void main(String args[])
    {
        UserSide myUserSide = new UserSide();
        myUserSide.runit(args);
    }
    private void checkStatus()
    {
        if (myBrokerHouse.prepareCheckStatus()==1) {
            System.out.println("Match found");
        }
        else {
            System.out.println("No match found");
        }
    }
    private void listStatus()
    {
        String sellerText, buyerText;
        sellerText = myBrokerHouse.getSellerText();
        buyerText  = myBrokerHouse.getBuyerText();
        System.out.println("BUYERS");
        System.out.println(buyerText);
        System.out.println("SELLERS");
        System.out.println(sellerText);
    }
    private void prepareBuyOrder()
    {
        String name, item;
        int price;
        System.out.println("");

        name =  readLine   ("What is your name?   ");
        item =  readLine   ("What are you buying? ");
        price = readNumber("What will you pay?    ");
        System.out.println("");
        myBrokerHouse.prepareBuyOrder(name, item, price);
    }
```

```
    private void prepareSellOrder()
    {
        String name, item;
        int price;
        System.out.println("");

        name =  readLine  ("What is your name?     ");
        item =  readLine  ("What are you selling? ");
        price = readNumber("What is your price?    ");
        System.out.println("");
        myBrokerHouse.prepareSellOrder(name, item, price);
    }
    private int seeWhatToDo()
    {
        int next = -1;
        while (next < done || next > list) {
           next=readNumber("0-Quit, 1-Buy, 2-Sell, 3-Check, 4-List: ");
        }
        return next;
    }
}
```

Just to complete the picture, here is the batch file I used for preparing this system:

```
rem Create Broker.tlb
midl Broker.idl

rem Create CBrokerHouse.class and IBrokerHouse.class
javatlb /d . /p Broker /p:b- Broker.tlb

rem del classes from trustlib
del %SystemRoot%\java\trustlib\Broker\*.class

rem Compile local class
jvc Broker\*.java
```

```
rem Compile client
jvc UserSide.java

rem Copy local class to trustlib
copy Broker\*.class %SystemRoot%\java\trustlib\Broker\

rem Register java class
javareg /register /class:Broker.BrokerHouse /progid:BrokerHouse
/clsid:{C414B3D3-DB01-11d0-BAFB-000000000000}
```

Problems

There are several problems with our brokering system as it now exists. The most immediate one is that this is a one-shot deal. Once you exit the system, the state of the system is lost. The next time you start up the system, it will be as if it was the first time. Any new buyers will not be matched up with sellers registered the last time the program ran. In the next chapter, we will discuss how this problem can be solved.

Summary

Object technology is a good technology, as far as it goes. Unfortunately, many people do not understand the purpose of object technology, and attempt to apply it in inappropriate areas. Object technology is *not* appropriate for high-level systems packaging. This is the realm of *component* technology. If Microsoft has contributed nothing else to the computer industry, their long-term advocacy for component technology earns them a place in the history books.

COM/DCOM is the basis for Microsoft's component technology. This technology is far from perfect in its details. It uses a confusing language (IDL) for defining interfaces. It requires the use of a set of nonintuitive tools. It has historical baggage in the arbitrary distinction between COM and DCOM.

But the basic idea of COM/DCOM is very sound. You package a bunch of object code into a component. You make this component the separation point between user interface and business logic. You provide this component the ability to move to another process, or even another machine, at the whim of the system administrator.

Java fits in very well with the general idea of components. Java has good support for interfaces, and for writing classes to support those interfaces. The biggest problem is the poor match between Java and IDL.

Visual Basic is an important part of the MDCA. Although there are other tools available for designing and implementing user interfaces, Visual Basic is still the most advanced. Microsoft has done a good job of integrating components into the Visual Basic environment.

We are slowly making our way out of the MDCA onion. We have looked at Java, components, and Visual Basic, and found at least an intellectual compatibility among these three technologies. Now we will start looking at higher-level coordinating technologies, and the problems they solve.

PERSISTENCE

5

All programs have data. What elevates programs from the puerile to the practical is the *persistence* of that data. It's hard to imagine any program of purpose without persistence.

Imagine a word processor that can't store its words, a designer that can't store its designs, a spreadsheet that can't store its spreads. We have all worked with programs that, at some critical moment, failed the persistence test. We have all heard sob stories about how it would have been on time "if only my computer hadn't lost the file." "My disk crashed" has become the 1990s' equivalent to "The dog ate my homework."

In the business community, persistence is taken seriously. Networks can go down. Computers can blow up. Whole departments can disappear overnight. But if a single byte of data is lost, heads roll. Even Ronald Reagan (or at least one of his speech writers) recognized this. "Information is the oxygen of the modern age," he said. Information is, indeed, the oxygen of the modern age. It is the fuel upon which the fire of commerce depends. And Commerce is what the MDCA is all about.

In this chapter we will look at some of the issues involved with making your components persistent. We will then look at some of the Microsoft frameworks that are (or at least, will be) in place to support persistence. Then we will use these frameworks to add persistence to our brokering system. This chapter focuses on storing data in file systems. Later, we will look at using databases as storage devices.

What Is Persistence?

There are really three goals of persistence systems. The first goal is to give the illusion that a software system is always running, even when it isn't. I call this the *illusion of perpetuity*, and this is where we will be focusing our attention in this chapter. The second goal is to allow a system to work with a much larger collection of data than it could if it had to store all its data in memory at once. The third goal is to provide a mechanism for multiple processes (often, but not always, running the same basic software system) to share data with each other.

Figure 5.1 contrasts some common persistence systems with respect to how they see each of these goals.

There are many different persistence systems. They differ by how much weight they give each of these goals. Sequential files, for example, give a reasonable illusion of perpetuity, as long as nothing too serious goes wrong. Journaled files are able to maintain this illusion even in the face of disk failure. Some keyed file systems maintain the illusion of perpetuity and allow systems to organize huge collections of data. High-performance databases not only maintain the illusion of perpetuity and give the ability to organize huge collections of data, but also provide high-quality mechanisms for data sharing.

Figure 5.1 Contrasting persistence systems.

	Goals		
	Illusion of Perpetuity	Large Data Collections	Multi-process Access
Sequential Files	Yes, but no Failure Protection	No	No
Journaled Files	Yes	No	No
Keyed Files	Yes	Yes	Sometimes
Databases	Yes	Yes	Yes

Persistence and MDCA

In Chapter 3 we talked about Java objects. In Chapter 4 we talked about turning these objects into components. The first step toward making these components useful is giving them persistence. This is by no means the last step. We still have to deal with making these components shareable, scaleable, reliable, secure, and fault tolerant. These are the requirements of commerce, the focus of MDCA, and the raison d'être of this book. We will cover these topics in future chapters. But first things first. And once we have created a component, its first stop on the commerce-enabling assembly line is persistence.

The Great Fraud

For most of my career in software, I have been involved, in one way or another, in the persistence of objects. Nobody can work that long in an area without picking up a healthy complement of prejudices. Rather than deny them, I figure it's best to be up front about them. Besides, as William Hazlitt said over 100 years ago, "No wise man can have a contempt for the prejudices of others; and he should even stand in a certain awe of his own, as if they were aged parents and monitors. They may in the end prove wiser than he." We'll soon see how wise *my* prejudices are. Especially my Big Prejudice.

For many years, object-oriented database vendors have been touting their products as the answer to object persistence. If you want to use objects, they say, you must use an object-oriented database. Storing objects in a file system, they say, is like trying to store an airplane in a garage. Storing objects in a relational database, they say, is like storing a car by taking it apart every evening and putting it back together every morning. "Objects," they emphatically shouted, "Belong in Object-Oriented Databases!"

Corporate MIS departments bought into this argument, although not exactly the way the vendors intended. Fine, they thought. If we are doing object-oriented programming, we need object-oriented databases. We have as much interest in object-oriented databases as we have in having our eyeballs extracted. If objects mean object-oriented databases, then forget objects.

Why, you may ask, were the MIS departments so warmly receptive to using object-oriented databases? What's the matter with adopting a new technology?

The answer is simple. Information drives commerce. Commerce depends on information, and lots of it.

To give you an idea of how many gobs of information it takes to drive a big corporation, consider this. If a byte of information is equivalent to a drop of water, the amount of information stored by a typical large corporation will fill a lake 100 feet deep, 200 feet wide, and 9 miles long. (If you want to try this calculation, you can start with the assumption there are 30,720 drops of water per gallon, calculate the volume of a few hundred trillion drops, and go from there.)

Most corporations do not have lakes this size, so they store all of this information in two places: file systems and traditional databases. They do *not* store this information in object-oriented databases. The amount of information stored in object-oriented databases would not quench a thirst on a hot day.

So, when the object-oriented database vendors ask MIS departments to switch over to object-oriented databases, they are asking the equivalent of the following:

1. Take your one-billion-cubic-foot lake (which is working just fine right now, by the way).

2. Drain out all the water, saving it in some intermediary one-billion-cubic-foot location.

3. Replace the lake with a one-billion-cubic-foot tank made of some new fancy space-age material.

4. Train your staff for six months on how to operate the new tank.

5. Transfer the original water into the new tank.

6. Do all of this without losing a single drop of the original water.

If you do all of this perfectly, with no mistakes, nobody will be able to tell the difference between the original lake and the new tank!

Now MIS departments are known for being somewhat strange. But they do like their sleep. And they do like their paychecks. Neither of which is compatible with this proposal.

So, my Big Prejudice is this: Object-oriented databases are a fraud! The idea that objects should be stored in object-oriented databases is ludicrous. The object-oriented database vendors have done the world a great disservice by convincing people that object-oriented programming necessitates object-oriented databases. This has been the single greatest impediment to the acceptance of object technology by corporations that could have otherwise greatly benefited from it.

But don't worry. Dante has reserved a special circle in Hell for these vendors. They will find themselves spending eternity moving one billion cubic feet of water from one location to another, with nothing but a teaspoon carried in their teeth. Revenge shall be ours!

Okay. Enough. Sorry about the digression. But there is no point in having prejudices unless they are going to be big, and unless you can share them with your friends.

Microsoft's Position on The Great Fraud

Where does Microsoft stand on The Great Fraud? Are they pushing for natural lakes or artificial holding tanks?

It turns out that Microsoft understands this issue perfectly. They have been hard at work developing great technology to allow your COM components to be stored in the lake of your choice. You can choose flat files, architected files, all flavors of traditional databases. The only thing you *can't* choose is object-oriented holding tanks. I have yet to see a single word indicating that Microsoft could care less about object-oriented databases. While IBM was out spending millions of dollars buying up stock in object-oriented database companies, Microsoft was making sure that their COM objects had the best possible access to the data storage technologies that MIS cares about. Payoff time is now here.

File Systems

There are many types of files systems. All of them are layers on top of the most basic file architecture, which is shown in Figure 5.2. Essentially, this architecture is an infinitely long string of bits with the following characteristics:

- Each bit has a unique address.
- Given the address, one can read the value (1 or 0) of the corresponding bit.
- Given the address, one can change the value (to 1 or 0) of the corresponding bit.

Figure 5.2 Basic file systems.

address	0	1	2	3	4	5	6	7	8	9	10
value	0	0	1	1	0	1	0	0	0	1	0

Within these basic constraints, an amazingly rich collection of storage algorithms can be built. This collection is built layer upon layer. First, we organize our collection of bits into collections of bytes. Then we build directory systems, so we can partition this endless stream into logical files. Then we design buffering schemes, so that we can store pieces of these files in main memory, from which access is much faster, but within which much less can be stored. Then we build keyed index systems. Then we build transactional controls. And so on and so forth. But underneath it all is a simple bitstream and direct-access mechanism.

Relationships between Objects and Data

In the past, we have distinguished between component objects and language objects. We are not going to be so careful about this distinction in this chapter. It turns out that the problems faced by component objects and language objects are very similar, so the discussion is basically the same for either.

As we discussed in the last chapter, objects have state, or data, associated with them. Assuming that we want to preserve the illusion of perpetuity, we are going to need to store the object's data is some persistence system whenever anything significant happens to the object. We will also need to restore the object's data before anything of significance happens to the object. The illusion of perpetuity depends on doing these two things, and doing them consistently. This is shown in Figure 5.3, which shows a system maintaining the illusion of perpetuity in the face of a system failure.

A given object is going to be mapped onto some finite collection of data in a persistent system. As shown in Figure 5.4, this mapping could go to a file within a directory, a record within an indexed file, a row within a relational database, or even some combination of these.

Figure 5.3 The illusion of perpetuity.

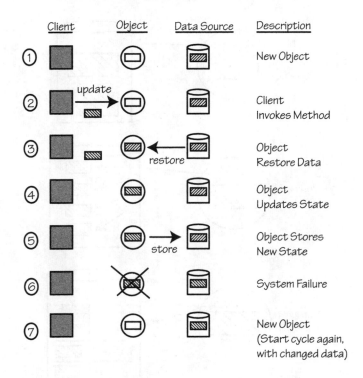

Regardless of where we store the object's data, there will be some name that uniquely identifies that data collection (or at least, uniquely identifies someplace where the key can be found). If the data is stored in a file, the data is identified by a file pathname. If the data is stored in an indexed file, the data is identified by a file pathname and a key. If the data is stored in a relational database, the data is identified by a database name, a table name, and a unique row identifier.

The name of the object's persistent state uniquely identifies a specific potential instance of an object. If we are storing a dog whose state is named lassie.dat, then when we restore that state named lassie.dat into a new dog object, that object becomes for all intents and purposes the same object as the original object that stored the data. It may or may not be true that the restored dog is precisely the same instance as the stored dog, but they might as well be the same because, behaviorally, there is no perceptible difference.

Figure 5.4 Mapping of object data.

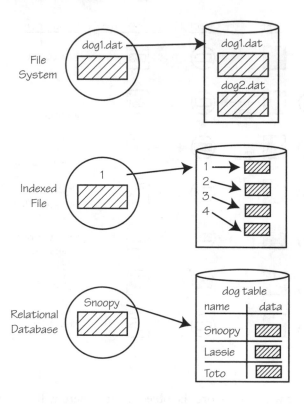

Names and Monikers

You can see that if you are working with persistent objects, this concept of *name* becomes rather interesting. So interesting, in fact, that we can package the idea of *name* into a class with its own behaviors. This allows us to have an object called, say, LassieName, whose class is name. We will think of LassieName as capturing the idea of the name of Lassie's state. If Lassie's state is named lassie.dat, then this will somehow be represented inside the object LassieName. Let's explore LassieName.

Every persistent object has an associated name. A given name can refer to a single persistent object (or more precisely, to the persistent data for the persistent object). Therefore, we can guess that there will be a once-to-one correspondence between persistent objects, like Lassie, and name objects, like LassieName. This relationship can be pictured as shown in Figure 5.5.

We can make these name objects more useful by adding some more intelligence. Let's assume we can figure out how to teach these objects to return to us their associated persistent object. This is a significant gain, because we don't need to keep both the persistent object and the name around. It is sufficient to keep only the name because, given the name, we can always get the associated persistent object. In other words, we don't need to keep Lassie around as long as we have LassieName, and as long as we can ask LassieName for Lassie whenever we need her.

Figure 5.5 Relationship between persistent objects and name objects.

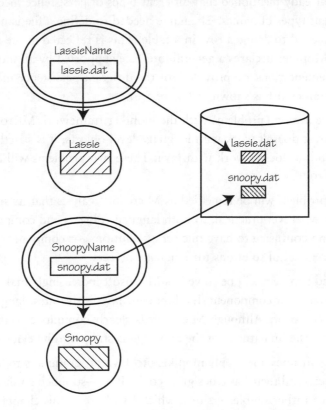

How would we go about teaching name objects to return their associated object? In other words, how do we add a method, say, getObject, that will return the persistent object associated with this particular name? One thing we might do is add a private data member to the name class, say, myObject, that will be an internal reference to the associated persistent object. Then implementing getObject is just a matter of returning myObject.

Microsoft defines an interface that does just this. Instead of calling it *name* they call it *moniker*, which, according to my dictionary, means "a personal name or nickname." The formal interface that describes a moniker is IMoniker. The I stands for interface. IMoniker supports an equivalent to getObject, which they call BindToObject. BindToObject does exactly what we have described for getObject. It returns a reference to the associated persistent object.

We have already mentioned that different types of persistence mechanisms require different types of names. The name needed to define a file is not the same as the name needed to define a row in a table. This is reflected in the moniker framework. IMoniker declares a general interface supported by all monikers, and different implementations are provided for the different persistence mechanisms. This general framework is shown in Figure 5.6.

Now, there are two problems with the moniker framework Microsoft has provided. First, it doesn't work with language-level objects; it is strictly for components. Second, it doesn't work with Java. These two problems will be solved, and probably soon.

The first problem will be remedied as Microsoft realizes that its solutions need to apply, wherever practical, to both language objects and component objects. It is too confusing to have one set of solutions for component objects and a totally different set of solutions for language objects.

The second problem will be solved as Microsoft increasingly makes Java its preferred language for component development. Java is the latest language to be embraced by Microsoft. Although Microsoft is clearly committed to the future of Java and COM, the immaturity of the marriage is still painfully evident.

So, Microsoft does not supply monikers to Java programmers today. Still, the idea of monikers and their basic design is compelling—so much so that I have written my own rather simple versions, which I will use in this chapter. Having

Figure 5.6 The moniker framework.

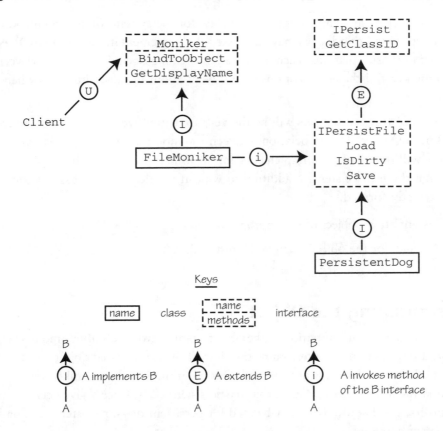

studied the design of monikers as they are made available to other languages, I believe the versions I am presenting will be close, at least from an interface perspective, to what eventually will be made available to Java programmers. So, by using home-brewed monikers patterned after Microsoft monikers, we get to both reuse a good design and prepare for a likely future.

I said that Microsoft will provide different classes implementing the IMoniker interface, each designed to support different persistence systems. In this chapter, we are going to focus on using file systems for persistence. The moniker implementation for file systems is FileMoniker, a simple version of which I have also created.

Creating an Association

Let's go back to an analysis of the name class for file systems or, as we now know it, the FileMoniker class. We have discussed the implementation of BindToObject, at least in those situations when we already have an association formed between the moniker and the persistent object. But what about in those situations when we don't?

One of those situations will be the very first time we ask the FileMoniker to BindToObject. The association between the moniker and the persistent object will not exist. The implementation of BindToObject will have go through these three steps in addition to what it would do if the association was already formed:

1. Instantiate an object of the appropriate class.

2. Arrange for the object's state to be restored.

3. Set up the association.

Instantiating the Object

The first step, the instantiation of the object, implies two facts about monikers. First, it implies that monikers know the class of their associated object, even before the object has been instantiated. Second, it implies that monikers can request the instantiation of any arbitrary persistent class, since a given class of monikers, say, FileMoniker, may be used for persistent dogs, persistent cats, or persistent mangoes.

In fact, Java does not provide a mechanism for the instantiation of an arbitrary class. In Java, you must explicitly declare the name of the class at instantiation time, using code such as

```
dogInterface lassie = new dog();
```

Although Java does not support arbitrary instantiation, COM does. We saw this back in Chapter 4, when we examined this code:

```
Set myHello = CreateObject("HelloTest.Hello")
```

The string passed to CreateObject determines the class of the instantiated object. This string is completely arbitrary. If I pass a string that refers to a class that COM can't figure out how to create, then this function will fail. However, COM is certainly willing to give it the old college try.

So, Java does not support arbitrary instantiation, a feature required for monikers (and extremely useful in many situations). I suspect that Microsoft will eventually add this feature to Java. In the meantime, I am faking this in my FileMoniker implementation.

Restoring the Object's State

The second step in the three-step program to form an initial association is to cause the object's state to be restored. How will a moniker arrange this?

One can assume that restoring an object's state is going to require accessing data that is private to the object. Let's look at a simple Dog class:

```
class Dog {
    private String name;
    public Dog()
    {
        name = "Unknown";
    }
    public String myName()
    {
        return name;
    }
    public void myName(String newName)
    {
        name = newName;
    }
}
```

What does it mean to "restore" an object of this class? It means to go out to a disk file, read in a string, and set the private data member. It stands to reason that only an object of the Dog class can do this, since the data that needs to be set is private to the object. Now we could just add some arbitrary method to Dog, such as

```
class Dog {
    private String name;
```

```
public pleaseRestoreYourself(String fileName) {
   ...
}
```

Then the moniker would invoke this method on the newly instantiated dog object to cause the restore to occur. However, there is a problem with this. Suppose cat then defined its restore like:

```
class Cat {
   private String noise;
   public timeToWakeUp(String fileName) {
   ...
}
```

If we allow classes to make up their own system for restore, then we can't write a generic FileMoniker that knows how to ask any object to restore itself. We need a standard contract that all persistent objects promise to support, so that FileMoniker knows how to communicate the restore request.

The way we write a contract in Java is by creating an interface. The interface defining the contract that all file-system-oriented persistent objects promise to support is called IPersistFile, which is defined like this:

```
interface IPersistFile extends IPersist {
   void Load(String fileName);
   ...

}
```

You can see that IPersistFile is derived from IPersist, which defines that part of the contract common to all persistent objects, regardless of where they are stored. We will look at the IPersist contract later.

If we want our Dog to be a persistent object using the file system, we need Dog to support the IPersistFile interface. This support will fulfill its contract requirements with the FileMoniker. In order to support this interface, the Dog class will look like this:

```
class Dog implements IPersistFile {
   private String name;
   public void Load(String newFileName)
   {
```

```
    . . .
    }
    . . .
```

Implementing Load

In order for a Dog object to be associated with a FileMoniker object, the Dog class must implement the IPersistFile interface and, in particular, the Load method. How Dog implements Load is its own business. Having implemented a large number of Load methods (or their equivalent) in my life, I have found some patterns that work well in a variety of situations. I'll show you this pattern in this section, but keep in mind you are free to do your Load any way you want. The code for this example (including the moniker implementations) can be found in the code zip file under Chapter05_01.

I suggest splitting the Load into two parts. The first part has to do with mapping an input stream to a file. The second part, invoked at the bold section, has to do with actually reading the Dog-specific data from that stream. So, my suggested implementation of Dog would look like this:

```java
import java.io.*;

class Dog implements IPersistFile {
    private String name;
    . . .
    public void Load(String newFileName)
    {
        try {
            FileInputStream file = new FileInputStream(newFileName);
            DataInputStream myStream = new DataInputStream(file);
            LoadState(myStream); /* Load Dog Data */
            myStream.close();
        }
        catch (FileNotFoundException e) {
            System.out.println("New File: " + fileName);
        }
        catch (IOException e) {
            System.out.println("Close Failure");
        }
```

```
        }
    }
    protected void LoadState(DataInputStream myStream)
        throws IOException
    {
        name = myStream.readUTF();
    }
    ...
```

If you look at the implementation of Load, you will see that it is generic to any persistent object. In fact, rather than actually have this code in the class, we could use any of the standard Java techniques for code reuse, such as implementation inheritance or delegation, to incorporate this code. But rather than confuse the issue with introducing more Java, we will keep it simple. In this implementation, it is the LoadState method that actually does Dog-specific reading.

This separation of file-manipulation code from data-manipulation code has a number of advantages. One of these is support for derived classes. Another is support for contained objects. We'll just briefly touch on both of these here, since this is getting into more detail than is really necessary at this point.

Support for Derived Classes

Suppose I have a new class derived from Dog, say, NoisyDog. The Java implementation of NoisyDog might look like this:

```
class NoisyDog extends Dog {
    private String noise;
    ...
```

If we want a NoisyDog to Load itself, how does it do so? It needs to read in data both for name (which is part of the Dog class) and noise (which is part of the NoisyDog class). The easiest way to accomplish this is to have NoisyDog override the LoadState method. Its version should look like this:

```
protected void LoadState(DataInputStream myStream) throws
IOException
{
    base.LoadState(myStream);
    noise = myStream.readUTF();
}
```

When the moniker asks the NoisyDog to load itself, it will do so by invoking Load, which will invoke LoadState. But the LoadState that is invoked will be the NoisyDog LoadState, not the Dog LoadState. The NoisyDog LoadState will then delegate to the base class (Dog), which will do its LoadState first. Then the NoisyDog LoadState can get its information from the same stream.

We would have a problem if we tried to do a similar design by overloading Load. There would be no way to create one DataInputStream that could be used both by the Dog Load and the NoisyDog Load.

Support for Contained Objects

If our object has references to other objects, we may or may not want those other objects (the *contained* objects) to load from the same stream as the original object (the *container* object). By splitting up the Load and the LoadState, we can either Load the container and contained objects from the same stream (by having the container invoke LoadState on the contained objects), or we can have the objects Load from different streams (by having the container invoke Load on the contained objects). Splitting up Load responsibilities as proposed gives us the most flexible options.

Other IPersistFile Responsibilities

The Microsoft IPersistFile includes several other methods, some of which we won't discuss. But there are two others we should at least look at briefly.

```
interface IPersistFile extends IPersist {
    void Load(String fileName);
    boolean IsDirty();
    void Save();
    ...
}
```

The interface IPersistFile inherits from IPersist, which contains this interface:

```
interface IPersist {
    String GetClassID();
}
```

The method GetClassID is actually supposed to return a COM-style class ID, but since this isn't working yet, and this is not applicable to Java anyway, we will just have ours return a String that identifies the class. Conceptually, this is what the definition calls for anyway.

The Save method defined in IPersistFile is the inverse of Load. It's fairly questionable as to whether or not this method should be in the same interface as Load. Load is necessary for the moniker's BindToObject method to be implemented. But there is no such requirement for Save. In a strict transactional setting, we would have the object do its own saving as necessary. But, Save is here, so we might as well implement it. If you do so, I suggest doing so using a similar strategy as for Load: in other words, splitting the Save into a file-management section and a data-management section.

The IsDirty method is intended to provide Save optimization. If a class implements IsDirty, the method should return True if the object has been changed but not saved, and False otherwise. In other words, a client could use IsDirty to determine whether or not the object even needs to be saved.

The GetClassID method can be used to determine the class of an object. Java normally doesn't provide such a capability, so this can be useful.

Here is an implementation of Dog, with the remaining methods implemented:

```java
import java.io.*;
class Dog implements IPersistFile {

    private String name;
    private String fileName;
    private boolean iAmDirty;

    public Dog()
    {
        name = "Unknown";
        fileName = null;
        iAmDirty = false;
    }
```

The constructor in the preceding code initializes the private data. iAmDirty is the variable that will be used to track the dirty status of the Dog.

```java
    public String GetClassID()
    {
        return "Dog";
```

```
}
```

The method just shown returns the name of the class.

```
protected void LoadState(DataInputStream myStream)
      throws IOException
{
   ...
}
public void Load(String newFileName)
{
   ...
}
```

We have already looked at the preceding two methods.

```
protected void SaveState(DataOutputStream myStream) throws
IOException
{
   myStream.writeUTF(name);
}
```

SaveState is exactly the inverse of LoadState. The two should mirror each other. The writeUTF method is part of the standard Java io stream package.

```
public void Save()
{
   try {
       FileOutputStream file = new FileOutputStream(fileName);
       DataOutputStream myStream = new DataOutputStream(file);
       SaveState(myStream);
       myStream.close();
       iAmDirty = false;
   }
   catch (FileNotFoundException e) {
       System.out.println("Load Failure: " + fileName);
   }
   catch (IOException e) {
       System.out.println("Close Failure");
   }
```

```
}
```

Save is the inverse of Load.

```
public boolean IsDirty()
{
    return iAmDirty;
}
```

Since our Dog always saves itself whenever a major state change occurs, it would be a reasonable implementation of IsDirty to always return False. However, we are trying to be consistent with the stated objectives of persistent objects.

```
public String myName()
{
    Load(fileName);
    return name;
}
```

This is the method used to ask a Dog for its name. It always does a load before it does anything else.

```
public void myName(String newName)
{
    name = newName;
    iAmDirty = true;
    Save();
}
```

This is the method used to tell the Dog its new name. It always does a Save once the name has been updated. The iAmDirty is being set to True, but only momentarily, since as a result of the Save it will be set back to False.

More on Monikers

Let's compare frogs and princes. If I were to sit a frog and a prince next to each other and ask you what these two things have in common, you would be hard-pressed to answer. On the other hand, if I were to ask you to list the advantages of being a prince and the advantages of being a frog, you would probably have no trouble coming up with a long list for each. Princes can awaken Sleeping

Beauty with but a brush of their downy lips. Frogs can eat flies. Both of these are useful tricks, given different circumstances.

Princes are not very useful when we have a room full of flies. Frogs are not very useful when we have Sleeping Beauty pining away on the sofa. Fortunately, frogs can be turned into princes, and vice versa. If you have a frog and a snoozing Sleeping Beauty, kiss the frog and, poof!, you have a prince. Once Sleeping Beauty wakes up, opens the windows, and lets in all the flies, just wave your magic wand at the prince and, poof!, you have a frog again. You can continue this indefinitely. Frog, prince, frog, prince. As long as neither your lips nor the magic wand wear out, you are set.

Let's compare two other things that appear at first to have nothing in common. Let's compare monikers and strings. You can probably think of lots of neat things that strings can do, and lots of neat things (well, at least one) that monikers can do, but nothing that both can do. Strings can be stored in files. They can be passed around in e-mail. They can be read on Web sites. Monikers can return objects. Strings can't do that. All of these are useful tricks, given different circumstances.

Wouldn't it be nice if, as with princes and frogs, we could turn monikers into strings, and vice versa? Then when I want to send you my moniker in some e-mail, I would just transform the moniker into a string and send it to you. If you wanted to bind to my object, you could just transform the string back into a moniker, and then ask the resulting moniker to BindToObject.

Fortunately, we can do just this. The magic wand that transforms a moniker into a string is the method GetDisplayName. All monikers support this method. This is even better than a magic wand. You just tell the moniker to turn itself into a string and, poof!, you have a string.

The kiss that turns the string back into a moniker is also a method. This method is MkParseDisplayName. This method is not a normal moniker method. It can't be, because we no longer have a moniker on which to invoke it. We have a string. So, this method (at least in my implementation) is static. Static methods, in Java, can be invoked anytime, whether or not there is an actual object of the class in question around.

So, GetDisplayName and MkParseDisplayName are inverse functions. The first transforms a moniker to a string. It takes one parameter, a moniker, and returns a string. The second transforms a string into a moniker. It also takes one parameter, but now the parameter is a string, and the return value is a moniker.

Admittedly, GetDisplayName and MkParseDisplayName are pretty droll names, especially compared to *kiss* and *magic wand*. That's what you get when you have Microsoft Nerds naming things rather than Walt Disney.

Here then, is a full definition of the IMoniker interface. Actually, the Microsoft version has more methods, but this is all we will use here.

```
interface IMoniker {
    Object BindToObject();
    String GetDisplayName();
    IMoniker MkParseDisplayName(String displayName);
}
```

Just for the fun of it, I will show you my implementation of FileMoniker. Now please, don't laugh. This is just temporary until Microsoft gets around to providing the real thing. But at least it will let us write some code. This is mainly for the benefit of the Java Heads out there. The rest of you are probably happy just knowing the interface just shown.

```
class FileMoniker implements IMoniker {

    private IPersist myObject = null;
    private String fileName;
    private String className;

    public Object BindToObject()
    {
        if (myObject != null) {
            myObject.Load(fileName);
            return myObject;
        }
        if (className.equals("Dog"))
            myObject = (IPersistFile) new Dog();
        else
            System.out.println("BindToObject: bad class name");

        myObject.Load(fileName);
```

```
        return myObject;
    }
```

The BindToObject method is definitely a kludge. Ideally, we would use arbitrary instantiation code here, but as I pointed out earlier, Java does not support arbitrary instantiation. This means the code we write here hard-wires the number of classes this moniker will support.

```
public String GetDisplayName()
{
    return className + ":" + fileName;
}
```

Here we have basically defined the architecture of the string. This must agree with the next method.

```
static public IMoniker MkParseDisplayName(String displayName)
{
    FileMoniker newMoniker;
    String fileNamePart;
    String classNamePart;
    int breakPoint;

    breakPoint = displayName.indexOf(":");
    classNamePart = displayName.substring(0, breakPoint);
    fileNamePart = displayName.substring(breakPoint+1);

    newMoniker = new FileMoniker();
    newMoniker.fileName = fileNamePart;
    newMoniker.className = classNamePart;
    return newMoniker;
}
```

Notice that this method is static, meaning it can be called with or without an instantiated FileMoniker object.

This code makes some assumptions about what the string looks like. The string starts with a class name, then has a colon, and then has a file pathname—for example, Dog:lassie.dat. The class name is the class of the associated persistent object. The file pathname is the pathname of the file containing the object's data.

Now, the Microsoft strings, when they come out, may not look exactly like this, but they will certainly contain similar information.

Knowing the architecture of the string is very useful. It allows you to create a string using any number of Java string-manipulation techniques. As long as the string you create is architected like a moniker string, you can create a moniker from that string by using MkParseDisplayName. And once you have done that, you can request the associated object by using the moniker method BindToObject, which will instantiate a new object of the appropriate class and invoke Load on that object. Isn't it amazing how the world all comes together sometimes?

Let's review, for the record, what we mean by a persistent object. A persistent object has the following characteristics:

- It implements the IPersistFile interface.
- It reads its data at the start of each method.
- It writes its data whenever a method invocation results in a significant change to the object's state.

An object that fulfills all of these requirements has a variety of neat tricks it can do. We will look at one of these tricks now, and another in the next chapter.

The Illusion of Perpetuity

The first of the neat persistent object tricks is presenting the *illusion of perpetuity*. Remember the illusion of perpetuity? We were discussing that at the beginning of this chapter. It is the illusion that a program never stops running. The following program (in the code zip file under Chapter05_01) demonstrates the illusion of perpetuity. This program creates a moniker and requests the associated persistent Dog object. If you start this program with an argument (for example, jview Main1 Lassie), the program will tell the Dog object that the argument is its name. Then the program asks the Dog its name and prints the answer. Here is the code:

```
public class Main1 {
    public static void main (String args[])
    {
        IMoniker m1 =
            FileMoniker.MkParseDisplayName("Dog:dog.dat");
        Dog dog1 = (Dog) m1.BindToObject();
```

```
        if (args.length > 0) dog1.myName(args[0]);
        System.out.println("My name is "+dog1.myName());
    }
}
```

If I run this program four times in a row, I get these results:

```
jview Main1 Lassie
My name is Lassie

jview Main1
My name is Lassie

jview Main1 Snoopy
My name is Snoopy

jview Main1
My name is Snoopy
```

You can see the illusion at work here. It's as if the program never stops. This program is behaving as if it's in a giant loop. I can shut off my machine and go to Hawaii for a month, and when I return, Snoopy will start up again exactly where he left off. To be honest, I should point out that I am only speculating that if I go to Hawaii for a month the program will continue working. I have never tried this. But I am accepting grants to test this hypothesis.

What is neat about the illusion of perpetuity is that it requires no special effort on the part of the client. The client never asks the Dog object to Load or Save itself. The client has no particular awareness that the object is even persistent, other than the fact that the object had a moniker for a mother.

We will develop this idea quite a bit over the next few chapters.

COM

This is all great for Java classes. But how does this relate to COM and the MDCA? From the Java perspective, COM is just another client. If my Java class is persistent, it is persistent as well from the perspective of COM.

We can see this by continuing work with the brokering system. When last we left the brokering system, we had packaged the Java classes into a neat COM called BrokerHouse. We then built a user interface to drive this component from Visual Basic. The biggest problem with this system was that when it shut down, it lost all of its work. And when it started back up, it did so from scratch. In other words, it did not support the illusion of perpetuity.

So, now we know what we must do. We must make the language objects of the broker system persistent. And that means the following:

- We must make the objects implement the IPersistFile interface.
- We must restore the objects before taking any important actions, and store them afterwards.
- We must acquire the objects using a FileMoniker.

Let's look through the steps. The code we are looking at here is in the zip file under Chapter05_02. You will see that the code is a little more complicated than that of the simpler Dog class, but it's just a matter of plodding through it. If you are not a hard-core Java Head, feel free to browse through this quickly.

Adding Persistence to the BrokerHouse

There are two classes to which we need to add persistence. These are the Gnome and Broker classes. First thing we need to do is to make sure both of these classes support the IPersistFile interface. I have taken slightly different approaches to ensure this. The Broker class, you may remember, implements the BrokerInterface. I have therefore extended the BrokerInterface to include the IPersistFile interface. My new version of BrokerInterface looks like this:

```
package Broker;
public interface BrokerInterface extends IPersistFile
{
    public EmployeeInterface getEmployee();

    public void registerBuyer(PersistentGnomeInterface newBuyer);
    public GnomeVector getBuys();
    public boolean anyBuys();

    public void registerSeller(PersistentGnomeInterface newSeller);
    public GnomeVector getSells();
    public boolean anySells();
}
```

The Gnome I have taken care of a little differently. I have added a new interface called the PersistentGnome interface, mainly because I felt it would simplify some of my code if I could count on a gnome to keep tabs on its own moniker. This interface is defined like this:

```
package Broker;
interface PersistentGnomeInterface extends IPersistFile
{
    IMoniker moniker();
}
```

I now change the Gnome interface to be derived from this. My new Gnome interface looks like this:

```
package Broker;
interface GnomeInterface extends PersistentGnomeInterface
{
    public String employee();
    public String item();
    public long price();
    public String otherName();
    public long negotiatedPrice();
}
```

My agent interface is totally unaffected:

```
package Broker;
interface AgentInterface extends GnomeInterface {
    public void negotiatedPrice(long newPrice);
    public void otherName(String other);
    public void moniker(IMoniker newMoniker);
}
```

as is my EmployeeInterface:

```
package Broker;
interface EmployeeInterface extends GnomeInterface{
    public void employee(String newName);
    public void item(String newItem);
    public void price(long newPrice);
}
```

My BrokerHouseInterface is unchanged, which implies that, whatever I am doing, it won't impact my COM clients:

```java
package Broker;
public interface BrokerHouseInterface
{

    public int prepareCheckStatus();
    public void prepareBuyOrder
        (String name, String item, int maxPrice);
    public void prepareSellOrder
        (String name, String item, int minPrice);
    public String getSellerText();
    public String getBuyerText();
}
```

This takes care of my interface definitions. Now let's see what changes we have to make in our class files. First we have the Gnome class, which now must implement the IPersistFile interface. Why must it implement the IPersistFile interface? The class only claims to implement AgentInterface and EmployeeInterface. But when you agree to implement an interface, you agree to implement *any* interface this interface extends (such as GnomeInterface), and any interface *that* interface extends (such as PersistentGnomeInterface), and any interface *that* interface extends (such as IPersistFile).

```java
package Broker;
import java.io.*;

class Gnome implements AgentInterface, EmployeeInterface
{
    private String myEmployeeName;
    private String myItemName;
    private long myPrice;
    private long myNegotiatedPrice;
    private IMoniker myMoniker;
    private String otherName;

    private String fileName;
    private String monikerString;
```

```
    private boolean iAmDirty;

    public void Save()
    {
        try {
            FileOutputStream file = new FileOutputStream(fileName);
            DataOutputStream myStream = new DataOutputStream(file);
            SaveState(myStream);
            myStream.close();
            iAmDirty = false;
        }
        catch (FileNotFoundException e) {
            System.out.println("Load Failure: " + fileName);
        }
        catch (IOException e) {
            System.out.println("Close Failure");
        }
    }
```

The Save method is identical to the one we showed for Dog.

```
    protected void SaveState(DataOutputStream myStream)
        throws IOException
    {
        myStream.writeUTF(myEmployeeName);
        myStream.writeUTF(myItemName);
        myStream.writeLong(myPrice);
        myStream.writeLong(myNegotiatedPrice);
        myStream.writeUTF(otherName);
        myStream.writeUTF(monikerString);
    }
```

We write out all the important data items. Notice we don't have to write out every item, only those that will need to be restored to return to this state.

```
    protected void LoadState(DataInputStream myStream)
        throws IOException
    {
```

```
        IMoniker m;
        myEmployeeName = myStream.readUTF();
        myItemName = myStream.readUTF();
        myPrice = myStream.readLong();
        myNegotiatedPrice = myStream.readLong();
        otherName = myStream.readUTF();
        monikerString = myStream.readUTF();
        m = FileMoniker.MkParseDisplayName(monikerString);
        moniker(m);
    }
```

LoadState is the inverse of SaveState, and is responsible for returning the object's state to what it was at the time of the SaveState.

```
public void Load(String newFileName)
{
    try {
        fileName = newFileName;
        FileInputStream file = new FileInputStream(fileName);
        DataInputStream myStream = new DataInputStream(file);
        LoadState(myStream);
        myStream.close();
    }
    catch (FileNotFoundException e) {
    }
    catch (IOException e) {
        System.out.println("Open Failure: " + fileName);
    }
}
```

Load is just like the persistent dog version.

```
public static String GetClassID()
{
    return "Gnome";
}
```

We never really use this method, but it is part of the IPersistFile contract (indirectly, via IPersist).

```
public boolean IsDirty()
```

```
    {
        return false;
    }
```

Again, part of the IPersistFile contract.

```
public void moniker(IMoniker newMoniker)
{
    myMoniker = newMoniker;
    monikerString = myMoniker.GetDisplayName();
}
```

This allows the Gnome to keep track of the associated moniker. It simplifies some of the coding later on.

```
public IMoniker moniker()
{
    return myMoniker;
}
```

We can use this method to get the associated moniker.

```
public Gnome()
{
    myEmployeeName = "Unknown";
    myItemName = "Unknown";
    myPrice = 0;
    myNegotiatedPrice = 0;
    otherName = "None";
    myMoniker = null;
}
```

The constructor is unaffected, other than the addition of another state variable (myMoniker) to initialize. Those are the interfaces. Now let's take a look at the classes. Here is the Broker class, which, remember, is an IPersistFile by virtue of BrokerInterface being an extension of IPersistFile.

```
package Broker;
import java.io.*;
public class Broker implements BrokerInterface
{
    private GnomeVector pendingBuys;
    private GnomeVector pendingSells;
```

```
private GnomeVector oldBuys;
private GnomeVector oldSells;

private String fileName;
private boolean iAmDirty;
private int lastID;
```

The three private variables just shown are all part of the persistence. The lastID variable will be used to create monikers for the employees.

```
protected void SaveState(DataOutputStream myStream)
    throws IOException
{
    pendingBuys.SaveVector(myStream);
    pendingSells.SaveVector(myStream);
    oldBuys.SaveVector(myStream);
    oldSells.SaveVector(myStream);
    myStream.writeInt(lastID);
}
```

SaveState, as usual, is responsible for saving the state of the object. Notice that we have simplified this method by adding a SaveVector method to the GnomeVector, which saves its gnomes out to the stream. We will come back to this.

```
protected void LoadState(DataInputStream myStream)
    throws IOException
{
    pendingBuys.LoadVector(myStream);
    pendingSells.LoadVector(myStream);
    oldBuys.LoadVector(myStream);
    oldSells.LoadVector(myStream);
    lastID = myStream.readInt();
}
```

As usual, LoadState is the mirror image of SaveState. Like LoadState, it is simplified by the addition of a new method to the GnomeVector.

```
public void Save()
{
    try {
```

```
        FileOutputStream file = new
            FileOutputStream(fileName);
        DataOutputStream myStream = new
            DataOutputStream(file);
        SaveState(myStream);
        myStream.close();
        iAmDirty = false;
    }
    catch (FileNotFoundException e) {
        System.out.println("Load Failure: " + fileName);
    }
    catch (IOException e) {
        System.out.println("Close Failure");
    }


}
```

Nothing unusual about Save.

```
public void Load(String newFileName)
{
    int size;
    String name;
    IMoniker m1;
    try {
        fileName = newFileName;
        FileInputStream file = new FileInputStream(fileName);
        DataInputStream myStream = new DataInputStream(file);
        LoadState(myStream);
        myStream.close();
    }
    catch (FileNotFoundException e) {
    }
    catch (IOException e) {
        System.out.println("Close Failure");
    }
}
```

And nothing unusual about Load.

```
public String GetClassID()
{
    return "Broker";
}
```

This is part of the IPersistFile interface (via IPersist). We have implemented it, although we aren't using it.

```
public boolean IsDirty()
{
    return iAmDirty;
}
```

Same here.

```
public Broker()
{
    pendingBuys = new GnomeVector();
    pendingSells = new GnomeVector();
    oldBuys = new GnomeVector();
    oldSells = new GnomeVector();

    iAmDirty = false;
    lastID = 0;
}
```

The constructor now sets up the persistence-related variables.

```
public void registerBuyer(PersistentGnomeInterface newBuyer)
{
    pendingBuys.addGnome(newBuyer);
    lookForMatches();
}

public void registerSeller(PersistentGnomeInterface newSeller)
{
    pendingSells.addGnome(newSeller);
    lookForMatches();
}
```

The preceding two methods are unchanged, except that I have changed the "generic" gnome interface to PersistentGnomeInterface.

```
public EmployeeInterface getEmployee ()
{
    IMoniker moniker;
    String name;
    AgentInterface gnome;

    moniker =
        FileMoniker.MkParseDisplayName("Gnome:"+lastID+".dat");
    lastID++;
    gnome = (AgentInterface) moniker.BindToObject();
    gnome.moniker(moniker);
    return (EmployeeInterface) gnome;
}
```

Our old version of getEmployee instantiated a new gnome. This new version not only instantiates one, but assigns it a moniker.

Now let's take a look at BrokerHouse. It is not a persistent object, but it uses persistent objects and, therefore, has some changes because of this.

```
package Broker;
import java.io.*;
public class BrokerHouse implements IBrokerHouse,
BrokerHouseInterface
{
    private IMoniker brokerM;
```

Since the broker object is now a persistent object, we are going to keep track of its moniker, rather than the broker itself.

```
public BrokerHouse()
{
    String monikerString = "Broker:broker.dat";
    brokerM =
        FileMoniker.MkParseDisplayName(monikerString);
}
```

When we first create the BrokerHouse, we set up the moniker for the broker.

```
private BrokerInterface getBroker()
{
```

```
BrokerInterface broker;

broker = (BrokerInterface) brokerM.BindToObject();
return broker;
}
```

Since our version of BindToObject automatically does a Load, we know when getBroker is invoked, and our Broker object is up to date.

```
public String getSellerText()
{
    BrokerInterface myBroker = getBroker();
    GnomeVector v = myBroker.getSells();
    myBroker.Save();
    return getGnomeVectorString(v);
}
```

Because this method results in a significant state change to the broker object, we do a Save. This is a slightly different strategy than we used with the Dog. The Dog automatically saved its own state whenever a method was invoked that resulted in a state change. Here the "client" is saving the object. The reason we have chosen this strategy is to minimize the number of Saves. We have some opportunities to bunch up work. We are doing this because we know that the component as a whole (from the COM client perspective) will be following the rule to save itself after every significant state change.

```
public String getBuyerText()
{
    BrokerInterface myBroker = getBroker();
    GnomeVector v = myBroker.getBuys();
    myBroker.Save();
    return getGnomeVectorString(v);
}
```

The same discussion we had with getSellerText applies here as well.

```
public void prepareBuyOrder
        (String name, String item, int maxPrice)
{
    BrokerInterface myBroker = getBroker();
```

```
        EmployeeInterface agent = myBroker.getEmployee();

        agent.employee(name);
        agent.item(item);
        agent.price(maxPrice);

        agent.Save();
        myBroker.registerBuyer((PersistentGnomeInterface) agent);
        myBroker.Save();
    }
```

Our agent Save strategy is similar to our broker. Here you can clearly see an optimization. Rather than have the agent save itself each time an employee name, item name, or price has been set (each of which result in significant state changes), we do the Save only once, after the last update has been made.

```
public void prepareSellOrder
     (String name, String item, int minPrice)
{
    BrokerInterface myBroker = getBroker();
    EmployeeInterface agent= myBroker.getEmployee ();

    agent.employee(name);
    agent.item(item);
    agent.price(minPrice);

    agent.Save();
    myBroker.registerSeller((PersistentGnomeInterface) agent);
    myBroker.Save();
}
```

The prepareBuyOrder discussion applies here as well.

Now we are ready to look at GnomeVector. Generally, we have made two changes. First, we are assuming the gnomes are PersistentGnomeInterface gnomes, rather than just GnomeInterface gnomes. Second, rather than storing gnome references in the underlying vector, we are storing moniker references.

```
package Broker;
import java.util.Vector;
```

```
import java.io.*;

class GnomeVector
{
    private Vector myVector;

    public PersistentGnomeInterface getGnome(int n)
    {
        IMoniker m;
        PersistentGnomeInterface gnome;
        m = (IMoniker) myVector.elementAt(n);
        gnome = (PersistentGnomeInterface) m.BindToObject();
        return gnome;
    }
```

The getGnome method rebinds the object associated with the moniker each time it is invoked.

```
    protected void LoadVector(DataInputStream myStream)
        throws IOException
    {
        IMoniker m1;
        String name;
        int size = myStream.readInt();
        for (int n = 0; n < size; n++) {
            name = myStream.readUTF();
            m1 = (IMoniker) FileMoniker.MkParseDisplayName(name);
            myVector.addElement(m1);
        }
    }
```

The LoadVector method is invoked by the broker object when it is asked to load itself. Notice what it actually reads from the stream—not monikers, but the strings associated with the monikers. It then recreates the moniker and places it in the underlying vector.

```
    protected void SaveVector(DataOutputStream myStream)
        throws IOException
    {
```

```
IMoniker m1;
String name;
myStream.writeInt(myVector.size());
for (int n = 0; n < myVector.size(); n++) {
    m1 = (IMoniker) myVector.elementAt(n);
    name = m1.GetDisplayName();
    myStream.writeUTF(name);
}
}
```

The SaveVector method is the inverse of LoadVector. It is invoked by the broker object when it is asked to save itself. Notice what it actually stores into the stream. You could predict this if you knew what LoadVector is expecting to find in the stream: moniker strings. Why am I storing moniker strings rather than monikers? Because object references cannot be stored in streams. Object references have no meaning once this process goes away. The only guarantee the system makes is that the string will still be valid in another process, and can be used in that process to create a new moniker that will be valid.

Figure 5.7 Brokering system interface.

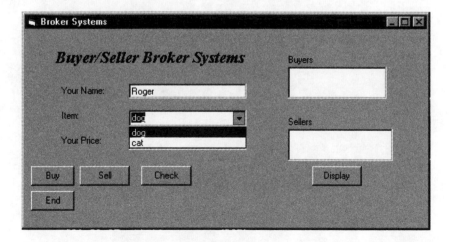

Summary

We have done a lot of work in this chapter, and made a lot of changes in our brokering system. What, exactly, has it brought us?

At the end of the last chapter, we had a brokering system that was well componentized, and had a great user interface. But it was useless. Why? Because it didn't store its state. In this chapter, we have discussed the major issues involved with making objects, but of the component and of the language type, persistent. Then we went through the brokering system, and made the BrokerHouse component persistent. We have used file systems as our data repository, but the same issues apply for many other storage mechanisms.

The user interface looks like Figure 5.7. It hasn't changed. But what *has* changed is what happens when we click the End button. Now this program presents the illusion of perpetuity. The next time the program comes up, it will be as if it never stopped. We are well on the way toward having a usable system.

Keep in mind that the frameworks I have described here don't exist yet. However, I have taken an educated guess as to what they will look like, and have provided implementations here that you can get started with.

SHARING AND SCALABILITY

6

I hate driving to the airport. Parking is terrible. Traffic is often backed up. I always worry about my car overheating, or having an accident on the way, or even getting sidetracked. Getting sidetracked? Once I missed a flight because I saw a new bagel shop on the way to the airport. I stopped in and by the time I decided what I wanted my flight had left. I tried to explain this to the attendant at the airline ticket counter and received no sympathy. Bagels weren't in the company manual. "But it was an *everything* bagel, and it was loaded with cream cheese," I tried to explain.

I could ask my wife to drive me. But she is no more fond of driving to the airport than I am. So what am I to do?

My best option is to take a taxi. When I want to go to the airport, I phone the taxi company. The company radios the nearest available taxi. The taxi comes to my house and drives me to the airport. I pay the taxi. I get on my flight. When I return, it's even easier. I don't even have to call. I just step outside the airline terminal and there is a taxi waiting for me.

In this chapter, we are going to discuss how to organize taxis efficiently. And gnomes. And components.

The Loyal Taxi Strategy

If you have no idea how taxis work, and you are trying to figure it out from watching me come and go at the airport, you might have trouble. All you know is that I arrive at the airport in a taxi, and when I return to the airport, I step out of the terminal and into a taxi. Here is one hypothesis you might come up with to explain this.

You might form the hypothesis that taxis in Austin are very loyal. They bring people to the airport who travel perhaps several thousand miles. The taxis wait through rain and shine, turning away any attempt to entice them away, until their beloved passengers return days or weeks later. When passengers finally return, their taxis are right there, waiting right where they left them. Taxis, you might think, are incredibly loyal in Austin. The loyal taxi strategy is shown in Figure 6.1.

If you watch my trip carefully though, you might observe some details that are hard to fit with the loyal taxi hypothesis. For example, the driver. The one who took me to the airport was clean shaven. The one who took me home had a beard. Of course, it *had* been a week. And then there is the taxi itself. The one that took me to the airport didn't look exactly like the one that took me home. Or did it?

Figure 6.1 The "loyal taxi" strategy.

You might also observe details that would fit perfectly with the loyal taxi hypothesis. You might, for example, fingerprint the two drivers and find that they are indeed the same person. And you could find that the license plates on the two taxis are the same. This could happen. Austin is a small city.

The most important clue that the loyal taxi hypothesis is not correct is right outside the airline terminal. It is not the identity of the drivers or the license plates on the taxis. It is the number of taxis.

At any given time, there are about 50 taxis waiting at the airport. There are about 10,000 people taking off from the airport every day, with probably one third of them using taxis to get to the airport. Let's say the average trip away from Austin is about a week. If the loyal taxi hypothesis is correct, you would expect to see about 1/3 taxis × 10,000 trips/day × 7 days/trip, or 20,000 taxis waiting at the airport at any given time. Considering that the airport has total parking for only 5300 cars, 20,000 taxis hanging around twiddling their thumbs would turn the airport into a giant perpetual gridlock. Which it almost is anyway, but that is another story.

The Disposable Taxi Strategy

Having discarded the loyal taxi hypothesis, you might think about the disposable taxi hypothesis. This hypothesis says that when I call the taxi company, the taxi company goes out and buys a new taxi and hires a new driver. The driver and taxi take me to the airport. The driver is then fired and the taxi disposed of. When I arrive back at the airport, a new driver is hired and a new taxi is purchased and I am brought home. Then the driver is fired and the taxi once again discarded. This strategy is shown in Figure 6.2.

This system is much better from the perspective of the airport administrator. It means that very few taxis will be hanging around the airport. Of course, the landfill administrator may not be thrilled, but that's somebody else's problem.

If taxis and drivers aren't too expensive, this system might be workable. It is certainly much better than dedicating a taxi to every person going to the airport. For one thing, it makes it possible to get to the airport, which would be precluded by 20,000 taxis blocking every available access road. The only downside of this system is the cost. Is the cost of taxis, you might wonder, so cheap that purchasing a new one for every trip is really feasible? It is likely, you might conclude, that this system will be even more expensive than the original system.

Figure 6.2 The "disposable taxi" strategy.

But you can prove that the disposable taxi hypothesis is also false. All you need to do is to hang around the airport and surreptitiously mark every taxi with a big red X on the rear window as it drives by. At first, every taxi will arrive at the airport unmarked. But after a while you will notice something interesting. More and more taxis arriving at the airport will already have big red Xs on the rear window. After a while, virtually *every* taxi will arrive at the airport premarked. If the disposable taxi hypothesis was correct, you would *never* see a taxi arriving premarked. So there must be another explanation.

The Taxi Pool Strategy

I am not rich, but I can afford to take taxis—which I couldn't afford if either the loyal taxi or the disposable taxi hypotheses were true. I can afford taxis because the taxi companies have evolved an even better system for running taxis.

Taxi companies have pools of available taxis. When I call for a taxi to go to the airport, the taxi dispatcher checks the pool to find an available taxi. The dispatcher assigns that taxi to me for the duration of the ride to the airport. While I am using the taxi, it is mine, and mine alone. But once I arrive at the airport, the dispatcher puts the taxi back in the available taxi pool. I may get the same taxi when I next call, but if so, it will be a coincidence. I call this strategy the taxi pool strategy, for obvious reasons, and it is shown in Figure 6.3.

From my perspective, there is one huge advantage to the pool strategy. I can afford it. Thirty dollars, one way. I can live with that. Especially when I am billing it to a client.

The reason taxi pooling is so cheap is that taxis are used very efficiently. A given taxi spends relatively little time just hanging around. Most of the time it is

Figure 6.3 The "taxi pool" strategy.

being used by a customer. And even though the taxi driver has no idea who the next customer will be, he or she can be reasonably certain that there *will be* a next customer within a short time. And all customers are the same, from the driver's perspective. They all pay cash.

But the system also works well from the customer's perspective. We don't know which taxi will come when we call, but we can be reasonably certain that *some* taxi will come within a few minutes. And they all work equally well, from the customer's perspective. Any taxi will successfully transport the customer to the airport.

There is a balancing act that the dispatcher must perform. If there are too few taxis in the available pool, then taxis won't be available when they are needed by customers. And if customers have to wait too long, they will find other taxi companies. On the other hand, if there are too many taxis in the available pool, then taxis will be spending too much time waiting for customers, and this drives (so to speak) up the cost of running the taxi company. So the available taxi pool can't be too big, and it can't be too small. It must be just right.

There is one thing I hate about taxi pools, though. Drivers in a taxi pool are paid by the trip, and will not be sidetracked by bagel shops. Even those with *everything* bagels.

State

There are a few disadvantages to taxi pools from my perspective. For one thing, I can't leave something in the taxi on my way to the airport and expect it to be there for my ride home. For another thing, I can't just say to the driver, "Home, Charles," and expect him to have any idea of what I am talking about. Since he most likely wasn't the driver who initially took me to the airport, he doesn't know where home is. And her name may not even be Charles!

Taxi pooling is basically incompatible with "Home, Charles." The reason is that "Home, Charles" depends on some specific information being available in the taxi I enter. The necessary information is the location of my home. And there is only one place from which this information could have come, and that is from my original trip to the airport. So, in order to be able to say "Home, Charles," I must be sure that the taxi I take home is the same taxi I took to the airport. And this is incompatible with taxi pooling. And incompatible with my expense account.

So I have a choice. I can either choose a taxi company that will dedicate a taxi to me for my entire round trip, which will cost me dearly, or I can agree to give the taxi driver my exact address. I need to make absolutely sure that when I get in that taxi, the trip depends in no way on my ever having entered that taxi before, or that I will ever enter that taxi again. No "Home Charles." No personal items left in the cab. No commitments. No strings.

This is not to say I need to be cold-hearted about my trip to the airport. I can give the driver directions, start a conversation, take out my books and do reading, continue the conversation, double-check the directions, do some more reading. This is all fine, and compatible with taxi pooling. The only important point is that once I leave a taxi, I leave it totally and completely, with no expectation of ever returning.

We can categorize my relationship with the taxi by calling it a *stateless* relationship. In other words, every time I enter a taxi, I have no dependency on the state in which I last left it. The term *stateless* is a bit of a misnomer, because it seems to imply that the taxi has no state. It may have plenty of state, including directions I have given the driver, books I have lying around on the seat, the current value of the fare box. All of these things are part of the state of the taxi. But there is no long-term dependency on that state. When I enter the next taxi, I give new directions, I lay out my books again, and the fare box starts again from zero.

If you have been paying close attention, this whole conversation might be sounding a little familiar. We had a similar discussion about Gnomes back in Chapter 1. There we discussed how pooling of gnomes was necessary to keep them working at 100-percent efficiency, and that the overall cost of the system was closely correlated with the efficiency of the gnomes. If the efficiency of the gnomes dropped from 100 percent to 10 percent, the cost of the system went up by a factor of 10.

This is very similar to our taxi analysis. The main cost of running a taxi company is the cost of the taxis. So, if we can transport 1000 customers per day with only 50 taxis, our cost (and therefore our customer's cost) will be much lower than if we need 1000 taxis. If our company requires 1000 taxis to conduct the same business that our competitors can conduct with only 50 taxis, we won't be in the taxi business very long.

From the discussion about taxis, pooling, state, and efficiency, we can draw some important conclusions. Pooling is the most efficient mechanism available for increasing efficiency. And statelessness is a prerequisite for pooling.

Object State

Objects, like taxis, can be designed to be stateful or stateless. If an object is implemented in such a way that consecutive method invocations must be routed to the same object in order to work, that object is said to contain state, and is described as a *stateful* object. It is called stateful because the object contains state that is changed as methods are invoked on that object, and the proper functioning of those methods is dependent on knowing previous state changes of the object.

A good example of a stateful object is our MicrognomeCalculator class introduced back in Chapter 3.

```
class MicrognomeCalculator {
    private long first;
    private long second;
    public void setFirstMultiplier(long n1)
    {
        first = n1;
    }
    public void setSecondMultiplier(long n2)
    {
        second = n2;
    }
    public long multiplyNumbers()
    {
        long result = 0;
        long n;
        for (n=0; n<second; n++) {
            result += first;
        }
        return result;
    }
}
```

A program using this calculator would go through code like this:

```
MicrognomeCalculator calc = new MicrognomeCalculator();
/* ... */
calc.setFirstMultiplier(n1);
calc.setSecondMultiplier(n2);
n = calc.multiplyNumbers();
```

This code works only if these three method invocations all go to the same calculator object. This is because the object stores state between method invocations, and this state is necessary to the proper functioning of methods. This calculator is a *stateful* object.

Imagine that we have a grab-bag of 50 such calculators, and every time I invoke a method, I randomly choose one of these calculators on which to invoke the method. If I invoke setFirstMultiplier on calculator #1, setSecondMultiplier on calculator #21, and multiplyNumbers on calculator #8, I don't know what I am going to get, but it is unlikely to be the correct answer. This is shown in Figure 6.4.

The other calculator introduced in Chapter 3, the ObjectWatchCalculator, did not have this problem. Its implementation looked like this:

```
class ObjectWatchCalculator {
    public long multiplyTwoNumbers(long n1, long n2)
    {
        return n1 * n2;
    }
}
```

A program using this calculator uses code like this:

```
ObjectWatchCalculator calc = new ObjectWatchCalculator();
/* ... */
n = calc.multiplyTwoNumbers(n1, n2);
```

If we have 50 of these calculators, we can randomly grab any one of them for the method invocation. The calculator is completely independent on our ever having seen it before. We can invoke the multiply method on this as many times as we like, and regardless of how we randomly grab calculators, the code will still work fine. So the ObjectWatch calculator can work well in a pooled environment, whereas the MicrognomeCalculator can't. Pooling works only when we can randomly grab any object at any time.

Figure 6.4 Random calculators.

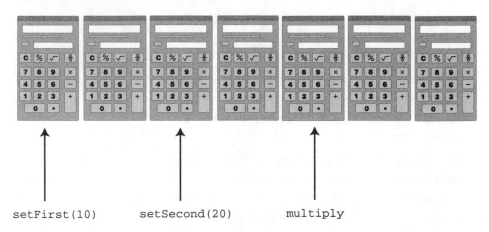

setFirst(10)　　　setSecond(20)　　　multiply

The difference between the two calculators is how they store state. The ObjectWatchCalculator does not store state between method invocations; it doesn't even declare any private variables. The ObjectWatchCalculator is an example of a *stateless* object. The MicrognomeCalculator not only declares private variables, but uses these variables to store state between method invocations.

This is not to say that you can't write stateful objects. You can. You just can't manage them with object pools. You are limited to a loyal taxi strategy, and this strategy is hugely inefficient. Therefore, the creation of stateful objects should be seen as a very poor programming practice, to be avoided whenever possible. The creation of stateful objects means every client needs a dedicated object, even if they aren't returning to the airport for a month.

So it is very important that we make our objects stateless. Writing a stateful object is like throwing a wad of gum into a crankshaft. The system might survive one or two, but it won't be long before the system grinds to a complete halt.

State and COM Objects

Where do object pools come from, and who manages them? They are part of the MDCA and, specifically, part of *Microsoft Transaction Server* (MTS). The MTS has other purposes as well, but for now we are going to focus on its role in allowing distributed objects to work efficiently.

The MTS coordinates COM objects exactly like a taxi dispatcher coordinates taxis. It maintains a pool of objects. When a client wants to invoke a method on a remote object, the MTS randomly assigns an object to that client from the pool. When the method invocation has completed, the object is returned to the pool. But don't leave anything in those objects. The next time you invoke a method you are likely to get a totally different object.

Actually, the current release of the MTS isn't quite this advanced, but this is the direction in which the MTS is rapidly headed. Perhaps by the time you read this, the MTS will fully support object pooling. At this point in time, the MTS supports a more rudimentary form of pooling, the disposable taxi model. Remember that model? Taxis are created as needed and disposed of upon reaching their destination. With MTS as it exists today, objects are instantiated as needed, and deinstantiated upon completion of their method invocation. This is not great, but it is still much better than clogging up the airport with 20,000 objects waiting for their next method request. And creating objects is a lot cheaper than creating taxis.

In this chapter, I will describe how to create objects that can be pooled. Or at least, can be pooled once the MTS pooling mechanism is available. In the meantime, I will show you how the disposable taxi model works today.

Designing a component so that it is poolable means designing a component that can operate efficiently, especially in a distributed environment. Designing a component that it can run efficiently means designing it so that it is stateless. Statelessness, efficiency, and poolability are not exactly the same thing, but they are so close that for all intents and purposes, we can consider the three to be synonymous. Since statelessness seems to me to be the most natural and least overused of these three descriptions, that is what I shall use to describe such objects.

If you think you don't care about statelessness in component objects, then either you don't understand distributed objects or you don't understand statelessness, or both. This concept is absolutely fundamental to efficient distributed objects. In the future, designing an object with state will seem as anachronistic as filling a program with goto statements does today.

What does it mean to design a component to be stateless? Earlier in this chapter I showed you a stateless calculator. Creating a calculator that is stateless is easy, because calculators don't need state to function. In fact, as that example showed, they function better without state. But what about brokering systems? If they don't have state, how are they going to keep track of buyers and sellers?

Remember the discussion about state in taxis? We said that statelessness doesn't really mean that taxis don't have state, just that the state is limited to the time during which they are physically occupied by a customer. Similarly, for components, statelessness doesn't mean that the underlying objects don't have state, just that the correct operation of their methods does not depend on maintaining that state from one invocation to the next.

Object Efficiency

Why do we say that objects must be stateless in order to be efficient? The answer is that only stateless objects can be pooled. And pooling is as necessary for efficient objects as it is for efficient taxis, or for efficient gnomes (as we discussed back in Chapter 1).

In modern commerce-oriented architectures, we will have thousands of client machines being serviced by server clusters. This is shown in Figure 6.5. The efficiency of the overall architecture will be largely driven by the efficiency of the server clusters. And it is on these server clusters that our component objects will live.

In Chapter 1 we described how the cost of the gnome systems was driven mainly by the cost of the rooms in which the gnomes lived. And the cost of these systems was largely driven by the efficiency of the gnomes living on those systems.

This is exactly the same situation we have with component objects. The cost of the component systems will be driven mainly by the cost of the systems in which the component objects exist. And they will live on server clusters. The efficiency of these objects will determine the efficiency of the server clusters, and that will determine their cost.

We might also consider the flip side of cost—that is, how many clients can be serviced by a given server cluster configuration. Any server cluster can efficiently manage only a limited number of component objects. Let's say that for a representative server cluster that number is 5000. If no pooling is used at all, then a given component object can service exactly one client, and the number of clients that that server cluster can service is 5000.

Figure 6.5 Commerce-oriented architecture.

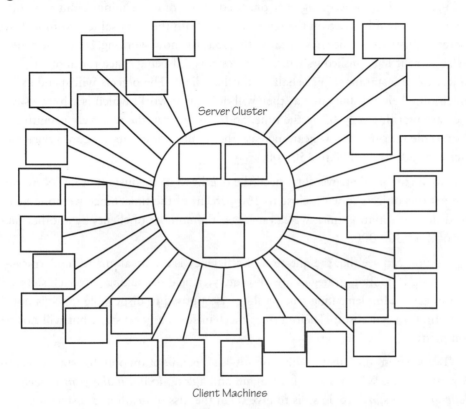

If these clients are typical, then for the great bulk of the time they are running, the component object is hanging around waiting for something to happen. Remember that that "something" will be the next method invocation from Visual Basic. Even if the human at the other end is typing as fast as possible, the component object will be spending very little time doing anything. And very often that human will be doing something other than typing as fast as possible, such as taking a coffee break or talking to the human in the next cubicle (who also, then, will be doing nothing). But let's be optimistic and say the human is working as fast as possible. Let's say it takes one minute to fill in a form in preparation for a component method invocation, one second to execute the method, and one second to instantiate an object.

With these numbers and no pooling, our system is running at 1/60 efficiency because the object is working only one second out of every minute. But it is still taking up valuable space on the server cluster. With the disposable taxi model, we increase this to 1/2 efficiency because the object is now working 1/2 of the time. As soon as it has finished its work, it is destroyed, freeing space for another object to be instantiated on behalf of another client. The objects will spend as much time being instantiated as they will doing real work, which is why we say they are working only 1/2 of the time. So by using even the relatively primitive disposable taxi strategy, we can increase the number of clients we can service by a factor of 30, from 5000 to 150,000.

With true pooling, we don't need the overhead of the instantiation. Now we can get our objects to work close to 100 percent of the time. Since we no longer need the instantiation time, we can increase the number of clients by another factor of 2, to 300,000.

So you can see that the question of efficiency is a critical one to modern systems design. Pooling strategies are absolutely critical to making server clusters cost-effective. Implementing true pooling, as opposed to disposable taxis, is not an option for Microsoft. Their current mechanism is a good start, but will not be competitive in the long term.

But keep in mind that pooling of any kind is an option only for stateless component objects. Which is why I say again and again, *do not make your objects dependent on state*. To do so is to give them the kiss of death in a distributed environment. To do so means you will have to explain to your management why your system's design peaks out at 5000 clients, while your competitor's, at the same cost, doesn't peak out until 300,000. I would like to be a fly on the wall for that particular discussion.

Making Objects Stateless

So by now you are convinced that you want to make your component objects stateless. There are typically four steps in the path of taking a run-of-the-mill language object and turning it into an efficient, stateless component object. These steps are as follows:

1. **Adding persistence.** Makes the language object persistent.

2. **Componentizing.** Redesigns the language object to be a logical component.

3. **Wrapping.** Wraps the newly componentized language object as a COM component.

4. **Packaging.** Packages the COM component so that it can be managed by the MS-DTC.

Let's go through these steps with a very simple example.

Adding Persistence

In Chapter 5 we added persistence to a simple dog class. Before persistence, the class looked like this:

```
class Dog {
    public Dog()
    {
        ...
    }
    public String myName()
    {
        ...
    }
    public void myName(String newName)
    {
        ...
    }
}
```

Life was so simple back then! By the time we finished adding in persistence, the class had turned into this:

```
import java.io.*;
class Dog implements IPersistFile {
    ...
    public Dog()
    {
        ...
    }
    public String GetClassID()
    {
        ...
    }
```

```
protected void LoadState(DataInputStream myStream) throws
IOException
    {
        ...
    }
public void Load(String newFileName)
    {
        ...
    }
protected void SaveState(DataOutputStream myStream) throws
        IOException
    {
        ...
    }
public void Save()
    {
        ...
    }
public boolean IsDirty()
    {
        ...
    }
public String myName()
    {
        ...
    }
public void myName(String newName)
    {
        ...
    }
```

Although this class is much more complicated than our starting class, it is much more useful. For one thing, this class gives the illusion of perpetuity, meaning that an object of this class gives the illusion of living forever.

There is another useful illusion that this class supports, and that is the *illusion of shareability*. Two programs using an object of this class can have the illusion of sharing the same object. The illusion is shown in Figure 6.6.

Let's explore the illusion of shareability with the following program, which can be found in the zip file under Chapter06_01a.

```java
import java.io.*;
public class Main2 {
    public static void main (String args[])
    {
        DataInputStream input = new DataInputStream(System.in);
        String name;
        IMoniker m1 =
            FileMoniker.MkParseDisplayName("Dog:dog.dat");
        Dog dog1 = (Dog) m1.BindToObject();
        try {
            for (;;) {
                System.out.print("Hit <return> to continue");
                input.readLine();
                System.out.print("My name is "+dog1.myName()+"...");
                System.out.print("New Name? ");
                name = input.readLine();
                if (name.length() == 0) break;
                dog1.myName(name);
            }
        }
        catch (IOException e) {
            System.out.println("Error");
        }

    }
}
```

This program goes into a loop. In each iteration of the loop, the program shows the current name of the dog, and gives the user an opportunity to change it. If the user enters a blank line, the program terminates.

If I were to run this program, I might get the following, with user input shown in bold:

```
jview Main2
Hit <return> to continue
```

```
My name is Snoopy...New Name? Lassie
Hit <return> to continue
My name is Lassie...New Name? Snoopy
Hit <return> to continue
My name is Snoopy...New Name?
```

But I also might get a very different result. I might get this:

```
jview Main2
Hit <return> to continue
My name is Snoopy...New Name? Lassie
Hit <return> to continue
My name is Snoopy...New Name? Lassie
Hit <return> to continue
My name is Snoopy...New Name?
```

In this last run, the program seems to be refusing my attempts to rename Snoopy to Lassie. How can the exact same program give these two very different results? This is because of the *illusion of shareability*. If I have two processes running this same program, the two processes appear to be sharing the same dog

Figure 6.6 The illusion of shareability.

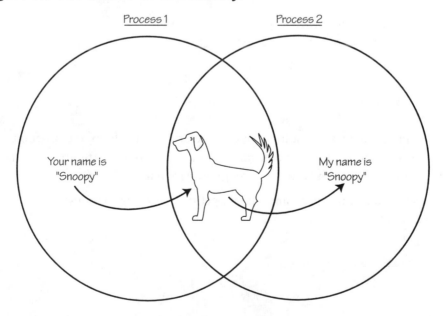

object. So the last program results could have been caused by two processes running the same executable interleaving in the following manner:

```
jview Main2
Hit <return> to continue
                                Jview Main2
                                Hit <return> to continue

My name is Snoopy...New Name? Lassie
Hit <return> to continue
                                My name is Lassie...New Name?
Snoopy
                                Hit <return> to continue
My name is Snoopy...New Name? Lassie
Hit <return> to continue
                                My name is Lassie...New Name?
Snoopy
                                Hit <return> to continue
My name is Snoopy...New Name?
```

You can see that these two processes appear to be fighting over the Dog's
name. We might rename this trick the *illusion of dueling objects*.

This illusion of sharing objects can be a very useful trick when developing
distributed applications. For example, if we add this illusion to our brokering
system, we could have a buyer matched up with a seller, even when the two
individuals are on completely different machines. We will do exactly this later in
this chapter.

Componentizing

We are going to be heading toward making our dog a COM object. There are
four immediate reasons for this. We will discover others later in the book, but
already we know that turning our Java object into a COM object will improve it
in the following ways:

1. We will have the capability of adding a nice Visual Basic interface.

2. We will make the object usable from any COM supporting language,
    rather than just Java.

3. We will be able to run the object remotely, on a different machine.

4. We will be able to manage the objects in a pooled, and therefore highly efficient, environment.

But our Dog class now is overly complicated. It has many methods that we aren't going to want to make visible to our Visual Basic programmer. In fact, the only methods a Visual Basic programmer cares about are those involved with naming the dog.

Wouldn't it be nice to return to the innocence of our original dog without giving up persistence? Life would be much easier for our poor Visual Basic programmer. So, our first step is going to be to reorganize this class as a component, but a component with persistence. The code shown here is from the code zip file Chapter06_01a.

To do this, we create another class, which will be our component-level class. It looks like this:

```
package DogLib;

public class DogComponent {
    public String getMyName(String dogID)
    {
        IMoniker m1 =
            FileMoniker.MkParseDisplayName("Dog:dog"+dogID+".dat");
        Dog dog = (Dog) m1.BindToObject();
        return dog.myName();
    }
    public void setMyName(String dogID, String newName)
    {
        IMoniker m1 =
            FileMoniker.MkParseDisplayName("Dog:dog"+dogID+".dat");
        Dog dog = (Dog) m1.BindToObject();
        dog.myName(newName);
    }
}
```

Although we have added to the complexity of the overall system, by adding another class, we have simplified it in another more fundamental way. First of all, our client program doesn't need to know anything about the persistence of the class. Second, the client program sees only the most basic subset of the original methods (two of the original nine).

You can see how much simpler the Java client has become. This was our client code using the original class:

```
public class Main1 {
    public static void main (String args[])
    {
        IMoniker m1 =
            FileMoniker.MkParseDisplayName("Dog:dog.dat");
        Dog dog1 = (Dog) m1.BindToObject();
        dog1.myName("Lassie");
        System.out.println("My name is "+dog1.myName());
    }
}
```

and this is the equivalent version, using our new component:

```
import DogLib.*;
public class Main1 {
    public static void main (String args[])
    {
        DogComponent dog = new DogComponent();
        dog.setMyName("1", "Lassie");
        System.out.println("My name is "+dog.getMyName("1"));
    }
}
```

You can see that the new version shows no awareness of the object's persistence. It treats the dog component as a standard Java object. Any Java programmer can figure this code out! No monikers to deal with. No object binding. Just run-of-the-mill Java code.

You may have noticed that there is a new parameter that has been added to the DogComponent methods. This is an ID for the dog. The ID will actually be used for linking the dog to a particular file. You can look back at the DogComponent methods to see how this is used.

Wrapping

With our new DogComponent class, we are well positioned to create our COM wrapper. This code can be found in the code zip file Chapter06_01b. We will start by showing the IDL file, which by now should look reasonably familiar. If not, review Chapter 4. This file is just an IDL equivalent of the Java DogComponent:

```
#include <JavaAttr.h>
[
    uuid(A582C761-F7A9-11d0-BB07-204C4F4F5020),
    version(1.0),
    helpstring("Dog Library Version 1")
]
library DOGLib
{
    importlib("stdole2.tlb");
    [
        object,
        uuid(A582C762-F7A9-11d0-BB07-204C4F4F5020),
        dual,
        helpstring("IDogComponent Interface"),
        pointer_default(unique)
    ]
    interface IDogComponent : IDispatch
    {
        import "oaidl.idl";
        HRESULT setMyName([in] BSTR dogID, [in] BSTR name);
        HRESULT getMyName([in] BSTR dogID, [out, retval] BSTR*
            name);
    };
    [
        uuid(A582C763-F7A9-11d0-BB07-204C4F4F5020),
        helpstring("DogComponent Class"),
        JAVACLASS("DogLib.DogComponent"),
        PROGID("DogComponent")
    ]
    coclass CDogComponent
    {
        [default] interface IDogComponent;
    };
};
```

The batch file we use for creating the COM component looks like this:

```
rem Create DogLib.tlb
midl DogLib.idl

rem Create CDogComponent.class and IDogComponent.class
javatlb /d . /p DogLib /p:b- DogLib.tlb

rem del classes from trustlib
del %SystemRoot%\java\trustlib\DogLib\*.class

rem Compile local class
jvc DogLib\*.java

rem Compile client
jvc Client.java

rem Copy local class to trustlib
copy DogLib\*.class %SystemRoot%\java\trustlib\DogLib\

rem Register java class
javareg /register /class:DogLib.DogComponent /progid:DogComponent
/clsid:{A582C763-F7A9-11d0-BB07-204C4F4F5020}
```

We have already discussed these commands back in Chapter 4, so we won't spend any more time on them here.

Now we can go ahead and create a Visual Basic interface. Figure 6.7 shows Visual Basic being used to create such an interface.

This interface is designed to allow a client to type in a dog ID and an optional name. There are three buttons: Change, Check, and End. These have the following purposes:

Change. Changes to the name of the dog identified by the dog ID to the name entered in the Name area.

Check. Displays the name of the dog identified by the dog ID in the Name area.

End. Ends the program.

On the Visual Basic side, the code is very simple. We declare a public reference to the COM dog interface in the module section:

```
Public dog As IDogComponent
```

Then in the form view, we have the following code:

```
Private Sub Command1_Click()
    Call dog.setMyName(Text1.Text, Text2.Text)
    Text2.Text = ""
End Sub

Private Sub Command2_Click()
    Text2.Text = dog.getMyName(Text1.Text)
End Sub

Private Sub Command3_Click()
    Set dog = Nothing
    End
End Sub

Private Sub Form_Load()
    Set dog = CreateObject("DogComponent")
End Sub
```

Pretty simple, isn't it? If we save this as an executable from Visual Basic, we get a program that we can run without even starting Visual Basic. The next figures show a few successive loops of this program. In Figure 6.8 we are about to change the name of dog #1 to "Lassie." In Figure 6.9 we are about to check the name of dog #1, and in Figure 6.10 we have just clicked the Check button, and the system has displayed the result.

Although I have said that these last three figures represent successive loops of the program, in fact, you would get exactly the same result if you clicked End after each command and restarted the program. This is because this component gives the illusion of perpetuity, which is the least we can expect, after all the work we have done.

This component also gives the illusion of shareability. In Figure 6.11 we see a whole screen full of clients, all working in different processes, all seemingly sharing access to the same underlying dog objects.

There is no reason the clients shown in Figure 6.11 can't all be on different machines. We would need only a minor modification in the DogComponent to

Figure 6.7 Preparing the interface.

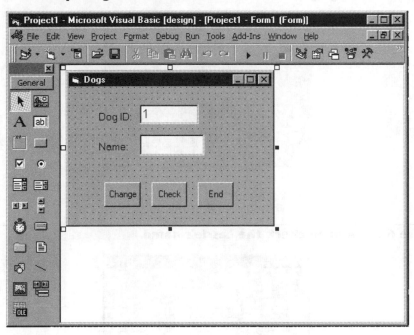

place all of the dog files in a single, shared directory space. Then we could have clients all over the world arguing about how they want to name their dogs.

Packaging

Now we are ready to package our Java classes for consumption by the Microsoft Transaction Server (MTS). The easiest way to work with the MTS is through the Transaction Server Explorer. This program supports the more or less standard explorer interface. When you first bring it up, it looks like Figure 6.12.

The first thing we will do is start up the Microsoft Distributed Transaction Coordinator (MS-DTC), if it hasn't been configured to come up automatically. To do this, highlight MyComputer, pull down the Tools menu, choose MS-DTC, and click on start.

The next thing we need to do is to create a package, which is the MTS container for our components. To do this, expand MyComputer, and click on Packages Installed. At this point the window should look more or less like Figure 6.13.

Figure 6.8 Changing Lassie's name.

Figure 6.9 About to check the Lassie's name.

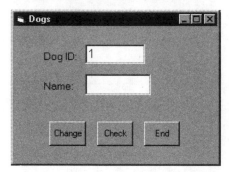

Figure 6.10 Having checked the Lassie's name.

Figure 6.11 A screenful of clients.

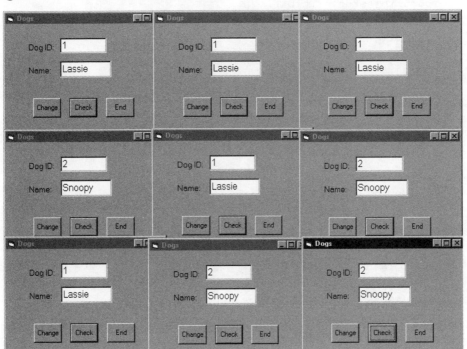

We are now ready to install a new empty package. To do this, pull down File and choose New. Then choose Empty Package, and a name of your choice (usually related to the functionality you are installing).

We have now primed the MTS to run the package. Now we must create the package. We are temporarily finished with the MTS.

We need to make a change in the IDL on the COM side. The new version will have only two changes, and they are shown in bold:

```
#include <MtxAttr.h>
#include <JavaAttr.h>
[
    uuid(A582C761-F7A9-11d0-BB07-204C4F4F5020),
    version(1.0),
    helpstring("Dog Library Trans Version")
]
library DOGLib
```

```
{
    importlib("stdole2.tlb");
    [
        object,
        uuid(A582C762-F7A9-11d0-BB07-204C4F4F5020),
        dual,
        helpstring("IDogComponent Interface"),
        pointer_default(unique)
    ]
    interface IDogComponent : IDispatch
    {
        import "oaidl.idl";
        HRESULT setMyName([in] BSTR dogID, [in] BSTR name);
        HRESULT getMyName([in] BSTR dogID, [out, retval] BSTR* name);
    };
    [
        uuid(A582C763-F7A9-11d0-BB07-204C4F4F5020),
        helpstring("DogComponent Class"),
        JAVACLASS("DogLib.DogComponent"),
        PROGID("DogComponent"),
        TRANSACTION_REQUIRED
    ]
    coclass CDogComponent
    {
        [default] interface IDogComponent;
    };
};
```

The new header file is needed to resolve the new macro. The macro, TRANS-ACTION_REQUIRED, will tell the MS-DTC to automatically start up a new transaction when this component is started. There are a few other options but this is the most common.

We also need to slightly modify the DogComponent Java file. The new version has a few lines added, which are shown here in bold:

```
package DogLib;
import com.ms.mtx.*;
```

```java
public class DogComponent implements IDogComponent {
    public String getMyName(String dogID)
    {
        String name;
        IMoniker m1 =
            FileMoniker.MkParseDisplayName("Dog:dog"+dogID+".dat");
        Dog dog = (Dog) m1.BindToObject();
        name = dog.myName();
        MTx.GetObjectContext().SetComplete();
        return name;
    }
    public void setMyName(String dogID, String newName)
    {
        IMoniker m1 =
            FileMoniker.MkParseDisplayName("Dog:dog"+dogID+".dat");
        Dog dog = (Dog) m1.BindToObject();
        dog.myName(newName);
        MTx.GetObjectContext().SetComplete();
    }
}
```

Figure 6.12 Transaction server explorer.

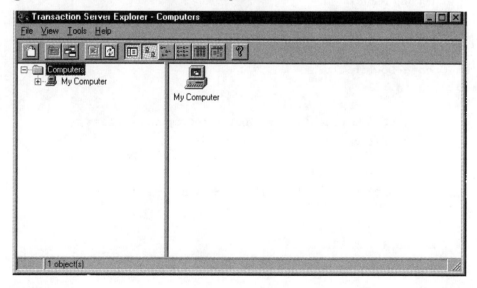

Figure 6.13 Packages view.

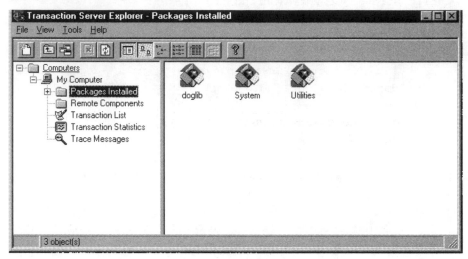

We need to add the import statement shown, which gives us access to the Java transaction package. MTx.GetObjectContext is a static method that returns what is called a *context object*. We will discuss some of the other context methods later. For now, the one we are interested in is SetComplete, which tells the MS-DTC that this object has finished its work, and can be used by other processes or discarded, at the discretion of the MS-DTC. This method tells MS-DTC that we are leaving the taxi.

The build process is different for Java classes destined for MS-DTC control. This is the batch file I used:

```
rem Create DogLib.tlb
midl DogLib.idl

rem Create CDogComponent.class and IDogComponent.class
javatlb /d . /p DogLib /p:b- DogLib.tlb

cd DogLib
JAVAGUID CDogComponent.class IDogComponent.class
cd ..

rem Compile local class
```

```
jvc DogLib\*.java

rem Compile client
jvc Main1.java

C:\MTX\TOOLS\EXEGEN /d /r /out:doglib.dll doglib.tlb *.class
```

The use of the midl and javatlb tools are the same as before. We now have to run javaguid on the files javatlb generated from the DogLib.idl file. This is a kludge, which has to do with incompatible uses of the UIDs in the class file. Then we are ready to compile the Java code. Finally, we must create a dll file that can be used by the MS-DTC. The tool used to create the dll is exegen. For now, exegen comes as part of the transaction package. The exegen options have the following meanings:

- **d:** Generate MS-DTC-compatible dll.
- **r:** Recurse into subdirectories when looking for files to include.
- **/out:** Generated file.

The files that will be included in the creation of the dll are listed after the options. We are using the doglib.tlb and any class files in this directory or subdirectories. We include the subdirectories because we are creating this as a Java package, which always involves subdirectories.

At the end of this batch file we will have generated doglib.dll, which is ready to be added to our transaction package. The easiest way to add this is through drag and drop. Bring up the Transaction Server Explorer and the Windows Explorer. In the Transaction Server Explorer, highlight the empty package you created earlier. In the Windows Explorer, drag the doglib.dll over to the Transaction Server Explorer and drop it in the right-hand portion of the screen. Figure 6.14 shows the state of these two explorers before the drag, and Figure 6.15 shows their state after the drop.

At this point we have packaged our Java implementation of our COM component so that it can be managed by the MS-DTC. We have also modified the Java implementation to allow the MS-DTC to use pooling. The crucial change that enabled pooling is the invocation of SetComplete. Without this invocation, MS-DTC would have no way of knowing when it is safe to release the object.

Figure 6.14 Before drag.

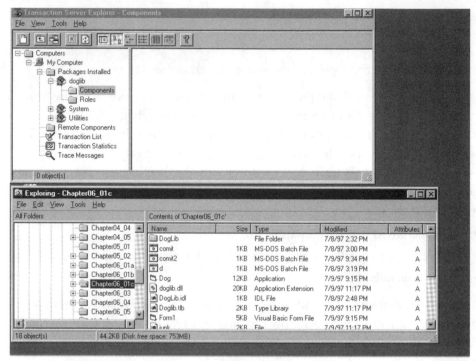

It is important to invoke SetComplete in every component-level method. It should always be the last statement in the method. It is only invoked in component-level Java classes (i.e., the class that directly implements the COM IDL definition—in this case, DogComponent).

Having done all this, we can rerun our Visual Basic interface. Now not only can we have dueling objects, but we can manage them efficiently and run them using a state-of-the-art interface!

Investigating Managed Objects

If you look closely, you may notice that there is no difference from the client perspective between standard COM objects and those managed by the MS-DTC. For that matter, how do we even know that these objects *are* being managed by the MS-DTC?

Figure 6.15 After drop.

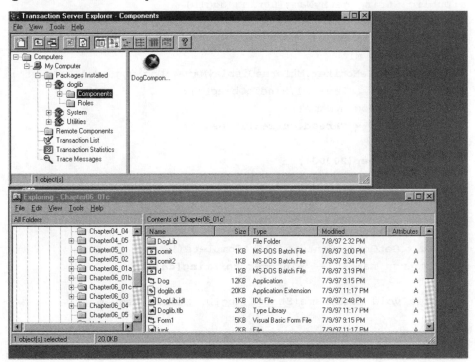

Let's spend a little time investigating the relationship between these objects and the MS-DTC. I am going to make two changes in the DogComponent class to help in this investigation. First, I am going to add a 20-second sleep cycle, so that the DogComponent methods take a long time to complete. Second, I am going to add a little note to the dog name returned by the getMyName method to tell us how many times this method has been invoked. The new version of DogComponent, with changes shown in bold, is this:

```
package DogLib;
import com.ms.mtx.*;

public class DogComponent implements IDogComponent {
    private int calls;
    public DogComponent()
    {
        calls = 0;
```

```
    }
    public String getMyName(String dogID)
    {
        String name;
        IMoniker m1 =
            FileMoniker.MkParseDisplayName("Dog:dog"+dogID+".dat");
        Dog dog = (Dog) m1.BindToObject();
        name = dog.myName();
        Thread t = Thread.currentThread();
        try {
            t.sleep(20000);
        }
        catch (InterruptedException e) {
        }
        calls++;
        MTx.GetObjectContext().SetComplete();
        return name+" - "+Integer.toString(calls);
    }
    public void setMyName(String dogID, String newName)
    {
        IMoniker m1 =
            FileMoniker.MkParseDisplayName("Dog:dog"+dogID+".dat");
        Dog dog = (Dog) m1.BindToObject();
        dog.myName(newName);
        Thread t = Thread.currentThread();
        try {
            t.sleep(20000);
        }
        catch (InterruptedException e) {
        }
        MTx.GetObjectContext().SetComplete();
    }
}
```

Now let's bring up the interface executable. The first time we click on the Check button we get the result shown in Figure 6.16 (after a 20-second wait). Notice that a 1 has been appended to the name, indicating that this is the first time the method was invoked.

Figure 6.16 The first check.

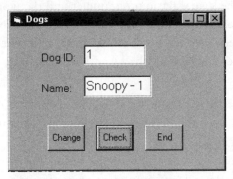

Now here is a very important question. What will this window look like the *second* time we click Check? Before you answer this, let's look again at the Visual Basic code controlling these buttons, with the Check code shown in bold:

```
Private Sub Command1_Click()
    Call dog.setMyName(Text1.Text, Text2.Text)
    Text2.Text = ""
End Sub

Private Sub Command2_Click()
    Text2.Text = dog.getMyName(Text1.Text)
End Sub

Private Sub Command3_Click()
    Set dog = Nothing
    End
End Sub

Private Sub Form_Load()
    Set dog = CreateObject("DogComponent")
End Sub
```

Notice that the object is instantiated once, when the form is first loaded. From then on we are just invoking methods on the same object. The second time we click the Check button we are invoking this on the same object as that on which we invoked the first Check. Or are we? What do you think the screen will show?

These two windows clearly show a discrepancy between the world as seen through the eyes of the Visual Basic programmer and the world as seen through the eyes of the component object. The Visual Basic programmer thinks that the Check method has been invoked on the DogComponent object twice. The DogComponent object thinks it has had Check invoked only once. How do we explain this?

In fact, this is exactly the result we would predict based on the MTS management policy available as of this release. Remember, the only management strategy now supported is the disposable taxi strategy. We create the object, use it, and destroy it. So, when our Visual Basic program begins the invocation of Check, the MTS creates and allocates a DogComponent object for its exclusive use. When the invocation is complete, the MTS destroys the object. The second time we invoke Check, the MTS goes through the same cycle with a brand-new object.

How would you expect the results to change once MTS supports true object pooling? Would you expect to always see a 1, or would you expect the number to increase sequentially? Remember, the difference between the disposable taxi model and true pooling is that in the latter, we don't discard objects that have completed their work. Instead, we add them back to the pool of available objects.

We definitely don't expect to see a 1 come up every time. This is a symptom of an object always being destroyed and recreated. But we also don't expect to see a sequential increase. The true answer depends on what else is happening on the system. With 10 client processes, we will have some unknown number of component objects, depending on how many the MTS decides are necessary. And these objects will be randomly assigned to the client processes.

So what we expect to see is a random number appearing. The first time we check the name we might be the first person using that object. The second time we may be using an object that has already been used by five other clients. Or we might be the first person using that object. There is no way to predict, and we would expect to see the number fluctuate randomly.

One final quiz. Suppose we make one more change in our DogComponent. Let's comment out the SetComplete invocation, as shown here:

```
package DogLib;
import com.ms.mtx.*;
```

```java
public class DogComponent implements IDogComponent,
IObjectControl {
    private int calls;
    public DogComponent()
    {
        calls = 0;
    }
    public String getMyName(String dogID)
    {
        String name;
        IMoniker m1 =
                FileMoniker.MkParseDisplayName("Dog:dog"+dogID+".dat");
        Dog dog = (Dog) m1.BindToObject();
        name = dog.myName();
        Thread t = Thread.currentThread();
        try {
            t.sleep(20000);
        }
        catch (InterruptedException e) {
        }
        calls++;
        // MTx.GetObjectContext().SetComplete();
        return name+" - "+Integer.toString(calls);
    }
    public void setMyName(String dogID, String newName)
    {
        IMoniker m1 =
                FileMoniker.MkParseDisplayName("Dog:dog"+dogID+".dat");
        Dog dog = (Dog) m1.BindToObject();
        dog.myName(newName);
        Thread t = Thread.currentThread();
        try {
        t.sleep(20000);
        }
        catch (InterruptedException e) {
        }
        // MTx.GetObjectContext().SetComplete();
    }
}
```

This small change has a dramatic effect on the result shown in the user interface window. But now, every time we click on Check the number increments by one. This will happen regardless of whether or not the MTS supports object pooling. Can you see why this number now increments?

The number now increments because the object is never destroyed. It becomes permanently glued to this client. The SetComplete invocation is required to let the MTS know that the object can safely be returned to the pool (if pooling is supported) or can safely be destroyed (if it isn't). Since this method is never called, the MTS keeps the object permanently assigned to this client. And this results in a huge loss of efficiency, because now the number of clients we can support is limited to the number of component objects we can support.

The removal of these two lines of code results in a precipitous decline of efficiency. Based on our earlier analysis, we can expect a decline in the number of clients we can support from 300,000 to 5000—a greater than 99-percent decline.

Monitoring the Pool

We can use the Transaction Server Explorer to monitor the object pool. In the Transaction Server Explorer you can expand My Computer, and click on Transaction Statistics. Now you have a gauge that shows you how many objects are currently active. The screen shot in Figure 6.17 shows this monitor with three clients all having clicked Check, and waiting their 20 seconds. If we were to remove the 20-second delay in the methods, this number would probably go down to one, since it would be hard to catch the system with more than one object in play.

When the 20 seconds is up, and the method invocation has completed, the monitor changes. The active transactions are back down to 0, and the aggregate has increased by 3.

More on the Illusion of Shareability

The illusion of shareability is quite powerful. Some of the special features of this illusion are as follows:

- There is no limit to the number of processes that can be "sharing" the same object.

- There is no requirement that the processes all be running the same program. The only requirement is that they are all mapped to the same underlying data storage. I could, for example, have a ne'er-do-well that goes into an endless loop, waking up every five seconds and unconditionally resetting the Dog's name to "Jumbo." That would certainly amuse the other processes.

• There is no requirement that the processes all be running on the same machine, as long as they have a shared file system.

But keep in mind that this illusion, like all illusions, is a sleight of hand. These processes are not sharing an object, they are sharing a data source. The illusion is shown in Figure 6.18. The reality of this illusion is shown in Figure 6.19.

Activation/Deactivation

The MTS manages objects through four stages of their existence. These stages are instantiated, activated, deactivated, and deinstantiated. An *instantiated* object is one that has been created, but never yet been assigned to a client. When an object is assigned to a client, it becomes *activated*. When the client is

Figure 6.17 Monitor and three clients.

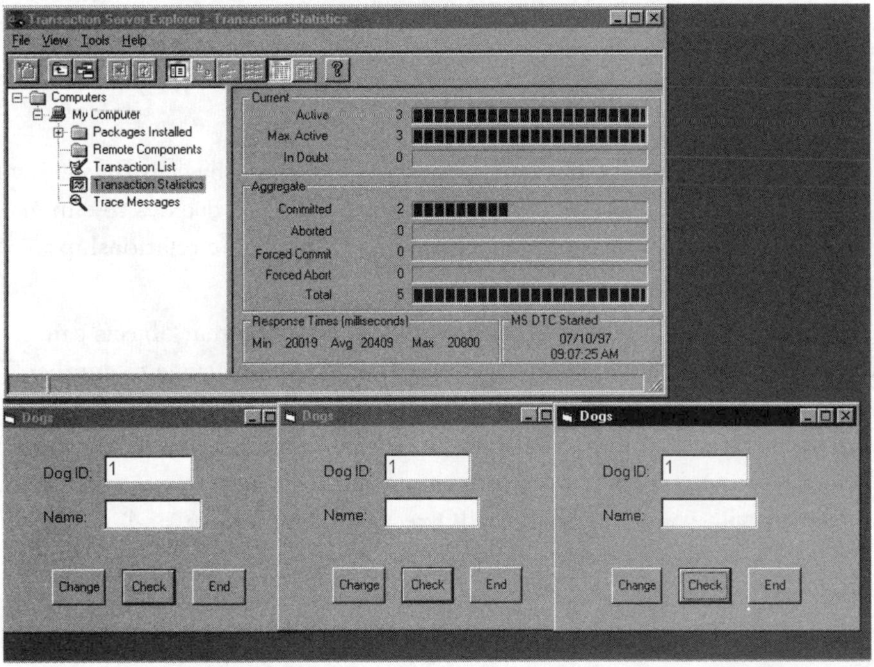

Figure 6.18 The illusion again.

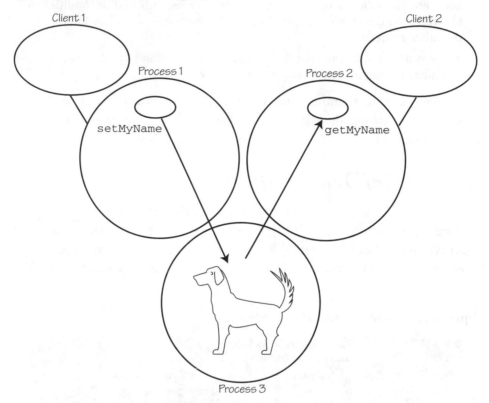

finished with the object, or perhaps more accurately, the object is finished with the client, the object becomes *deactivated*. When the MTS decides to eliminate the object, it becomes *deinstantiated*. Figure 6.20 shows the relationship between these four stages.

The Microsoft Java implementation provides hooks so that objects can be made aware of, and participate in, their transition from one stage to another. The constructor and destructor are provided as part of the normal Java language. These two methods are invoked as objects become instantiated and deinstantiated, respectively. Objects that want to control events at their activation and deactivation stages will want to support the IObjectControl interface, and implement the two methods Activate and Deactivate.

Figure 6.19 The reality of the illusion.

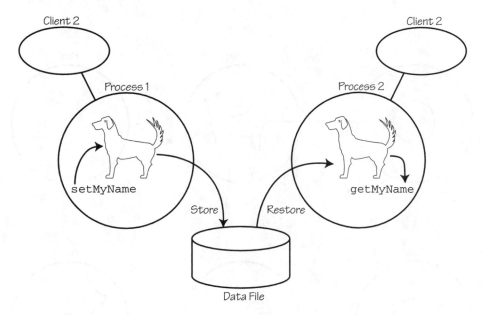

Activate/Deactivate affects only the server process. Proxies are maintained on the client side. During an object's activation phase these proxies actually forward method invocations off to the object living in the remote server. During the

Figure 6.20 The four stages of the object life cycle.

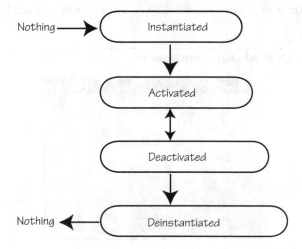

Figure 6.21 Proxies and activation.

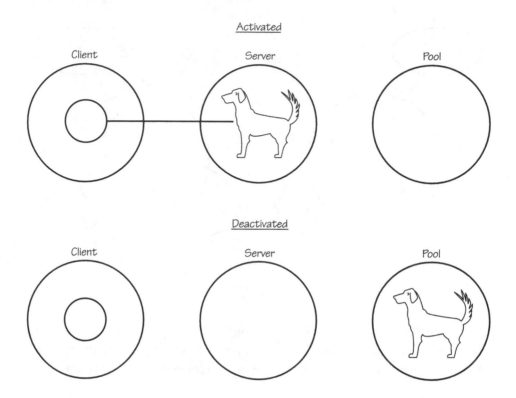

object's deactivation phase these proxies contain the information needed to reactivate the object on a moment's notice. This is shown in Figure 6.21.

Figure 6.22 Activated dog component.

The importance of Activate and Deactivate is much less important now than it will be once true pooling is supported. For now, there is no real difference between instantiation and activation, on the one hand, and deinstantiation and deactivation, on the other. However, you should write your objects as if true pooling is supported, so that they can take advantage of it when it becomes available. Depending on how you have designed your objects, you may never need to add any real code to Activate/Deactivate. Or perhaps you will move the code that you would normally place in the constructor to Activate, and the code you would normally place in the destructor to Deactivate. You can experiment with different approaches.

There is another important reason for objects to support the IObjectControl interface. This is because of another method in that interface called CanBePooled. When pooling is supported, Microsoft will invoke this method to ask the object if it is willing to be pooled. Objects that either do not support this method, or support it but return false, will not be considered eligible for pooling. And we know what that means.

In order to demonstrate the IObjectControl interface, I have modified the DogComponent. In the following code, I have reduced the sleep time and added a trace String variable, which we can use to demonstrate the invocation of the constructor and Activate. I temporarily return this string for the getMyName. This helps prove to us that the Activate is actually invoked. The modified lines are shown in bold. The only changed lines are in the DogComponent Java file. There are no changes necessary in the IDL definition or the Visual Basic code.

```java
package DogLib;
import com.ms.mtx.*;

public class DogComponent implements IDogComponent,
IObjectControl {
    private int calls;
    private String trace;
    public DogComponent()
    {
        calls = 0;
        trace = "1";
    }
    public boolean CanBePooled()
    {
```

```
        return true;
    }
    public void Activate()
    {
        trace = trace + "2";
    }
    public void Deactivate()
    {
    }
    public String getMyName(String dogID)
    {
        String name;
        IMoniker m1 =
            FileMoniker.MkParseDisplayName("Dog:dog"+dogID+".dat");
        Dog dog = (Dog) m1.BindToObject();
        name = dog.myName();
        Thread t = Thread.currentThread();
        try {
            t.sleep(1);
        }
        catch (InterruptedException e) {
        }
        calls++;
        MTx.GetObjectContext().SetComplete();
        // return name+" - "+Integer.toString(calls);
        return trace;
    }
}
```

Now we run our user interface program again. When clicking Check, we get the window shown in Figure 6.22. The "12" shown as the dog name is the trace variable. The "1" comes from the constructor and the "2" from the Activate. We never invoked Activate. This was automatically invoked by the MS-DTC.

Let's be clear on the relationship between MTS object management, Activate/Deactivate, and object pooling. MTS object management refers to either the disposable taxi strategy (all that is supported now) or true pooling (which will be supported). Activate/Deactivate refers to the stage changes.

Figure 6.23 Diagram of a buy request.

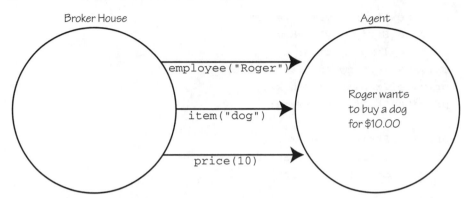

In the current release of MTS, objects make a one-way trip from instantiation, activation, deactivation, and deinstantiation. In order to assign an object, MTS instantiates and activates it. In order to deassign an object, MTS deactivates and deinstantiates it.

When MTS supports true pooling, objects will pass pack and forth frequently between activation and deactivation. The MTS will instantiate an object only when first putting it in the pool. It will then activate the object when assigning it to a client, and deactivate it when the client is finished. When and if it decides the object is no longer needed in the pool, it will deinstantiate the object.

A Closer Look at State

Some people will read the preceding discussion as my recommending a ban on private object variables. This is not true for three reasons. First, the use of private variables is not the only way to make an object stateful, although it is by far the most common. Second, one can use private variables without making objects stateful. It should be noted, however, that any object that uses private variables should be considered highly suspect. Finally, and most important, I have no issue with private variables in Java objects, as long as those Java objects are not implementations of IDL defined components. It is component-level objects that must be made stateless, not low-level Java (or C++) objects.

Let's take a closer look at the idea of a stateless component using a stateful object. Our brokering system, as last we left it in Chapter 5, includes many objects with state. For example, our gnome class had state every place you look:

```
class Gnome implements AgentInterface, EmployeeInterface
{
    private String myEmployeeName;
    private String myItemName;
    private long myPrice;
    private long myNegotiatedPrice;
    private IMoniker myMoniker;
    private String otherName;

    private String fileName;
    private String monikerString;
    private boolean iAmDirty;

    public void Save()
    {
        /* ... */
    }
    public void Load(String newFileName)
    {
        /* ... */
    }
```

Does this mean our BrokerHouse will be stateful? No, because before a gnome is updated, it is restored. And after it is updated, it is stored. Let's look again at the BrokerHouse method prepareBuyOrder(), which will be invoked directly by the Visual Basic Client. Remember that BrokerHouse is described by an IDL file and used by a Visual Basic Client, so clearly it is a component. The code for this method, as we left it in Chapter 5, is:

```
public void prepareBuyOrder
        (String name, String item, int maxPrice)
{
    BrokerInterface myBroker = getBroker();
    EmployeeInterface agent =
            myBroker.getEmployee();

    agent.employee(name);
    agent.item(item);
    agent.price(maxPrice);
```

```
        agent.terminalID(terminalID);

        agent.Save();
        myBroker.registerBuyer((PersistentGnomeInterface) agent);
        myBroker.Save();
    }
```

If we were to diagram a buy request, we would get the diagram shown in Figure 6.23. You can see from both the diagram and the code that gnome *must* be stateful. The gnome who is told the item we want purchased must be the same gnome as the one who was just told the name of the person making the purchase, and must be the same gnome as the one we will soon tell the price we are willing to pay.

Although the gnome is obviously stateful, this does not violate the rule that the component as a whole is stateless. The BrokerHouse code is not dependent on

Figure 6.24 Original and new gnome relationship.

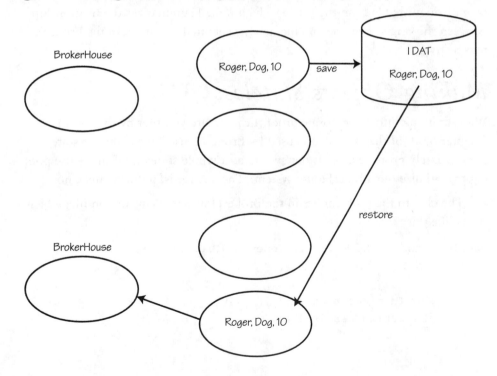

the state of the gnome lasting beyond the time it takes to invoke the *component level* method prepareBuyOrder(). At the end of this method invocation, the gnome's state is carefully tucked away in a persistent data store, and the internal state of the gnome is no longer important.

Why, you may ask, is the internal state of the gnome no longer important? After all, eventually we will need to check with that gnome to see what it wants to sell, and for how much. But we need to get this information from the gnome, we will at that time reread the gnome's state. If you recall, in Chapter 5 we made our brokering system persistent. One of the steps we took was to make both the Gnome and the Broker persistent. We used the IMoniker technology because it was convenient and hopefully compatible with the future Microsoft Java direction.

The key benefit of IMoniker technology is that the state of any object can be described by a string. This string can later be rebound to a new object whose state is identical to the original object. It is these strings that are stored in the Broker data structures. The broker doesn't care about finding the same gnome again. It will simply recreate one using this string, and that new gnome will then be indistinguishable from the original. Figure 6.24 summarizes the relationship between the original gnome and the newly generated gnome from the broker's perspective.

Making Objects Stateless

Without going into an elaborate proof, I can assure you that by the end of Chapter 5, all of the Java objects used by BrokerHouse have had their state appropriately protected. So, is our system as a whole stateless? Can we use pooling to optimize our BrokerHouse system? The answer is, unfortunately, no.

The clue to the problem lies in the BrokerHouse implementation file, which starts like this:

```
public class BrokerHouse implements IBrokerHouse,
BrokerHouseInterface
{
    private IMoniker brokerM;
    private String terminalID;
```

```
private static final String CLSID =
    "C414B3D3-DB01-11d0-BAFB-000000000000";
```

You should be able to spot the problem right off. We have private data, or state, in a class that implements a component. Gnome, of course, also has state, but Gnome is not a component-level object. Private data in a component-level object is almost certainly bad news.

There are two common techniques used to rid components of private data. I call the first of these *Date Parameterization* and the second *Key Parameterization*.

The Date Parameterization approach involves rewriting methods so that every method invocation receives all of the state it needs in the form of parameters. This was the approach used by the ObjectWatchCalculator discussed earlier in this chapter. The multiplyTwoNumbers(), whose purpose is to multiply together two numbers, received those numbers at the time of the method invocation. There is no need for private data because there is nothing to store between method invocations.

The Key Parameterization approach involves rewriting methods so that they receive a key they can use to find the data they need for their implementation. Typically this key identifies data in some persistent data store. If the persistent data store is the file system, then we would expect that key to be a string containing a pathname. If the persistent data store is a relational database, then we would expect that key to be a string identifying a row in a table.

Key Parameterization is the only technique we have to mimic the idea of object state in nondistributed objects. Almost any object of consequence will need to use some form of key parameterization.

The Micrognome calculator is now stateful. If we rewrite this calculator to use Key Parameterization, we might expect the new methods to look something like this:

```
class MicrognomeCalculator {
    public void setFirstMultiplier(string key, long n1)
    {
        writeData1(key, n1);
    }
    public void setSecondMultiplier(string key, long n2)
    {
        writeData2(key, n2);
```

```
    }
    public long multiplyNumbers(key)
    {
        int n1, n2;
        long result = 0;
        long n;

        n1 = readData1(key);
        n2 = readData2(key);
        for (n=0; n<second; n++) {
            result += first;
        }
        return result;
    }
}
```

Of course, this doesn't solve any of the other problems with the MicrognomeCalculator, but it does at least solve its problem of statefulness, thereby allowing it to be efficiently managed by the MS-DTC.

Historical Perspective on State

The question of state in objects has undergone an interesting historical metamorphosis. When programmers first adopted object-oriented programming, they thought of objects as almost necessarily composed of both state and behavior (or methods). For example, in my own book (*Class Construction in C and C++*), I said "A class such as a linked list is defined as being a collection of data, much like C's structures, and a set of functions that can be applied to that data. These functions are called methods." This statement reflected the common view of objects; that objects are a combination of state and behavior.

Now that we are starting to understand what it means to run component objects efficiently in a distributed environment, we are rethinking this view. Certainly objects still have behavior, and certainly objects still need data, or state. But now we don't think of that data as being part of the object. Indeed, part of the purpose of the behavior is to know how to find the data!

Base Clients, Components, and Java Objects

When we are designing and implementing a large system, we are working with many different types of software. Let's review these different types, and review the special features associated with each.

Clients. A *client* is a broad description of anything invoking methods on a component. A client can either be a component client or a base client.

Component clients. A *component client* is a client that is itself a component. All of the features associated with components are also associated with component clients.

Base clients. A *base client* is a client that is not a component. A base client is a client that is driving the whole system, usually through its direct interactions with a human being. It is not a component, and is not described by IDL. It is not distributed, although it makes use of distributed components. It is typically written as an executable.

Components. A *component* is a software entity that is described by an IDL file and can be distributed. Components can be further categorized as either managed or nonmanaged.

Managed component. A *managed component* is a component that is written so that it can be managed by the MS-DTC. It is stateless and supports IObjectControl interface. It is always packaged as a DLL, which is loaded into processes automatically by the MS-DTC.

Nonmanaged component. A *nonmanaged component* is one that is not written so that it can be managed by the MS-DTC. It most likely has long-term state, and either does not support the IObjectControl interface, or if it does so, returns false from the CanBePooled method.

Language-level object. A *language object* is something that is defined and written entirely in some object-oriented programming language. It is not described in IDL, and cannot be distributed outside of the component in which it is packaged (at least, using the MDCA). For our purposes here, we are assuming that the language of choice for implementing language-level objects is Java.

A Shareable Brokering System

For our grand finale, we will look at the modifications necessary to the brokering system to make it poolable. For those of you down in the pits, you will probably want to study this whole section, since you will probably have to go through similar exercises with your own components sooner or later. For those of you interested only in a high-level view of the necessary changes, you can look just at the interface changes. For those of you interested only in the basic ideas behind the MDCA, you can skim or ignore this entire section.

When we last left the brokering system, in Chapter 5, we had turned it into a persistent system. This allowed us to leave the system, turn off the machine, return the next day, and start up right where we left off. However, the system was not well organized for large-scale sharing.

Had 100 terminals all been working on the brokering system, we would have found a problem. The brokering system would have been shared, in that any one terminal would have looked like any other, and that anybody would have access to all the completed deals. But this isn't really what we want. We would really like partial sharing. We would like our terminal to be able to broker deals with any other terminal, but we don't want to be swamped with information about deals in which our terminal wasn't involved.

This is a common issue with commerce systems. We want our client to interact with other clients, but we don't want them to view information that doesn't concern them.

To solve this problem with the brokering system, we are going to start keeping track of terminal IDs. When a person first starts up a client process, we will ask them for a terminal ID. In a real system, we would read this from a configuration file, but the idea is the same. We will then flag our buyer/seller gnomes with this terminal ID, and when requesting information on pending buy/sells, we will only check for those matching terminal IDs. When it comes to deal-making, though, we will not be limited to clients on our terminal. We will deal with anybody, from any terminal.

Of course, the addition of terminalIDs alone will not be sufficient for large-scale sharing. We also need to enable pooling. So at the same time, we will be making the changes necessary to support pooling.

Let's go through the code and see what needs to happen. The code shown here is in the zip file under Chapter06_04. We will highlight changes with bold.

Brokering System Interfaces

The first change is in PersistentGnomeInterface. As we said, we need to track the terminalID. Since looking at the terminalID is pretty fundamental, we will put the read method in the most basic interface. Here is the change:

```
package Broker;
interface PersistentGnomeInterface extends IPersistFile
{
    IMoniker moniker();
    String terminalID();
}
```

Neither GnomeInterface nor AgentInterface is changed, so the next change is in EmployeeInterface, where we add the ability to set the terminalID:

```
package Broker;
interface EmployeeInterface extends GnomeInterface{
    public void employee(String newName);
    public void item(String newItem);
    public void price(long newPrice);
    public void terminalID(String newID);
}
```

The BrokerInterface has the terminalID added to all method definitions that have to do with finding information:

```
package Broker;
public interface BrokerInterface extends IPersistFile
{
    public EmployeeInterface getEmployee();

    public void registerBuyer(PersistentGnomeInterface newBuyer);
    public GnomeVector getBuys(String terminalID);
```

```
    public boolean anyBuys(String terminalID);

    public void registerSeller(PersistentGnomeInterface newSeller);
    public GnomeVector getSells(String terminalID);
    public boolean anySells(String terminalID);
}
```

The BrokerHouseInterface, which is our component-level interface, has the terminalID added to all of its methods:

```
package Broker;
public interface BrokerHouseInterface
{
    public int prepareCheckStatus(String tid);
    public void prepareBuyOrder(
        String tid, String name, String item, int maxPrice);
    public void prepareSellOrder(
        String tid, String name, String item, int minPrice);
    public String getSellerText(String tid);
    public String getBuyerText(String tid);
}
```

Brokering System Classes

The first set of class changes are to the Gnome class. I will show only those methods that have changes, and again, show those changes in bold. In a nutshell, we will be making the following changes:

- Implement the set and get methods for the terminalID.
- Update the LoadState and SaveState methods to write out the terminalID.

```
package Broker;
import java.io.*;

class Gnome implements AgentInterface, EmployeeInterface
{
    ...
    private String tID;
    ...
    public String terminalID()
    {
```

```
        return tID;
    }
    public void terminalID(String termID)
    {
        tID = termID;
    }
    protected void SaveState
        (DataOutputStream myStream) throws IOException
    {
        myStream.writeUTF(myEmployeeName);
        myStream.writeUTF(myItemName);
        myStream.writeLong(myPrice);
        myStream.writeLong(myNegotiatedPrice);
        myStream.writeUTF(otherName);
        myStream.writeUTF(tID);
        myStream.writeUTF(monikerString);
    }
    protected void LoadState(DataInputStream myStream) throws
        IOException
    {
        IMoniker m;
        myEmployeeName = myStream.readUTF();
        myItemName = myStream.readUTF();
        myPrice = myStream.readLong();
        myNegotiatedPrice = myStream.readLong();
        otherName = myStream.readUTF();
        tID = myStream.readUTF();
        monikerString = myStream.readUTF();
        m = FileMoniker.MkParseDisplayName(monikerString);
        moniker(m);
    }
    public Gnome()
    {
        myEmployeeName = "Unknown";
        myItemName = "Unknown";
        myPrice = 0;
        myNegotiatedPrice = 0;
        otherName = "None";
        myMoniker = null;
```

```
        tID = "None";
    }
}
```

The next class is Broker. The methods affected here are those that need to get information related to this particular terminal. Actually, the changes here are much less invasive than one might expect. This is because most of the changes have been consolidated into the GnomeVector class. Changed methods only are shown, with changes in bold:

```
package Broker;
import java.io.*;

public class Broker implements BrokerInterface
{
    public boolean anyBuys(String tID)
    {
        GnomeVector v = oldBuys.duplicateVector(tID, false);
        if (v.size() > 0) return true;
        else return false;
    }
    public boolean anySells(String tID)
    {
        GnomeVector v = oldSells.duplicateVector(tID, false);
        if (v.size() > 0) return true;
        else return false;
    }
    public GnomeVector getBuys(String tID)
    {
        GnomeVector v = oldBuys.duplicateVector(tID, true);
        return v;
    }
    public GnomeVector getSells(String tID)
    {
        GnomeVector v = oldSells.duplicateVector(tID, true);
        return v;
    }
}
```

As long as we are talking about the GnomeVector, we might as well look at that. Believe it or not, only one method is affected. Here it is, with changes in bold.

```java
package Broker;
import java.util.Vector;
import java.io.*;


class GnomeVector
{

    public GnomeVector duplicateVector
        (String terminalID, boolean remove)
    {
        GnomeVector newVector = new GnomeVector();
        PersistentGnomeInterface gnome;
        String tid;
        for (int n=size()-1; n>=0; n--)
        {
            gnome = getGnome(n);
            tid = gnome.terminalID();
            if (terminalID.equals(tid))
            {
                newVector.addGnome(gnome);
                if (remove) myVector.removeElementAt(n);
            }
        }
        return newVector;
    }

}
```

Now for the last of our classes, BrokerHouse. Remember that this is the Java class that implements the COM component. So we will have two sets of changes here. The first set will be changes involved with the terminal ID. The second set will be changes involved with pooling.

Among the changes related to pooling are three methods defined in the IObjectControl interface. Two of these actually require no code. These are Activate and Deactivate. They require no code because we have already ensured that saving and loading is appropriately handled elsewhere in the code. Even though no code is required, we must provide empty implementations since the methods are defined in the IObjectControl interface, and if we totally ignore them, we will get complaints from the Java compiler.

The third IObjectControl method, CanBePooled, is the only one we really care about, and the implementation of that is quite trivial. All we need it to do is to confirm that we are willing to be pooled.

Here is the new version of BrokerHouse:

```java
package Broker;
import java.io.*;
import com.ms.mtx.*;

public class BrokerHouse implements
    IBrokerHouse, BrokerHouseInterface, IObjectControl
{
    public boolean CanBePooled()
    {
        return true;
    }
    public void Activate()
    {
    }
    public void Deactivate()
    {
    }
    public String getSellerText(String tid)
    {
        String value;
        BrokerInterface myBroker = getBroker();
        GnomeVector v = myBroker.getSells(tid);
        myBroker.Save();
        value = getGnomeVectorString(v);
        MTx.GetObjectContext().SetComplete();
        return value;
    }
    public String getBuyerText(String tid)
    {
        String value;
```

```
        BrokerInterface myBroker = getBroker();
        GnomeVector v = myBroker.getBuys(tid);
        myBroker.Save();
        value = getGnomeVectorString(v);
        MTx.GetObjectContext().SetComplete();
        return value;
    }
    public int prepareCheckStatus(String tid)
    {
        int value = 0;
        BrokerInterface myBroker = getBroker();
        if (myBroker.anyBuys(tid)) value = 1;
        if (myBroker.anySells(tid)) value = 1;
        MTx.GetObjectContext().SetComplete();
        return value;
    }
    public void prepareBuyOrder
        (String tid, String name, String item, int maxPrice)
    {
        BrokerInterface myBroker = getBroker();
        EmployeeInterface agent =
            myBroker.getEmployee();

        agent.employee(name);
        agent.item(item);
        agent.price(maxPrice);
        agent.terminalID(tid);

        agent.Save();
        myBroker.registerBuyer((PersistentGnomeInterface) agent);
        myBroker.Save();
        MTx.GetObjectContext().SetComplete();
    }
    public void prepareSellOrder
        (String tid, String name, String item, int minPrice)
    {
        BrokerInterface myBroker = getBroker();
        EmployeeInterface agent= myBroker.getEmployee ();
```

```
        agent.employee(name);
        agent.item(item);
        agent.price(minPrice);
        agent.terminalID(tid);

        agent.Save();
        myBroker.registerSeller((PersistentGnomeInterface) agent);
        myBroker.Save();
        MTx.GetObjectContext().SetComplete();
    }
}
```

Component Definition Changes

Our component definition needs the same two sets of changes needed by our BrokerHouse Java class. The first set enables pooling, and the second set enables the terminalID. Here is the new version, with changes shown in bold:

```
#include <MtxAttr.h>
#include <JavaAttr.h>
[
    uuid(C414B3D1-DB01-11d0-BAFB-000000000000),
    version(1.0),
    helpstring("Broker Type Library Version 1")
]
library BrokerLib
{
    importlib("stdole2.tlb");
    [
        object,
        uuid(C414B3D2-DB01-11d0-BAFB-000000000000),
        dual,
        helpstring("IBrokerHouse Interface"),
        pointer_default(unique)
    ]
    interface IBrokerHouse : IDispatch
    {
        import "oaidl.idl";
```

```
        HRESULT getSellerText([in] BSTR tid,
            [out, retval]BSTR *text);
        HRESULT prepareSellOrder
            ([in] BSTR tid, [in] BSTR p1, [in] BSTR p2,
            [in] long p3);
        HRESULT prepareCheckStatus
            ([in] BSTR tid, [out, retval]long* status);
        HRESULT prepareBuyOrder
            ([in] BSTR tid, [in] BSTR p1, [in] BSTR p2,
            [in] long p3);
        HRESULT getBuyerText([in] BSTR tid, [out, retval]BSTR
            *text);
    };
    [
        uuid(C414B3D3-DB01-11d0-BAFB-000000000000),
        helpstring("Broker House Class"),
        JAVACLASS("Broker.BrokerHouse"),
        PROGID("Broker.Broker"),
        TRANSACTION_REQUIRED
    ]
    coclass CBrokerHouse
    {
        [default] interface IBrokerHouse;
    };
};
```

Build Changes

The new build process is the same as the dog build process, but for completeness, here it is:

```
rem Create Broker.tlb
midl Broker.idl

rem Create CBrokerHouse.class and IBrokerHouse.class
javatlb /d . /p Broker /p:b- Broker.tlb

cd Broker
JAVAGUID CBrokerHouse.class IBrokerHouse.class
```

```
cd ..

rem Compile local class
jvc Broker\*.java

rem Compile client
jvc UserSide.java

C:\MTX\TOOLS\EXEGEN /d /r /out:broker.dll broker.tlb *.class
```

Client-Side Changes

On the Visual Basic client side, the main change is the creation of a public variable called tid. We will set this up in the loading of the form, as shown here:

```
Private Sub Form_Load()
    Set mybh = CreateObject("BrokerHouse")
    Text1.Text = ""
    Text3.Text = ""
    Text4.Text = ""
    Text5.Text = ""
    Label7.Caption = ""
    Combo1.Text = "dog"
    Combo1.AddItem ("dog")
    Combo1.AddItem ("cat")
    tid = InputBox$("What is your Terminal ID?")
    Form1.Caption = "Broker Systems - Terminal (" + tid + ")"
End Sub
```

The remaining changes are just adding this variable to each method invocation.

```
Private Sub Command1_Click()
    Label7.Caption = ""
    Call mybh.prepareBuyOrder
        (tid, Text1.Text, Combo1.Text, Text3.Text)
    Label7.Caption = "Buy Accepted"
End Sub

Private Sub Command2_Click()
    Label7.Caption = ""
```

```
        Call mybh.prepareSellOrder
            (tid, Text1.Text, Combo1.Text, Text3.Text)
        Label7.Caption = "Sell Accepted"
End Sub

Private Sub Command3_Click()
    Dim result
    result = mybh.prepareCheckStatus(tid)
    If (result = 0) Then
        Label7.Caption = "No Matches Found"
    Else
        Label7.Caption = "Matches Found"
    End If
End Sub

Private Sub Command4_Click()
    Text4.Text = mybh.getBuyerText(tid)
    Text5.Text = mybh.getSellerText(tid)
    Label7.Caption = ""
End Sub

Private Sub Command5_Click()
    Set myby = Nothing
    End
End Sub
```

A Client's Perspective

Despite all these changes, from a client's perspective, very little has changed. The only new interface issue is that when they first bring up the form, they will have to tell the system the ID of their terminal. This is done through a popup window created by this Visual Basic command located in the Form Load routine:

```
tid = InputBox$("What is your Terminal ID?")
```

This command pops up the window shown in Figure 6.25.

After accepting the terminal ID from the user, the identification window goes away, and the rest of the session looks just as it did before, as in Figure 6.26.

Although the brokering system looks almost like it did at the end of the last chapter, it behaves differently in two areas. First of all, it behaves as a semi-shared

Figure 6.25 Terminal identification window.

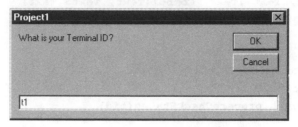

system, with an appropriate mix of shared and unshared characteristics (as we discussed earlier). Second, it is much more efficient. BrokerHouse components can now be efficiently managed using the disposable taxi strategy, and they are all set up for true pooling, whenever Microsoft gets it together.

Figure 6.26 Client broker system.

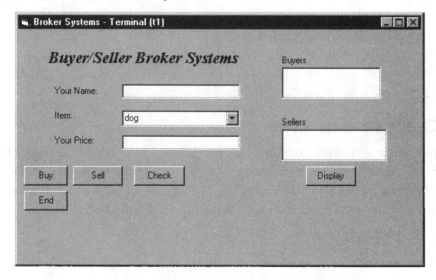

Summary

You can learn a lot from watching taxis. Taxi companies have known how to design efficient component systems long before any of us ever heard of objects, or distributed systems, or cluster efficiency. Back when Bill Gates was designing BASIC compilers to run on his Etch-a-Sketch. Back when Java was something you bought for 25 cents a cup. Taxi companies have always understood that efficiency requires pooling, and that pooling requires statelessness. And what is a taxi, but a component on wheels?

I suspect that any taxi driver could become a distributed systems designer with little or no training. They have been walking the walk for a very long time. But this is going to be our little secret. There are a lot of taxi drivers out there, and we really don't need the competition. So the next time your taxi driver asks what your job is, do what I do. Mumble something about being a consultant specializing in polymorphic resolution of heterogeneous cluster efficiency. Then change the subject. As quickly as possible.

Transactions and Databases

I n 1687, Sir Isaac Newton discovered the first law of commerce. He didn't call it that. He called it the third law of motion. He said that every action gives rise to a reaction of equal strength, but opposite direction. Jet pilots are greatly indebted to Newton. Without his third law of motion, jets couldn't fly. They would just sprawl around on the ground like so many sleeping cats.

But this law describes commerce as well. In fact, it is the cornerstone of commerce. For every buy, there is a sell. For every withdrawal, there is a deposit. For every loan, there is a debt. Commerce is every bit as dependent on this law as are jets. I can't explain who (or what) is responsible for enforcing the third law of motion. I will leave that to loftier books than mine. But I can explain who is responsible for enforcing the first law of commerce. Gnomes. In this chapter, I am going to explain how they do it. And how, on the backs of such gnomes, Microsoft is going to build its next empire.

The First Law of Commerce

Let's start by taking a closer look at the first law of commerce. We can restate this law as, "Every movement of commerce in one direction is accompanied by an equivalent movement in the opposite direction." In Chapter 1, I described buying airline tickets. This is a good illustration of the first law of commerce. The airline gives me an airline ticket. I give the airline money. Two movements that are equivalent, but opposite. The airline would be violating the first law if they took my money, but didn't give me a ticket. I would be violating the first law if I took a ticket, but then didn't pay my money.

There are many corollaries of the first law. Here are some of the most important.

Corollary 1. The If Either, Both Corollary. If one of these equal but opposite movements occurs, the other must as well. If I pay my money, the airline must give me the ticket.

Corollary 2. The If Not One, Neither Corollary. If one of these equal but opposite movements does not occur, the other must not either. If for any reason I do not pay my money, the airline must not give me the ticket.

Corollary 3. The Balanced World Corollary. There may be more than two movements, as long as the overall balance is maintained. I can pay for half my ticket with American Express, and half with Visa, as long as the two payments together total the cost of the ticket.

Corollary 4. The Changes are Forever Corollary. The future cannot undo the past. Once I have my ticket, I have my ticket. Nothing can change that.

Corollary 5. There No Excuses Corollary. There are no excuses for a failure of the first law. Everything must work perfectly regardless of rain, snow, sleet, hail, or your dog eating the disk drive.

Let's look at a few scenarios that violate one or more of these corollaries using the airline ticketing example. I call the airline to order a ticket. The agent charges the payment to my credit card and books my flight. The next day, the file cabinet containing the record of my purchase burns down. When I show up for my flight, the airline has no record of the purchase. They offer to refund my money. Sorry, I say. This is not acceptable. This is a violation of Corollary 4.

Let's say I order my ticket at the same time my wife buys her new Mercedes. The agent checks my credit availability and finds that I am flush with credit. So I am handed the ticket and I leave. At the next instant, the dealer at Max's Mercedes and More charges my wife's purchase. By the time the ticket purchase goes through, it is rejected because my available credit has suddenly gone to zero. But too late, I have already left the terminal with my ticket. Not fair, says the airline. This is a violation of Corollary 2.

You can see that the first law of commerce is very easy both to state and to understand. And anybody can design a system that works according to this law

99 percent of the time. But 99 percent isn't good enough, says Corollary 5. The system must work correctly 100 percent of the time. And that itsy bitsy 1-percent difference has occupied the best minds in our industry for the last half century. Including some that now work for Microsoft.

Let's look at one example of a commerce system that works 99 percent of the time, but not 100 percent: the brokering system as we last left it. Sure, it usually works. But there are dozens of things that can cause the system to violate the first law. Failures are possible on the component, the process, the machine, the communications, or the file level. Would you want to bet your life savings on the proper working of this program?

If I am charged with making the brokering system first-law compliant, I have two choices. One, I can insert into my components a huge amount of code to deal with problems so complex that they are probably only really understood by a handful of people in the world. Or I can run my components within a framework that automatically provides first-law compliance. It should take very little time to make this choice. If for no other reason that now when something fails, I have somebody else to blame.

Transactional Systems

Commerce people have a special term to describe the collection of balanced forces described by the first law. They call this collection a *transaction*. So if my money transfer requires a savings withdrawal balanced by a checking deposit, we say that these two account updates are contained within one transaction. Based on our discussion of the first law, we know that all of the elements of the transaction will either take place *in toto* or *in zilcho*. And we know that once the transaction has completed, it will never be undone. And we know that the correct balance of elements will be preserved, no matter what. This is shown in Figure 7.1.

To better understand the issues faced by transactional systems, let's look at how such a system could be designed with what we know about our favorite furry little creatures, gnomes.

Record Management Gnomes

At the simplest level, we need a gnome to do some record management. Let's say I am designing the system that will manage my airline ticket sales. I am going to

Figure 7.1 Transactions.

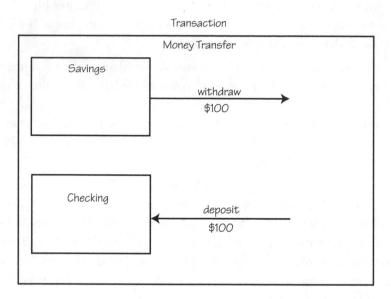

have airline agents selling tickets at the counter, and in the back room, our record management. This is shown in Figure 7.2.

My basic algorithm for selling a ticket looks as follows:

```
sell(customerID, flightID, costOfTicket)
{
    check flightID for availability;
    if (available) {
        check available credit for customerID;
        if (available credit is at least costOfTicket) {
            update available credit for customerID;
            Add cost to charges for customerID;
            update flight availability for flightID;
        }
    }
}
```

We can assume there are three collections of records used by this system. To make this as simple as possible, let's say a record is a 3 × 5 card, and a collection of records is a card file. Each card in a file has a unique sequence number.

Figure 7.2 Airline system.

We have three card files. The first, the flight file, contains a card for each flight. Each card contains information about the flight including the number of seats still available on that flight. The second, the customer file, contains a card for each credit card customer. Each card contains information about the customer, including their current credit limit. The third, the charge file, contains a card for each charge. It shows information about a particular purchase. Figure 7.3 shows representative cards from each of these files.

Now let's put all these files in a room, and assign a gnome, say Rick, to be the record manager. Keep in mind that Rick is managing not just records for one agent, but for the whole airline and perhaps the credit card company as well. How is Rick going to manage this system in accordance with the first law of commerce without losing his mind (which would likely lead to a violation of the No Excuses Corollary)?

Figure 7.3 Representative cards.

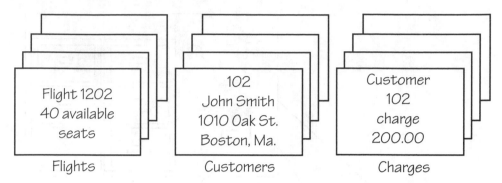

If Rick is responsible for ensuring the first law of commerce, he has a lot to do. Let's consider, for example, just the flight file. If Andrew, an agent, is told that Flight 1212 has one seat left, Andrew is likely to hand somebody a ticket based on that bit of information. Once Andrew has updated the customer's credit line and charged the customer's card, Andrew will update the seating availability of Flight 1212 to indicate that there are no more seats available.

What if Rick allows Anne, another agent, to check the availability of Flight 1212 after Andrew has checked the availability but before he has completed the sale and updated the flight record? Then Anne is likely to sell a ticket based on inaccurate information, or information that is about to become inaccurate. And this will violate the If Either, Both corollary: money will be paid, but the ticket that is sold will not, in fact, exist. So once Andrew has checked the flight availability, Rick needs to stall Anne's check until Andrew has had a chance to complete his sale.

But Rick should not stall Anne unnecessarily. There are a lot of agents out there, and a lot of customers. Work needs to proceed as quickly as humanly possible. If Anne's work is not in contention with Andrew's, it should not be impeded. So Rick has a lot of pressure on him. On the one hand, he must make sure Anne's work does not invalidate Andrew's work (or vice versa). And on the other hand, he is under pressure to minimize the time people are unable to access information.

Another way to think of this is that both Andrew and Anne have a series of record updates packaged together in a transaction. There is the Andrew transaction, and the Anne transaction. Perhaps there is contention between these two transactions, and perhaps not. If Anne is working with a completely different customer than is Andrew, and the two customers' flights do not overlap, then there is no problem, and Rick should allow Andrew and Anne immediate access to the records they need. But if there is contention between the two transactions, Rick needs to make sure that neither person pulls the rug out from beneath the other.

Does this sound like Rick has a high-pressure job? But that's not the end of it. Think of it. From Rick's perspective, this system is a cacophony of shouting, ordering, and pleading for one record or another to be updated. "Rick, how many seats does Flight 1212 have available?" "Rick, change the number of available seats on Flight 501 to 20." "Rick, how much credit does customer 15a have?" "Rick, change the credit balance on customer 100d to 50." "Rick, change the number of available seats on Flight 1212 to 9." Rick! Rick! Rick!

If Rick is to have any hope of sorting this out, he needs more information than just shouted orders. He needs to know specifically the following:

- Which requests are associated with which transactions, so he knows when a request needs to be protected, and when it doesn't.
- When each transaction ends, so that he can stop worrying about protecting its work.

Transaction IDs

Let's assume that agents have three buttons. The first is labeled Start, which is pressed when the agent starts a new sale. The second is labeled End, which is pressed when the sale has been completed. The third is labeled Quit, which is pressed if the agent wants to quit the sale; if—for example, the customer has inadequate credit or just changes his or her mind. The agent's counter is shown in Figure 7.4.

When the Start button is pushed, an electronic gizmo automatically creates a new unique number. We will call this number the transaction ID. From then on, when that agent pushes the intercom button to bark an order to Rick, a panel

Figure 7.4 Attendant's counter.

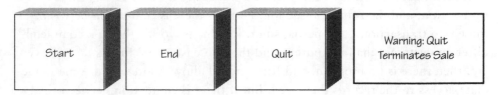

above Rick's desk shows the assigned transaction ID. The number is also displayed whenever either of the End or Quit buttons is pushed, along with a message saying which of the two buttons was pushed.

An agent's intercom is enabled by the Start button and disabled by both the Quit and End buttons. This effectively guarantees that all orders passed on to Rick will have an associated transaction ID.

Rick still has a tough row to hoe. But at least he now has the tools he needs to do his job. Look again at the pseudocode used to describe a ticket sale, with Start and End buttons added.

```
sell(customerID, flightID, costOfTicket)
{
    push Start button;
    check flightID for availability;
    if (available) {
        check available credit for customerID;
        if (available credit is at least costOfTicket) {
            update available credit for customerID;
            Add cost to charges for customerID;
            update flight availability for flightID;
        }
    }
    push End button;
}
```

Let's say Rick gets two requests in a row, the first to read information for some flight, and the second to update information for some flight. He processes the first request. What does he do with the second? The answer depends on two things. First, whether the flight numbers are the same for both requests. Second, whether the requests have the same or different transaction IDs.

If the two requests are for different flight numbers, then there is no problem. Regardless of from which agent they originate, there is no possible contention and Rick can process both requests. But what if the flights are the same?

If the flights are the same, then there is a possible collision in progress. In this case, Rick needs to consider the transaction IDs associated with the respective requests. If both requests have the same transaction ID, then he can assume that the agent updating the flight information is the same as the agent who just finished reading that flight's information. This is the normal state of affairs, and Rick can process the two requests. But if the transaction IDs are *not* the same, then Rick knows that the second request is coming from some other agent, say Anne. And he should stall Anne until one of two things happens. Either the first agent pushes the Quit button, or the first agent pushes the End button.

Locks

Keep in mind that poor Rick has to cope with lots and lots of requests. He may be trying to process hundreds of transactions at the same time. How can he remember which ones have requested what information? Rick needs a system. And the system he uses is one we call *locking*. Here is how he does it.

Rick has two colors of stickers: green and red. He also has a large whiteboard in his office. Rick follows the following procedures in dealing with data requests.

When Rick's panel lights up with a transaction ID that he has never seen before, he assumes he is getting the first request of a new transaction. When this happens Rick goes over to his whiteboard and writes the transaction number.

When a request comes over Rick's intercom to *read* some card, he does these five things.

1. He pulls the card from the appropriate file.

2. He puts a green sticker on the card, and writes the transaction ID on the sticker. A green sticker indicates that a transaction has requested a read of this card.

3. He writes the card sequence number on the whiteboard under the transaction ID associated with this request.

4. He reads the information back to the agent.

5. He returns the card to the file (with the sticker still attached).

When a request comes over his intercom to *update* the information on some card, he does these five things:

1. He pulls the card from the appropriate file.

2. He puts a red sticker on the card, and writes the transaction ID on the sticker. A red sticker is used to indicate some transaction has requested an update of the card.

3. He writes the card sequence number on the whiteboard under the transaction ID associated with this request.

4. He updates the information on the card.

5. He returns the card to the file (with the red sticker still attached).

When Rick's panel shows a transaction ID with the word "End," he does these five things:

1. He finds the transaction ID on the whiteboard.

2. One by one, he picks every card whose sequence number is written below that transaction ID.

3. As he picks the card, he removes the sticker with that transaction ID.

4. He returns the card to the file.

5. When all the cards have had their stickers removed, he erases the transaction information from the whiteboard.

When Rick's panel shows a transaction ID and the word "Quit," he follows the same sequence as for "End" for those cards with green stickers. But if the card has a red sticker and this transaction ID, that means the card has been updated, and the agent then changed his mind. Now Rick has to undo any changes made to this card by this transaction before removing the red sticker. We will talk about how he does this later. Figure 7.5 shows a card with several green stickers. Production costs being what they are, you'll have to imagine the color green.

Now how does this system help manage contention by two competing transactions? Well, so far, it doesn't, We need to add some more rules to govern what

Figure 7.5 Card with stickers.

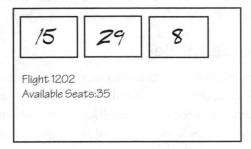

happens when Rick draws a card that already has an attached sticker. We will have four rules: the green on green rule, the green on red rule, the red on green rule, and the red on red rule.

The Green-on-Green Rule

Cards are allowed to have any number of green stickers. If Rick is about to add a green sticker (for a read request) and the card already has a green sticker (for another read request), then he adds the new green sticker to the card and allows the agent to read. The card now has two (or more) green stickers, each with a different transaction ID.

The Green-on-Red Rule

Cards with a red sticker cannot take a green sticker. If Rick is about to add a green sticker (for a read request), and the card already has a red sticker (for an update request), then Rick doesn't add the new green sticker. Instead, he goes to the whiteboard and writes the sequence of the card, the requesting transaction ID, the ID of the transaction on which it is waiting, and the color of the sticker the transaction wants to add. He writes this all under a column labeled "waiting."

That agent whose transaction requested the green sticker will then be blocked until the red sticker is removed. They can now go on a coffee break, although they shouldn't plan on being gone for more than a few tenths of a second.

The Red-on-Red Rule

Cards with a red sticker cannot take another red sticker. If Rick is about to add a red sticker (for an update request) and the card already has a red sticker (for another update request), then Rick doesn't add the new red sticker. Instead, he follows the same procedure outlined in the green-on-red rule. Again, the new transaction is blocked until the offending red sticker has been removed.

The Red-on-Green Rule

Cards with one or more green stickers cannot take a red sticker. If Rick is about to add a red sticker (for an update request) and the card already has one or more green stickers (for one or more read requests), then Rick doesn't add the new red sticker. Instead, he follows the same procedure outlined in the green-on-red rule, and the new transaction is blocked until all of the green stickers have been removed.

Rick's whiteboard can get pretty hectic. Rick's Figure 7.6 shows Rick's whiteboard at a typical time of the day.

Now let's summarize the states in which a card might find itself. The vast majority of cards will have no stickers, meaning no transaction is working with this card. Some will have one or more green stickers, meaning one or more transactions are currently reading this record. Some will have exactly one red sticker,

Figure 7.6 Rick's whiteboard.

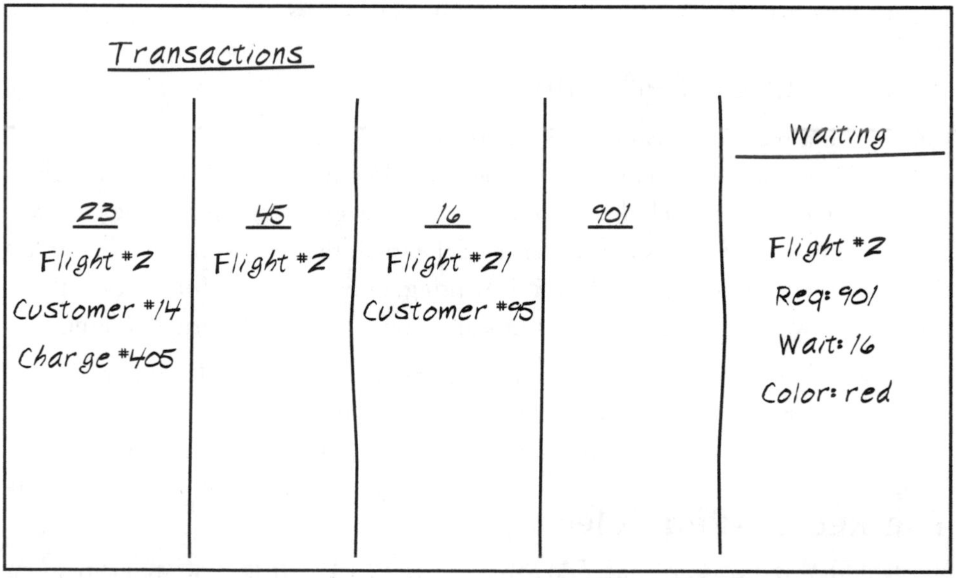

meaning one transaction is currently updating this record. Cards can never have more than one red sticker, and can never have a red sticker and any green stickers.

Remember that when a transaction either quits or ends, Rick is going to go through all the cards and remove stickers with that transaction ID. As he does this, he also needs to check the whiteboard to see if any transactions were waiting for this card.

If the sticker he is removing is green, then there are definitely not any transactions waiting to add a green sticker, because a card can hold any number of green stickers at once. But there may be a transaction waiting to add a red sticker. If so, and if there are no more green stickers on the card, then Rick can add the waiting red sticker the card, and allow that transaction to proceed.

If the sticker he is removing is red, then there may be transactions waiting to add either green or red stickers. If so, Rick chooses one of the transactions and allows its sticker to go on the card. He then erases the entry from the wait column.

If you can follow this system, you can see how this solves the problem of contentious transactions. Once Andrew has requested information from the Flight 1212 card, he will have his green sticker added to the card. This sticker will not be removed until he either pushes the End or the Quit button. Any other transaction trying to update that card will need to first place a red sticker on the card, and that won't be allowed until Andrew's green sticker has been removed. So Andrew can read the information, knowing its data cannot change until Andrew is finished with his work.

On the other hand, if Anne wants to read while Andrew is reading, then that requires the addition of Anne's green sticker. The rules allow multiple green stickers on a card, so Anne can go ahead and read even though Andrew hasn't yet finished his work. But that's okay, because his work doesn't require updates.

If Andrew requests an update on Flight 1212, then he places a red sticker on the card. If he already had a green sticker, then the green sticker is changed to a red sticker. If someone else had a green sticker on the card, then Andrew is out of luck. He must wait.

This system guarantees two important things. The first is that once a transaction had read some data, that data won't change until the transaction has completed. The second is that a transaction that updates a piece of data will block any other transactions from reading that data until it has brought its own work to completion.

We call this system a *record locking system*, and we call the stickers we place on the cards *record locks*. The green stickers are called *read locks* and the red stickers are called *write locks*. The stickers are just one way to implement locks. The important point is not how locks are implemented, but how read and write locks, along with the rules governing their use, are able to protect transactions from interfering with each other.

Logging

The sticker system has solved one of Rick's problems, how to deal with the barrage of data management requests and still manage to keep people from stepping on each other's toes. Now let's move on to the next problem: Corollaries 4 (Changes are Forever) and 5 (No Excuses). Even if Rick's file system burns to the ground, his data cannot be lost. How can Rick guarantee this?

One thing Rick could do is periodically shut down his system and make copies of all his files. He could then move these copies to a new location, so that if anything happens to his live data, he can go to a copied set.

This works fine as far as it goes. But if Rick made his last copy at midnight, and then a fire broke out at 5:00 P.M., Rick needs a way to restore all of the changes made between those times.

Rick uses a technique called *logging*. Anytime Rick makes a change to one of the cards, he logs the change on another piece of paper. He stores this log in another room, so that if there is a fire, he might lose the log, or he might lose the data, but he is not likely to lose both. Now if there is a fire, Rick takes his last copy and his log and, one by one, reapplies all of the changes in the log to the data copy. At the end of this, the copy is up to date with the lost original. Then Rick reopens for business.

Undo

We also pointed out that Rick needs to be prepared to undo changes made to records if the agent quits the transaction. There are two ways Rick can do this.

Rick can write changes to a temporary area, and apply them to cards only upon a normal transaction end. Or Rick can make a copy of the original record before updating it, and save this copy until the transaction either ends or quits. If Rick is really smart, he can combine this operation with what the logging process is doing anyway to ensure data stability.

Deadlocks

Rick is making good progress. His system now guarantees two things. One, that transactions will not interfere with each other. Two, that data won't be lost due to system failure. Rick's next problem is transactions that block each other.

Let's say Andrew and Anne are working with two different customers both flying Flight 1212. Based on the sell algorithm, the first thing they do is read the record for that flight. This results in two green stickers being placed on the card, one for Andrew and one for Anne. The last thing the two agents do within their transactions is to update the flight record. This means they want to exchange their green stickers for red ones.

The rules governing sticker placement say that a red sticker can only be placed on a card with no green stickers (unless they are from the same transaction). Anne's green-to-red sticker upgrade is blocked by Andrew's green sticker, and Andrew's green-to-red upgrade is blocked by Anne's. So both transactions get added to the wait list on Rick's whiteboard, and neither can proceed.

How long will they stay in this state? Basically, forever. These two transactions are in what we call a *deadlock* state. Anne cannot do anything until Andrew finishes his work. Andrew cannot do anything until Anne finishes her work. Andrew and Anne (and their two customers) can spend the rest of their lives waiting for a response from Rick. They are all trapped together in a world beyond time and dimension, in the Twilight Zone of data management.

Rick could leave these unfortunates floating in limbo. After all, from his perspective, this is just two fewer agents to bark orders at him. But beyond any immediate twinges of conscience, the deadlock will probably grow. Not only are Andrew and Anne blocked, but so is anybody else who wants to update Flight 1212. This tie-up on Flight 1212 will sooner or later prevent other transactions from releasing locks on other cards, so the problem will quickly multiply.

Soon there will be no agents getting any work at all done. Everybody will be waiting for everybody else to do something. Eventually, even management may notice that all of the agents are just sitting around with blank looks on their faces. And whose fault is this, they will want to know? And everybody will say, "We are waiting for Rick!"

So Rick needs to deal with the issue. He does so by periodically checking his whiteboard to see which transactions are waiting for which, and if any of those waiting are deadlocked.

One technique Rick might use to look for deadlocks is to draw a bunch of circles on his whiteboard, one for each active transaction. In the center of the circle, he writes the ID of the transaction that circle represents. He then draws arrows from that circle to every other circle representing transactions on which that transaction is waiting. He then looks for cyclic paths, in other words, paths that start at a given circle and lead back to that same circle. If, for example, there is a path that starts with Andrew's transaction circle and eventually leads back to Andrew's transaction circle, then Rick knows that all of the transactions on that particular path are deadlocked. Figure 7.7 shows a wait graph with no deadlocks, and Figure 7.8 shows a wait graph with Andrew and several others involved in a deadlock.

Figure 7.7 Wait graph with no deadlocks.

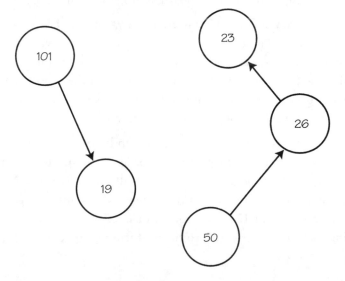

Figure 7.8 Wait graph with deadlocks.

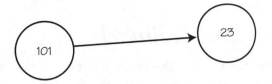

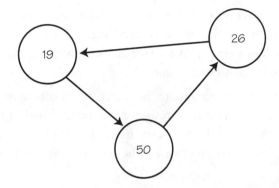

As soon as Rick detects the characteristic deadlock pattern, he jumps into action. He chooses one of the transactions to terminate. Let's say he decides to terminate Andrew's transaction. He terminates it exactly as if Andrew had pressed the Quit button. In other words, he goes through the following steps:

- He finds Andrew's transaction ID on the whiteboard.

- He picks every card shown as locked by Andrew and removes the lock stickers from the cards.

- If any of the cards had been updated, he erases the changes and replaces the original data.

- He returns the cards to their files.

- He erases any notations from the wait list on his board involving Andrew.

- He allows any transactions waiting on Andrew to continue.

- Finally, he calls Andrew and tells him the bad news.

Andrew may not be happy about this outcome. He now has to apologize to his customer and start the whole sale again. But this is a lot better than telling his customer he will be spending the rest of his life in the airline terminal, waiting for his sale to go through. And that is the only alternative.

Commitment and Rollback

A transactional package has two possible outcomes. It can either complete successfully, or it can be terminated. In our system, the airline agent decides to complete the transaction, by pushing the End button. But either the agent or Rick can decide to terminate the transaction.

The agent can terminate the transaction by pushing the Quit button. Andrew, for example, might find that the customer's credit is too low, or decide that the customer's face looks exactly like a face he just saw on a wanted poster, or the customer may change his or her mind.

Rick might decide to terminate the transaction because Andrew was involved in a deadlock, or was tying up a resource too long, or maybe Rick was just sick of being yelled at. In fact, Rick has the right to terminate the transaction for any reason, at any time, up to the moment he acknowledges processing an end request.

When Andrew presses his End button, he is requesting what we call a *commit*. A commit means he is finished with his transaction, and wants any changes made to cards as part of that transaction made permanently. He promises he will not change his mind for any reason. They don't call it *commit* for nothing.

Once Rick receives the commit request, he can make one of two choices. He can accept the commit, which means he makes all of Andrew's data changes permanent and signals Andrew a successful completion. Or he refuses the commit, removes all of Andrew's data changes, and tells Andrew the deal is off. This is called a *rollback*. Once the rollback has finished, it will be as if Andrew's transaction never existed. Locks are gone. Data changes are undone.

When Andrew requests the commit, it's very important that Rick think through his response carefully. He should not accept the commit if there is even the slightest chance that something might prevent him from making *any* of the data changes requested during this transaction. He should be holding the necessary cards in his hand, with a sharpened pencil, with a note from his doctor certifying his good health. Like I said, once he says yes, there are no excuses.

So commit is tricky business for Rick. But it does free him up in one way. Up until he commits the transaction, he must be able to perform a rollback and undo any record changes requested by that transaction at any moment. Rick never knows when Andrew or Anne may change their minds about a sale. Rick will need to keep original copies of any records modified by the transaction, so that they can be restored in the event of a rollback. But once Rick has finished the commit, he no longer needs to worry about rollback. An agent requesting a rollback after a commit would be violating Corollary 4, the Forever corollary. And we know how Rick feels about the Forever corollary. So after the rollback, Rick can kick back, breathe a sigh of relief, and toss the original data copies in the trash.

More Data Management Gnomes

At some point, even Rick can't keep up with this hectic lifestyle. Maybe he can manage the data for 20, or 40 agents. But sooner or later, we are going to need more Ricks. And we are going to reorganize our data. One way to do this is to place each of the three files in a room of its own, and put Rick clones in charge of each. Let's say we have Rick overseeing the flight files, and Rick clones Randy to oversee customer files, and Rita to oversee the charge file.

This newly partitioned system should be able to process a lot more agent requests. But now we have a lot more record manager gnomes involved in any given transaction. And the first rule of commerce hasn't changed. Just because the data is now spread out and involves multiple record management gnomes, transactions still need to be processed in an all-or-nothing manner.

Record management has just gotten more complicated. Let's say Andrew has one transaction that requires Rick to update a flight card and Rita to update a charge card. Suppose in response to a commit request, Rick updates the flight card. There is no requirement that Rick be able to undo after a commit, so he tosses out his original card copies. Then Rita needs to commit her change. But let's say she can't, for whatever reason, and decides instead to roll back. This is fair. Until she agrees to commit, she can do whatever she wants. But in the meantime, Rick has performed the commit. Now we are in a very bad situation. Rick has already updated his records, and Rita has refused to update hers. On Rick's side, this violates Corollary 1 (If Either, Both) and on Rita's side, this violates Corollary 2 (If Not One, Neither).

We solve this problem the way we solve all problems. We add another gnome type. This gnome type will be responsible for coordinating transactions that span rooms. We will call this gnome type the *transaction manager*.

The Society of Transaction Managers

Transaction manager gnomes need to maintain close relationships with record manager gnomes. In order to do this, every room that contains a record manager will also contain a transaction manager. Let's say our three transaction managers are Trix, Tammy, and Tina, and are assigned to the rooms of Rick, Randy, and Rita, respectively.

Now transaction managers have a very close-knit society. They share information. They talk to each other all the time. They have no secrets. If you tell Trix something, she will immediately call Tammy and Tina.

As in the single-room system, when Rick gets a read or update request, it is accompanied by its transaction ID. And as before, when a new transaction ID first arrives, Rick starts a new column on the whiteboard. But now Rick needs to do one more thing. He needs to tell Trix that he is involved with this transaction. And of course, when he tells Trix, she immediately tells Tammy and Tina. So now the whole world knows.

Let's assume that a given transaction is going to update records managed by both Rick and Randy. When Rick gets his first request, he will talk to Trix, as described earlier. When Randy gets her first request, she talks to Tammy, who talks to Trix and Tina. So the society of transaction managers now knows that for a particular transaction ID, both Rick and Randy are involved.

Now let's assume the agent pushes the Quit button midway through the order. We know that this translates to a rollback request. But now the rollback request will go to the society of transaction managers, along with the ID of the transaction being rolled back. Since the society knows that both Rick and Randy are involved with this transaction, the society issues rollback requests to both Rick and Randy. Rick gets his request through Trix, and Randy gets hers through Tammy.

The bottom line is that the agent pushes the Quit button, and both Rick and Randy roll back. So Corollary 2 (If Not One, Neither) is intact.

We know that rollbacks can also originate from a record manager. If Randy decides that for some reason she can't allow the transaction to proceed (for example, if the transaction is deadlocked on her machine), then Randy can make the rollback decision. But now she also lets Tammy know about her decision. Tammy calls for an immediate summit of the society. "Who else was involved in this transaction?" the society asks, and up pops Rick's name. So the society tells Trix to issue a rollback order to Rick. And all is well with the world.

Commits are a little more complicated. Remember, commits are the result of an agent pushing the End button. A commit request by a human being does not necessarily result in a commit being done by the record manager. The record manager, remember, can refuse the commit request. But with both Rick and Randy involved in the transaction, we need to make sure that either both Rick and Randy commit, or neither Rick nor Randy commit. How does the society manage this trick?

They do it by having an extended dialog with the record managers. Here is how it works.

When any member of the society gets a commit request for a particular transaction, the society holds a meeting and generates a list of all the record managers involved. In this case, that list consists of Rick and Randy. The appropriate society members are charged with asking Rick and Randy how they feel about doing a commit on this transaction.

So Trix asks Rick if he is willing to commit the transaction and Tammy asks Randy. Now this is a very serious question. If Rick says he is willing to commit, then he had better be able to commit. He should have his cards in hand, pencil sharpened, and doctor's certificate, just as he did when asked to commit in the single-room system. If Rick says yes, he should freeze, poised to perform the commit on a moment's notice. He must let nothing happen that will prevent him from committing. He is fully committed to commit, so to speak. And of course, this goes for Randy as well.

Once Rick has agreed to commit a transaction, he adds that transaction to a special column on his whiteboard. This is the list of committed-to-commit transactions, that is, those transactions to which Rick has agreed to commit, but hasn't yet been told how the rest of the record managers feel about it. If anything goes wrong, this list will come in handy.

Rick and Randy report their answers back to Trix and Tammy, who then discuss the situation together. If Rick and Randy both agreed to commit, then Trix and Tammy issue the actual commit orders to both Rick and Randy. But if either Rick or Randy say they are unwilling to commit, then Trix and Tammy issue rollback orders instead. So even though Rick said he was willing to commit, the final result may be a rollback order. Therefore, Rick should have been ready to commit, but not to do the commit.

Once the record managers are asked if they will commit, any who agree to commit are left in limbo. Let's say Rick agrees to the commit, and Randy declines. Rick has no idea what will happen next. In fact, Rick doesn't know if any other record managers are even involved in this transaction. Randy, on the other hand, knows exactly what is going to happen next. Randy knows that the transaction will only commit if every record manager so agrees, and she knows that she has not agreed. So while Rick has to wait with bated breath for the next word from Trix, Randy can go ahead and start the rollback. Figure 7.9 diagrams this situation.

Figure 7.9 Waiting for the commit.

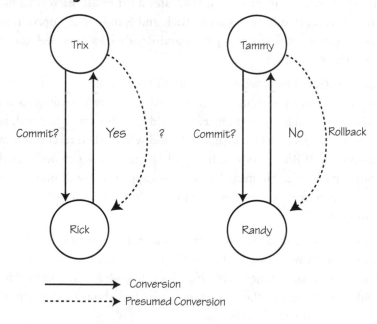

How long does Rick have to wait in this state of limbo? Usually, not long. The society has had a lot of practice, and knows the rote. But occasionally something will go wrong, such as a communications line going down. But whatever it takes, Rick has no choice but to wait. He holds onto his locks, and make no changes that would prevent him from going through with the commit, should the order come down from Trix.

There are other things that can go wrong with this system, and Corollary 5 (No Excuses) says that all must be dealt with. For example, Rick can die. Any time a record manager dies, another is sent in to take his or her place, but this can take a while.

Suppose Rick bites the big one in the middle of a transaction, but before he has been asked if he is willing to commit. This is not a big problem. As soon as the society of transaction managers realizes Rick has departed, they can collectively roll back any transactions in which he was involved.

Suppose Rick dies after he has agreed to commit, but before he got the final word on the outcome of the transaction. Now Rick Junior comes on board. He needs to check Rick's whiteboard, in particular, the list of committed-to-commit transactions. Rick Junior will check with the society of transaction managers to find out what the outcome of those transactions was, and process them accordingly.

The relationship between the record manager gnomes and the society of transaction managers is critical in ensuring compliance with the first law. Without this relationship, we would have transactions spanning record managers with some record managers committing, and others rolling back. One nice thing about this relationship is that it is a straightforward extension of what record managers already do: commit and roll back.

Multi-Room Locking

Earlier we discussed how deadlocks are handled when they occur in a single room. Deadlocks within a room are the responsibility of the record manager, say Rick, in that room. Rick is responsible for periodically checking to see who is waiting on whom, and noticing if any of those waiting are caught in a mutual deadlock. When Rick finds a group of such transactions, he chooses a sacrificial victim who is flushed for the general good of society.

How does this work in a multi-room environment? Let's say Rick is managing flight records and Randy is managing customer records. Anne starts a new transaction that results in a read request to Rick for Flight 1013 and an update request to Randy for Customer 007. Then Andrew starts a transaction that results in an update request to Rick for Flight 1013 and read request to Randy for Customer 007. Let's assume that Rick and Randy receive these requests in the following order.

1. Rick gets the Flight 1013 read request from Anne. He places a green sticker on the Flight 1013 card.

2. Randy gets the Customer 007 read request from Andy. He places a green sticker on the Customer 007 card.

3. Rick gets the Flight 1013 update request from Andy. Rick can't place Andy's red sticker on the card, because Anne has a green sticker on the card. So he places Andy on his blocked list, and Andy becomes blocked.

4. Randy gets the Customer 007 update request from Anne, who isn't blocked. But Randy can't place Anne's red sticker on the card, because Andy has a green sticker on the card. So Randy places Anne on his blocked list, and Anne becomes blocked.

At this point, Andy is blocked by Anne, and Anne is blocked by Andy. This is shown in Figure 7.10.

So Andrew can't go any further until Anne finishes her transaction. And Anne can't go any further until Andrew finishes his transaction. Deadlock!

The problem is that neither Rick nor Randy know what is happening in the other's room. For that matter, neither has any way of knowing that anybody else is even involved in the transaction. If Rick and Randy both diagram the wait states of Anne and Andrew, they will get the two diagrams shown in Figure 7.11. Neither of these diagrams shows the cyclic path that is symptomatic of a deadlock.

Now if somebody could take a higher-level look at the locks, they would see a different picture. They would see the diagram shown in Figure 7.12, which clearly shows a deadlock. But who is going to take this higher-level view?

If you have been following along with the architectural ideas discussed in this book, you will have no trouble answering this question. "Time for a new gnome type," you will answer. Unfortunately, you will be wrong.

Figure 7.10 Multi-room deadlock.

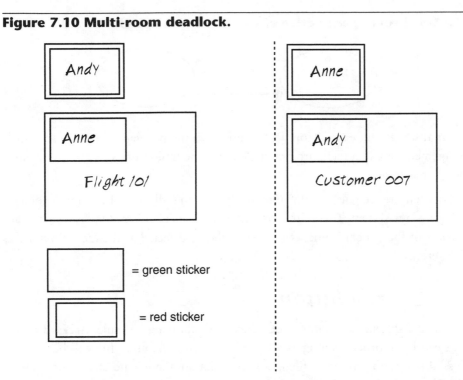

Creating a gnome that can perform multi-room lock management is much more difficult than creating a gnome that can perform multi-room transaction management. One of the biggest problems is performance. The speed with which one can add, delete, or change a lock is absolutely critical to the overall performance of the system. It is several orders of magnitude more critical than the speed of negotiating multi-room commits, for example. A single transaction may manipulate hundreds or even thousands of locks. There is no way the system could survive the overhead of record managers having to communicate remotely with lock managers, and lock managers having their little tête-à-têtes every time a lock needs changing.

Figure 7.11 Single-room perspective of multi-room deadlock.

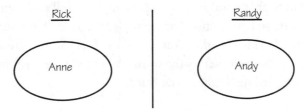

7.12 Multi-room perspective of multi-room deadlock.

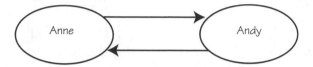

So although there are theoretical solutions to the problem of multi-room lock management, none of them are practical, given the limitations of currently available gnome systems.

So what are we going to do? Obviously we can't allow multi-room deadlocks to clog up our system. There are two answers to this problem. One is directed at the users of the system (Anne, et al.). The other is directed at the record managers (Rick, et al.).

The User Solution

Users of the system can eliminate deadlocks by following one rule: Access files in an agreed-upon order. As long as all users agree that the flight file will be accessed before the customer file in any transaction, there is no chance of deadlock. This is the bottom line of this section. For the rest of this section, I will try to show why this is true. Those of you who are impatient are welcome to skip to the next section.

We can prove this in two ways. One, by exhaustingly listing all possibilities for two transactions, each of which reads a record in one file and updates a record in another. This is done in the table in Figure 7.13. The first row in the table represents Anne reading the flight record. The second row represents Anne updating the customer record. The third row represents Andy reading the customer record. And the fourth row represents Andy reading the flight record.

The numeric value indicates the order that that particular event occurred in the sequence. There are a total of four events, and the full table shows every possible ordering of these four events. For example, the seventh numeric column reads 4, 1, 2, and 3. This says that Anne read the flight information as the fourth event and updated the customer as the third. Andy read the customer as the second event and updated the flight as the third.

Figure 7.13 Exhaustive deadlock analysis.

```
--------------------+--------------------------
Anne read    flight   + 111111 434232 342423 223344
Anne update  customer + 223344 111111 434232 342423
Andy read    customer + 342423 223344 111111 434232
Andy update  flight   + 434232 342423 223344 111111
                      + --D-D- --D-D- --D-D- --D-D-
```

The final row shows which columns result in a deadlock. You can walk through any column with a "D" at the end to verify that it does indeed result in a deadlock.

If you study the deadlock columns, you will notice every one of them violates the rule about each transaction following the same order. Column 3, for example, has Anne accessing first flight, then customer, but Andy accessing first customer, then flight.

This is not to say that every violation of the deadlock rule will result in an actual deadlock. But it is true that every obedience of the deadlock rule will avoid deadlocks. And when it comes to multi-room transactions, avoidance of deadlocks is the name of the game.

We can also try generating enthusiasm for the deadlock rule through a less exhaustive (maybe) and more logical (maybe) analysis. Consider two transactions, transaction 1 and 2, racing to update record A. One of them will get to the record first. That transaction will place either a read or an update lock on the record.

Let's say the first transaction places a read lock on record A. The second transaction reaching it will also attempt to place a read lock or a write lock. If it places a read lock on the record, then neither transaction is blocked. Then we follow this same analysis for record B. On the other hand, if the second transaction tries to place a write lock on that first record, then it becomes blocked. Since the second transaction is blocked, it cannot do anything to block the first transaction. Since the first transaction cannot be blocked, it will eventually complete the transaction, at which time the second transaction can place the update lock on record A and continue normally. Therefore, there is no possibility of a deadlock.

On the other hand, let's say the first transaction places a write lock on record A. Then the second transaction is blocked regardless of what it wants to do. And since the second transaction is blocked, it can't do anything to block the first transaction, which must therefore continue, and eventually allow the second transaction to do its work.

So users can avoid deadlocks by following an agreed-upon path for table access.

The Record Manager Solution

The user solution works fine, as long as users cooperate. But users are known to be a bit feeble-minded. What happens if a user ignores the rule and causes a deadlock? How can the record manager (Rick) figure out that something has gone amiss, if he is unable to examine locks in other rooms?

Although Rick can't tell directly that one of his transactions is involved in a deadlock, he can be on the lookout for the symptoms of a deadlock. The main symptom of a deadlock is a transaction that is going nowhere fast. If Rick notices that a particular transaction is making no progress after some arbitrary period of time, he can decide that the transaction is probably deadlocked, and terminate it after duly notifying Trix of his decision. If he's wrong, then oh well . . . that's life. That's just one of the risks you take when using a record manager. Andy will tell the customer there was a "system glitch," which is the technical term for an unanticipated rollback. Then Andy will start the sale from the beginning. His customer may be a little annoyed, but so what? She is young. She will get over it.

MDCA

It's time to leave the wonderful world of gnomes and return to the much more boring world of the Microsoft Distributed Component Architecture. How are these two worlds related?

Microsoft's goal with the MDCA is to make Microsoft operating systems the platform of choice for running distributed commerce applications. We have talked about some of the pieces to this puzzle. Java is providing the component-building technology. COM/DCOM is providing the distribution and language independence. The Microsoft Transaction Server provides scalability through component object pools. We have also talked about some general ideas of object persistence, and how basic file systems can be used to give the illusion of perpetuity.

File systems are fine for many simple data management problems. But when we are talking serious distributed commerce, we are talking about massive data spread out over networks of machines, with guaranteed reliability, high-speed multiuser access, and distributed transaction support. This is far beyond the capability of any file system. For this we need a serious database system and a serious distributed transaction system.

Microsoft's premier offering in the serious database department is SQLServer. Microsoft's only offering in the serious distributed transaction department is Microsoft Distributed Transaction Coordinator, also known as MS-DTC, part of the Microsoft Transaction Server, and now part of SQLServer.

We have already seen one of the functions of the Microsoft Transaction Server. This is to provide component object pooling, a prerequisite for efficient three-tier architectures. We will talk more about three-tier architectures later, and we discussed object pooling in the last chapter.

In the rest of this chapter we are going to discuss the Microsoft distributed data access strategy. This strategy includes three related technologies: the distributed transaction support of MS-DTC, the database capability of SQLServer, and the data model presented by Active Data Objects (ADO).

If you study the Microsoft data access strategy, you will find it very confusing. Microsoft supports many database products, both those made by Microsoft and those made by competitors. Microsoft defines many data models for accessing databases. A full perspective on this picture would include VBSQL, ODBC API, DAO, RDO, and ADO on the data model side, and Jet, SQLServer, Oracle, Sybase, and ISAM files on the database side.

I have tried to simplify this whole story by looking at the preferred Microsoft solution for building large distributed commerce systems over the next few years. In my opinion, this means one distributed transactional model (MS-DTC), one database (SQLServer), and one data access model (ADO, or Active Data Objects). Although there are dozens of combinations that Microsoft will support to varying degrees, this is the combination that I believe will be stressed, and the one that will get the most attention from Microsoft in our lifetimes (in a field where "lifetimes" are measured in months).

The weakest link in this whole equation is the data access model. ADO is not yet available for Java, and is still unproved on other platforms. At the very least, I would expect a name change, as Microsoft shies away from words like "Active," which seem indicative of the increasingly quaint ActiveX technology and less and less relevant to the new worlds Microsoft is striving to conquer.

The Three Layers of Data Access

Figure 7.14 shows the three layers of the Microsoft data access strategy.

At the lowest level of the data access strategy is a system for accessing data, guaranteeing transactional stability (or the first rule of commerce) on a single machine, and coordinating as efficiently as possible the conflicting demands of different users. This level corresponds to the record manager gnomes. It is the database and, in the preferred Microsoft solution, the database is SQLServer.

At the next level is the ability to coordinate transactions across machines (the high-tech equivalent of a gnome's room), and even across different databases. We call a transaction that spans machines a *distributed* transaction, and the

Figure 7.14 The three layers of the Microsoft data access strategy.

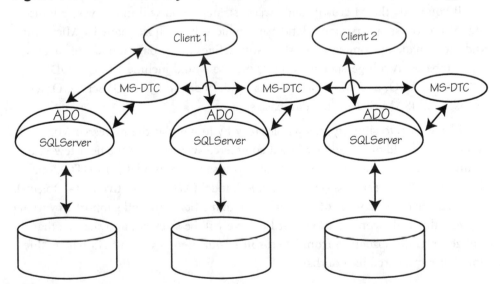

Microsoft technology that is able to coordinate distributed transactions is the MS-DTC. The level corresponds to the society of transaction manager gnomes.

At the client level is the data model. This is the way data is presented to clients. In the gnome's world, this corresponds to the language ticket agents used to read and update records. The Microsoft preferred data model is ADO.

In the context of data access, the word *client* does not refer to the Visual Basic client of a component, but rather the client of the data access technologies. In most cases this client is actually going to be the Java implementation of a business component. Visual Basic clients rarely access data directly. Instead, they access business component objects that make use of data. Figure 7.15 shows the typical relationship between the Visual Basic client, the business object, and the data access layers.

Relational Databases

Let's start with a close look at the lowest level of the Microsoft distributed data access strategy, the database level, *SQLServer*.

SQLServer is named after SQL (usually pronounced either "sequel" or just "SQL"). SQL stands for Structured Query Language, a language developed orig-

Figure 7.15 Clients, objects, and data access.

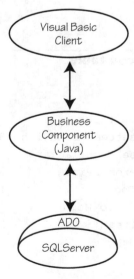

inally by IBM. It was intended to be an easy-to-use language for accessing relational databases.

The concept of a relational database was originally developed by E. F. Codd, then of IBM. He published his ideas in a landmark paper titled "A Relational Model for Data for Large Shared Data Banks" in 1970. This paper has since become one of the most heavily cited papers in computer science. Ironically, even though IBM invented relational databases, it took IBM more than 20 years to come out with a relational database product, lagging far behind Oracle and Sybase. Some things, I guess, never change.

So what is a relational database? It is a database that models data as tables. A table consists of both columns and rows. The columns in a table define the type of data being stored. They are sometimes described as *fields*. The rows are groupings of related data. They are sometimes described as *records*.

As I am writing this, I am sitting in the food court of the Lakeline Mall in Austin, Texas. There are nine food booths around me. Figure 7.16 shows an example of a table that describes just a few of the delectable offerings within my reach.

The table in Figure 7.16 has four columns. Typically, the number of columns doesn't change, or at least it doesn't change very often. The table also has seven rows. The number of rows does change, as food booths open or close, or discover new and improved technologies for loading food with grease.

Figure 7.16 Lakeline Mall food table.

Restaurant	Item	Cost	Fat_Level
Philly Grill	French Fries	1.25	High
Philly Grill	Cheesesteak Sandwich	3.99	Very High
Jalapeno's	Cheese Enchiladas	3.99	High
Villa Pizza	Pepperoni Pizza	3.19	Very High
Hot Dog On A Stick	Hot Dog	1.60	High
Panda Express	Veggie Lo Mein	2.79	Medium High
Dippin' Dots	Ice Cream	2.25	High

Relational databases have operations that allow one to manipulate tables. Logically, these operations allow one to create new tables from old tables.

Once such command allows me to select a subset of the rows in a table. For example, if I wanted a table showing me all of the healthy food available at the mall, I would look for only those rows describing menu items whose fat level is "Low." It would be a very short list. The SQL statement for this is "select * from Lakeline where Fat_Level = "Low"."

I can also eliminate columns in which I have no interest. Let's say it's my birthday, and I don't care about fat or cost today. I can show just the restaurants and the items with this SQL statement: "select Restaurant, Item from Lakeline". This statement will show the table in Figure 7.17.

When a query returns multiple identical rows, the multiple rows are eliminated from the results. So if I wanted to look at the range of healthy food available at Lakeline Mall, I could use this command: "Select Fat_Level from Lakeline". The result is shown in Figure 7.18.

I can also combine two or more tables. Let's say I have another table, shown in Figure 7.19, given to me by my rather humorless doctor.

This new table, shown in Figure 7.19, and the original Lakeline Food table have a column in common. This column is Fat_Level. Relational databases allow me to form queries that require linking two or more tables together. The linkage is shown in Figure 7.20. I can show the restaurants, menu items, and health ratings with this command: "Select Restaurant, Item, Frequency from Lakeline,

---

Figure 7.17 Selected columns of Lakeline Mall food table.

```
Restaurant              Item
----------              ----
Philly Grill            French Fries
Philly Grill            Cheesesteak Sandwich
Jalapeno's              Cheese Enchiladas
Villa Pizza             Pepperoni Pizza
Hot Dog On A Stick      Hot Dog
Panda Express           Veggie Lo Mein
Dippin' Dots            Ice Cream
```

Figure 7.18 Health range at Lakeline Mall.

```
Fat_Level
---------
High
Very High
Medium High
```

Guidelines where Lakeline.Fat_Level = Guidelines.Fat_Level". The result of this query is shown in Figure 7.21.

We can also add new rows to tables. So when the new culinary Mecca, Chick-FilA, opens up selling deep fried chicken wings for only $4.99 a bucket, I am ready for them with this statement: Insert into Lakeline ("Chick-FilA", "Wings", 4.99, "Very Very High").

And I can also delete data from tables. So when the only remotely healthy food available is pulled from the menu, I can chronicle its demise with this obituary: Delete from Lakeline * where Item = "Veggie Lo Mein".

This gives you a quick introduction to relational database theory, the basics of the SQL programming language, and a brief message from your doctor.

SQLServer

Microsoft has designed SQLServer to be much more than a relational database. They have designed it to be highly competitive for distributed commerce applications. Microsoft's goal is to make SQLServer the database of choice for distrib-

Figure 7.19 Health guidelines.

Fat_Level	Health_Guideline	Frequency
Low	Excellent	Very Often
Medium	Good	Often
Medium High	Bad	As Little As Possible
High	Very Bad	Never
Very High	Very Very Bad	Less Than Never

Figure 7.20 Linkage between Lakeline and health.

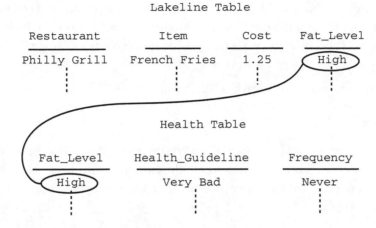

uted commerce applications. To do this, they have focused on these three areas, the same three areas on which they have focused at all levels of the MDCA:

1. Incorporating the best features of their competitors.

2. Pricing the product below the competition.

3. Designing the product to run on hardware platforms that cost a fraction of the cost of their competitors' platforms.

Among the more important features Microsoft has incorporated into SQLServer are cursors, clustering, indexing, efficient locking, stored procedures, and triggers. None of these technologies were invented by Microsoft. But keep in

Figure 7.21 How often Lakeline's foods can be safely eaten.

Restaurant	Item	Frequency
Philly Grill	French Fries	Never
Philly Grill	Cheesesteak Sandwich	Less Than Never
Jalapeno's	Cheese Enchiladas	Never
Villa Pizza	Pepperoni Pizza	Less Than Never
Hot Dog On A Stick	Hot Dog	Never
Panda Express	Veggie Lo Mein	As Little As Possible
Dippin' Dots	Ice Cream	Never

mind that the finance community that is developing these distributed commerce applications is not particularly interested in innovation. It wants to use technology that is well established. Microsoft has a huge job ahead convincing this conservative community to make the switch from mainframes to desktops. Its best hope is to show that the technology is exactly what they have been using all along. The only thing that has changed is the cost.

Let's take a brief look at each of these features.

Cursors

Cursors are how one programmatically navigates through a collection of records in a database. A cursor is used to indicate the current record in the collection, and commands are provided that allow one to move the cursor forward, backward, or to specific records.

Clustering

Ultimately, records are stored on a disk drive. A disk drive is a mechanical device designed to read magnetic disks. Inside the disk drive, the disk is spinning. A disk takes up physical space. When a disk drive reads a record from the disk, it must first physically move its read/write head to the location at which the record is stored. When a disk drive reads two records from the disk, it must first physically move the read/write head first to the first location and then to the second location.

The amount of time it takes to move the read/write head is the single most important determinant for the overall time it will take to read records. If the second of two records is located physically far away from the first, then there will be a long delay between the time it takes to read the first record and the second, as the read/write head has to mechanically move from one location to the other. If the second record is located physically close to the first, then there will be a very short delay between the time it takes to read the two records. This is shown in Figure 7.22.

A database that supports *clustering* allows an administrator to specify which records should be stored physically close to which other records. The administrator does not get to specify where on the disk these records should be stored (this is a very low-level function controlled by the operating system). But the administrator does get to say where the records should be stored relative to each other.

When clustering is used efficiently, overall system performance can be greatly improved. By locating related records near each other, the administrator can

Figure 7.22 Physical placement of records.

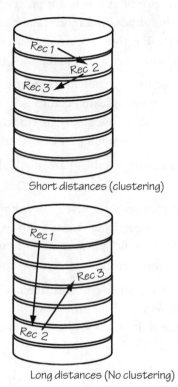

Short distances (clustering)

Long distances (No clustering)

increase the likelihood that when asked for the next read, the read/write heads will require very little, if any, movement.

Clustering is never seen by either Visual Basic clients or the components storing their data in SQLServer. But it does provide the system administrator an important tool in improving overall performance.

Indexing

The reason one uses databases is because one wants to store a lot of data. And if one wants to store data, it stands to reason one will want to find it later. In fact, typically one spends much more time reading existing data than one does creating new data. Even the generation of a new sales record probably requires a lot more looking up than writing. One needs to find the customer information, credit information, past sales information, and inventory information.

When there are a small number of records, one can just read through them all to find the necessary information. But this is not practical when the number of records is numbered in the hundreds, and most databases contain records numbering in the millions at least. For these records, we need very efficient ways of finding the information for which we are looking.

The most efficient way of finding individual records out of large collections is through *indexing*. There are many indexing algorithms, and we won't try to cover any of them here. But they all share the ability to quickly find one record out of a very large collection based on some small part of that record.

Let's assume we have a customer table, part of which is shown in Figure 7.23.

We can set up multiple indexes for a given table. Each index will allow one type of key to be used to find a particular record. For example, we might set up an index for Last_Name. This would allow us to find the record(s) for a given last name very quickly. You can picture the index as shown in Figure 7.24.

Having an index makes an unbelievable difference in lookup time, as long as the lookup we are doing is based on an indexed field. So if we have an index for last name, last-name lookups will go very quickly, but that index won't help if we are trying to find a particular row by first name or phone number.

An administrator can set up any number of indexes for a table, but there is a trade-off. On the one hand, looking up a row on a non-indexed field will be slow to the point of being unworkable. But every index used exacts two prices. First, indexes take up significant disk space, and the more indexes one creates for a table, the more disk space that table will take up. Second, indexes significantly slow down both new record creation and record updates, and the more indexes the table has, the slower these operations become.

Figure 7.23 Customer table.

```
First_Name   Last_Name   Phone_Number   SSN          Balance
----------   ---------   ------------   ---          -------
John         Smith       512-555-1234   064-55-1234  10,000
Jane         Brown       512-555-1235   055-44-5432  9,980
Joan         Oak         512-555-9876   044-55-1212  0
...
```

Figure 7.24 Index and table.

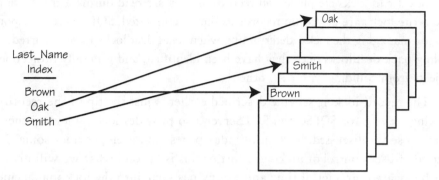

Either too many indexes or too few will slow down the overall system. Too many indexes slow down record creation and update, because these operations need to update both the record table and the index. This is shown in Figure 7.25. Too few will make queries horribly slow.

There is no right answer as to what fields should be indexed. It depends on how the applications will be looking for their data.

The presence or absence of an index has no direct impact on the implementation of a component. There is no programmatic difference between searching for records with or without an index. The impact will be limited to the performance of the system. But for a large collection of records, searching without an index will simply not be practical.

SQLServer has looked very carefully at indexes, and, like all commercial-grade databases, has studied how best to use them when optimizing lookups.

Efficient Locking

Any commercial grade database has to lock records. It is impossible to support multiple applications reading from and writing to the same data without locking. This is a requirement of the first law of commerce and its corollaries.

Figure 7.25 Inserts and updates in indexes.

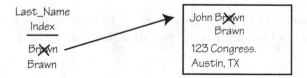

The most basic record-locking scheme is the one described earlier for the gnomes. Read locks are placed on records as they are read during a transaction and write locks are placed on records as they are updated. SQLServer is responsible for managing the locks, determining when local deadlocks have occurred, rolling back deadlocks once they have been identified, and generally protecting objects from colliding with each other.

The record-locking scheme described earlier is just the tip of the record-locking iceberg for SQLServer. SQLServer also provides locking levels other than those we discussed, locking of index pages, and even provides some degree of user control of locking. Most of this is beyond what we will discuss, but be aware that a lot of time and energy has gone into the lock management in this product.

Stored Procedures

SQLServer allows bits of SQL code to be stored in the database itself. These code segments can then be invoked directly from a component. This is primarily for segments of code that need to examine large amounts of data, such as daily sales totals. As we will discuss in the chapter on three-tier architecture, component objects typically do not live on the same machine as the database, just as our gnome record managers do live in the same room as the ticket agents.

Shipping large amounts of data from one machine to another is expensive. It is much cheaper to run the query on the machine where the data lives. But normally the query must run on the machine where the component object is, since this is where the query is coming from. So in order to determine daily sales totals, hundreds of thousands of records would have to be transferred from the machine with the database to the machine with the object component, where they could then be processed to calculate the daily sales total.

Stored procedures allow code to run on the database machine rather than on the component object machine. So rather than having to ship all the records from the machine where they are stored to the machine where they will be analyzed, we can analyze them on the machine where they live, and just ship back the results.

Stored procedures are generally considered to be *de rigueur* for today's database system. And of course, they are part of SQLServer.

Triggers

Triggers are something like stored procedures. They are also code segments that are stored on the database machine. But whereas stored procedures are set off on request by a component object, a trigger is set off by an event within the database itself. Triggers are often used to enforce validity checks. Triggers are the latest craze in databases, and therefore part of SQLServer.

This concludes our tour of SQLServer. The main point is not to exhaustively go through every feature. We have given only the briefest overview of a product that can easily be the subject of a book (and in fact, is the subject of many). The point is that Microsoft wants to own the platform for distributed commerce applications. And one important piece of this puzzle is the data storage component. It is no accident that Microsoft's premier database product is designed to be a perfect match for the needs of this new breed of applications.

ADO

Any database has a model for storing data. For relational databases, and therefore SQLServer, this model is the *relational* model, which is why they are called *relational databases*, in case you were wondering.

The model the database uses for storing data and the model components use for storing data are not necessarily the same. Typically, the database will be wrapped with a layer that is responsible for presenting data in a format designed for simple and efficient use by components. Many wrapping layers can be supported on a given database, and a given wrapping layer can be supported on many different database products. This gives the component some degree of independence of the underlying database.

Microsoft supports many data wrapping layers. The one that appears headed for prominence is the ADO (Active Data Object) layer. As of press time, ADO is not available for Java components, but its release should be very soon. So the code I will discuss in this section will be my conjecture based primarily on C++ interfaces, but the details are not as important as the high-level concepts.

The ADO model is built around a concept called *recordsets*. A record set is a collection of records that can be manipulated as a group. You can read records from the record set, add new records into the record set, update records in the

record set, and delete records from the record set. All of these actions are translated by ADO into operations on the underlying SQLServer database. The relationship between ADO record sets and the underlying SQLServer database is
shown in Figure 7.26.

ADO also provides some relatively advanced capabilities in addition to the
basic read, add, update and delete functions. These include the following:

**Support for independently created record sets, and returning recordsets
from Java procedures.** This allows for the encapsulation of database
activity.

Support for stored procedures with in/out parameters and return values.
This allows efficient use of stored procedure code, which we discussed
earlier

Support for different cursor types. These types include *forward only* cursors, which are optimized for batch processing; *dynamic* cursors, which
can move forward or backward and show updates by other users; *keyset*
cursors, which can move forward or backward but do not show updates
by other users; and *static* cursors, which return a snapshot of the database, primarily for use in generating reports.

Support for database-specific cursors. This allows database vendors to
define their own cursors.

Figure 7.26 Relationship between record sets and database.

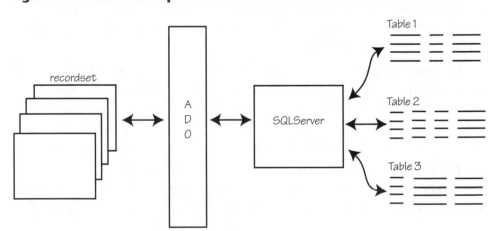

Advanced recordset cache management. This minimizes the amount of data that has to be sent back and forth between the component and the database.

Support for limits on number of returned rows and other query goals. This helps components guard against runaway queries that take much longer, or return much more data than expected.

Support for multiple recordsets returned from stored procedures.

ADO also allows the component to give some hints to the underlying database about what kind of locking is preferred. The locking options are as follows:

ReadOnly. The component promises not to try to update any of the records.

Pessimistic. The database should assume the worst case, and that the application will be editing most of the records.

Optimistic. The database should lock only those records that are specifically updated.

BatchOptimistic. The client will be doing batch updating rather than immediate updating.

The ADO Model

ADO defines seven different objects, which together allow one to access records in the underlying database (in this case, SQLServer). These objects, and their purpose, are these:

Connection. Represents a session with the database.

Error. Contains information about an error resulting from an ADO operation.

Command. Represents a specific command that can be executed against the database, such as an SQL command.

Parameter. Represents parameters needed by specific queries, or the in/out arguments or return values of stored procedures.

Recordset. Represents the set of records, or rows, returned by the last ADO command.

Field. Represents one column of the table.

Property. Represents a dynamic characteristic of an ADO object as defined by a specific database.

One can simplify this whole model by working only with recordsets. In this case, Connection and Command objects are automatically created. We will look only at the methods of recordset, since these are the main methods you will be using as you work with the database. The methods supported by Recordset, and their purpose, are currently these:

AddNew. Create and initialize a new record in the recordset. Various options allow one to specify the value of the new record. This will effectively add a row to a table in the underlying database.

CancelBatch. Used to change your mind about a bunch of updates that were going to be done *en masse*.

CancelUpdate. Used to change your mind about a single new record or record update.

Clone. Create a copy of this recordset, including all of its records.

Close. Close this recordset and free system resources.

Delete. Delete the current record in the recordset.

GetRows. Copies records from a recordset into a two-dimensional array.

Move, MoveFirst, MoveLast, MoveNext, MovePrevious. Various flavors of moving around in the recordset. Returns an EOF indication if the move has exceeded the size of the recordset.

Open. Opens the cursor on the recordset.

Requery. Reissue the original command and refresh the contents of the recordset.

Resync. Similar to Requery, but used to resync a static database.

Supports. Used to query a recordset to see if it can perform some specific functionality. This is in recognition of the fact that not all databases will be able to support all of the ADO capabilities.

Update. Save changes made to the current record.

UpdateBatch. Save changes made to the entire recordset when updating in batch mode.

The recordset object also defines some properties. Properties, in Visual Basic and IDL, are the equivalent of public data in Java. I doubt that the eventual Java implementation of properties will use public data. Most likely, they will use paired set and get methods for each property member. Some of the more useful properties for recordset are listed here:

ActiveConnection. Most useful to get a reference to the ActiveConnection object.

BOF/EOF. BOF indicates that the current record position is before the first record in the recordset; EOF indicates that it is after the last record position.

CursorType. Returns the type of the cursor being used. This is especially helpful if you are using a recordset that you didn't create.

EditMode. Used to determine if records in the recordset have been changed, but not stored to the database.

Filter. Allows you to specify views on various subsets of the full set of records in the recordset.

LockType. Used to declare the lock type, before the recordset has been opened, or to determine the lock type after.

MaxRecords. Used to determine the maximum number of records returned by a query, to avoid runaway queries.

RecordCount. Tells how many records are in the recordset.

Status. Used to determine the status of the current record with respect to bulk updates. Useful to figure out whether or not the record has been updated, and if not, why not.

The Java programmer will use the following steps with ADO:

1. Define an SQL statement that will find the appropriate records.

2. Decide on the locking mechanism.

3. Create a recordset using the defined SQL statement.

4. Move through the recordset, working with one record at a time.

5. Close the recordset.

Again, since the exact Java mappings are still not released, and because ADO in general is undergoing changes, we will have to wait for the next edition of this book for some actual code samples, although we will look at some pseudocode later in this chapter. And perhaps direction will change on the database wrapper of choice. At this point, however, all indications are that ADO is here to stay.

The Distributed Transaction Coordinator

If everybody would act rationally, not go overboard with their data, and organize all of their data on a single machine, there would be no need for the Microsoft Distributed Transaction Coordinator (MS-DTC). But commerce applications have a voracious appetite for data. Servicing the needs of a typical large distributed commerce application with one database on one machine would be like trying to put out a burning building with a water pistol. So if we are going to build these large systems, we need many machines, and we need them coordinated.

We talked about the first law of commerce. We think of a transaction as being a unit of work. It is acceptable that none of the work be done. It is far preferable that *all* of the work be done. But it is totally unacceptable that only part of the work be done. I mustn't be charged for tickets I didn't get. I shouldn't be able to withdraw money without my balance being reduced. I can't buy your pork bellies without your pork going belly up.

The first law of commerce is no less true when the data is spread between two machines than it is when it is neatly packaged in one machine. Just because you choose to store savings accounts on one machine and checking accounts on another is no excuse to forget to credit my deposit if you debited my withdrawal.

But just as Rick, the record managing gnome, has no way of knowing what other record managing gnomes are involved with the agent's work, SQLServer on a single machine has no way to communicate with SQLServers (or other databases) running on other machines. So just as we added the society of transaction managers for our gnomes, we add an overseeing layer to monitor the distributed transactions. This layer is the MS-DTC.

The Transaction Framework

The best way to think of the MS-DTC is as a framework within which different database products can work. The purpose of this framework is distributed transaction support, so that the data involved with a transaction on one machine and one database will not commit unless the data involved with that same transaction on all machines and in all databases commits.

Frameworks are always based on interfaces. A piece of software plugs into a framework by supporting a specific interface. In the case of the MS-DTC, this piece of software is a database product, and the interfaces have to do with negotiating transactional commits. The MS-DTC discusses the commit plans with the databases through these interfaces. At press time for this book, the only database product that supports the MS-DTC transactional interface is SQLServer, but the interface is designed so that any database product that wants to can implement these interfaces.

The idea of having a standard interface for distributed transaction coordinators to communicate with databases is not unique to Microsoft. This idea has been around for a long time. The industry standard interface is called the XA. However, Microsoft has chosen to support its own interface, and leave XA for a future release. By what I can only attribute to an incredible coincidence, SQLServer just happens to support the Microsoft proprietary interface.

The conversation between the MS-DTC and SQLServer is just like the conversation between Trix, the transaction manager, and Rick, the record managing gnome. This conversation is often described as a two-phase commit, because there are two phases to the conversation. In the first phase, the MS-DTC asks the involved databases whether or not they are willing to commit. In the second phase, the MS-DTC tells the databases whether or not they *should* commit.

The algorithm is the same we looked at with the record managers and the transaction society gnomes. All of the databases get to say whether or not they will commit, and if any refuse, then MS-DTC tells all to terminate the transaction. Figure 7.27 shows the two-phase commit protocol with a successful commit, and Figure 7.28 shows the protocol with a rollback.

The component object is unaware of all these conversations. From its perspective, it reads data, updates data, and either commits or rolls back. If it commits, it gets one of two answers back. Either the commit is accepted, or it isn't. Little does the component object know that the decision as to whether the commit is to be accepted involves a consensus decision by a whole series of databases and transaction managers.

Much of the work that goes into the implementation of the MS-DTC and the cooperating databases has to deal with situations that rarely happen. But rarely is too often, when these rare situations may be involving transfers of millions of dollars. Microsoft, if it is to be taken seriously in the high-stakes world of commerce, must make sure these situations never happen.

One such situation is lost communications. A particularly critical period is after a database has said it is willing to commit and before the transaction manager responds with the final outcome. This period normally lasts less than a second, but if something goes wrong, like communications are lost, the transaction manager crashes, or the resource manager crashes, this period of limbo may last a long time.

This state of limbo is the same situation Rick the gnome found himself in with Trix the transaction manager. And like Rick, the database has to wait. It

Figure 7.27 Two-phase commit protocol with commit.

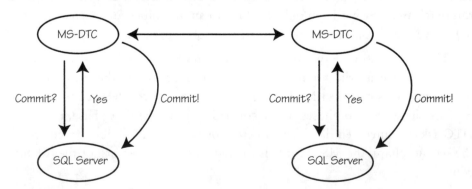

Figure 7.28 Two-phase commit protocol with rollback.

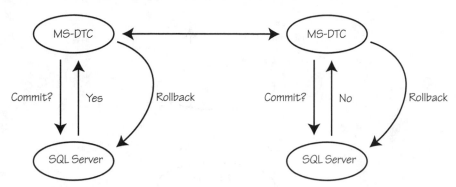

may or may not elect to accept more work, but if it does, it must make sure this work doesn't impede its ability to eventually carry through with the commit, if that is the final decision, or the rollback, if that is the decision. This period of limbo is shown in Figure 7.29.

Resource Managers and Resource Dispensers

MS-DTC doesn't understand much about databases, but it knows how to talk about transactions. And databases that are willing to participate in its conversations, it calls a *resource manager*. The term resource manager effectively means a database that knows how to participate with the MS-DTC in the distributed transaction protocol. A resource manager could be SQLServer or any other database, relational or otherwise, that can participate in the protocol. Being a resource manager in no way commits you to a specific data model, only a specific distributed transaction model.

There is another implicit requirement on resource managers, but one that isn't enforced by MS-DTC. This is the requirement of permanence. The whole point of two-phase commit is to ensure that either every database has permanently stored the data involved in the transaction, or that none of them have. But the database is responsible for figuring out how to store that data, and doing it in a way that allows it to recover from disasters. All the MS-DTC can do is pass around the ID of the transaction needing committing. The database is on its own to fulfill its covenant.

Actually, there is another type of conversation in which MS-DTC can participate. This is with software that manages nonpersistent resources. Such software

---

Figure 7.29 Period of limbo.

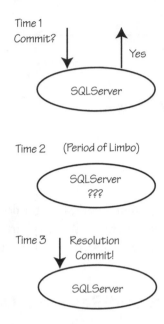

is called a *resource dispenser*. We aren't going to spend a lot of time on resource dispensers here, but we will give a quick overview. All in all, they are much less important than resource managers, the true backbone of the distributed commerce world.

Resource dispensers simplify access to shared resources in a server process. Resource dispensers manage nondurable shared state. They are like resource managers, but without the guarantee of durability. The two that come with the Microsoft Transaction Server are the ODBC Resource Dispenser and the Shared Property Manager.

The ODBC Resource Dispenser (ODBC 3.0 Driver Manager) is responsible for managing pools of database connections for Transaction Server components that are using ODBC interfaces. Pooling of database connections has the same advantages as object pooling, which we discussed in the last chapter. It allows a much larger number of clients to access a given database. The ODBC Resource Dispenser pools database connections and automatically allocates them on an as-needed basis similar to the pooling of objects for clients discussed in the last chapter. When the database connections are no longer needed, they are reclaimed by the ODBC Resource Dispenser.

The Shared Property Manger is used to organize shared data among the different components of an application. It allows reads and updates of the shared data to be done transactionally. In the brokering system, we could use it to maintain a count of the total amount of commissions we have made.

Automatic Transactions

As you are well aware by now, all commerce interactions occur within the context of a transaction. Somebody has to decide which interactions are part of which transactions. There are three possibilities as to who will take this responsibility. The first is the Visual Basic client. The second is the component object itself. The third is the Transaction Server.

Placing the responsibility on the Visual Basic client can be a problem. It places a burden on the client to understand when transactions are needed. If the client gets this wrong, serious and unexpected problems can result.

Placing the responsibility on the component object can also be a problem. The very nature of building software systems out of preexisting components means that component objects don't always know about the transactional context in which they will be used.

In many of these situations, allowing the Transaction Server to start the transactions is the best of all worlds. We can tell the Transaction Server that the component requires a transaction. Then if a transaction is already running when the component starts its method, it will piggyback off of that transaction. If a transaction isn't already running, the Transaction Server will start one on behalf of the component. But in either case, the database access will be guaranteed to be within a transaction.

The capability of the Transaction Server to automatically start a transaction is called an *automatic transaction*. How the Transaction Server should make this decision is stored in the *transaction attribute* for the component package. We discussed component packages in the last chapter.

There are several ways to set the transaction attribute. You can do this either with configuration options within the Transaction Server Explorer, or within the

IDL. However you set the transaction attributes, the possible values are as follows:

Requires a transaction. Methods on the component must execute within the scope of a transaction. If the client doesn't have a transaction, then one is created automatically by the Transaction Server. This is the most common option.

Requires a new transaction. Methods on the component must execute within the scope of their own transaction. When such a component is instantiated, a new transaction is started even if the client did have a transaction. This is used when the component should commit independently of the commit of its client.

Supports transactions. When such a component is instantiated, it inherits the transaction status of its client. This is used for components that don't care whether or not they run within a transaction. If the client wants a transaction, fine. If the client doesn't, that is also fine.

Does not support transactions. When such a component is instantiated, its context is created without a transaction, regardless of the transactional status of its client. This is primarily for the backward compatibility with old components that were developed prior to the availability of transactions.

Components that use only one transactional resource, such as a database, will still have transactional support on that resource even when transactions are not in effect, but will not be able to participate in two-phase commits.

If you choose to define the attribute at component definition time, you do so inside the IDL file. The possible values are defined in the Microsoft include file MtxAttr.h, which includes this segment:

```
#define TRANSACTION_REQUIRED
    custom(TLBATTR_TRANS_REQUIRED,0)
#define TRANSACTION_SUPPORTED
    custom(TLBATTR_TRANS_SUPPORTED,0)
#define TRANSACTION_NOT_SUPPORTED
    custom(TLBATTR_TRANS_NOTSUPP,0)
#define TRANSACTION_REQUIRES_NEW
    custom(TLBATTR_TRANS_REQNEW,0)
```

To set one of these attributes, modify the IDL file to #include the MtxAttr.h file and invoke one of these four macros. The changes we would make to our BrokerHouse definition would be these:

```
#include <MtxAttr.h>
/* ... */
[
    uuid(C414B3D3-DB01-11d0-BAFB-000000000000),
    helpstring("CBrokerHouse Object")
    TRANSACTION_REQUIRED
]
    coclass CBrokerHouse
    {
        [ default ]
        dispinterface IBrokerHouse;
    };
```

Contexts

Objects are instances of components. If the component is defined to be a Transaction Server component, meaning it is run as a Transaction Server package, then instances of that component are Transaction Server objects. Every Transaction Server object has an associated context object, which supports the IObjectContext interface. Any method can find its associated context object through the method GetObjectContext, a static method on the MTx class. Typical Java code to do this looks like:

```
import com.ms.mtx.*;
IObjectContext context;
context = MTx.GetObjectContext();
```

Once you have a reference to the context object, you can invoke any of the IObjectContext methods. The most important include the following:

void DisableCommit(). Says that the transaction associated with this object cannot be committed yet. This is used to create stateful objects, which we have already recommended against.

void EnableCommit(). Used when we want an object to maintain its state for now, but that transactions in which it is participating can be committed. This is also recommended against.

boolean IsSecurityEnabled(). Used to check to see if security has been enabled, which can only be true if the object is running in a server process. We will talk more about security later.

boolean IsCallerInRole(Sting role). Used to determine the role of the client of this method invocation. Roles are described in the security section, but they refer to the group of the client. We might, for example, assign a "Buyer" role to a category of users. The code for PrepareBuyOrder of BrokerHouse could then check to make sure it is being invoked by a client who has been validated as a buyer. The code for this would look like:

```
if (!context.IsCallerInRole("Buyer")) {
    /* Refuse to cooperate */
}
```

This method can only be relied upon when security has been enabled. Therefore, these two methods should be paired, as in

```
if (!context.IsSecurityEnabled() ||
    !context.IsCallerInRole("Buyer")) {
    /* Refuse to cooperate */
}
```

boolean IsInTransaction(). Used to determine if a transaction is active. Methods that think they must work within a transaction context can use this method to determine if the expected transaction has, in fact, been made active.

void SetAbort(). Used to indicate that the transaction associated with this method invocation should abort (or quit) as soon as this method completes. This is often placed in error handling code. We might expect to see this, for example, in a gnome's store method. If the gnome decides that its internal state is not acceptable, it could invoke SetAbort rather than complete the store.

When a method aborts itself, it will automatically abort all objects associated with contexts that share this transaction.

void SetComplete(). Used to indicate that the transaction associated with this method invocation has successfully completed. The object can now be deactivated. If the object started transaction, the Transaction Server will attempt to commit the transaction immediately upon return. If it just piggybacked off of another transaction, then the Transaction Server will wait until the rest of the transaction has completed.

Components may, but do not have to, actively participate in the outcome of transactions in which they are involved. They do so by using the SetComplete or SetAbort methods of their Context Object. We would expect to find this code in the BrokerHouse methods, such as

```
import brokerhouselib.*;
import java.io.*;
import com.ms.mtx.*; // Required for transactions


public class BrokerHouse implements IBrokerHouse,
BrokerHouseInterface
{  /* ... */
   public void prepareBuyOrder(
        String tid, String name, String item, int maxPrice)
   {
      boolean errors;
      // ... (Check for Errors)

      if (errors) Mtx.GetObjectContext().SetAbort();
      else Mtx.GetObjectContext().SetComplete();
   }
}
```

Server Processes

Robert Frost said "Home is the place where, when you have to go there, they have to take you in." A component object might say something similar about a server process. The server process is the place where, when you have to go some place, they have to take you in.

Everybody has to live some place. Component objects must live in a process. A server process is a special process that runs under control of the Transaction Server. A given server process can host many components which, through pooling, can be servicing any number of clients. The Transaction Server determines which objects will be instantiated by a given server process, and how many clients those objects will serve. The actual instantiation is done by the server process.

Changes to Brokering System

How does the material in this chapter impact our brokering system? Obviously, we are going to want to use MS-DTC and SQLServer. How shall we modify our brokering system?

There are many approaches we could take to this project. My own personal feeling is that a large amount of the work we have been doing can now be relegated to the database. So I will completely rewrite the BrokerHouse class, eliminating all of the lower-level classes.

The first thing I will do is to create two tables in the database, one for sellers and one for buyers. They will actually look identical, except for the table name. Some people might just put them in one table with an additional field identifying which rows are sellers and which are buyers. I think it is a bit more straightforward to use two tables, but either approach is acceptable. The tables, with some sample data, are shown in Figure 7.30.

The tables shown in Figure 7.30 are a little naïve in that we are assuming that the name of the employee is unique. If we wanted to be more realistic, we would use something like social security number here, but that is overkill for this example.

Now let's go through the code, discussing the changes. The first few lines are the same. They are:

```
package Broker;
import java.io.*;
import com.ms.mtx.*;
```

Next we define the class. This will not change at all. It is important that it not change, since this is the contract with the Visual Basic programmer, and

Figure 7.30 Buyer and seller tables.

```
Table: Buyer
Employee   Item    Price   NegotiatedPrice   TID   PartnerName
--------   ----    -----   ---------------   ---   -----------
Michael    dog     20                        t1
Roger      cat     10                        t2
Rachael    bird    100                       t3

Table: Seller
Employee   Item    Price   NegotiatedPrice   TID   PartnerName
--------   ----    -----   ---------------   ---   -----------
Emily      dog     10                        t2
Chris      whale   1000                      t3
John       VW bug  250                       t3
```

we definitely want to make these changes without affecting any Visual Basic code.

```
public class BrokerHouse implements
      IBrokerHouse, BrokerHouseInterface, IObjectControl
{
```

The old BrokerHouse code made use of a private variable for tracking the broker. We are going to eliminate the broker, so we can delete the next line:

```
private IMoniker brokerM;
```

The first method is private, and is no longer needed. Out it goes:

```
private BrokerInterface getBroker()
{
    BrokerInterface broker;

    broker = (BrokerInterface)
    brokerM.BindToObject();
    return broker;
}
```

The next three methods are use by the Transaction Server for pooling. They were discussed in the last chapter, and they remain as is:

```
public boolean CanBePooled()
```

```
{
    return true;
}
public void Activate()
{
}
public void Deactivate()
{
}
```

The next method is the constructor. It is no longer needed. Bye!

```
public BrokerHouse()
{
    String monikerString = "Broker:broker.dat";
    brokerM = FileMoniker.MkParseDisplayName(monikerString);
}
```

The next method, prepareBuyOrder, actually serves two functions. First, it prepares a buyer record. Second, it checks to see if any trading partners can be matched (as a side effect of invoking registerBuyer). The original version looked like this:

```
public void prepareBuyOrder(String tid, String name,
    String item, int maxPrice)
{
    BrokerInterface myBroker = getBroker();
    EmployeeInterface agent = myBroker.getEmployee();

    agent.employee(name);
    agent.item(item);
    agent.price(maxPrice);
    agent.terminalID(tid);

    agent.Save();
    myBroker.registerBuyer((PersistentGnomeInterface) agent);
    myBroker.Save();
    MTx.GetObjectContext().SetComplete();
}
```

The new version will do the equivalent work by updating records in the database. We will be using pseudocode to show the ADO manipulation.

```
public void prepareBuyOrder(String tid, String name,
     String item, int maxPrice)
{
    sqlStatement = select * from buyers where PartnerName = "";
    rs = instantiate new recordset;
    open recordset with sqlStatement;

    add new record where Employee = name,
         Item = item, Price = maxPrice, TID = tid;
    update recordset;
    close recordset;
    checkForMatches();
    MTx.GetObjectContext().SetComplete();
}
```

We will add a new private method to do the match check, since this will need to be invoked from two places:

```
private void checkForMatches()
{
    sqlStatement = select * from buyers, sellers where
         Buyer.PartnerName = "" and
         Seller.PartnerName = "" and
         Buyer.Item = Seller.Item and
         Buyer.Price >= Seller.Price

    for each record in recordset {
         Buyer.PartnerName = Seller.Employee
         Seller.PartnerName = Buyer.Employee
         Buyer.NegotiatedPrice =
               (Buyer.Price + Seller.Price) / 2
         Seller.NegotiatedPrice =
               (Buyer.Price + Seller.Price) /2
    }

}
```

The old prepareSellOrder looked similar to the old prepareBuyOrder:

```
public void prepareSellOrder(
    String tid, String name, String item, int minPrice)
{
    BrokerInterface myBroker = getBroker();
    EmployeeInterface agent= myBroker.getEmployee ();

    agent.employee(name);
    agent.item(item);
    agent.price(minPrice);
    agent.terminalID(tid);

    agent.Save();
    myBroker.registerSeller((PersistentGnomeInterface) agent);
    myBroker.Save();
    MTx.GetObjectContext().SetComplete();
}
}
```

The new one will look similar to the new prepareBuyOrder:

```
public void prepareBuyOrder(String tid, String name,
    String item, int maxPrice)
{
    sqlStatement = select * from buyers where PartnerName = "";
    rs = instantiate new recordset;
    open recordset with sqlStatement;

    add new record where Employee = name,
        Item = item, Price = maxPrice, TID = tid;
    update recordset;
    close recordset;
    checkForMatches();
    MTx.GetObjectContext().SetComplete();
}
```

The next method actually has two purposes. The first is to prepare text showing any sellers that correspond to this terminal ID. The second is to remove the sellers, once displayed, from the list of sellers that still need to be maintained. They have been assigned a trading partner, and the result has been displayed. So they should become history. We can tell if they have been assigned a trading partner by whether they have been given a negotiated price. The original version of this method looked like this:

```
public String getSellerText(String tid)
{
    String value;
    BrokerInterface myBroker = getBroker();
    GnomeVector v = myBroker.getSells(tid);
    myBroker.Save();
    value = getGnomeVectorString(v);
    MTx.GetObjectContext().SetComplete();
    return value;
}
```

The new version will look like this:

```
public String getSellerText(String tid)
{
    String value = "";
    sqlStatement = select * from Seller
        where TID = tid and partnerName <> "";
    open recordset with sqlStatement;
    for each record in recordset {
        concatonate value with new record;
        delete record;
        update recordset;
    }
    MTx.GetObjectContext().SetComplete();
    return value;
}
```

The getBuyerText goes through a similar metamorphosis:

```
public String getBuyerText(String tid)
{
    String value = "";
    sqlStatement = select * from Buyer
        where TID = tid and partnerName <> "";
    open recordset with sqlStatement;
    for each record in recordset {
        concatonate value with new record;
```

```
    delete record;
    update recordset;
}
MTx.GetObjectContext().SetComplete();
return value;
```

}

The next method is responsible for checking to see if there are any matched buyers and sellers waiting to be displayed at this terminal. The original version was:

```
public int prepareCheckStatus(String tid)
{
    int value = 0;
    BrokerInterface myBroker = getBroker();
    if (myBroker.anyBuys(tid)) value = 1;
    if (myBroker.anySells(tid)) value = 1;
    MTx.GetObjectContext().SetComplete();
    return value;
}
```

The new version is:

```
public int prepareCheckStatus(String tid)
{
    int value = 0;
    sqlStatement = select * from Buyers
        where TID = tid and partnerName <> "";
    open recordset with sqlStatement;
    if RecordCount > 1 return 1;

    sqlStatement = select * from Buyers
        where TID = tid and partnerName <> "";
    reopen recordset with sqlStatement;
    if RecordCount > 1 return 1;

}
```

The remaining methods are private, and no longer needed.

Costs and Benefits

We have made a lot of changes in the BrokerHouse and, in many ways, the new code is more complicated than the old code. But the new code has many advantages, which all in all, far outweigh the costs of the change and the increase in complexity.

First of all, there is much less of the new code. Although the BrokerHouse itself has not decreased in size, we have lost all of the lower-level classes. Although in most complex systems, we will still use lower-level Java classes (and we could have considered doing so here), it will still be true that the amount of code can be considerably lessened.

The new code is much more robust. It is built on top of a highly reliable database that understands the meaning of commitment. You can be sure that once you successfully return from one of the BrokerHouse methods, the data updates will never be lost.

The new code handles multiuser contention. Our old code could easily fail with multiple-user collisions on the updates. For example, two people could both attempt to buy a dog from the same person, and if the timing is right, one would overwrite the changes made by the other. Our new system uses automatic record locking to absolutely positively eliminate any chance of multiuser collisions.

The new code has more flexibility as to data placement. We could have both buyers and sellers in one database, or spread out over several. Because we are using the MS-DTC, our transactions can span as many databases and machines as we like.

The new code is relatively independent of the underlying database. It uses ADO for data access, which is compatible with SQLServer, other relational databases, and even databases using completely different data access models.

The new code handles many more records. Our old code would peak out at a few hundred pending deals. With appropriate index use, our new code could easily handle millions of pending deals. For these volumes of data, we would add indexes on the following fields:

Terminal ID, so that we can quickly find records in which our terminal is interested.

Item, because this is the field used to match buyers and sellers.

The Item Cost is a debatable field for indexing. If we often find ourselves with thousands of potential matches based on compatible items and doing large-scale filtering based on cost, then an index on this field might improve performance. This would be one of those many judgment calls based on an *a posteriori* analysis of the performance and the intuition of the database administrator.

Summary

To summarize this chapter, let's look again at the various players in this drama, and the responsibilities of each.

Application components are like the BrokerHouse. They model the activity of a business. They implement business rules and coordinate the data representing the state of the business. Some of these update transactional databases, and often more than one transactional database. When they update more than one transactional database, they must use the Microsoft Distributed Transaction Coordinator (MS-DTC) to guarantee that transactions spanning databases are coordinated.

The Microsoft Transaction Server has its fingers in many pies. In the last chapter, we discussed its role in object pooling. Later we will see what it has to offer in security and thread management. Here it has responsibility for managing context objects and server processes.

The Microsoft Distributed Transaction Coordinator (MS-DTC) coordinates transactions spanning resource managers and even machines, ensuring that the rules of commerce are followed. It implements the two-phase commit protocol, which offers multiple resource managers the opportunity to participate in a consensus decision on commits.

A resource manager is a database that knows how to participate in the two-phase commit protocol; specifically, the two-phase commit protocol as defined by Microsoft. Resource managers are responsible for knowing how to commit and roll back data as requested during the final phase of the two-phase commit protocol.

Databases and transactions are absolute requirements for distributed commerce applications. Microsoft has designed products that run on small, cheap, NT machines that compete feature for feature with their counterpart products running on large, expensive machines. Microsoft has filled the trough with water and shown the horses the way. Now the question is, will they drink?

MULTI-TIER ARCHITECTURE

8

I often work in the mall, as I am right now. My son seems to have an endless fascination for the artificial air, sounds, and food that make up the mall experience. So he goes off and plays videogames. And I sit in the food court, and write. I have noticed that I am not the only one who uses the food court of the Lakeline Mall as an auxiliary office. I often see people with cell phones, writing pads, and technical papers, ready to hunker down until either they are called for dinner or their kids' quarters run out—whichever happens first.

However, I suspect that my portable office is more unusual than most. Not only do I have my cell phone, writing pads, and technical papers, but I also have with me an industrial-strength database, a distributed transaction coordinator, and an entire distributed object environment, not to mention enough disk space to automate a small city. You might say that I epitomize Mark Twain's advice: "Put all your eggs in the one basket and—WATCH THAT BASKET."

Most people seem to get by with baskets quite a bit smaller than mine. In fact, most of these baskets are able to run little more than a Web browser and a game of solitaire. They are certainly not capable of running the equivalent of a metropolitan computer department on a laptop. The computers in most of the mall stores, for example, are able to do little more than display and total customer purchases. Yet every purchase is tied into some fairly large business systems and underlying databases. How do they do this?

Today, these itsy bitsy computers work by delegating the real work to large mainframe computers. They do this through what is known as *multi-tier architectures*. Today, only mainframe computers have the tools necessary to support large, multi-tier applications. These mainframe computers do not run Microsoft software. Microsoft is not happy about this.

In this chapter, we are going to explore multi-tier architectures, discuss the technologies Microsoft is offering to compete with the big boys, and describe how this technology integrates with the rest of the Microsoft component strategy.

History

Most large, business-oriented applications have a lot of code. This code can functionally be divided into three areas: the user interface, the business logic, and the data management. The user interface is responsible for getting information from and displaying information to a human being. The business logic is responsible for the algorithmic expertise of running a particular business. The data management is responsible for reliably storing data, and sorting out and managing conflicting access demands to that data. Figure 8.1 shows a typical commerce-oriented application.

Once upon a time, a long, long time ago, there were no personal computers or workstations. There were only very big mainframes and very dumb terminals. Terminals could do little more than display characters. All work of significance was done on the mainframes. The mainframe was responsible for deciding how to get information to and from the user, how to process the business algorithms, and how to manage data.

We could describe these systems as a *single-tier architecture*. It is single tier because there is only one monster computer involved. The single-tier architecture for these systems is shown in Figure 8.2.

From an end-user perspective, single-tier user interfaces had two significant problems. First, they were sluggish. Information transfer rates between computers

Figure 8.1 Typical commerce-oriented application.

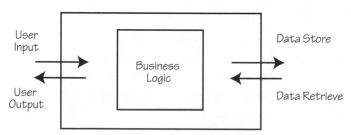

Figure 8.2 Single-tier architecture.

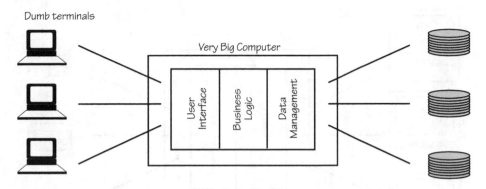

and terminals were very slow, and one could literally watch the characters individually appear on the terminal. The second problem with single-tier user interfaces was that they were ugly. Terminals were very limited in how they could display information, and nobody wanted to waste valuable computer cycles on complex interfaces anyway.

Slowly, terminals became more intelligent. They could do more sophisticated displays, and they could take over some of the work involved with creating and processing the user interface. Eventually these terminals transformed into personal computers. These small computers were dedicated to presenting a user interface to a single human being.

This new architecture was called a *two-tier architecture*. It is called two-tier because two types of computers are involved. Small computers are used for running the user interface, and the large mainframes are responsible for the business logic and managing the data. The two-tier architecture is shown in Figure 8.3.

In the two-tier architecture, the user interface computer would collect significant blocks of information from the human being, and send that information en masse to the mainframe. The mainframe would then process that information, and eventually send back new data or results code to the user interface computer, which would then decide how best to show that information to the human being.

The small user interface computers in the two-tier architecture had two important advantages in their ability to work with humans. First, since they were

Figure 8.3 Two-tier architecture.

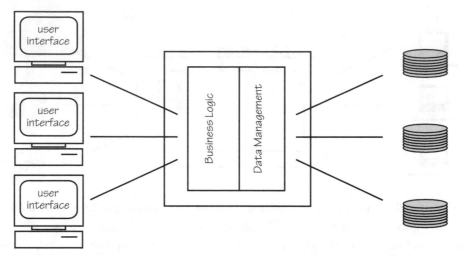

dedicated to a single user, nobody treated their CPU cycles as a corporate resource. This allowed unparalleled power to be dedicated to figuring out how to present information in the most ergonomic way possible. Second, the data transfer rate between the main CPU and the monitor was unbelievably fast, so fast that whole screens of complex information could be updated instantaneously.

The two-tier architecture also had an important effect on the computer industry. IBM, which dominated the market for the one-tier architecture, understood nothing about small computers and had no vision for their use. This opened up the first major opportunity for new companies to find a niche in the computer market. One person who did understand small computers, and had a vision for the impact they could have, was Bill Gates. But you probably already know that story.

As time went on, the user interface computers became more and more powerful. Eventually, people discovered they could move more and more of the business logic from the mainframe to these computers. The mainframes were perceived more as data servers to the real workstations supporting individual people. This architecture was called the *client/server architecture*. The workstations were the clients. The mainframes were the servers. The client/server architecture is shown in Figure 8.4.

Figure 8.4 Client/server architecture.

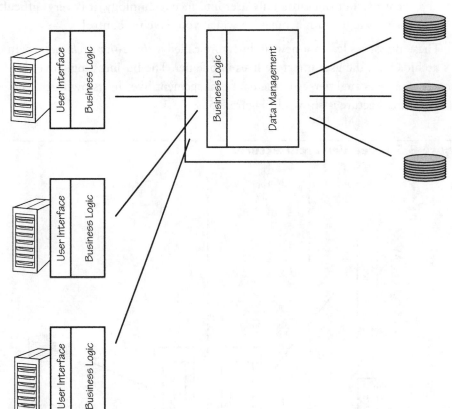

The client/server architecture worked as long as business logic was kept relatively simple and the business algorithms changed relatively infrequently. But soon, business systems got more complicated. Business pressures required the ability to update algorithms quickly.

Traditional client/server architectures had two problems. First, the business logic was getting so complex that it was difficult to contain on small workstations. Second, client systems were too difficult to update as business algorithms required frequent adaptation.

Recently, there has been an new pressure on client/server architectures. More and more, we are seeing the Internet included in commerce applications. When the client is working with an application through the Internet, one has to assume that the client machine includes only user interface technology. It is very difficult to place business logic on machines on which you have no control.

These pressures led to a new architecture called a *three-tier architecture*. In this architecture, the user interface lives in one tier. The business logic lives in another one dedicated tier. And the data management lives in its own tier. The three-tier architecture is shown in Figure 8.5.

Figure 8.5 Three-tier architecture.

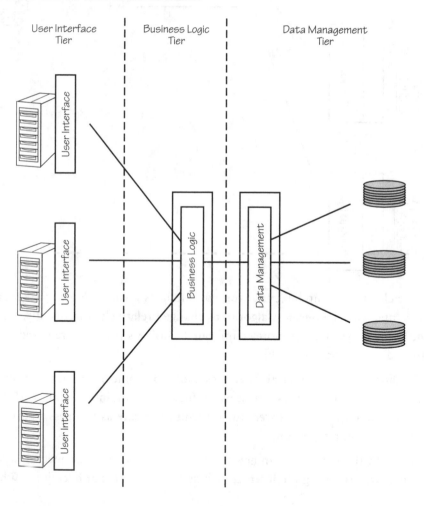

Three-tier architectures offer a major advantage over two-tier or client/server architectures. Business logic is consolidated on one large machine, where it can be easily managed.

Around this time, objects came into vogue, and then their close relatives, components. Components turned out to be an excellent packaging technology for encapsulating business logic. We discovered how to build higher-level components out of existing components. And we also discovered how to distribute these components across networks of machines.

Microsoft was an early advocate of component technology, and proposed COM as its solution. Microsoft also quickly realized the power of distributing these components across machines, and proposed DCOM.

With the advent of distributed components, new pressures began to be felt on three-tier architecture. Suddenly, one machine was not enough to contain the business logic. We needed components on one machine to communicate with components on other machines. There seemed to be no limit to the number of ways to split up this middle tier.

At the same time, the database tier was under attack. It had always been assumed that businesses stored data in large, monolithic databases. More and more businesses were turning to heterogeneous collections of databases. Logically, it became difficult to view the database tier as anything but collection of sub-tiers.

In recognition of these basic architectural changes, we now have a multi-tier architecture, or what some call an *N-tier architecture*. In this architecture, small computers are still used for the user interface, but now there are many computers involved in the running of the components that model the business. We will start calling this tier the *component tier*. One, for example, might be running customer components. Another might be running inventory components. Another might be running accounts. There may also be many machines involved in storing data; some storing to indexed files, some to relational databases, and some to hierarchical databases. This new multi-tier architecture is shown in Figure 8.6.

Even though we use the term multi-tier architecture, it's worth keeping in mind that this is just a variant on the three-tier architecture. The only difference is how many computers are involved in the various tiers. Some people don't even distinguish between three-tier and multi-tier architectures.

Figure 8.6 Multi-tier architecture.

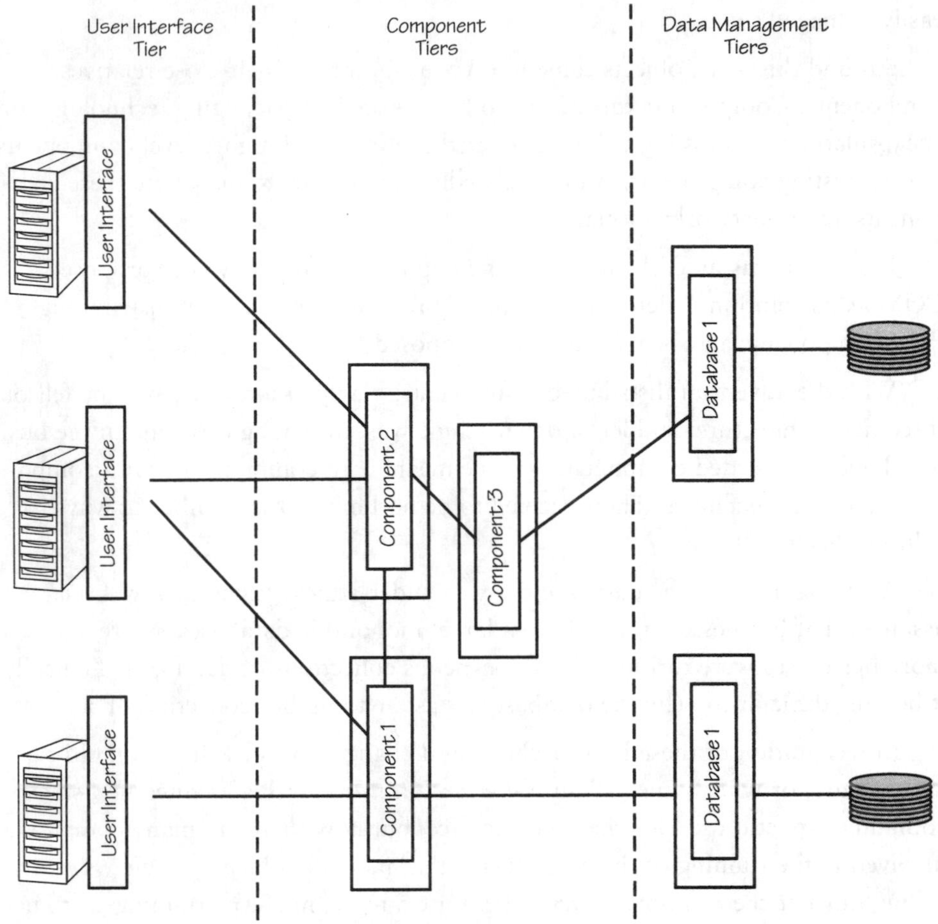

And that pretty much brings us to today. The term *multi-tier architecture* seems sufficiently vague that it may be with us for a while. So we will spend the rest of this chapter looking at this architecture, and how Microsoft is addressing its needs.

The Client Tier

So let's look at each of these tiers, from Microsoft's perspective.

The *client tier* is where the human being works. It will be running a Visual Basic interface, or a Web browser, or quite possibly, both. From Microsoft's perspective, there is little to say about the client tier. Microsoft won the battle for this tier a long time ago. Virtually all machines in this tier run Microsoft operating systems, and many use Microsoft tools, such as Visual Basic, to create the actual interface.

The future of this tier will be impacted more and more by the Internet, as more and more commerce systems are set up to be accessible from the growing Web. This means the client tier will be growing thinner and thinner, with little on these machines other than the basic HTML page processing systems. The HTML pages, as well as all business logic, will reside elsewhere. Eventually the low end of machines in this category will probably not even have their own disks. Everything will come from the Web.

So the client tier can be subdivided into machines running Visual Basic interfaces and machines running Web browsers. The latter group can either be issuing DCOM requests directly or indirectly through another technology called the Microsoft Internet Information Server (IIS). The relationship of browsers to the overall multi-tier architecture is shown in Figure 8.7.

The Component Tier

The *component tier* is where we run the business logic. Since I am assuming we are going to encapsulate the business logic into components, I have been calling this the *component tier*.

Microsoft's component technology, COM, is especially well suited to the needs of the component tier. It has the following important features:

- Components are very natural to those familiar with object-oriented programming.

- Components are well encapsulated, with well-defined interfaces.

- These interfaces can be discovered at run time.

- The components are language neutral, so code running in the user interface tier can make use of the component tier without regard for programming language.

- Components can be built on each other, allowing richly layered software designs.

Figure 8.7 Browser architectures.

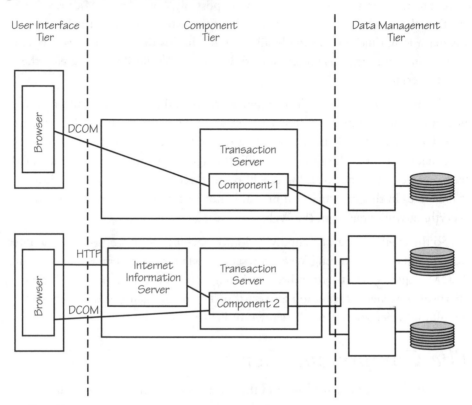

DCOM extends this to provide a very simple distribution model. Once people understand components in general, the extension to having code in the user interface tier make remote requests to components on the component tier is straightforward, as shown in Figure 8.8. The DCOM model for distribution is much easier to understand than, say, TCP/IP sockets, or even Remote Procedure Call—two other technologies commonly used for communicating between client and component tiers.

The use of the DCOM layer for inter-tier communication provides another important advantage. It shields the clients from the underlying communications protocol. Today, the underlying communications protocol is a form of RPC, but this could change as Microsoft seeks to provide communication models that are not well served by RPC. The fact that DCOM is the component visible communication layer means that RPC is never seen by clients or components. Future

Figure 8.8 Moving components from client to component tiers.

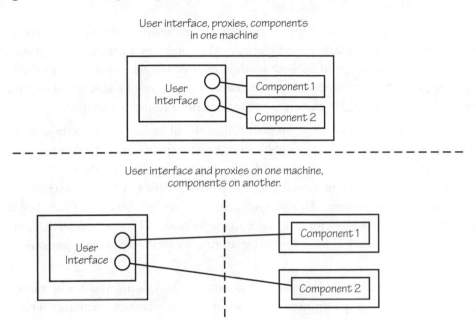

implementations of DCOM could be built on something quite different with minimal or no client impact.

Today, the equivalent to the component tier is run on expensive machines running obscure operating systems (like Unix and MVS) on proprietary hardware. Microsoft is making an aggressive bid for this market.

If Microsoft takes over the component tier, two things will happen. First, business systems will become much cheaper to build, as expensive hardware can be replaced by standard off-the-shelf systems. Second, Bill Gates will own an even larger share of the earth's wealth than he does today.

The Microsoft assault on the component tier is led by the Microsoft Transaction Server (MTS). We have already discussed this product's role in the absolutely critical areas of object pooling and distributed transactions. In addition to these important functions, MTS provides the ability to administer components on this peer network of computers, and the ability to keep these components secure, which we will discuss later.

The MTS is also responsible for providing a framework into which different data management products can be plugged. MTS provides a general description of a resource manager, and product vendors provide resource managers for their specific products. Any of these resource managers will then be able to play within the distributed two-phase commit protocol described in the last chapter.

The value of the two-phase commit protocol will be largely determined by the number of database products with working resource managers. Microsoft has already provided a resource manager for its flagship database product, SQLServer. It has also announced a resource manager for CICS, a popular IBM data management product. This resource manager has been named *Cedar*. And it has also announced plans for a resource manager that will support any XA-compliant database, which is the industry standard for distributed transaction support.

Most commercial databases are XA compliant. So you might ask why these databases would ever go through the effort of writing a resource manager. The reason is that a resource manager written specifically for a database is going to be more efficient than that same database using a generic XA resource manager. Market pressure will encourage vendors to work as fast as possible with MTS, once MTS becomes a widespread, middle-tier environment. You can be sure Microsoft will be adding pressure with SQLServer, which will be tightly integrated with MTS.

MTS also has the ability to manage a database connection pool, which is similar to its ability to manage object pools. This allows applications to make use of pools of preconnected SQLServer sessions, rather than having to establish dedicated database connections.

The use of connection pools has two important benefits. First, the processing overhead associated with creating and terminating database connections occurs all at once when MTS is initialized and terminated, which usually occurs at system boot-up time. Second, this allows the total number of connections to be much smaller than what is required if one statically assigns a connection to each client. Database connections are a limited resource in a large system.

The importance of MTS in the multi-tier architecture cannot be overemphasized. It is an extremely advanced technology that goes well beyond the concept of Transactions. Do not be misled by its poorly chosen name. It is *the* environment for the component tier. MTS is what makes components work in a multi-tier architecture. It is, more than anything else, the technology that distinguishes the MDCA from competitive technologies. If your business is commerce, MTS is your first, second, and third reason for buying into the Microsoft strategy.

Figure 8.9 shows the role of MTS in the component-tier network.

The Data Management Tier

Finally we have the *data management tier*. This is the critically important layer in which data is stored and retrieved. Microsoft's offering for this tier is SQLServer.

This is going to be by far the toughest nut for Microsoft to crack. There are many well-established data management products, and although SQLServer is

Figure 8.9 The role of MTS in the component-tier network.

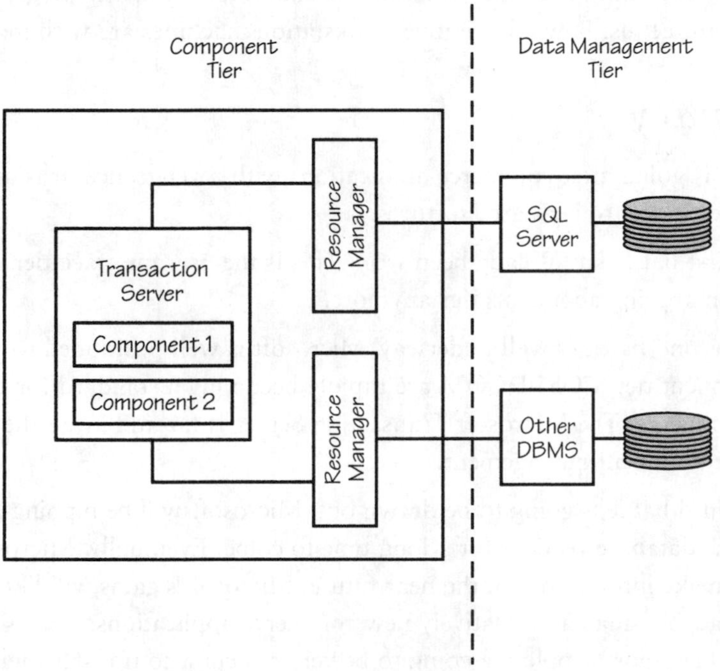

extremely competitive based on price, performance, and functionality, there is a great deal of data out there. As we discussed in the last chapter, companies are very reluctant to replace data management products. It is not a fun project.

The strategy Microsoft will have to play here will be coexistence and gradual replacement. Microsoft will undoubtedly offer tools to simplify the migration of data, but these are not likely to meet with any widespread enthusiasm on the part of their customers. The long term will be to convince customers to use Microsoft for the user interface tier (which all do now, anyway) and Microsoft for the component tier (for which they have a compelling story). Then use Microsoft for the data-management tier for new projects.

There are two arguments that Microsoft can make for SQLServer on the data-management tier. The first is that it will probably be the only data management product supporting connection pools, as we discussed earlier. The second is the cost of ownership.

The cost of ownership will be much less for SQLServer for two reasons. First, Microsoft will be pricing SQLServer very competitively, and second, SQLServer will be able to run on workstation-class machines, which, as we have discussed, are a fraction of the cost of their mainframe counterparts. When we get to clusters, we will see just how competitive workstation machines are with mainframes.

Summary

Microsoft is going after commerce applications with a vengeance. It is attacking at all three tiers of today's architectures.

The first battle has already been won. This is the user interface tier. There is no point in arguing about this tier anymore.

The second battle is well underway. Microsoft is well positioned to take over the component tier. COM/DCOM are rapidly becoming a standard for distributed components. The Microsoft Transaction Server is far and away the market leader in component management.

The third battle is going to be drawn out. Microsoft will be nipping at the heels of the database vendors for a long time to come. Eventually, Microsoft will probably make inroads, but in the near future, Microsoft's gains will likely be limited to relatively small and relatively new commerce applications. This is one basket into which most people are going to be very reluctant to transfer their eggs.

SECURITY

Commerce people seem to be a bit paranoid about their money. I have noticed that when bank presidents go to MacDonald's, they don't leave boxes of hundred-dollar bills lying about. When I try to buy a new car with $5000 bills from my old Monopoly game, salespeople give me a pained expression. For some reason, business people seem to take their money rather seriously.

It seems that nobody trusts anybody. Or maybe, everybody trusts nobody. When I write a check for the week's groceries, the clerk wants me to prove I am who I say I am. When someone asks for my credit card over the phone, I make sure I know who is at the other end of the line. When an envelope arrives in the mail with payment for a consulting job, the first thing I do is open the envelope and make sure the check has not been removed. You just can't be too sure.

And it's no different with computers. Just because I am a business component selling stock shares and Joe Blow is a Visual Basic program on another computer doesn't make me or Joe Blow any more trustworthy. And just because the payment arrives in a neat little electronic packet doesn't make the contents any safer than if they had arrived in a paper envelope. Just like there are bad people, there are bad computers in this world.

If we are going to conduct commerce over computer networks, we need a mechanism to make sure the Visual Basic program claiming to be logged in as Joe Blow really is logged in as Joe Blow. Joe Blow needs a mechanism to make sure the component in the other room merrily deducting money from his checking account is one he trusts to deliver real stock shares. We both need mechanisms for verifying that the information sent between us has not been manipulated by unscrupulous third parties.

So if Microsoft is going to take over the field of electronic commerce, it had better be prepared to deliver some serious security capabilities. And so it has. In this chapter, we are going to explore the various techniques components can use to placate paranoia.

NT Security

Overall, NT is a relatively secure operating system for business purposes. Version 3.5 is rated C2 by the National Computer Security Center, and 4.0 is being evaluated now. A system rated C2 is evaluated on the following capabilities:

Discretionary access and control. An administrator must be able to define and control its users' access to system resources like files and directories. NT does this through the use of ACLs (Access Control Lists).

Identification and authentication. The system must be able to determine the identity of processes making requests. NT does this through requiring all users to log on in a tightly controlled manner. NT, for example, requires you to hit CTRL/ALT/DEL before logging on to eliminate the possibility of Trojan Horse programs.

Auditing. The system must be able to audit security events and user actions (such as file access).

Resource reuse. Allocation and deallocation of resources must be protected, and when these resources are reused, they must have the ability to be first zeroed out to prevent people from reading old data.

It is important to know that NT is secure overall, because the MDCA is built on NT, and can only be as secure as the underlying operating system. Much of the security of the MDCA is built on the identification and authentication capabilities of NT.

Everything runs in a process. When a component is running, it is running in a process. When a client is running, that client is running in a process. All processes have a user ID, which is guaranteed by the underlying NT. So when we are talking about identity validation, we are talking about the identity of these processes.

MTS Authorization

I am going to assume that you are running your components under control of the Microsoft Transaction Server (MTS). In general, I see little compelling reason for using the MDCA without MTS. We have already discussed the many important functions MTS provides to the overall MDCA.

MTS Explorer is used to place components in packages, as we discussed earlier. A package will run as a whole in some process. MTS Explorer is used to configure the user ID under which the package will run. So the user ID under which the package will run needs access to any system resource used by any method of any component of the package. This often adds up to considerable security allowances, since its needs are a superset of all the needs of its constituent methods.

This causes a problem. If our package is required to have broad security access, how can we restrict what users (such as the Visual Basic programs running remotely) can do using this package?

Let's consider an example based on our brokering system. In IDL, our current system looks like this:

```
/* ... */
library BrokerLib
{
    interface IBrokerHouse : IDispatch
    {
/*    Methods to buy and sell stuff */
    };
    coclass CBrokerHouse
    {
        [default] interface IBrokerHouse;
    };
};
```

Let's add a few more interfaces and another component definition. IAdmin will be an interface used to add and delete valid buyers and sellers. IReport will be an interface used to prepare summary reports of brokering system activity. We can combine this all into one IDL file like this:

```
/* ... */
library BrokerLib
```

```
{
    interface IBrokerHouse : IDispatch
    {
/*     Methods to buy and sell stuff */
    }
    interface IAdmin : IDispatch
    {
/*     Methods to administrate user IDs.
    }
    interface IReport : IDispatch
    {
/*     Methods to report on system usage.
    }
    coclass CBrokerHouse
    {
        [default] interface IBrokerHouse;
    }
    coclass CAdministrator
    {
        [default] interface IReport;
        interface IAdmin;
    }
}
```

In Chapter 7, we described how we might use SQLServer to store information for our brokering system. We proposed setting up buyer and seller tables to contain information on unfulfilled negotiations. To refresh your memory, these tables are shown again in Figure 9.1.

Based on our discussion of the IReport and IAdmin interfaces, we might assume we have an accounting table, such as the one shown in Figure 9.2.

Let's assume we have the following five users authorized to use the system:

Bill: authorized to buy or sell with the system.

Bev: authorized to buy or sell with the system.

Anne: authorized to use the administrative (add/delete user) functions.

Andy: authorized to use the reporting functions.

Arnold: authorized to use the reporting and administrative functions.

Figure 9.1 Buyer and seller tables.

```
Table: Buyer
Employee   Item     Price    NegotiatedPrice    TID    PartnerName
--------   ----     -----    ---------------    ---    -----------
Michael    dog      20                          t1
Roger      cat      10                          t2
Rachael    bird     100                         t3

Table: Seller
Employee   Item     Price    NegotiatedPrice    TID    PartnerName
--------   ----     -----    ---------------    ---    -----------
Emily      dog      10                          t2
Chris      whale    1000                        t3
John       VW bug   250                         t3
```

What kind of access do these users need to the SQLServer tables? Buying and selling requires both read and write access to both the buyer and seller tables. Reporting requires read access to the account table. And administrating requires read and write access to the account table.

If we assume these users are logging directly into SQLServer, and directly using the tables, we would assign them the SQLServer permissions shown in Figure 9.3.

Figure 9.2 Accounting table.

```
Table: Account
Account Name    Balance Due
------------    -----------
Bill            100
Michael         50
Roger           0
Rachael         10
Emily           5
Chris           120
John            100
Bev             98
```

Figure 9.3 SQLServer permissions.

Tables

	Buyer	Seller	Account
Bill	RW	RW	None
Bev	RW	RW	None
Anne	None	None	RW
Andy	None	None	R
Arnold	None	None	RW

Users

Access
R = Read
W = Write

However, we are not going to have these users logging directly into SQL-Server and updating tables. We are going to have them updating the tables through the brokering system components. Bill and Bev will be updating tables through the IBroker interface of the CBrokerHouse component, Anne and Arnold through the IAdmin interface of CAdministrator component, and Andy and Arnold through the CReport interface of the CAdministrator component. The update situation will really be like that shown in Figure 9.4.

We have already stated that the package as a whole will run inside a single process, and that the process will be assigned a user ID. This package includes both CAdministrator and CBrokerHouse components,

How shall we go about organizing the security of this system? There are two possibilities: *client impersonation* and *client authorization*. MDCA supports both of these options, but only one works well. Why don't you see if you can guess which technique works and which doesn't as we describe each.

In client impersonation, the package process temporarily takes on the user ID of the client, invoking a method as long as that method is working. As soon as the method is completed, the user ID of the package reverts to its original user ID. Using client impersonation, we would set up the table permissions as shown

Figure 9.4 Updating through brokering components.

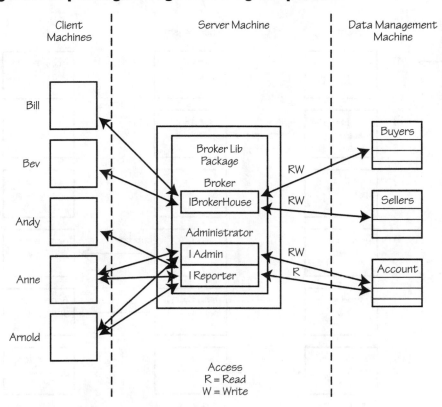

back in Figure 9.3 and let SQLServer sort out who can do what. Client imperson-ation is shown in Figure 9.5.

In client authorization, the package starts up with the user ID configured with the Transaction Explorer, and never changes. SQLServer is set up to grant the package user ID all permissions it needs to perform any of its methods. So if the package can do anything, how do we limit what clients can do using that package?

In client authorization, access is controlled at the interface level. In other words, we define which users are allowed to make use of which interfaces. Then from the SQLServer side, the only user allowed to update tables is the user ID of the package process. Figure 9.6 shows how we would set up user rights for the interface.

Figure 9.5 Client impersonation.

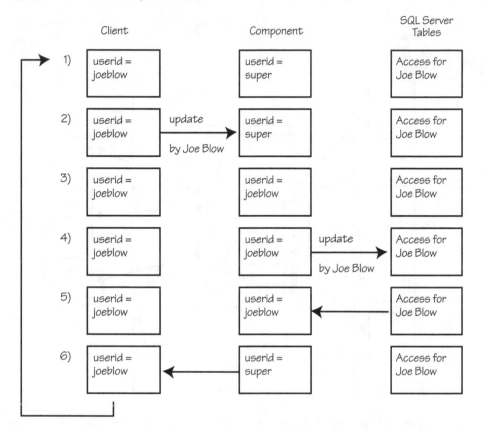

In both client impersonation and client authorization, unauthorized clients are unable to access the database, but the block occurs at different levels. In client impersonation, the block occurs at the database level, and security is controlled by the database security. In client authorization, the block occurs at the interface level, and security is controlled by MTS. Figure 9.7 contrasts blocking in client impersonation and client authorization.

Client Impersonation versus Client Authorization

Okay. Now back to our quiz question. Which is a better technique? Client impersonation, in which access is given explicitly to each user to access exactly those

Figure 9.6 User rights for client authorization.

Interface

	IBrokerHouse	IReport	IAdmin
Bill	Yes	No	No
Bev	Yes	No	No
Anne	No	No	Yes
Andy	No	Yes	No
Arnold	No	Yes	Yes

Users

Access to Interface
Yes = Can use interface
No = Cannot use interface

Figure 9.7 Blocking of impersonation versus authorization.

Blocking in impersonation

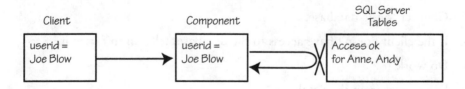

Blocking in authorization

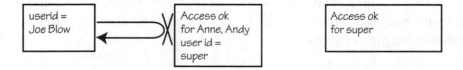

system resources he or she needs? Or client authorization, in which the component process runs as a superuser and clients are sorted out based on access rights to the component interfaces? Let me give you a few clues.

Clue 1: From SQLServer's perspective, your identity is established at the time you first create the connection to the database.

Clue 2: Creating a connection to the database is a very expensive operation.

Clue 3: We cannot afford to dedicate an object to each user. Instead, we will use object pooling, as described in Chapter 6.

Clue 4: Because creating a connection to the database is very expensive, we will create pools of database connections. Like all connections, these connections will be dedicated to particular user IDs. We haven't discussed connection pooling in depth, but we have mentioned it in Chapters 7 and 8.

Let's compare the efficiency of these two security techniques. We can assume we are using object pooling (Clue 3). This is one of the most important reasons for using the MDCA. So let's compare client impersonation and authorization in light of the fact that we will be using object pooling.

If we were to use client impersonation in conjunction with object pooling, we would have to take the following steps with each method invocation:

1. Figure out the user ID of the client invoking this method.

2. Change the user ID of the component to the user ID of the client.

3. Connect to the database.

4. If the client doesn't have access to the database, tell 'em to forget it.

5. Do work.

6. Disconnect from the database.

7. Change the user ID of the component back to its original user ID.

There is a problem here. Connecting and disconnecting are very expensive operations (see Clue 2).

If we use client authorization, we eliminate the need to connect and disconnect with every method invocation. The steps we need to follow with client authorization are as follows:

1. Figure out the user ID of the client invoking this interface.

2. If the client doesn't have access to this interface, tell 'em to forget it.

3. Borrow a connection from the connection pool. They will all have been created using the component's user ID.

4. Do work.

5. Return connection to the connection pool.

Much better, isn't it? And there are other problems with client impersonation. For example, imagine how much work is involved if you rewrite the component code. Suddenly the component needs to update a few more tables.

With client impersonation, you have to figure out everybody who ever might use that interface, and go and change all of their table access rights within SQLServer. If we have 1000 users and two table authorization changes, client impersonation will require 1000×2 authorization changes. That's 2000 changes, for those of you who are math impaired.

With client authorization, we only need to change the table access rights of the user ID of the component process for each table, a total of 1×2 authorization changes. That is two changes, again, for the math-impaired readers.

The interface hasn't changed, only the implementation. So if they were able to access the interface before, they still can now. If they couldn't before, they still can't. If you are the system administrator, would you much prefer to make 2 changes or 2000?

So client authorization is better than client impersonation for the following reasons (plus more, but this will at least give you a taste):

- It is compatible with object pooling.
- It is compatible with database connection pooling.
- It is much easier to administer.

Roles

By now I hope I have convinced you that client authorization is the way to go. But we can do even more to simplify the administration of the system. We can make use of *roles*.

Every user is assigned one or more roles. Roles are assigned using the Transaction Explorer. A role is a just a way of interacting with the system. A role is a lot like a user group. In fact, it's not clear to me why Microsoft didn't just use user groups instead of inventing a new concept. But who knows why things work the way they do up on Mount Olympus?

When deciding which users can access which interfaces, I actually decide which *roles* can access which interfaces. Then I assign specific roles to individual users as they are added to the system. It does sound a lot like user groups, doesn't it?

Administering interface by role is much easier than administering by user ID. It is much easier to remember that Brendan takes the buyer role than it is to remember that Brendan needs access to the IBrokerHouse interface. It is also much easier, if Brendan gets promoted, to remember to just change Brendan's role from buyer to reporter than it is to remember to remove his access from the IBrokerHouse interface and add it to the IReporter interface.

The MTS Explorer is used for all role administration. It includes the following functions:

- Creating new roles
- Assigning roles to user IDs
- Assigning interface access to roles

Access can also be assigned at the component level rather than the interface level. This is just a shorthand way of assigning access to all of the interfaces of that component.

Programmatic Interface to Roles

You may also check roles in component code. We got a preview of this back in Chapter 7 when we discussed the context object. Remember that the context object is an object that is associated with the transaction. Assuming you are running your components within the MTS (and who wouldn't be?), your components automatically have a context object whenever they are active. The Java code to get your context object is:

```
import com.ms.mtx.*;
IObjectContext context;
context = MTx.GetObjectContext();
```

Once you have the context object, you can use it to determine whether or not the client is associated with a particular role. This is used to achieve finer security granularity than what MTS provides, which is interface granularity. MTS lets you decide which roles can access which interfaces, but does not let you assign access by individual methods.

If your interfaces are well designed and chosen with security in mind, then interface granularity is all you will ever need. But in those rare cases where you must take control on a method by method basis, the programmatic interface is your ticket.

The two context object methods you will use are:

- **boolean IsSecurityEnabled()**. Used to check to see if security has been enabled.

- **boolean IsCallerInRole(Sting role)**. Used to determine the role of the client of this method invocation. This method is only reliable if security has been enabled, so it is often used in conjunction with the last method.

We might, for example, have a super administrator role that is the only one allowed to invoke a method initializing the buyer system. The code to ensure the client is a valid super administrator looks like:

```
if (context.IsSecurityEnabled() &&
    context.IsCallerInRole("SuperAdmin")) {
/* Initialize system */
}
```

Authentication

Client authorization tells you that the system believes a client is authorized to use the interface(s) being used. But who believes the system? After all, just because you are paranoid, doesn't mean they *aren't* out to get you.

So MTS Explorer allows you to specify your paranoia level or, to put it in another light, how much confidence you want that a particular method is coming from where it says it's coming from and that it has not been tampered with.

There is an inverse relationship between your level of paranoia and the ultimate performance you will get out of your system. You don't get nothing for nothing. Levels of paranoia are called *authentication levels,* in MTS jargon. MTS supports the following levels of paranoia:

None. You are an extremely trusting individual. You believe everything you hear. Could I hold on to your American Express card for a few days?

Packet. You are mildly paranoid. You trust the message but not the messenger. You want the system to verify that the method invocation is from whom you think it is from.

Packet integrity. You are quite paranoid. You don't trust anything. You want the system to verify the source of the method request *and* that nobody has tampered with the contents. You might want to consider investing in therapy.

Packet privacy. You are probably delusional, and beyond the reach of therapy. You don't trust anything and, by the way, you don't want anybody looking over your shoulder. You want the message source verified, the contents proven untampered, *and* the parameters to the method encrypted. According to the Microsoft documentation, this authentication level is available every place but France. Presumably because the French are already beyond therapy.

MTS Explorer allows you to set authentication level at the package level. All methods of all interfaces of all components in that package then share the same authentication level. Think of it as the MDCA equivalent of group therapy.

Advanced Security—CryptoAPI

Most people are going to be more than happy with the basic security provisions of MTS. But if you really want to get into the business of writing absolutely, positively secure applications, you are probably going to wander into the CryptoAPI sooner or later. The CryptoAPI is an extensive API giving you the ability to work directly with all kinds of algorithms having to do with protecting information and keeping it super secret.

There are two aspects to the CryptoAPI: the client side and the Cryptographic Service Provider (CSP) side. On the user side, the CryptoAPI defines an API framework that can be used to do everything from very basic to advanced cryptographic work. On the CSP side, the CryptoAPI defines a specific API that must be implemented in order for a cryptographic product to work within the context of the MDCA.

Eventually, the CryptoAPI is intended to support many different CSPs. At this time, the only CSP supported is the one that comes with NT, the Microsoft RSA Base Provider (RSA). RSA, by the way, stands for Rivest, Shamir, and Adleman—the three people who developed this well-known cipher algorithm in the late 1970s.

CryptoAPI consists of five functional areas. We won't attempt to go through them in any depth here. The important point is to understand the basic algorithms provided by the CryptoAPI, which we are about to cover, and how the architecture is organized. These are the five areas:

Certificate encode/decode functions. Used for encoding and decoding certificates and related data.

Certificate store functions. Used for certificate management.

Base cryptographic functions. Used for a wide range of functions, including connecting with a particular CSP, generating and customizing cryptographic keys, exchanging and transmitting keys, encrypting and decrypting data, and computing cryptographically secure data signatures.

Low-level message functions. Used for very low-level message functions. Most applications will use the simplified message functions.

Simplified message functions. Used for working with messages, including encrypting and decrypting messages, signing messages, and verifying signatures.

The CryptoAPI architecture is shown in Figure 9.8. Now let's look at some of its basic algorithms.

Encryption/Decryption

Encryption refers to the ability to take a piece of data and turn it into a meaningless pile of gibberish. *Decryption* refers to the ability to take a meaningless pile of gibberish and turn it back into a piece of data.

Encryption/Decryption is used to ensure privacy. Let's say I have a Visual Basic client who is going to invoke a method on a remote component, and that

Figure 9.8 CryptoAPI architecture.

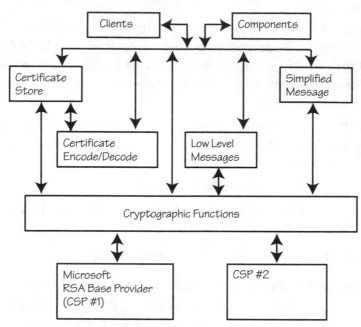

CSP = Cryptographic Service Provider

one of the input parameters is a credit card number. I don't want this credit card number floating around in cyberspace, just waiting for some nasty process to intercept it and sell it to the highest bidder. So I will use encryption/decryption to ensure the privacy of the credit card number.

The Visual Basic client will use encryption algorithms (provided by the CryptoAPI) and an encryption key to turn the credit card number into gibberish. We will then pass that gibberish to the component.

The component can't work with gibberish, so it uses decryption algorithms (also provided by the CryptoAPI) and a decryption key to turn the gibberish back into a credit card number. Anybody intercepting the message between the client and the component will have nothing but gibberish, and gibberish (regardless of how big the pile) generally doesn't get very high bids on the open market. This process is shown in Figure 9.9.

Figure 9.9 Encryption/decryption algorithm.

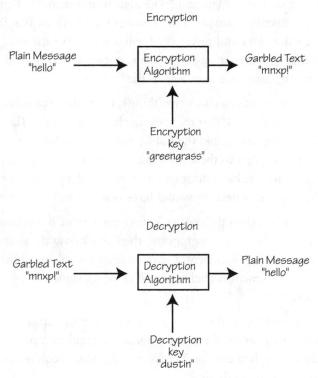

Verification

Verification refers to the ability to determine that a particular individual or company has intentionally sent out a particular piece of data, and to verify that the data has not been changed since it was sent. This can be used for software signatures on legal documents. It can also be used to verify that the software you just downloaded from the Internet was really written by the company you think it was written by, and not by some hormone-impaired teenage hacker.

Verification is a two-stage process. The first stage is the creation of a digital signature. This is done by the person creating the data and sending it out. The second stage is done by the person checking to see if the data is properly signed and unchanged.

In the creation stage, the data and the person's private key (such as a password) is fed into a signature algorithm. The algorithm returns a digital signature. That signature is effectively unique, and is determined both by the data and the private key. The same data and private key will always give the same signature. But if either changes by even a single bit, the resulting signature will be different. The data and the signature are then sent to the verifier.

The verifier now wants to check two things. First, that the message came from whom it claims. Second, that the message hasn't changed. The verifier feeds the data, the digital signature, and the public key into a validation algorithm. The public key is a key assigned to the sender that anybody can find out. The validation algorithm returns a value indicating whether this data signed by the person whose public key you are checking would have resulted in this signature.

If the answer is yes, then the verifier knows the sender is as claimed and the data is unchanged. If the data is a program, then you know the source of the program. If the data is a legal document, then you know who signed the document, and you know the document is unchanged since being signed. This whole process is shown in Figure 9.10.

Notice that the verifier can only check to see if the signature is valid. The verifier cannot create a signature. Creating a signature requires a private key, which is available only to the data creator. Verifying a signature requires only a public key, which is available to anybody.

Certificates

You can verify the signature of somebody only if you have their public key. From where do you get their public key?

The obvious answer to this is that you get it from the sender, the same place from where you get the signature. But do you really want to do this? The reason you need the public key in the first place is because you don't trust the sender and you want to verify his or her signature. If you get the public key from the sender, then you don't know if the public key you are getting is the one you really want.

So, if you can't get it from the sender, from where can you get it? The correct answer is that you get it from a highly trusted third party. Someone who is 100 percent above reproach. Someone like a Certificate Authority (CA). These are

Figure 9.10 Signature validation algorithm.

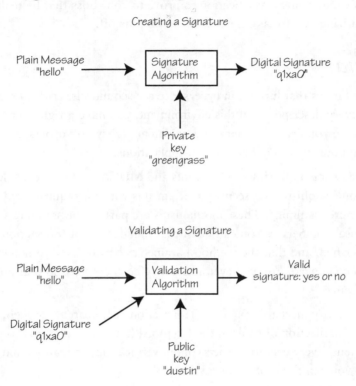

Creating a Signature

Plain Message "hello" → Signature Algorithm → Digital Signature "q1xaO"

Private key "greengrass"

Validating a Signature

Plain Message "hello" → Validation Algorithm → Valid signature: yes or no

Digital Signature "q1xaO"

Public key "dustin"

parties from whom anybody can get anybody's public key. A good business to be in, if you happen to be perfect.

Encryption/Decryption versus Verification

Although similar algorithms are involved in encryption/decryption and verification, the two techniques have very different purposes.

Encryption/decryption is used to ensure data is available only to authorized users. An encrypted program cannot be run. An encrypted credit card number cannot be used. An encrypted file cannot be read.

Verification is used to allow people to determine the origin of a file, and that the file has not been tampered with. You use verification to make sure the program you just downloaded is not a virus (or if it is, at least you know where it came from). You use verification to make sure the purchase order you are about to fulfill is valid. You use verification to prove to your boss that he really sent the note authorizing you to take the next three months off.

Summary

Everybody knows that lurking in cyberspace are scoundrels, criminals, and nasty people of every description. In this environment, you have a right to be paranoid. In cyberspace, you are either paranoid or you are crazy. Yet cyberspace is where we must run our distributed commerce applications.

We need some powerful security tools and MDCA is at the ready. MDCA provides some sophisticated security mechanisms without requiring any client or component programming. These mechanisms are part of the standard repertoire of the Transaction Server. You can insist that the identify of transaction participants be verified, and that the method parameters be validated to make sure they haven't been changed. You can even insist they be encrypted, so that nobody else can read them.

If the security mechanisms of the Transaction Server aren't enough, you have an incredible collection of tools in the CryptoAPI. You can play spy to your heart's content. Every encryption/decryption, verification, validation, and certificate-based tool you can think of is yours.

Cyberspace is here. CyberCriminals are here. And now, so is CyberCop.

CLUSTERING

10

I wonder how many readers remember the original *Candid Camera*. The show consisted of a collection of unrelated episodes in which a hidden camera captured the embarrassment, humiliation, or mere degradation of some unsuspecting patsy caught in a set-up situation. It starred Alan Funt. It was in black and white. Or maybe it was just in black and white on *my* TV—I can't remember. I was only a babe at the time, you understand.

In this chapter, I am going to tell you about one of my favorite episodes of *Candid Camera*. In order to give you the background to understand this episode, I am going to explain a bit about how banks organized their teller queues back when I was a babe, and how they do this today. It turns out that the same principles that apply to teller queues apply to a technology called *Clusters*. So we might as well discuss Clusters in this chapter as well.

Clustering is a technology that is of particular importance to applications that demand high throughput and high reliability, and want these at the lowest possible cost. Distributed commerce applications are prime examples of such applications. And, as you can guess from previous discussions, once we identify a need of distributed commerce, we have also identified an area in which Microsoft is very interested, and one on which MDCA will focus.

So it should be no surprise that *Candid Camera*, bank tellers, distributed commerce applications, Clusters, and MDCA are all closely related. But let's start at the beginning.

My Favorite Episode of Candid Camera

My favorite *Candid Camera* episode took place in a bank. Before I explain the episode, I have to explain how banks worked, way back when. First of all, this was before ATMs (and that's not Asynchronous Transfer Mode, for you total dweebs). Back in those days, when you wanted money, you had to physically enter the bank. This meant that you had to go to the bank when it was open, which alone resulted in great inconvenience to yourself. Bank hours were not chosen for your convenience, unless you happened to be a bank president with a very heavy golf schedule.

When you entered the bank, you faced an phalanx of teller windows. In front of each teller window was a long queue of supplicants. As you entered the bank, you chose one of these queues to join. As each supplicant completed his or her business with the teller, the queue would gradually move up. This organization is shown in Figure 10.1.

Once you joined a teller queue, there were only three ways out. You could eventually make it to the head of the queue, in which case you were entitled to plead your case to the teller. Or you could eventually give up, leave the queue, and join the end of another queue, in the hope that it would move faster. Or you could just give up, period, a not infrequent event.

This particular *Candid Camera* episode was filmed at a bank with three teller queues. Both the length and the speed of these queues were manipulated by the *Candid Camera* crew. Here is a typical denouement. Paul, the patsy, enters the bank. Tellers Terry and Tom have five people in queue and Teller Therese has three people in queue, as shown in Figure 10.2.

Figure 10.1 Bank organization in the bad old days.

Figure 10.2 The bank when Paul enters.

Naturally, Paul chooses Therese's queue. Immediately two things happen. First, three more people each join Terry and Tom's queue, swelling their queues to eight people each. Second, Therese turns into the slowest teller this side of the border (*any* border). By the time Therese finishes one customer, all eight of Terry and Tom's customers have been serviced, and another eight have joined each of their queues. Ten minutes have passed, and the bank now looks like Figure 10.3.

Paul, of course, is very unhappy, being much too important a person to spend his time in bank queues. Therese shows no sign of speeding up. Even though there are only two people ahead of him, Paul eventually gives up and joins Tom's queue with its eight people. Then three things happen:

1. Therese gets ten more people in her queue.

2. Therese becomes the epitome of efficiency.

3. Tom becomes a lesson in lethargy.

Figure 10.3 The bank after 10 minutes.

In no time, Therese has serviced all ten people in her queue, and Tom is still struggling to get through one. Of course, by then Therese has another long queue at her window.

This continues indefinitely. No matter what Paul does, he can't make any progress toward getting his work accomplished. Whatever queue he joins immediately slows to a crawl. Whatever queue he leaves immediately becomes the Daytona racetrack. Now if this were the real world, Paul would eventually go crazy. But this is a setup, so just before Paul totally loses it, Alan Funt steps out and declares, "Smile, you're on *Candid Camera*!"

This scenario could not happen in today's banks. First of all, nobody enters a bank anymore. But even those few who do face a different teller organization. Banks today do not have long queues before teller windows. Instead, they have a single queue for all the tellers. As tellers become available, they take the next person in the queue. This organization is shown in Figure 10.4.

The old queuing organization, the one that victimized poor Paul, is still used universally by grocery stores, so I will call this *grocery store queues*. The new queuing organization is used universally by airlines to check in airline passengers, so I will call this *airport queues*.

I have never met anybody who prefers grocery store queues to airport queues. Here is a partial list of some of the problems inherent with grocery store queues.

Unpredictable wait times. The amount of time you will wait has nothing to do with the amount of work you need done or even the number of people in line. It seems to have more to do with factors like the speed of the cashier, how people in front decide to pay, and other factors that you just can't predict when you choose which queue to join.

Inherent unfairness. If a new queue opens up, it immediately fills up with new customers who haven't even been waiting in line (isn't this annoying!), and you, who any dolt can plainly see is the most deserving person in the store, get absolutely no benefit.

Total dependence. If the cashier has to go to the bathroom, or suddenly goes into a trance, or leaves the store in a huff, you have had it. You either wait until things get sorted out, or you give up and get in a new queue.

Figure 10.4 Bank queues today.

Poor Paul faced all of these problems. And because we have all faced them at some point or another, we sympathize with Paul. We know exactly how Paul felt, which is what made this episode so funny.

Airport queues work quite differently, and have none of these problems. Here is a look at the analogous issues with airport queues.

Predictable wait times. You can predict the amount of time you will be in line by knowing the average time it takes to service a customer, the number of customers, and the number of airline agents. You won't be exactly right in your estimate, but you probably won't be far off.

Inherent fairness. If a new agent comes on board, everybody on line benefits. The whole queue moves faster.

Independence. If any one agent goes down for the count, you are minimally impacted. The queue will move a bit slower, but you will still eventually make it to the front and get your ticket.

What are the differences between these two queue types, and how do these differences cause these radically different results?

In grocery store queues, you are assigned to a cashier at the time you join a queue. You know exactly who you will get. From that point on, the universe consists of you, the queue, and the cashier. Nothing else happening in the store has any impact on your life.

In airline queues, you have no idea which agent you will get when you join the queue. From your perspective, the universe consists of you, the queue, and *the blob*, that amorphous collection of airline agents someplace Out There. As long as the blob continues working, you will eventually be serviced. The blob might get bigger, in which case the queue will move faster, or the blob might get smaller, in which case the queue will move slower. But as long as the blob exists, you will sooner or later get serviced. This organization is shown in Figure 10.5.

Airline queues are more efficient than grocery store queues from management's perspective as well. Here are a few of the issues management cares about.

Downtime. If a grocery store cashier takes a coffee break, you have a queue of angry customers. If an airline agent takes a coffee break, nobody notices.

Performance. If a grocery store queue is moving too slowly, there is nothing you can do to speed it up. If an airline queue is moving too slowly, management just goes to the nearest airline agent store and buys a few more units.

Serviceability. If a grocery store cashier needs servicing, that queue comes to a halt until servicing is complete. If an airline agent needs servicing, the queue continues with only a little impact.

So from everybody's perspective, a blob of agents is much better than individual agents. Figure 10.6 compares the important characteristics of airline queues and grocery store queues.

Figure 10.5 Airline terminals as blobs.

Figure 10.6 Airline queues versus grocery store queues.

	Grocery Stores	Airline Terminals
Predictability	Very Low Dependent on individual cashiers	Very High Based on average statistics
Reliability	Very Low System fails when just one cashier fails.	Very High System fails only when all agents fail
Serviceability	Difficult Cashier cannot leave without customer impact	Easy Cashier can leave at any time

You can see that this *Candid Camera* episode is completely dependent on grocery store queues. This episode could never have been filmed at a bank using airline queue organization.

Blob Prerequisites

It is possible to structure an airline terminal so that the blob organization can't work. Here are two types of structure that would prohibit the treatment of agents as blobs.

Let's say that people call in advance to order their tickets, and tickets are held by the agents who took the phone call. In order to get your ticket you must go to the same agent who took your phone call. If you must see a specific agent by name, the agents are not interchangeable. This is no good for blobs. Blobs only work if we can think of an agent as *an agent*, rather than some individual.

Let's say the airline terminal is organized like many conference check-ins, where each agent has access to information only for people whose last names start with certain letters of the alphabet. Agent Anne, for example, can see only people with last names starting with A–C, because that is the credit information she has. If your agent must have access to specific information (your last name), and the information is not uniformly available to all agents, then you are constrained in whom you can see. These agents are effectively not interchangeable. This is no good for blobs. Blobs work only if all of the blob constituents (agents, in this case) have access to all of the information.

So we can see two requirements. Agents must be interchangeable. And all of the information must be available to all of the agents.

Blob Performance

Are blobs really the best way to organize airline terminals? Let's say we are upper management. We have a single airline agent and a single queue for customers. It is clear to us that we need more help.

We have two possible strategies we might follow. We can buy a new airline agent, say Super Agent. Super Agent is the latest model of a new breed of genetically engineered ticket agents. Super Agent takes no breaks, makes no chit chat, and moves with the speed of greased lightning. Or for the price of one Super Agent, we can buy ten Vanilla Agents, the nongenetically engineered variety. Which would be better?

On a well-known travel industry benchmark, Super Agent performs at 1000 MIPS (Muddleheaded Itinerants Per Shift) whereas Vanilla Agent (the nongenetically engineered variety) performs at 50 MIPS. But Super Agent costs $10,000 per shift, while Vanilla Agent costs $1,000. So Super Agent processes itinerants at a cost of $10 each (10,000/1000) while Vanilla Agent processes them at $20 each (1000/50). So which is the better deal? Super Agent, right?

Not so fast. Industry benchmarks are measured in vitro. Let's look at how agents interact with customers in vivo. We start by breaking down the interactions between customers and agents into their various components, and time each. We get the following:

- Customer fumbles for ticket—15 seconds
- Customer tries to explain that he is late for the flight because he stopped at the bagel shop—20 seconds
- Customer tries to decide which luggage to check—10 seconds
- Customer looks for ID—15 seconds
- Agent processes ticket—3 seconds for Super Agent, 60 seconds for Vanilla Agent
- Customer puts ticket in pocket and picks up carry-on luggage—10 seconds

You can probably start to see the pattern here. In vivo, it takes Super Agent 73 seconds to process a customer (15+20+10+15+3+10) and Vanilla Agent 130 seconds (15+20+10+15+60+10) to process a customer. It doesn't take a degree in math to figure out that a blob of only two Vanilla Agents will exceed the performance of one Super Agent. In fact, even if you could make Super Agent a million times faster, it would have an insignificant impact on the outcome. The best Super Agent in the world cannot process a customer in less than 0 seconds. At that rate, our blob of two Vanilla Agents will still process two customers every 130 seconds, while it will take Super Agent 140 seconds to process those same two customers.

So our end result is that a blob of two Vanilla Agents outperforms Super Agent, and does it at 1/5 the cost (10,000 / 2 × 1000). Or another way to look at this is that for the cost of one Super Agent, we could buy a blob of 10 Vanilla Agents. Then we would have a blob-based system that performs at 10 customers per 130 seconds, or 4.6 customers per minute, as opposed to our Super Agent processing 1 customer per 73 seconds, or .82 customers per minute. Five times the performance for the same cost. Not bad, right?

A Brief Word from Your Math Teacher

We are about to talk about blob reliability. Reliability means the chances of something going wrong. When we talk about the chances of something happening, we are talking about probability. So before we get into blob reliability, we will spend a moment reviewing basic probability. If you are reasonably well versed in probability theory, feel free to skip this section.

If you flip a coin, there is a 1-in-2 chance it will come up heads. See, that wasn't too bad, was it? There are many ways we can describe 1-in-2 chance of heads. We can say that on average, the coin comes up heads 1/2 the time. We can say the coin has a .5 chance of coming up heads. We can say the coin has a .5 chance of coming up tails. If you flip the coin once per day, we can say that the coin will come up heads one out of every two days.

If you throw a die, there is a 1-in-6 chance it will come up with a 3. We can say that it comes up with a 3 1/6 of the time, or that it has a .167 chance of coming up 3, or that if you throw a die once per day, it will typically come up with a 3 one day out of every six.

If you are told the chances of something happening, you can figure out how often that something will happen and vice versa. If something has an X chance of happening at any given time, then it will happen on average 1/X times. A coin, for example has a .5 chance of coming out heads on a given throw. Therefore, it will come out heads every 1/.5 throws. Since 1/.5 is equal to 2, we know it will come out heads on average once every 2 throws.

If you flip two coins, the outcome of the first coin has no impact on the outcome of the second. If I were to tell you that the first coin came up heads, and asked you, based on that information, what the second coin was likely to come up, you would have no idea. Knowing the outcome of the first coin in no way helps you predict the outcome of the second. The reason you can't predict one coin toss knowing the result of the other is that the two events are completely independent.

If you flip two coins, what are the chances that the first coin will come up heads and the second tails? We have already said that these two outcomes are independent. When two outcomes are completely independent, the chances of both happening are the chances of the first happening times the chances of the second happening. So, the chances of the first coming up heads and the second tails is $.5 \times .5$, or .25, or 1 in 4.

If you flip two coins, what are the chances that the first coin will come up tails and the second heads? This is basically the same as the last case, so the chances again are $.5 \times .5$, or .25, or 1 in 4.

If you flip two coins, what are the chances that exactly one, but not both, of the two coins will come up heads? There are two ways this could happen. The first coin could come up heads and the second tails, or the first could come up tails and the second heads. We know the probability of each of these, .25, so the chances of either one happening are the two chances added together, or .25 + .25, or .5. Just to complete the cases, there is also a .25 chance that both coins could come up heads, and a .25 chance that neither could come up heads.

Something always happens. We can restate this rule by saying there is a 1.0 chance that something will happen. If we enumerate all the possible things that can happen, and list the chances that any of them will happen, the sum of them all must equal 1.0. If it doesn't, we made a mistake someplace. With the two coins, there is a .5 chance of one coin coming up heads, a .25 chance of both coins coming up heads, and a .25 chance of neither coin coming up heads. These are all the possibilities, and the sum of the chances (.25 + .25 + .5) equals 1. One of these three things is guaranteed to happen.

Let's say you take a die and color every side black except one. If you roll that die, what are the chances it will come up black? The chances of any one of the black sides coming up is the same as the original die coming up 3: 1 in 6, or .167, or on average, once every six throws. But now there are five sides, so we multiply the chances of one side coming up black by five. There are therefore $5 \times .167$ chances, or .835 chances. Or we could say it will come up black on average five out of every six throws.

Let's say you take two of these colored dice. What are the chances that the first will come up black and the second white? Since these are independent events, the chances of this combined event are the chances of the first coming up black (5/6) times the chances of the second coming up white (1/6), or 5/36. This is also the chances of the first coming up white, and the second black. The chances of both coming up black are $5/6 \times 5/6$, or 25/36. And the chances of both coming up white are $1/6 \times 1/6$, or 1/36. This enumerates all the possibilities, so we can check our answer. The sum of these (1/6 + 5/6 + 5/6 + 25/6) is 36/36, which is 1, so we are okay.

What are the chances of exactly one of the two dice coming up black? This can happen by either the first coming up black and the second white, or the first white and the second black. So we add the chances of these two events, and we get 5/36 + 5/36, or 10/36.

What are the chances of at least one of the two dice coming up black? This is the chances of exactly one of the two dice coming up black plus the chances of both dice coming up black. The former we just calculated as 10/36, and the latter we already know is 1/36. So the chances of at least one of the two dice coming up black is 10/36 + 1/36, or 11/36.

This concludes the word from your math teacher. It should be enough to get you through the next section.

Blob Reliability

Before we were so rudely interrupted by your math teacher, we had analyzed the performance of blobs compared to Super Agents. We found that even a small blob outperforms Super Agent. But this isn't the end of the story. All agents get sick, even Super Agent. What if we absolutely positively must know that our system will work. We cannot afford to bring our business to a halt, even for one day. Perhaps here Super Agent offers an advantage.

Let's say Super Agent gets sick 1 day per year, but Vanilla Agents, coming from inferior stock, get sick 74 days per year. Surely this is a good argument for buying Super Agent. Or is it?

Let's compare a five-member blob of Vanilla Agents against one Super Agent. We know from our previous analysis that the five-member blob will perform at more than twice the speed as the Super Agent at one-half the cost. But what about system reliability?

A given agent in the blob has about a 1/5 (.2) chance of getting sick on any given day, and about a 4/5 (.8) chance of being well. We can calculate the probability on a given day of a given number of agents being up. For example, the chances of all five agents running is

$$(.8 \times .8 \times .8 \times .8 \times .8) = .32768$$

In general, the chances of exactly M agents running and N agents not running are

$$(P_r{}^M) \times (P_{nr}{}^N) \times P$$

where P_r is the chances of an agent running and P_{nr} is the chances of an agent not running, and P is the number of permutations of M agents running and N agents not running. Since M (agents running) and N (agents not running) must equal the total number of agents (T), we can rewrite this equation in terms of T and M:

$$(P_r{}^M) \times (P_{nr}{}^{(T-M)}) \times P$$

In our example of all five agents running, this equation is

$$(.8^5) \times (.2^{(5-5)}) \times P$$

which simplifies to

$$(.8^5) \times (.2^0) \times P$$

Since any number raised to the power of 0 is 1, this equation simplifies to

$$(.8^5) \times P$$

There is only one combination of agents working and not working that yields all five agents working (namely, all five agents working). Therefore, P is 1, and this equation becomes

$(.8^5)$

This equation is just a rewrite of

$(.8 \times .8 \times .8 \times .8 \times .8)$

So you can see that in this simple case, when M is 5 and N is 0, this equation for calculating the chances of M agents working and N not working is correct.

The situation is a little more complicated when M is 4 and N is 1 only because we have to figure out what P should be. There are five ways we could have four agents working and one not working, namely, any one of the five agents could be the malfunctioning agent. There are ten ways we could have three agents working (agent 1 and 2 could not work, agent 1 and 3 could not work, and so on). There are also ten ways we could have two agents working. There are five ways we could have one agent working. And there is only one way to have all agents not working. These are all the possible values of P.

Based on this, Figure 10.7 shows the chances that a given number of agents will be working (and not working) on any given day.

On any given day either five, four, three, two, one, or zero agents must be working. There are no other possibilities. Therefore, we can check the calculations in Figure 10.7 by verifying that final numbers all add up to 1, which they do:

$.32768 + .4096 + .2048 + .0512 + .0064 + .00032 = 1.0$

Figure 10.7 Chances of different number of agents working.

Working	Not Working	Chances
5	0	$(.8^5) \times (.2^0) \times 1 = .32768$
4	1	$(.8^4) \times (.2^1) \times 5 = .4096$
3	2	$(.8^3) \times (.2^2) \times 10 = .2048$
2	3	$(.8^2) \times (.2^3) \times 10 = .0512$
1	4	$(.8^1) \times (.2^4) \times 5 = .0064$
0	5	$(.8^0) \times (.2^5) \times 1 = .00032$

Now let's look at the chances of *at least* M agents working on any given day. Up until now we have been calculating the chances of *exactly* M agents working on any given day. The chances of *at least* four agents working is equal to the chances of exactly four agents running plus the chances of exactly five agents running. These are all the possibilities of at least four agents running. Using this logic, Figure 10.8 shows the chances of at least M agents working, for different values of M.

Blob versus Super Agent Reliability

Super Agent gets sick 1 day out of 365. The blob goes down only when all five agents are out, which, according to Figure 10.7, has a .00032 chance of happening on any given day, and therefore happens on average once every 3125 days. Therefore, our blob is almost 10 times as reliable as Super Agent, even though Super Agent is far more reliable than any one of the blob components (74 times to be precise).

To be fair, although the blob as a whole will fail with 1/10 the frequency as Super Agent, there will be additional times when the blob will not work as well as Super Agent, namely, when four out of five of the blob agents are sick, and only one is holding down the fort.

When four out of five agents are out, the blob performs at about one-half the speed of Super Agent. From Figure 10.7 this has a .0064 chance of happening on any given day, and therefore happens on average once every 156 days, or about twice a year.

Figure 10.8 Chances of M agents working on a given day.

M	
0	.00032 + .0064 + .0512 + .2048 + .4096 + .32768 = 1.0
1	.0064 + .0512 + .2048 + .4096 + .32768 = .99968
2	.0512 + .2048 + .4096 + .32768 = .99328
3	.2048 + .4096 + .32768 = .94208
4	.4096 + .32768 = .73728
5	.32768 = .32768

We can reasonably assume that when we were thinking of purchasing Super Agent, we based our performance needs on peak performance needs in our busy season. For an airline, this is Thanksgiving and a small handful of other high-travel days. Let's assume that we have 12 high-travel days per year. Then the chances of any one day being a high-travel day are 12/365, or .033. The chances of both the blob running slower than Super Agent and having a high-travel day are

.033 × .0064 = .0002112

How often does this event occur? We find this by dividing 1 by .0002112.

1/.0002112 = 4734 days = 12.97 years

These two events will therefore occur on the same day on average, about once every 13 years.

And the Winner Is . . .

We can summarize the comparison of blobs versus Super Agent by stating the following:

- Super Agent brings our entire business to a standstill 1 day per year.

- The blob brings our entire business to a standstill 1 day every 10 years.

- The blob slows down our business to one-half Super Agent's capacity 1 critical day every 13 years. It also slows down twice a year, but on days when nobody is likely to notice.

- The rest of the time (363 days of the year), the blob runs between one-and-a-half to three times faster than Super Agent.

- This particular blob configuration (five agents) costs about one-half of what Super Agent costs.

These results are quite remarkable, considering that the agents making up the blob are very inexpensive, and individually not very reliable (they are sick 20 percent of the time, after all).

There are a few odd situations when Super Agent is a better fit for a business. But it seems clear to me that for the overwhelming majority of commerce applications, blobs greatly outperform Super Agents, are much more reliable, and cost much less. I declare blobs the winner.

Microsoft's Interest

So why does Microsoft care about all this? Microsoft is in the Vanilla Agent business. It is not in the Super Agent business. Every time a Vanilla Agent is sold, Microsoft makes a few bucks. Every time a Super Agent is sold, two bad things happen to Microsoft:

- Microsoft makes no money.
- Microsoft's competitors make money.

You can see that Microsoft would like nothing better than for everybody to buy Vanilla Agents and for nobody to buy Super Agents. But Vanilla Agents can only compete with Super Agents if they can work together in a blob. So Microsoft is entering the blob business. The sooner Microsoft can create blob-enabling technology, the sooner it can eliminate the Super Agent menace.

The computer industry, of course, doesn't deal with travel agents. It deals with computers. The computer equivalent to a Vanilla Agent is a small cheap workstation. The computer equivalent to a Super Agent is a big expensive mainframe. The computer industry also has a special name for blobs. It calls them *clusters*.

Clusters

What exactly is a cluster? Here is my definition of a cluster: A *cluster* is a blob of computers.

Gregory F. Pfister, who wrote the bible on clusters*, defines a cluster as "a type of parallel or distributed system that consists of a collection of interconnected whole computers that is utilized as a single, unified computing resource," which is just a high falootin' way of saying a cluster is a blob of computers.

When you use a cluster, you don't know which computer you will use. You don't care. All you care about is that sooner or later (preferably sooner) you will be using some computer.

There are a lot of times you want to use a very specific computer. When I want to write another chapter in this book, I can't use just any computer. I want my laptop. I want my disk drive. No other computer will do.

In Search of Clusters: The Coming Battle in Lowly Parallel Computing, by Gregory F. Pfister, published by Prentice-Hall PTR, 1996.

But there are a lot of other times you don't care which computer you use. When you execute a buy order with a brokering system, you don't care which computer executes the buy order. Any computer that can give you equivalent results is fine with you.

However, Microsoft *does* cares what kind of a computer you are using. They want you running some computer that is running Microsoft software. And if that software has anything to do with commerce, that computer is going to have to have high performance and high reliability. And the only way Microsoft can deliver that combination is through a cluster. Which, as we have seen, gives Microsoft a very compelling story.

The code name Microsoft has been using for its cluster technology is *Wolfpack*. This name comes from the cover artwork of Pfister's book, which shows a pack of wolves (dogs, actually, but who's looking closely?) attacking a multiheaded dog. You may ask what this artwork has to do with clusters, or anything else, for that matter. It turns out Pfister is being allegorical. The dog/wolf pack represents clusters of computers. The multiheaded dog represents parallel processors. Microsoft identifies with the clusters. In the picture, the dog/wolf pack is winning, by the way.

Clusters in Multi-Tier Systems

We talked about multi-tier architectures. Clusters fit in very well with multi-tier architectures. Figure 10.9 shows a typical systems-level view of multi-tier architectures. This view shows one machine presenting the user interface sending requests up to a business object server, which sends requests up to a database engine machine. But from the user's perspective, there is no such thing as multi-tier architectures. There is only the user interface.

The user cares a lot about the machine presenting the user interface. If the user interface is presented on a computer in the next room, the user isn't going to be too happy. But why should the user care which computer processes the business object? And why should the user care which computer manages the data storage?

As far as these nonuser tiers go, the user only cares about three facts:

• Requests are processed quickly.

• The computers are available whenever they are needed.

• The cost of using these computers is low.

Figure 10.9 Systems-level view of multi-tier architecture.

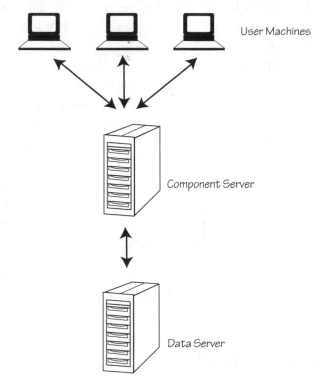

Do these needs sound familiar from our earlier discussion? These are exactly the areas in which clusters (or blobs) shine! Clusters are fast. Clusters are highly available. And clusters are cheap.

At least conceptually, it is very easy to see how to incorporate clusters into multi-tier architectures. All we need to do is redraw the architecture with clusters at each of the nonuser tiers. This is shown in Figure 10.10.

Why Clusters?

Why do we care about clusters? For the same reason we care about agent blobs:

Performance. We want the best possible performance from our computers, which implies load balancing.

High Availability. We want our systems guaranteed to work when we need them, which implies we need system redundancy.

Scaleability. We want to be able to add new machines as needed, which implies we need a linear growth path.

Price/Performance. We want to pay as little as possible for our system, which implies we are cheapskates.

These are same arguments we have been hearing since the first abacus replaced fingers as a computational device.

There is another, more subtle reason for buying clusters. Clusters allow you to purchase highly predictable availability. There is no such thing as 100-percent guaranteed reliability 100 percent of the time. There is probably no 100-percent guarantee of anything in life, other than death and taxes, which we discussed back in Chapter 2. However, clusters allow you to do a simple cost/reliability model. As long as you know the reliability and the cost of units making up the cluster, you can calculate the cost and reliability of the N cluster as a whole.

Figure 10.10 Multi-tier architecture with clusters.

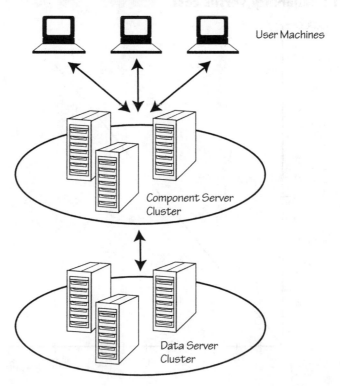

User Machines

Component Server
Cluster

Data Server
Cluster

Figure 10.11 Cost and failure analysis of typical cluster.

Unit cost = $5,000
Chance of failure = .20

N Unit	Cluster Cost	Chance of Failure	Mean Time to Failure
1	5,000	$.20^1$ = .20	$1/.20$ = 5 days
2	10,000	$.20^2$ = .04	$1/.04$ = 25 days
3	15,000	$.20^3$ = .008	$1/.008$ = 125 days
4	20,000	$.20^4$ = .0016	$1/.0016$ = 625 days
5	25,000	$.20^5$ = .00032	$1/.00032$ = 3125 days
6	30,000	$.20^6$ = .000064	$1/.000064$ = 15625 days

Figure 10.11 shows an analysis of an N cluster unit where the individual units cost $5,000 and have a 20-percent chance of failure on any given day.

Figure 10.12 Reliability versus cost.

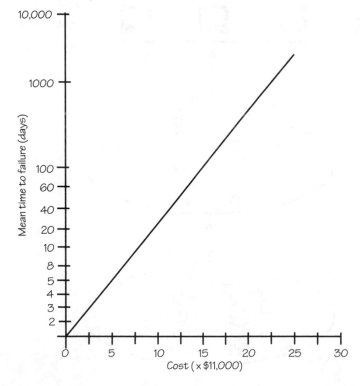

Based on Figure 10.11, you can see that you can choose the reliability you want and the price you can afford. You buy failure, but predictable failure. If you spend $15,000, your cluster will fail approximately once every 125 days, whether it needs to or not. If you spend $30,000, your cluster will fail approximately once every 42 years.

If you graph the data shown in Figure 10.11, you will get the graph shown in Figure 10.12. This is a graph that is guaranteed to warm the very cockles of the hearts of management. This graph shows an exponential increase in reliability with cost. Wouldn't it be wonderful if the whole world worked like this!

So when your management tells you they want at least 20 years between failures, you can whip out Figure 10.12 and show them exactly what it will cost. Skillfully used, this graph alone is worth the cost of this book.

The predictable nature of failure in clusters is a major plus for businesses, which need to know how often disasters will strike. Now when you convince management to spend the $30,000 and the cluster fails the next day, you can assure them that there will be no more downtime until long after they have all retired. But it wouldn't hurt to start polishing your résumé. After all, one can't be too safe.

Of course, every ointment has its fly. The data presented here is idealized. It assumes a perfect cluster implementation. We are a long way from being able to judge how perfect Microsoft's cluster implementation will be. It may well be that their architectural overhead piddles out at a very small number of nodes, or that the cluster system itself adds an unacceptable degree of instability. But Microsoft clearly understands the issues, and has hired some of the best in the business to build a cluster system nonpareil.

Microsoft Cluster Design

It's very easy to enumerate the user requirements of clusters. These requirements closely mirror the requirements we discussed for agent blobs. These requirements are:

1. All computers in the cluster must be interchangeable.

2. All computers in the cluster must have access to all the data (which is just another way of stating requirement 1).

The user really wants only one thing. The user wants the cluster to look like a single computer. Now surely that's not much to ask.

Now, you may have noticed that computers are not airline agents. It's one thing to take a bunch of airline agents and convince them to act as a blob. It's quite another thing to take a bunch of computers and convince them to act as a cluster. Here are just a few of the problems that must be solved:

- Data must be universally available to the cluster.

- Every machine on the cluster must be capable of running any program submitted to the cluster.

- Work is submitted to the cluster, not to machines within the cluster. The cluster must decide how to assign workloads to the computers within the cluster.

- Administrative programs are needed to add machines to and remove machines from the cluster.

- The cluster needs mechanisms to determine when a machine has died, and to reapportion the dead machine's workload to the remaining machines.

- Any user-visible names, such as filenames or process names, must be defined at the cluster level, rather than the machine level. Users don't know about individual machines in a cluster. From the user's perspective, the individual machine doesn't exist.

In addition to these generic cluster requirements, there are certain requirements that Microsoft will want to lay on its cluster solution. These include:

- The individual machines in the cluster should be running Microsoft software and Microsoft operating systems. This implies a cluster architecture layered on top of a generic NT operating system.

- The cluster strategy should be tightly integrated within the overall Microsoft Distributed Component Architecture (MDCA). This implies integration with Java, DCOM, SQLServer, object pooling, distributed transactions, and messaging, to mention the bare-bones minimum.

- Systems designed around the MDCA should work on Microsoft clusters without modification. Or maybe this is what I just said in the last bullet.

Microsoft has been working on this problem for a number of years, and the final solution is still at least a year away. But at least some information of the Microsoft Cluster Architecture is already available, although I recommend you not get too hung up on the details.

The Pieces

Microsoft calls the individual computers in the cluster *nodes*. A node is a fully functional computer. It has its own memory, its own disk drivers, and its operating system. It is also running the Microsoft Cluster Service, which is a collection of software that is responsible for coordinating the activity of this computer within the context of the overall cluster. A node can be part of one and only one cluster. Nodes can shift which cluster they are nodes of, as long as they are never part of more than one cluster at a time.

A *cluster resource* is a physical or logical component that is conceptually owned by the cluster, rather than a specific node on the cluster. A cluster resource can be a disk, a database, a Web site, or an application. A cluster resource is something that *must* be available if the cluster is to do its work. A *resource monitor* serves as an intermediary between the cluster service and the cluster resource. The resource monitor runs in its own process to protect the cluster service from resource failures, and to protect itself from failures of the cluster service.

The *cluster database* is a database that resides on each node in the cluster. It contains information about the physical and logical elements in the cluster, the nodes currently participating in the cluster, the cluster resources, and other related cluster information.

The Microsoft Cluster Service has seven subsystems. Their names and purposes are as follows:

Membership Manager. Keeps track of which other nodes are actively running within the cluster of record. The membership manager is sometimes also called the *node manager*. The membership manager continually sends out messages to other nodes on the cluster letting them know that the node is alive and well. These messages are called *heartbeats*.

Checkpoint Manager. Responsible for managing the cluster database.

Global Update Manager. Provides a mini distributed transaction service, so that nodes across the cluster can keep their cluster databases in synchrony.

Failover Manager. Works with Resource Monitors (which are not one of the subsystems, but are involved with clusters) to manage cluster resources. The resource monitors are responsible for noticing that a cluster resource has become unavailable, and the failover manager is responsible for moving the resource to another node.

Event Processor. Supports event notification between applications and the various subsystems of the cluster service.

Database Manager. Maintains the cluster configuration database.

Communication Manager. Manages communications between the various nodes of the cluster.

The relationship between these pieces is shown in Figure 10.13.

Node States

Nodes can exist in any of three states. These are:

Offline. The node is down, and should not be considered an active member of the cluster. An offline node has to bring its cluster database up to date and formally rejoin the cluster before it can become online.

Online. The node is a fully functional member of the cluster. It knows who else is part of the cluster, and who is managing which resources.

Paused. The node is there, but temporarily unavailable, probably for system maintenance. Paused nodes can become online at a moment's notice. They keep their cluster databases up to date and communicate with the other nodes in the cluster.

Shared Nothing Design

Earlier we discussed the need to have all data available to all cluster machines. Yet clusters are based on a standard NT operating system, which doesn't support the idea of two machines being able to access one disk drive at the same time. How are these two facts reconciled?

Microsoft clusters use a cluster architecture known as a *shared nothing* architecture. In this architecture, a given resource, such as a disk, is owned by a given computer. When another computer wants access to the data on a disk owned by some other computer, it forwards a request to that other computer. The other computer then accesses the data on behalf of the requesting computer. This architecture is called *shared nothing*, because a given resource can be accessed by one and only one computer. The shared nothing architecture is shown in Figure 10.14.

Figure 10.13 Architecture of Microsoft clusters.

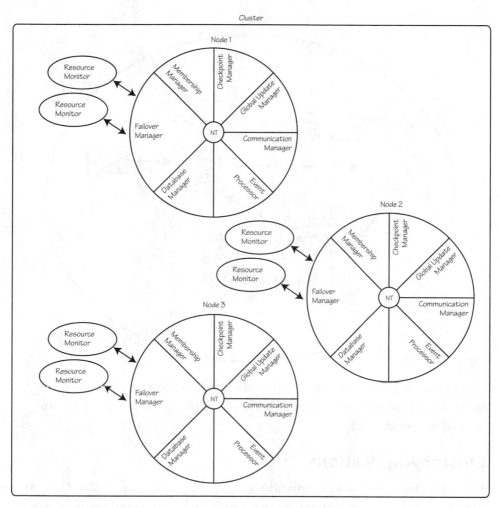

The resource ownership can be dynamically switched, if the node owning the disk (or other resource) fails. In that case, the remaining nodes negotiate to take ownership of the resource. Once a new node takes ownership of the resource, it notifies the other nodes so that future requests can be appropriately routed.

In contrast to the shared nothing architecture is the other common architecture. This is called a *shared everything* architecture, shown in Figure 10.15. In this architecture, any computer can access any disk (or other resource). There are many arguments Microsoft presents as to why the shared nothing architecture is

Figure 10.14 Shared nothing architecture.

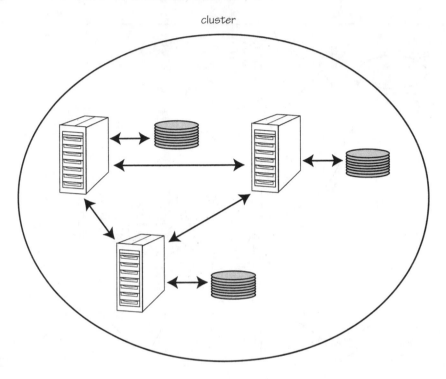

cluster

better than the shared everything architecture, but the bottom line is that Microsoft prefers the shared nothing architecture because it is much easier to layer onto standard NT.

Cluster Applications

There are three categories of applications, from the cluster perspective. These are *cluster management* applications, *cluster aware* applications, and *cluster unaware* applications.

The first category is *cluster management* applications. These are applications used to administer the cluster. They are used to add cluster resources, add and remove nodes to the cluster, and otherwise manage the overall cluster. It is highly unlikely any end user in his or her right mind would write such an application, but the necessary API (application programming interface) is there, should you ever choose to do so.

Figure 10.15 Shared everything architecture.

cluster

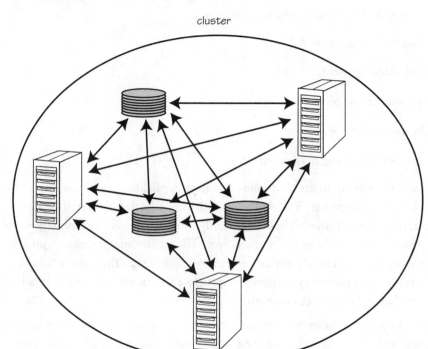

The second category is a *cluster aware* application. This is an application that knows it will be run on a cluster, and takes specific advantage of the cluster environment. It communicates directly with the subsystems of the cluster service. There are currently three requirements for cluster aware applications:

- The application must use TCP/IP as a network protocol.

- The application must maintain data in a configurable location.

- The application must support transaction processing.

The third category is a *cluster unaware* application. This is an application that doesn't care whether or not it will be run on a cluster. Such an application is managed as a generic application resource, and Microsoft provides tools necessary to manage such applications.

Cluster API

The Cluster API is divided into these five areas:

Cluster management

Node management

Resource management

Group management

Cluster database management

It seems unlikely to me that many business applications will use any of these APIs. At least, I hope not. The API set is a dense collection that will be quite intimidating to most users. These are mainly intended for cluster management applications and cluster aware applications. The cluster management applications are applications used by cluster administrators to manage the cluster. Cluster aware applications are very serious groupware applications, generally much more complex than a business component.

The majority of business components I believe will be cluster unaware, and as such, will not use these APIs. Business components will instead be managed by higher-level cluster applications, such as the Microsoft Transaction Server, which will coordinate the pooling of component objects within the cluster environment. However, my opinions on this are speculative, since the world as a whole has very little experience in this area.

So one might ask, why publish an API for something that nobody will use? I believe Microsoft's goal is to own the standard for cluster APIs. Nobody has claimed to own a standard for clusters. Microsoft realizes that the company that controls the standard for workstation clusters will own a valuable asset. Few other companies are in a position to put in a claim for control of this lucrative area, and those few that might, such as IBM, seem unaware of the high stakes involved.

Relationship to Object Pooling

We have discussed object pooling, and its importance in distributed commerce applications. Clustering is very similar to object pooling, except that it is on a machine basis rather than an object basis. In object pooling, we use multiple objects to satisfy client requests. In clusters, we use multiple machines to satisfy workload demands. In object pooling, we dedicate a single object to a client for the duration of a request. In clustering, we dedicate a machine to satisfy one or more workloads. In object pooling, objects are released when no longer needed. In clustering, machines are returned to a cluster pool once their workload permits it.

In the long term, I expect Microsoft to automatically use pools of machines (clusters) for the automatic management of pooled objects. Client requests to an object will then go to a pool of objects that has been disseminated throughout the cluster, rather than a pool of objects that is located on one single machine. This is shown in Figure 10.16.

Summary

Workstations have all of the following problems:

- They are slow.
- They are unreliable.
- They stop working when you try to service them.

Figure 10.16 Clusters and object pools.

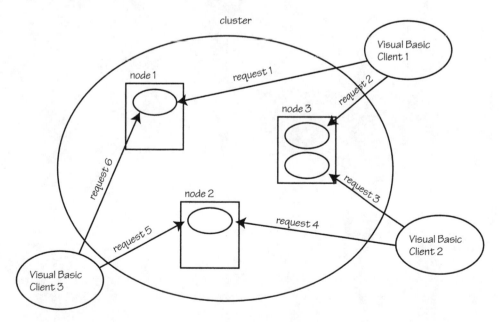

Distributed commerce does not appreciate any of these eccentricities. Enter clusters. Cluster technology is the magic bullet that transforms slow, unreliable workstations into fast, highly reliable production systems. So cluster technology is essential to the success of the MDCA. And therefore essential to the success of Microsoft.

Clusters do have one disadvantage. They are not very funny. You are not likely to see Alan Funt pop out of a cluster and say "Smile, you're on *Candid Camera*!"

MESSAGE QUEUING

Every once in a while a new technology is introduced that fundamentally changes the way we work. Not just improves it, but completely changes it. One such technology is e-mail. E-mail has done more than help us communicate better or faster. It has given us a whole new way of communicating.

What is new about e-mail is a unique combination of these four features:

- It is fast.
- It is reliable.
- Messages can be processed at times convenient for the sender and receiver.
- Parties can communicate without having to be on line at the same time.

There are other forms of communications that have some of these features, but no other communications technology offers all four. Telephones are fast and reliable, but they are inconvenient, and both parties need to be on line at the same time. The postal service is reliable, offline, and convenient, but is slow.

DCOM is like a phone line. It is fast and reliable, but it is not necessarily convenient, and everybody has to be on line together. If I am running an application on my computer, I am almost never on line. I am in the mall, or the coffee shop, or the woods. Then several times a day I plug the phone line in and attach to the network. If an application (or component) on my computer has to depend on DCOM to communicate with an application (or component) on your computer, it is probably going to be disappointed. It will be hard pressed to find a time when both of us are on line together.

We need a technology for software communications that allows fast, reliable, convenient, offline communications. Then if my application wants to ask yours to purchase an airline ticket for next week, it will use this technology to send yours a message. If I am not on the network, no problem. The message gets saved someplace, and the next time I plug in, off it goes. The next time your application wants to look for buy requests, it checks for messages, and there is the request from my application. Your application processes the purchase and sends my application back a message telling it the purchase was successful. The next time I return from the woods and plug in my laptop, my application gets the good news.

This type of message processing sounds a lot like e-mail. Of course, e-mail is designed for human beings. There are a lot of things human beings can do that software can't. We need a message-processing technology that has all of the advantages of e-mail, but is designed for software. And that's exactly what the Microsoft Message Queue Server (MSMQ), otherwise known as Falcon, is. MSMQ is e-mail for software.

How E-Mail Works

When I work with computer neophytes, I always have trouble explaining how e-mail works. They understand the idea of one computer passing off a message to another computer. But they always assume that both machines have to be on line for the message to be transmitted. We know that that isn't how e-mail works.

E-mail, at least the way most of us use it, involves at least these four computers:

- The sender's computer
- The sender's service provider's computer
- The recipient's service provider's computer
- The recipient's computer

Transferring e-mail is a multistep process. If I want to send you e-mail, I first create the e-mail. Then I queue the e-mail on my machine. Every once in a while I initiate a linkup with my service provider's computer, at which time my e-mail program transfers all queued e-mail from my computer to my service provider's computer. My service provider's computer then ships the e-mail to your service provider's computer.

Once my e-mail has made its way to your service provider's computer, this process reverses itself. You occasionally initiate a linkup with your service provider's computer. At this point, your e-mail program then downloads your e-mail to your machine. When you are ready to read that e-mail, your e-mail program presents the mail to you, one by one. This process is shown in Figure 11.1.

In reality, e-mail can get more complicated than this. First of all, I usually have many letters queued up and ready to send, usually each to a different recipient. You, on the other hand, are getting e-mail not only from me but from many others as well. Even leaving out the intermediate service provider machines, the e-mail network gets very complicated, as shown in Figure 11.2.

An e-mail message has an incredibly complicated path it must travel to get from my laptop to yours. It would be way beyond my ability as a human being to effect the transfer. But fortunately, all of this complexity is hidden from me. From my perspective, there are really only two things of which I need to be aware. One is the message I am sending. The other is the e-mail address of my intended recipient.

Figure 11.1 How e-mail works.

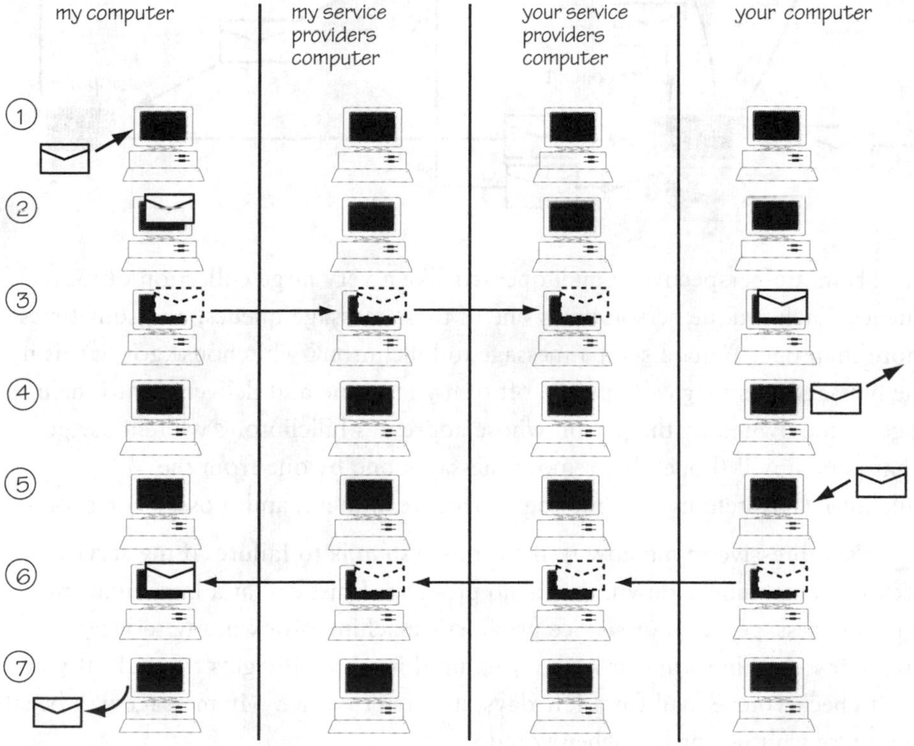

Figure 11.2 The e-mail network.

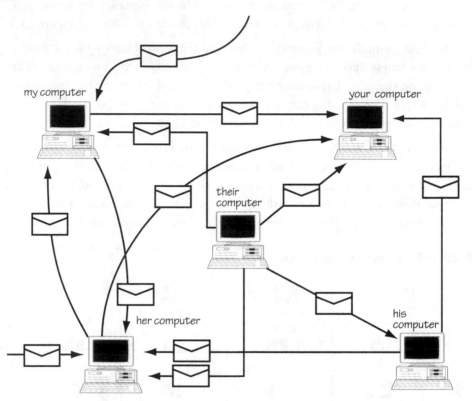

From my perspective, e-mail operates like a very large collection of message queues. Each unique person owns one of these message queues, and sometimes more than one. When I send a message to billclinton@whitehouse.gov, it's as if the message was magically picked off of my machine and delivered into the message queue owned by the person whose address is billclinton@whitehouse.gov . That person will (hopefully) remove messages one by one from the billclinton@whitehouse.gov message queue, read them, and (possibly) respond.

It's impressive to me how resilient this system is to failure. If my service provider's machine is down, that is no problem. I just call at a later time and transfer messages. If your service provider's machine is down, my service provider's machine will just keep trying until it eventually gets through. If you don't check your e-mail for a few days, it doesn't matter. My message will be sitting there waiting for you when you do.

Let's look at the important characteristics of e-mail that make it so useful.

1. Messages are delivered reliably. I know that if I send you a message, sooner or later that message will get through.

2. Messages are delivered when possible. There is no requirement that sender and recipient be on line concurrently.

3. Messages are delivered as fast as possible. The system itself introduces very little delay in the delivery. Generally the delay is in waiting for the recipient to check the message queue.

4. Message delivery does not block the sender. Once I send you a message, I can continue with other work. I don't have to sit there and wait for a response.

Asynchronous versus Synchronous Communication

I said that in e-mail, message delivery does not block the sender. In software we call this form of communications *asynchronous*, in contrast to *synchronous* communication.

Telephones are a form of synchronous communications. Once you ask me a question on the phone, you must sit there and wait until I answer, or until you give up. I often use this feature to deal with telemarketers. No matter what they are selling I tell them I am very interested in it. I ask them to hold on, saying I'll be right back. Then I put the phone on the counter and walk away. I figure I save the world at least 30 seconds of aggravation while they try to figure out if I am ever going to return (which, of course, I don't). I highly recommend this strategy to my readers.

This strategy only works with *synchronous* intrusions on your privacy. It doesn't work for junk e-mail, because the sender is not blocked while waiting for your reply. In other words, junk e-mail is an *asynchronous* intrusion on your privacy, and asynchronous intrusions require a different approach. Which, I regret to say, I have yet discover.

Do you think COM/DCOM is synchronous or asynchronous? The answer to this is not necessarily obvious. But look back at some of our code from Chapter 4.

This Visual Basic code is triggered when the user asks to see if there are any matches for transactions involving this terminal:

```
Private Sub Command3_Click()
    Dim result
    result = mybh.prepareCheckStatus()
    If (result = 0) Then
      Label7.Caption = "No Matches Found"
    Else
      Label7.Caption = "Matches Found"
    End If
End Sub
```

The third line is a COM/DCOM call to a possibly remote object. The fourth line will not execute until the method invocation completes. This is a synchronous communication. The caller is blocked until the method completes. And in this case, we want this method invocation to be synchronous. Line 4 depends on the method not returning until the result has been determined.

But look at this other code, also from Chapter 4.

```
Private Sub Command1_Click()
    Label7.Caption = ""
    Call mybh.prepareBuyOrder(Text1.Text, Text2.Text, Text3.Text)
    Label7.Caption = "Buy Accepted"
End Sub
```

This is the code used when we have entered the necessary information for a buy. Now we are ready for the broker to go out and try to locate a qualified seller. Do we really want the method to be blocked? If the method is going to take a long time to execute, we would be perfectly happy if we could just continue on entering more buy/sell information. This is an example of a method we would like to execute asynchronously.

Unfortunately, COM/DCOM does not support asynchronous communication. All methods are invoked synchronously. If you are the client, you wait for the method to either complete or the system to give up. If that is what you want, you will be happy. If it isn't, you need something else. And for now, that something else is MSMQ.

MSMQ

As I said, MSMQ is e-mail for software. Visual Basic programs can use it to communication with other Visual Basic programs or with Java components (or even COM components implemented in a more primitive language). Components can use it to communicate with each other.

The general paradigm of MSMQ is message queues. A message queue is a public message delivery channel for software. Think of it as the equivalent of an e-mail address for software. Message queues are characterized by the following:

- Each message queue has a unique ID, called a *globally unique ID* (GUID), similar to the GUIDs we saw for component definitions back in Chapter 4.

- Each message queue has a name, which is designed for consumption by humans as opposed to a GUID, which is designed for a computer.

- Message queues have properties associated with them, which can be used in searching for message queues of interest.

- Message queues are global resources. Every message queue is available to any software running on the network.

- Each message queue is protected by permissions, which define how specific user IDs are allowed to interact with specific message queues.

- Any software process running under a permitted user ID can place messages into and remove messages from any message queue.

The MSMQ API

One interacts with message queues by using a collection of predefined and preimplemented COM/DCOM objects. At press time for this book, the interfaces to these objects are subject to change, but the current collection includes the following: MSMQQuery, MSMQQueryInfos, MSMQQueryInfo, MSMQQueue, MSMQMessage, MSMQEvent, MSMQTransactionDispenser, and MSMQTransaction.

These various interfaces describe objects you can manipulate in your Visual Basic programs or Java components to send and receive messages to and from message queues. But you need to think of these objects a little differently than other objects. You need to realize that these objects are logically shared with potentially many other processes on your network.

They are shared in the same sense that the BrokerHouse object we have been using throughout this book is shared. The state of the object changes as a result of overall system activity over which you have limited control. With our BrokerHouse object, we have to periodically check to see if new buyer/seller matches have been discovered, even if our particular process has been inactive. Buyer/seller matches can result from the activity of any process using the brokering system.

In the same way, message queues are highly dynamic. I could check my queue object one moment and find no messages, and then check it again in a few seconds and find 100 messages, even if my process has been completely dormant. This is because the queue object is effectively shared. Not shared in the sense that multiple processes have references to the same component object, but shared in the sense that multiple processes have objects that represent the same logical queue. So if we both have references to MSMQQueue objects representing the same queue, then when I add a message to my queue, your queue object gets that message. It is precisely this sharing of logical objects that allows our systems to communicate. This is shown in Figure 11.3.

In the following sections, we will discuss the methods and major properties of each of the MSMQ interfaces. A property is best thought of as a public data item. Properties can be either read/write or read only. In Java, properties will probably map into set/get methods (for read/write properties) and set method only (for read only properties). Unless specified otherwise, assume properties are read/write. In the interest of space and boredom, many properties, particularly those having to deal with security, have been left out.

MSMQQuery

An MSMQQuery object represents a specific query against the MSMQ directory of available queues. MSMQQuery includes methods to find queues based on queue properties. The MSMQQuery methods are:

LookupQueue. Returns an MSMQQueueInfos object that contains information on all of the queues that fulfilled this search request. The search request can be based on any of these queue characteristics: queue UID, service type, name, time created, or time modified.

There are no properties associated with the MSMQQuery interface.

Figure 11.3 Logical queue sharing.

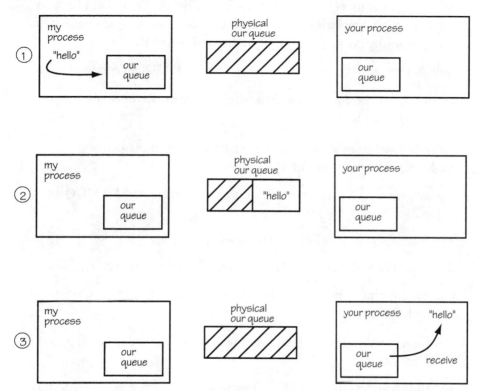

MSMQQueueInfos

An MSMQQueueInfos object is a collection of MSMQQueueInfo objects. The MSMQQueueInfos methods are:

Next. Returns the next queue in the collection. Returns NULL if the cursor is at the end of the queue collection.

Reset. Resets the cursor to the start of the results of a query.

There are no properties associated with the MSMQQueueInfos.

MSMQQueueInfo

An MSMQQueueInfo object represents information about a particular queue. The MSMQQueueInfo methods are:

Create. Creates a brand new queue with the name and properties of the MSMQQueueInfo object. Returns an error if the queue couldn't be created—for example, if the name conflicted with an existing queue. This is the equivalent of creating a new authorized e-mail ID.

Delete. Deletes the queue associated with this MSMQQueueInfo object.

Open. Opens the queue associated with this object. Returns an MSMQQueue object.

Refresh. Used to make sure the property values of the associated MSMQQueue object haven't changed.

Update. Used to change property values of the associated MSMQQueue object.

The MSMQQueueInfo interface has these properties:

dateCreateTime (read-only). The time the queue was created.

dateModifyTime (read-only). The time the public queue's properties were last updated.

isTransactional (read-only). Indicates whether or not the queue supports transactions.

strPathName. Specifies the MSMQ pathname of the queue. The MSMQ pathname specifies the name of the computer where the queue's messages are stored, if the queue is public or private, and the name of the queue.

MSMQQueue

An MSMQQueue object represents an instance of a queue. The MSMQQueue object has an implied associated cursor, which points to the "current" message. This cursor is updated by various peek methods, which allow you to iterate through the messages without removing them. The MSMQQueue methods all take a parameter saying how long to wait for a message, and all return an MSMQMessage object. These methods are:

Peek. Returns the first message in the queue without removing the message. An optional parameter is used to control how long the method will wait for a message to arrive. Peek does not move the cursor.

PeekCurrent. Like Peek, but peeks at the message at the current cursor location without changing the cursor location.

PeekNext. Like PeekCurrent, but updates the cursor location.

Receive. Retrieves and removes the first message in the queue.

ReceiveCurrent. Retrieves and removes the message in the current cursor location.

ReceiveNext. Based on the Microsoft documentation, this appears identical to ReceiveCurrent. I have no idea what the difference is.

Reset. Resets the cursor to the beginning of the queue.

The MSMQQueue interface has the following properties:

binSenderCert. An array of bytes representing the security certificate, used to authenticate messages.

isOpen (read-only). Indicates whether or not the queue is open.

lAccess (read-only). Indicates the access rights of the queue. Returns either MQ_SEND_ACCESS (messages can only be sent to the queue), MQ_PEEK_ACCESS (messages can be looked at but not removed from the queue), or MQ_RECEIVE_ACCESS (messages can be taken out of the queue or peeked at).

MSMQMessage

An MSMQMessage object represents a message in the queue. It is these objects that are placed into and removed from queues. The MSMQMessage methods are:

Send. Used to send this message to a particular queue, which is one of the parameters to the method. An optional parameter is an MSMQTransaction object, used to indicate that this send is part of a transaction.

Note that although you place a message on the queue by invoking send on the *message* object, you remove that message from the queue by invoking receive on the *queue* object. This gives an odd asymmetry to send/receive. A more logical place for the Send method would be in the MSMQQueue interface, and perhaps this will change before the product becomes finalized.

The MSMQMessage interface has the following properties:

binSenderId (read-only). An array of bytes that represent the identifier of the sending application.

body. The contents of the message. The body can be a string, an array of bytes, or any persistent object that supports the IPersist interface (see Chapter 5 for a discussion of this interface).

dateArrivedTime (read-only). The time the message arrived at the queue.

dateSentTime (read-only). The time the message was sent to the queue.

isAuthenticated (read-only). Indicates that the message was authenticated by MSMQ.

lenBody (read-only). Indicates the length of the message body in bytes.

lMaxTimeToReachQueue. Specifies a time limit (in seconds) for the message to reach the queue.

lMaxTimeToReceive. Specifies a time limit (in seconds) for the message to wait in the queue before being retrieved.

MSMQEvent

An MSMQEvent object is used to communicate events from the queue to the application. Two events are supported: message arrival and error notification.

MSMQTransactionDispenser

An MSMQTransactionDispenser object is used to create a transaction object. MSMQTransaction dispenser methods include:

BeginTransaction. (which returns an MSMQTransaction object).

MSMQTransaction

The MSMQTransaction represents the transaction in progress. MSMQTransaction methods include:

Commit. Commits the queue updates that have been part of this transaction.

Abort. Aborts the queue updates that have been part of this transaction.

Queue Types

Although message queues are the most common type of queue, there are other types as well. These include:

Administration queues. Used to store MSMQ-generated acknowledgments about message delivery.

Response queues. Used for application-generated response messages.

Journal queues. Used to store copies of application-generated messages.

Dead Letter queues. Used to store application-generated messages that cannot be delivered.

Report queues. Used to track the status of messages as they move through the system.

Private versus Public Queues

Queues come in public and private flavors. Public queues are queues that anybody can look up and make use of. Private queues are queues that can be used only by those who specifically know about them.

Using Message Queues in Applications

An MDCA application can make use of any number of message queues. Each one will have a purpose and a name. Our brokering system, for example, could use message queues to transfer information between the Visual Basic clients and the broker component. A message queue named "Buyers" might be used to place messages about people wanting to make buys, and a message queue named "Sellers" might be used to place messages about people wanting to make sells. Conceptually, this system looks like Figure 11.4.

MSMQ Transactions

MSMQ is integrated with the Microsoft Transaction Manager and its two-phase commit protocol, as described back in Chapter 7. This means that the sending of a message into a queue can be part of a transaction that includes updates to

Figure 11.4 Broker queues.

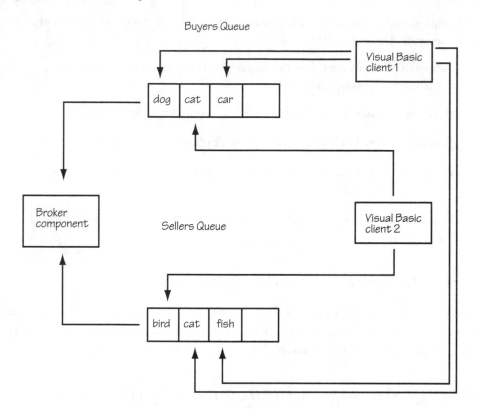

transactional databases. If the sending of the message fails, the database updates will automatically be backed up. If the database updates fail, the message will not be sent to the queue. This is the basic nature of the laws of commerce and their relationship to transactions, which was also part of the discussion in Chapter 7.

MSMQ works within a two-phase commit protocol the way anything works within a two-phase commit. It acts as a resource manager that understands the two-phase commit protocol coordinated by the Microsoft Distributed Transaction Coordinator (MS-DTC). Remember all of this from Chapter 7? At the time the client issues a commit request, the MS-DTC asks all of the involved resource managers if they are willing to commit, and if they all are, then the MS-DTC lets everybody know the commit is final. If any resource manager declines the commit, the MS-DTC tells everybody the deal is off. MSMQ queues, because they are managed by an MS-DTC resource manager, can be part of this algorithm. This is shown in Figure 11.5.

MSMQ transactions encompass the transmission of the message from the sender to the appropriate message queue. The transaction guarantees that the message will make it into the queue, and MSMQ guarantees that once a message makes it into the queue, it will eventually be delivered. But when? MSMQ has no control over the when. When will happen when the appropriate application decides to read the queue.

Two-phase commit transactions are intended to be short-lived. Remember that every resource manager involved in the transaction is left in a state of limbo until the transaction has resolved. The potential for delayed delivery (or perhaps it is better to say delayed receipt) prohibits the use of two-phase commit spanning

Figure 11.5 MSMQ and two-phase commits.

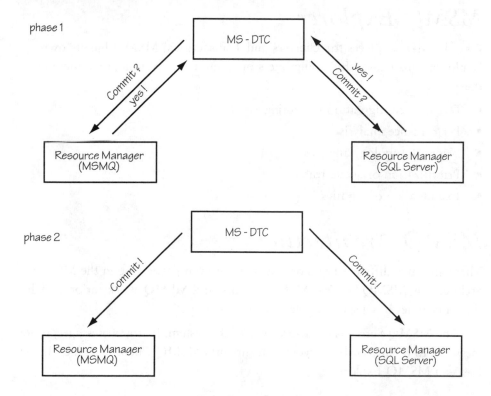

both send and receipt. We simply cannot tie up resource managers until I finally decide to return from the woods and check my messages.

Instead, MSMQ provides many mechanisms for returning information about the eventual delivery of the message. This allows applications to undertake what are called *compensatory* transactions, that is, transactions intended to undo the results of previous committed transactions.

MSMQ Security

MSMQ offers a full complement of security operations, similar to those we described back in Chapter 9. Messages can be encrypted, authenticated with various levels of reliability. The MSMQ security is built on the CryptoAPI discussed in Chapter 9, so that chapter will give you a good sense of what you can do to protect your messages.

MSMQ Explorer

Like the MDCA pieces for Clusters and Transactions, MSMQ has its own Explorer. This is used for doing one-stop administrative functions, including these:

- Dynamic configuration of routing
- Performance analysis
- Network topology analysis
- Prioritization of queue traffic
- Examination of log files

MSMQ Architecture

There are three different types of machines that can participate in the MSMQ architecture: MSMQ Servers, MSMQ Clients, and MSMQ Workstations. Each of these machines has a specific role to play.

The MSMQ Server is the workhorse of the system. It stores messages, routes messages to other MSMQ Servers, and supports MSMQ Client machines. It also hosts an MSMQ Explorer.

The MSMQ Client is a machine on which we have applications using queues. This machine can send and receive messages, but is very basic. It cannot store any queues of its own. It relies on an MSMQ Server to provide queues for its use. There will often be many MSMQ Client machines being serviced by one MSMQ Server.

The MSMQ Workstation is a hybrid between the MSMQ Server and the MSMQ Client. It can send and receive messages, like a client. It can also store messages, like an MSMQ Server. However, it cannot participate in routing. It is designed to operate in the occasional absence of a network. Its main purpose is to support mobile computing.

Figure 11.6 Shows the relationship between these three machine types.

Figure 11.6 Three MSMQ machine types.

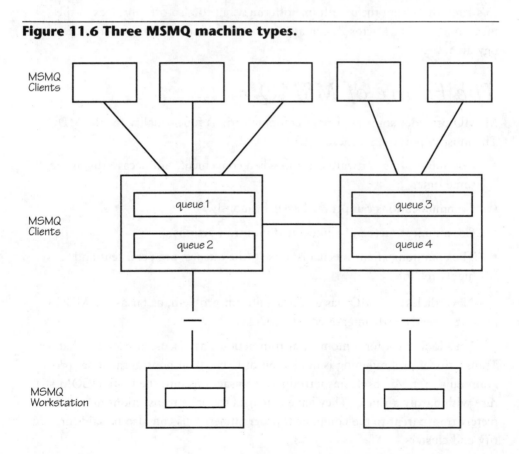

Microsoft is working with third parties to provide bridging technology to allow MSMQ to interoperate with non-Microsoft platforms. According to a recent Microsoft white paper, there are three main focuses for this activity:

- MSMQ API on Legacy platforms, including IBM mainframes (MVS/CICS), Unix platforms, and AS/400, allowing Windows NT clients to pass messages to these platforms.

- MSMQ to IBM MQSeries queue-to-queue gateway, allowing integration between MSMQ and one of the important mainframe competitors.

- MSMQ to CICS transient data queue gateway, allowing integration between MSMQ and CICS.

Microsoft's plan here is to offer competitive technology and encourage people to switch over from the mainframe offerings, but to also offer bridges in the meantime, so that Microsoft can at least find a toehold in this important technology area.

The Future of MSMQ

MSMQ provides some important communications functionality for the MDCA. The most important are these:

- Communicating software can run when convenient, not necessarily at the same time.

- Communications can proceed asynchronously.

- Communications can be integrated into transactions.

- The communications mechanism itself (the queues) are persistent and highly reliable.

Nevertheless, MSMQ has a very significant problem, as far as the MDCA goes. It is very poorly integrated into DCOM.

Let's look back for a moment at transactions, as discussed back in Chapter 7. Transactional programming is quite a bit different than nontransactional programming. Yet Microsoft has introduced transactions into the basic DCOM structure with hardly a ripple. They have managed to make transactions almost completely transparent to the component programmer. This can also be said for security and clusters.

But the use of MSMQ is nothing even close to transparent. You use one programming model for synchronous message passing (DCOM), and a completely different programming model for asynchronous message passing (MSMQ). These two models couldn't possibly be more different. Yet, as you can see from the brokering example, it would be very convenient to be able to invoke DCOM methods asynchronously.

MSMQ is not built on top of DCOM. The main reason for this is that DCOM is based on RPC (Remote Method Call), which is a form of synchronous communication. To build an asynchronous model on top of a synchronous architecture is very difficult.

However, Microsoft has discussed plans to build an asynchronous form of RPC on top of MSMQ. One might assume that the next step would be to base DCOM, or at least some version of it, on top of this new asynchronous RPC. The main reason they would want to do this is to support asynchronous DCOM methods, which would be a wonderful addition to DCOM and a much stronger integration story between MSMQ and DCOM.

However, this seems at least a year away. And many things can happen in a year in the computer industry. So we will have to wait and see. But at least there is hope that these two important technologies will become much tighter at some point within our lifetimes.

Summary

Reliable, transactional, asynchronous communications is a must for commerce systems. It is the only way to communicate between software that is not always on line at the same time, and not always working on totally reliable networks. It also is a big performance gain for applications that need to invoke long running methods on components. Reliable, transactional, asynchronous communications is the territory of MSMQ.

MSMQ is based on message queues. Message queues work very similarly to e-mail. One process communicates with another by placing a message in an agreed-upon queue. The other process reads the message by removing it from the queue. Like e-mail, messages queues are highly reliable, and very flexible when it comes to routing across unreliable networks.

MSMQ is not perfect. It has a programming model that is quite at odds with DCOM. However, there is hope that this will be fixed. And when it is, we will have both synchronous and asynchronous method invocation, which will be very cool. I will be waiting with bated breath for this announcement from Microsoft. But it looks like I had better wait in asynchronous mode. I do have another life.

Tour's over. Time to get off the bus.

We have gone through a lot of material. We can't cover everything in detail, but I have tried to give you enough information about all the pieces so that you can understand the Microsoft vision, and start planning how you might use this technology.

The last two years has been an incredible roller coaster ride. In that short time, Java has ignited the imagination of software developers, the Internet has exploded, distributed objects have become the latest dance craze, and Microsoft has quietly begun introducing a series of technologies designed to relegate mainframe computers to the trash heap. Let's take a look at where we are today, and where we are going.

It is only fair to point out that, although I have never been shy about sharing my opinions with you, I am especially vocal in this chapter. It would be unfair to assume that my opinions are shared by any of the companies I mention or, for that matter, anybody else.

Commerce on the Net

I could try to impress you by telling you that over the next two years the Web will become a driving force in commerce. But this is, by now, a platitude. Everyone knows this. Every large company is trying to figure out how to exploit the Web to increase sales. Although nobody really understands how best to make this a reality, the industry has come to a general consensus on these three ideas:

- A multi-tier (at least three-tier) architecture is a requirement (see Chapter 8).

- Distributed components are the natural mechanism for developing distributed applications (see Chapter 4).

- Java is the preferred language for developing distributed components (see Chapter 3).

The huge interest in the Web as a commerce-enabling technology has spawned three competing technologies for distributed component applications: CORBA, Java, and MDCA. Let's take a brief look at each of these.

CORBA

CORBA stands for Common Object Request Broker Architecture. It is a standard for doing distributed components that was developed by an industry consortium called OMG, for Object Management Group. The OMG started in 1989 with eight members and now includes over 700 members, including every major player in the computer industry, including Microsoft.

Strictly speaking, CORBA refers to the architecture of the ORB, or Object Request Broker, which is the lowest level of the OMG architecture, comparable to the DCOM level of MDCA. However, the term CORBA has come to be associated with the entire OMG architecture, including a whole collection of object services, although formally these services are called CORBAServices.

These services describe standard features of a distributed system upon which a programmer can theoretically depend. Some of the more important of these services include the following:

Life Cycle. How objects are born and how they die.

Naming. How shared objects can be located.

Concurrency. How object locking works.

Events. How objects notify each other of important events in their lives.

Externalization. How objects can create an externalizable package of their state.

Licensing. How objects can make sure they are being used by authorized clients.

Collections. How objects can be grouped together.

Query. How you can find objects within collections.

Security. How to make objects secure.

Trader. How to find objects based on what they can do for you.

Persistence. How to store objects.

Properties. How to assign general properties to objects.

Relationships. How objects can be associated with each other.

In addition to CORBA and the object services, OMG has defined its own interface definition language, which, like Microsoft's, is called IDL. However, there are two important differences between OMG IDL and Microsoft IDL. First, OMG IDL is much more intelligently designed, and quite natural for a Java or C++ programmer. Second, OMG IDL is probably a permanent feature of the OMG landscape, unlike the Microsoft counterpart, which is likely to eventually either go away or morph into something unrecognizable.

You may also hear the term IIOP (Internet Inter-Orb Protocol). Originally, OMG specified an interface for the ORB, but did not give any details on its implementation. It soon became apparent that in order for the technology to be competitive, ORBs from different vendors would have to interoperate. In order for the ORBs to interoperate, details about the communications needed to be specified. This became the IIOP specification from OMG. Today, virtually all vendors support the IIOP protocol.

I have a great fondness for OMG. I was one of the principal architects of the CORBA object persistence service, and spent my five years at IBM leading the development effort of the persistence portion of the SOM project. SOM was IBM's implementation of CORBA. I attended many OMG meetings throughout the world, and greatly respect the people involved.

CORBA shares many design goals with MDCA. Both are component oriented, rather than object oriented (although many members of the OMG club would deny this). Both are focused on distribution. Both are intended to be language independent. Both include an entire component run-time milieu.

But CORBA also has some significant differences from MDCA. Perhaps the most important is that OMG, unlike Microsoft, is a specifications, not an implementation organization. This means that members come together to agree on a set of standard interfaces. OMG has never written a line of code in its existence.

The implementation of the specifications is at the whim of the OMG members. In theory, OMG requires that any specifications OMG adopts be based on existing technology, and further requires that when members propose technology for standardization, they promise to provide full implementations of those standards shortly after the standards are approved.

In practice, neither of these occurs. The approval process encourages companies to make joint proposals that typically involve torturous political compromises, and the final submissions bear little resemblance to any existing technology, real or imagined. On the implementation side, companies have many ways to avoid spending development dollars they decide they have better use for. IBM, for example, has co-sponsored many proposals, and has yet to implement any of them. But because IBM is such an important member of OMG, it is highly unlikely that IBM will ever face any serious censure.

CORBA does differ from MDCA in one important respect: CORBA is based on shared objects. MDCA is based on pooled objects. This means that in CORBA, many client proxies can point to the same object. While this is theoretically true in MDCA as well, MDCA is oriented toward stateless objects that can be pooled. While both architectures allow sharing of object information, CORBA does this by sharing remote objects, and MDCA does this by sharing remote data. The MDCA version of this, and the reasons I think it is important, are described in Chapter 6.

OMG had a long head start on Microsoft. The first implementations of CORBA preceded DCOM by years. But Microsoft has rapidly made up for lost time. By now, Microsoft has a far more complete implementation of its overall architecture than any OMG member does of CORBA.

The main reason Microsoft has been able to pull ahead of OMG is because of the nature of the OMG process. A typical specification takes a year to finalize, and the overall OMG architecture is composed of dozens of such specifications. And when the specification is finally complete, the first line of code has yet to be written. This is an extremely slow process in an industry in which entire technologies can be made obsolete in months. In the time it takes OMG to agree on the interface of one minor object service, Microsoft can both define *and* implement huge architectural globs. You can see that there is little hope that OMG will ever catch up.

Another problem with the CORBA approach is the general lack of standard, cross-vendor programming tools. Any tools that do exist are vendor specific. This makes general CORBA programming only for those with a serious death wish. OMG describes their CORBA programming seminar series as "Extreme Programming." They aren't kidding.

You can get a general sense of the CORBA market by comparing the revenues of CORBA-based companies with those of Microsoft. This comparison isn't entirely fair, because Microsoft makes money from many different technologies, most of which are unrelated to MDCA. But I believe that over the next few years, MDCA will be driving a significant portion of Microsoft revenue stream, and more and more of its technologies will play some role, even if a minor one, in the overall MDCA strategy.

So how does CORBA stack up against Microsoft? To begin with, most companies today are losing money on CORBA. Neither IBM nor Sun, for example, are, in my view, likely to ever recoup even a fraction of their huge investment in CORBA. Of those companies that are making money in this area, IONA is probably one of the strongest. It has a well-respected ORB implementation and has one of the most complete collections of object services. IONA has a long history with CORBA, and has tightly tied its business strategy to CORBA.

In the 90-day period beginning April 1, 1997, IONA reported its best quarter ever. Revenues were up by 142 percent over the same 90-day period in 1996, and net income was up by 166 percent. Total income (profit) for that 90-day period was 1.7 million dollars.

How did Microsoft do in those same 90 days? Microsoft's income was 1.06 billion dollars. Microsoft had far exceeded IONA's income for the entire 90-day period before Bill Gates had even woken up on the very first morning of that quarter (and quite likely, before he had even gone to sleep the night before).

Java

In one sense, Java took over where CORBA left off. Not technologically, but politically. Up until Java took off, CORBA was seen as the world's line-in-the-sand against Microsoft. Once Java came on the scene, most of the world moved over to a new beach.

Java's claim to fame is its write-once-run-anywhere philosophy, as we discussed back in Chapter 3. This philosophy holds true, as long as one is willing to stick with the most marginal of all possible applications. Now SunSoft and its co-conspirators are adding a raft of libraries to its Java repertoire, but it is widely accepted that this collection can't possibly be ported to every possible Java platform. So much for write-once-run-anywhere.

Where Java the language ends and Java the smorgasbord begins is impossible to say with certainty. Microsoft has vigorously adopted Java the language, and looks with disdain on most of the rest of the Java offerings. Microsoft has announced support for JavaBeans, a technology that was introduced to compete with the traditional Microsoft ActiveX frameworks, an area in which I believe Microsoft is rapidly losing interest as it understands more and more of the promise of MDCA.

In one sense, Java has done more to ensure the success of MDCA than anything else. Java has essentially derailed the CORBA effort, and CORBA was the only architecture broad enough in vision and scope to have had a chance of competing with MDCA. But, thanks to Java, this won't happen. The major companies that supported CORBA have now all been completely distracted by Java.

IBM hasn't discussed OMG in months, and now actively discourages its customers from using SOM, once its flagship CORBA implementation. Sun is awash in Java, and nary a word is heard about CORBA. In July and August 1997, 20 percent of the Sun press releases were related to Java, and 0 percent were related to OMG or CORBA. I don't mean to continue to pick on IBM and Sun in these discussions, but these two companies are by far the largest and most visible supporters of the OMG effort. Once they lose interest in OMG, you can be sure the rest of the industry won't be far behind.

Java the smorgasbord is, in my view, fatally flawed in several key areas. First, it is very limited in its vision. This alone wouldn't be too bad if it were an open architecture, but it isn't. It works well as long as your needs can be satisfied by the Java womb, but as soon as you want to grow up, you have had it. Second, it is language centric, and no matter how good a language is, it must have bridges to other languages for legacy reasons, if nothing else. The industry has never bought into, and never will buy into, a single-language strategy.

MDCA

We have spent this whole book examining the MDCA. One thing we haven't discussed is the availability of this architecture on non-Microsoft systems, an area where both CORBA and Java have strong stories.

In July, 1996, Microsoft, amid much fanfare, transferred control of COM, DCOM, and other low-level parts of MDCA to The Active Group, a consortium of software and systems vendors dedicated to promotion and widespread adoption of ActiveX core technologies working under the auspices of The Open Group. Many cynics in the industry saw this as a ploy to one-up Sun in an attempt to win the "most open system" award in the public eye. In their press release at the time, Microsoft said:

"Microsoft Corp. today announced plans for fulfilling its vision of openness for ActiveX by transitioning specifications and appropriate technology to an industry-standards body. A working group of customers, ISVs, and platform vendors will convene shortly to determine the process for transitioning ActiveX technology to an independent organization. The group will be a customer-driven organization in which Microsoft is one of many members involved in decision making."

This "working group" finally got around to holding their first (and only) meeting four months later, and since then has gone into total hibernation. If there is now any activity to hold any of the MDCA up for public standardization, it has been well hidden.

DCOM is available on a few non-Microsoft platforms, most notably Unix systems, thanks to a port by Software AG. However, none of the MDCA supporting technologies, such as MTS, have been ported, nor has Microsoft publicly discussed any plans for doing so. Therefore, despite Software AG's highly publicized porting effort, we have to realistically consider MDCA an architecture that is limited to Microsoft operating systems for the foreseeable future. Of course, this is a very large group of very important operating systems.

Figure 12.1 compares Java, CORBA, and MDCA. This comparison is highly opinionated, but I hope not too biased. I have tried to make sure I insulted everybody at least once. I doubt anybody else in the world will agree with me 100 percent on all of these areas. In any case, be sure to read the notes carefully for my justifications on ranking the different areas the way I did.

Figure 12.1 Comparison of three technologies.

Feature	Java	CORBA	MDCA
Java language support	yes	no(1)	yes
Shared objects	yes	yes	no(2)
Pooled objects	no	no	yes
Relational DBs	yes	no	yes
Asynch. communications	no	no(3)	yes(4)
Cross language support	no	yes	yes
Cross operating system	yes	yes	no(5)
Persistence model	yes	no(6)	yes
Component availability	yes	no	yes
System managed threads	no	no	yes
Seamless transactions	no	no(7)	yes
Machine clustering	no	no(8)	yes(9)
Standards body involvement	no	yes	no(10)
Client tier support	no(11)	no	yes
Component tier support	yes	yes	yes
Data tier support	no	no	yes
Workstation focus	yes	no	yes
Mainframe focus	no	yes	no
Overall availability	yes	no(12)	yes
Major vendor support	yes	no(13)	yes(14)

Notes:

(1) The OMG is working on Java bindings, and these will probably be available soon.

(2) It is possible to share objects in DCOM, but the mechanisms are highly obscure compared to CORBA.

(3) It is possible to do asynchronous communications in CORBA, but the mechanisms are highly obscure compared to DCOM. Further, they do not integrate into the transaction framework.

Figure 12.1 Continued

(4) It is easy to do asynchronous communications in the MDCA, but the programming model is quite different from the programming model for synchronous communications (see Chapter 11).

(5) Although DCOM itself will run on many platforms, little, if any, of the critical MDCA support technology will. Without the availability of this support technology, DCOM will be uninteresting.

(6) The OMG has a persistence specification, but it is undergoing change and cannot at this time be considered stable.

(7) OMG has a specification for transactions, but it requires explicit control by either clients or components.

(8) OMG would say that their architecture doesn't address clustering one way or another.

(9) The MDCA clustering available at press time is still in beta, and is limited in functionality.

(10) Microsoft has allegedly turned over ownership of the DCOM specification to a standards body, but this is largely a joke (see earlier discussion in this chapter). This group has had very little activity, and isn't even looking at the critical question of MDCA support technology.

(11) Java has some client-tier support, but it is very weak and I have rated it closer to a "no" than to a "yes."

(12) Although the OMG has standardized a wide range of object services, few are actually available from vendors. The gap between what has been standardized and what is readily available is growing rather than shrinking. The reasons for this are discussed earlier in this chapter.

(13) All major vendors are members of OMG, but almost all (including SunSoft and IBM) are focusing their technical attention on Java and have largely lost interest in CORBA.

(14) The only major vendor supporting the entire MDCA is Microsoft, but that's major enough for me.

And the Winner Is ...

I'm going to have to call it Microsoft. Partly this is because of the incredible vision behind MDCA, although I'm not convinced there isn't a lot of serendipity behind this vision (but hasn't this been the story of Microsoft's life?). Partly this is because of problems with the competitive architectures.

But serendipity or not, and competitive flaws aside, what is coming together is very impressive. Microsoft has laid the groundwork for a whole new approach to creating distributed commerce applications. It has done this by taking traditional mainframe technologies, adding on a distributed component system, and putting the whole thing together on a hardware platform so cheap that, on a price basis alone, it will force people to take it seriously.

The biggest problem with MDCA is its Microsoft-only focus. However, there is lot of bridge technology to allow legacy systems, such as databases and message queues, to participate. There is also work going on to allow interactions between CORBA and DCOM, and, to a lesser extent, between Java the grab bag and DCOM, although each side has its own opinion on who is the home team and who is the visitor.

MDCA is not perfect. IDL is particularly imperfect. Clustering is minimal, and Falcon has a long way to go before we can call it a seamless integration with DCOM. But these problems are fixable and, I have no doubt, will be fixed. The basic architecture holds together, and holds together well.

Ten Rules for Distributed Component Programming

As my final words to you and, in part, to summarize this book, I have distilled my experience in implementing distributed component systems into a few (well, 10) rules I recommend to people implementing distributed component systems. Many of these are applicable to any distributed component technology, and several are specific to MDCA. Here they are.

1. *Separate your tiers.* In particular, separate your user interface from your business logic. Even if you think you will be running both in the same process (which you probably won't), you will have a much more flexible system if your user interface code can be managed independently of your business logic. Keep in mind that each tier is independent, and you never know what will be happening in the other tiers. So don't lock yourself into one technology. Use dual interfaces and standard Java data types that are compatible with Visual Basic.

2. *Distinguish components from objects.* Components are a packaging tool. Objects are an implementation tool.

3. *Distinguish interfaces from classes.* Interfaces define behaviors. Classes implement behaviors. Your interfaces are your contract. They are your word, your bond, your promise to your users. Agonize over them, get them right and don't change them. Classes are an ongoing sculpture. You can continue to mold them, tweak them, and improve them as often as you like. Don't worry about making them perfect the first time. You can change classes to your heart's content.

4. *Use tier-appropriate technology.* Java is great for implementing components, but weak for implementing user interfaces. Visual Basic is wonderful for user interfaces, but too primitive for implementing components. SQLServer is perfect for storing data, but has little to offer either user interfaces or components.

5. *Eliminate component state.* Look upon even the smallest state variable as an affront to your professional dignity. Treat state as the pariah it is, a conspiracy to reduce your sleek, high-performing objects to technological sloths. Make your components stateless. Even if your environment doesn't support pooling, you will open up important opportunities for performance tuning, object sharing, and object robustness.

6. *Enclose algorithms in transactions.* Transactions make error handling much, much easier. As your distributed systems increase in complexity (and they always do), they will quickly reach a point where you cannot hope to manage all possible error conditions without the use of transactional logic. The sooner you realize this, the better off you will be.

7. *Choose environments carefully.* When you make the decision to buy into MDCA, or Java, or CORBA, you are making a decision for life. You are not renting, you are buying. You are not dating, you are getting married. And there are no divorce courts where you are heading.

8. *Design decisively, implement incrementally.* Take your design very seriously. Bring in your best people for design reviews. If you are lacking expertise in distributed component technology, this is the place to spend your consulting dollars. Then once you have your design done, implement slowly and methodically. I recommend the following implementation plan:

- Implement prototypes of all interfaces using just Java interfaces and working within a single process. Don't use either COM or DCOM at this state. Testing and debugging will be much easier.

- Design and write some simple Java test programs. Save every test program you write, and use them as the basis for new test programs. Plan a strategy that allows you to rerun all of your test programs easily as you continuously look for newly introduced bugs. Use your test programs and prototype code to evaluate your interface design. If you need to change them (very likely), now is the time!

- Write IDL definitions of the interfaces. Implement and test using a single process. Do not add any new code except for the COM wrappers.

- Modify your test programs to work with the COM wrappers. Do not add any new code, and don't change a line of your prototypes until you have your test programs working again.

- Package for consumption by the Microsoft Transaction Server, but continue to test on a single machine. Make sure your test programs are all working correctly before you continue.

- Move the transaction package to a remote machine and retest, retest, retest.

- Start doing scalability tests. Make sure you can support the number of users you must eventually support.

- Slowly replace prototype implementations with live code. Rerun your test programs continuously. It is much easier to find a bug 10 minutes after it has been introduced than it is to find one 10 days after it has been introduced.

- Keep checking your design assumptions and scalability.

9. *Write 'em right.* Writing difficult-to-use systems is easy. Writing easy-to-use systems is difficult. Do it right, even if you don't think anybody will appreciate the effort. They will, in time.

10. *Allow time.* This is tough work. Most failure can be attributed to unrealistic expectations on how long it will take to implement systems, especially first systems. Give yourself plenty of time to write and rewrite pro-

totypes. If you aren't familiar with object-oriented programming, this is your first hurdle. Then you tackle components. Then distributed components. Then clusters, security, and the rest of the MDCA architecture. Nobody is going to learn this material overnight.

You are about to use some interesting technology. You are in for some interesting times. I hope you have enjoyed the tour. Good luck!

Index